ARIES

TAURUS

GEMINI

CANCER

LEO

VIRGO

LIBRA

SCORPIO

SAGITTARIUS

CAPRICORN

AQUARIUS

PISCES

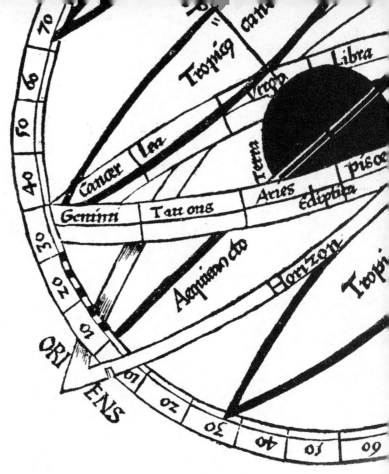

about the author

Raven Kaldera first began learning astrology in the eighth grade when he did the charts of all his classmates. He is currently a shaman, homesteader, herbalist, kitchen witch, intersexual FTM activist, and the founder of the First Kingdom Church of Asphodel. He is the author of *Hermaphrodeities: The Transgender Spirituality Workbook* (Xlibris Press, 2001), and the co-author (with Tannin Schwartzstein) of *The Urban Primitive* (Llewellyn, 2002) and *Handfasting and Wedding Rituals* (Llewellyn, 2003). 'Tis an ill wind that blows no minds.

mythastrology

RAVEN KALDERA

EXPLORING PLANETS & PANTHEONS

2004
Llewellyn Publications
St. Paul, Minnesota 55164-0383, U.S.A.

FIRST EDITION
First Printing, 2004

Book design and editing by Rebecca Zins
Cover design by Kevin R. Brown
Cover planet image by Brand X Pictures

Library of Congress Cataloging-in-Publication Data
Kaldera, Raven
    MythAstrology: exploring planets & pantheons / Raven Kaldera.—1st ed.
    p.   cm.
    ISBN 0-7387-0516-0
    1. Astrology. I. Title.

BF1708.1.K35 2004
133.5—dc22

2004044238

Llewellyn Publications
A Division of Llewellyn Worldwide, Ltd.
P.O. Box 64383, Dept. 0-7387-0516-0
St. Paul, MN 55164-0383, U.S.A.
www.llewellyn.com

PRINTED IN THE UNITED STATES OF AMERICA

contents

The Moon, 61

Mercury, 101

venus, 137

Mars, 179

Jupiter, 221

Saturn, 263

Uranus, 307

Neptune, 343

preface
How to Use This Book

I began this book with Psyche and ended it, years later, with Cybele. Writing it provided one of the most intense spiritual experiences of my life. I didn't choose who to write about; I made a list of all the planets in all the signs and studied it every night. I asked the cosmos, the myriad gods, who wanted to step forward and claim a placement, and explain to me why it was theirs. Inevitably, one figure detached itself from the undifferentiated mass of Spirit and visited my mind, telling their story and claiming their place.

I thought that I knew astrology pretty well until I began this book. It was the gods themselves who taught me how much I didn't know. They showed me nuances of each sign that I had been oblivious to. How many times had I tossed off a cookbook-entry description when confronted with an energy that was unfamiliar to me? "Venus in Aries means that you are assertive in love," I'd say, and leave it at that. While not untrue, these summations were certainly incomplete. It took the feisty Rhiannon to show me the real melodrama of an Aries Venus, and so on throughout all the planets. In some cases, my two-dimensional thinking included planetary placements that were to be found in my own chart. I had always glossed over my own Saturn in Pisces; it took Odin to explain to me why my life was the way it was and how Saturn had affected that.

On the other hand, even a deity myth of depth and complexity cannot encompass the entirety of any given planetary/sign energy. For all that the myths gave more understanding and complexity, they are not the whole story, and this should be kept in mind as you read them. They are simply archetypal patterns—ways of being human in this world—that fit within the energy of each placement. You'll have

your own personal "take" on each planet and sign; if you come u
with more myths that I've overlooked, I'd love to hear about them.

Of course, the easiest way to use this book is to look up your ow
chart, planet by planet. However, you can also go further. You ca
use the planet-sign combinations to find planets that are aspectin
each other—for instance, your Venus may be in Leo, but if it is als
conjunct Pluto you may want to check Venus in Scorpio for adde
depth of understanding. These myths are also helpful if you ar
undergoing a transit; if Uranus is going over your Moon, readin
Moon in Aquarius might be helpful in understanding the combina
tion of lunar and Uranian energies.

You can also just concentrate on what's going on in the sky at th
moment. If the biggest transit of the week is Saturn in aspect to Mer
cury, you could check either Saturn in Gemini or Mercury in Capri
corn. The more strongly aspected planet is likely to take the day, so i
Saturn is more intense you might decide that this would be Loki
week and meditate on his lessons, and plan accordingly.

If you are a polytheist, you might want to think of the deities o
your birth chart as your own personal pantheon. You might want t
make offerings to them, or create small altars for them, or meditat
and have conversations with them. They'll listen, and hopefully giv
you some advice on how to get through their lessons.

If you're a professional astrologer, you've probably already discov
ered how difficult it is to interpret a chart for someone who know
nothing at all about astrology. That spirograph with the funny littl
symbols all around it isn't the easiest thing in the world to make usei
friendly. You can use this book to do a reading the shaman's way—b
telling stories. Your clients may not understand what an Aquariu
Moon means, but the story of Mwuetsi will probably make ther
laugh knowingly, or nod sheepishly, or at least think hard abou
themselves and their motivations. They may not understand Mars i
Leo, but they will respond to the imagery of roaring Sekhmet. Usin

the myths as illustrations—and object lessons—can give them an easier vocabulary to take with them. To know that having Jupiter in Libra means that some part of them has similar goals, values, and pitfalls to the goddess Hera can be more useful than knowing that their Jupiter is in an air sign ruled by Venus, especially if you take the time to make the stories real for them.

Whether you're a deist or simply looking at archetypes as ways of being human, you'll find that the myths in this book can start to become real for you, if only in that you'll start seeing them in people all around you. You'll start to see the actions of the people you know in terms of the stories that they are living, and see your own life that way as well. And once you see them, you'll find that you've given yourself more choices about what paths you want to be on, and which you feel you're done with. It's how the right stories can change anyone's world.

The sun

Amon-ra

Sun in Aries

In the ancient land of Khent—the Black Land as its occupants called it—the greatest of all gods was Ra, the burning sun. He ruled over all the land like a great father, dispensing wisdom and putting down rebellions. Ra was the creator, the first god of the people of Khent, which today we call Egypt. Before there were any others there was Ra, the all-seeing eye in the unremitting hot sky over a parched desert land. He was the First, just as the Aries Sun is the first, and always will be. In his legend we see the sun with early eyes, those of people who first looked up and saw divinity, the source of life. Aries is primal instinct, survival, and he is very good at it.

Ra, as the sun, spent half the day soaring in the air, inspecting his kingdom below. In the morning he and his boat rose out of a lotus flower, and at night he sank into the depths of the underworld, bringing light for its dead inhabitants. This daily voyage was not without peril, however; there was a great serpent, Apep, living in the Nile, who sought to swallow Ra's boat and had to be constantly fought off. In the underworld there were other terrors, each attempting to devour his light. In some allegories, he is born as a little child each morning and ages to an old man each night.

We tend to think of Aries as a simple, straightforward sign, rather one-dimensional, without much depth. Nothing, however, could be further from the truth. For one thing, Aries combines apparently contradictory archetypes within him: the Innocent Child of springtime and the Warrior of Mars. We will come to the Warrior in a moment, but first we should look at Ra the sun god who lives each day as if it were his whole life, present in the moment. This is one of the gifts of Aries consciousness, especially in the solar placement. Ra also needs to fight daily battles in order to survive and bring light to both worlds, and here we can view the quintessentially Arian trait of courage. This is the energy of the daily battle that one emerges from victorious every time, and awakes fresh to every morning, all demons defeated for the time being. It is part of the Aries fire, and it is sustained by innocence. He does not believe that he can lose or that each day may not be an event to be lived with wonder.

Ra had a secret box locked away, which was the source of his power. In it, as his unfortunate grandson once found, were two items: a poisonous snake and a magical lock of blue hair. The snake had a tendency to leap out and kill anything that opened the box, and the lock of hair could heal any wound, even that of the deadly snake. The two together can be read as both the Achilles heel of Aries—the anger that leaps out impulsively, not caring who its random targets might be—and its salvation, the lock of hair as blue as the wide sky. The sky, in Egyptian mythology, is the place of the crying hawk, Ra's symbol, and Horus's as well. The flying bird looks down on things from a distance, a quality the tempestuous Aries Sun needs to learn—using his head (from whence comes the lock of hair) rather than his leap-and-strike survival instinct.

However, Ra made a few errors. Among them was his rather strange attitude toward children and grandchildren. He drew from himself the first two children, Shu the god of the air and Tefnut the goddess of the dew, as if they were a mere experiment. When they proceeded to have opinions and desires that did not mirror his, he was rather surprised and annoyed. Shu and Tefnut mated and produced two more children, Geb and Nut, and this upset Ra so much that he ordered them permanently separated from each other, a task Shu performed. When they managed to thwart him and produce five children, however, he gave in and grudgingly accepted his new brood. Aries likes new things, but only new things that go along with his idea of how things should be, which seems like an impossible contradiction and in fact is one. In spite of this, he recovers quicker than many signs and does not hold grudges.

When Ra grew old and weak, his subjects began to mutter against him. This is the worst fear of Aries the Child, who hates the idea of old age and lack of control. Ra decided to teach his rebellious subjects a lesson and sent Sekhmet after them, but she ate so many of them that he had to resort to getting her drunk in order to stop the extinction of his entire kingdom. This shows that even when Aries' anger seems like a good idea at the time, it often gets out of hand and has repercussions that the enthusiastic Aries never seems to guess at beforehand. Isis also took advantage of his old age, playing the feminine Venus-ruled Libra Moon to his masculine Mars-ruled Aries Sun and charming the words of power out of him. Once she had them in hand, she nullified his power and took it for herself, and he realized—as trusting Aries often does—that he had just been had.

Ra was the first god, and he was chief of the pantheon for millennia of Egyptian history, but somewhere in the twelfth Pharaonic dynasty a new god arose who would eclipse Ra and all the others, up until the Christian era. He was warlike and strong, and bore as patron animals the Arian ram and the aggressive goose. His name was Amon, and his priesthood gained ground with disconcerting speed. Pharaoh after pharaoh named himself after some relationship to Amon or built temples or obelisks to him. The most famous of them, the pharaoh who conquered more land than any other, was

named Ramses. Amon was Mars to the hilt; he was shown sometimes as a man with double plumes on his head and sometimes as a
ram-headed man. He ruled the Age of Aries with his chariot and
lance.

Seeing this, the priesthood of Ra agreed to combine the two gods,
and Amon-Ra came out of that agreement. The new composite
deity that was Amon-Ra owned so much of Egypt's wealth that his
priesthood was richer than the pharaoh. After the last of the Ramses dynasty died off, the chief priest of Amon-Ra ascended the
throne himself. In Ethiopia his priesthood chose the rulers; in Libya
they built him a great shrine. Child, Old Man, Great Warrior—he
held within himself all the archetypes of Aries, all of which any
Aries Sun can access and manifest, and neither he nor any of his
worshippers saw any contradiction.

Aries conquers less out of ambition than out of challenge—not of
others, but of himself. On some level, he knows that each trial will
improve his spirit a little more, and he is driven toward them. If he
can't find a worthy challenge to keep improving himself with, he
will find an unworthy one and pursue it anyway. He is the "I"
opposed to the Libran "Thou," and he can be self-centered, like Ra,
the sun that is the brightest thing in the sky. He can also fight to the
death for the right things, or the wrong ones. Aries' energy is not a
guided missile; it's a cannon that needs to be aimed properly or others will suffer. Aimed at obstacles, he plows through them as if they
don't exist. It isn't so much ambition as the thrill of the chase. After
all, there are many reasons why a king or general would conquer
other lands, but Ramses, the chosen of Amon-Ra, did it for one reason alone: glory. Aries understands glory. It's part of the secret of his
contradiction, you see . . . both the Child and the Warrior are surrounded by clouds of glory. Different kinds, perhaps, but glory
nonetheless. Glory is the heart of this most fiery of fire signs . . . and
after all this time, hawks still circle the glorious, blazing Sun.

ᏩᎯᏋᎯ

Sun in Taurus

The Earth is the place from whence all our bodies come. It can be thought of as the original body that we grow out of and that we will return to. It can even be thought of as the body that we are parasites living in, if you'd like to put it that way. However we put it, it comes down to the same thing: Earth and body are on some level one and the same. There is the fiery core of chemical reaction, there is the skin, and there is the place where Earth touches Sun. This surface is the place where most of the life is concentrated, green and growing, sessile and moving, constantly changing yet dancing in the same old patterns of birth and death and rebirth from the soil.

This interface of Earth and Sun is where we best experience the sacred being that we call Gaea. Unlike other deities, she is easy to see and touch. Other sacred beings can be experienced subtly in the wind or the flames or the cycle of life, but Gaea is the most obvious and tactile. We are never very far from her, unless we leave the planet. She is right there, where we can dig in her, feed from her, crumble her in our hands. And that's just the way Taurus likes it.

The ancient Greeks named her Gaea. She has other names, though—Tellus Mater, Erda, Artha, Hertha, and so forth. She is the one constant in every religion, because we are all born of her. Yet to reduce her simply to a personification of the ball of dirt we live on is to far underestimate her in our psyches. She is Mother as much as she is Earth, she is metaphorical as much as she is physical. In our collective unconscious she is the nurturing figure who is more powerful than our actual mothers, and to whom they never measure up. She is all-giving and maternal, but in a completely different way than that of, say, Demeter, whom I have associated with Cancer. Demeter loves personally and intensely, and is easily thrown off by changes in her children, mirroring Cancer's sensitivity in the face of trauma. Gaea mothers impersonally; she is all-generous, but none of her children is more special to her than any other. She is hard to shock. Like a secure Taurus individual, you can beat on her breast and scream and she will stand patiently, loving but unmoved, until you are done.

If this immense archetype seems a little difficult to live up to, it is. Yet every Taurean Sun has Gaea at the roots. Gaea's impersonal force of gravity illustrates the Taurean Sun possessiveness, which is strong but often seems impersonal. People sometimes become property-like, thing-like, in their hearts, and thus the confusion when their "things" get up and walk away. Although Taurus does have to guard against this, it does not come out of a sociopathic need to dehumanize or objectify; it is just the ripple of Gaea consciousness coming through them. To her, we are all her things.

At its worst, this can result in a kind of materialism where objects or money take the place of attention or loving words. This sort of Taurus is someone who, paradoxically, has not gotten away from the earth archetype but has gone too deeply into it, and perhaps needs to be dragged up and away by some other god who can show them the long view. Whatever else material goods become a replacement for, however, it will not be for physical affection. The most sensual and affectionate of all the signs, Tauruses need physical touch like they need water. It would do them well to remember that earth without water—Taurus without Venus's ruling power of love—is a desert. Sometimes just increasing the amount of loving touch they have in their lives, assuaging that skin hunger, is enough to bring them back from a dry world of materialism and drudgery. For Taurus, hugs and cuddles really can work wonders.

Like Gaea, who objected to Uranus the sky god spreading himself over her and stifling her, Taureans may object to more airy types who dominate the conversation, expect everything to move at their pace, and become impatient at the Taurus need to make decisions slowly and think things over carefully. Like the physical Gaea, Taurus prefers slow changes to fast ones. The Earth does not live at the same rate that we do, and it is as if Taurean Suns are tapped into that Gaian clock just enough to keep them slowed down a little more than the rest of us. Slow, of course, does not imply stupid. It is not the opposite of intelligent, but rather the opposite of impulsive, or rapid, or abrupt, or haphazard. Taurus would rather see that something is well thought through than go off half-cocked. And on a simple emotional level, it takes her longer to get used to things. That's why it's hard for her to let go of people and jobs and ideas— she'll have to get used to not having them around.

It seems that in most descriptions of Taurus, astrologers go to the trouble of emphasizing the bull rather than the cow, as if Taurus was the most masculine of signs. It's actually ruled by Venus, the most feminine planet of all, and is a supposedly "feminine" (meaning receptive rather than aggressive) sign. So why all the macho posturing? Perhaps in order not to offend male Taureans, who sometimes do a good deal of macho posturing themselves, as if to prove that they don't have any of those receptive qualities. Still, any sexism out of Taurean men is far less about Taurus-type beliefs about gender and far more about simply being socially conservative and uncomfortable with major world-view changes. If we lived in a matriarchy, Taurus men would probably be telling the rest of the boys not to act uppity or take on women's airs.

To change the mind of a Taurus, you have to be in their life, day after day, putting forth your best effort to be friendly, not getting into a lot of intellectual discussions (because even if you win them, it probably won't change her mind) and just putting in the time until she gets used to you and whatever your alternative ideas and lifestyle are about. You'll have to outwait her, which will not be easy. When you've become a fixture in her life, strange ideas and all, she'll accept you because it will be more effort for her to throw you out. You can even keep your strange ideas, because she's used to them now (on you, anyway), and she'll be more shocked if you ever change your mind.

But anyway, back to the bull. This livestock animal appears in hundreds of myths, from Europe to China, as the sacred earth-spirit. It seems (in the western half of the world, anyway) that if the Earth Goddess could appear as an animal, it would be a cow, and so the bull simply became Gaea's male incarnation. You will notice, however, that the bull is often sacrificed to Gaea. Part of this is the concept of giving back like to like, but the deeper meaning seems to be that the aggressive, trampling nature of Taurus needs eventually to be sacrificed to (read: cycle back into) the overarching archetype of Gaea's abundance and generosity.

Gaea gives abundantly because she has it to give, which describes a Taurus Sun who is secure in themselves. They are also associated with the archetype of the Builder, which they share with Capricorn and occasionally Virgo. However, the motivations are different: it is said that Taurus builds up because there are mountains, and levels flat because there are fields, and digs deep because there are caves. In other words, Taurus builds like the Earth makes its own natural features and for the same reasons. Capricorn is more likely to build high in order to dwarf the mountains, not become them.

Taurus is strong. She has the solidity of earth and stone, tree and bone, and when her anger erupts, as it rarely does, it is like hot lava leaping from a crack that has just appeared in the ground. Taurus takes a long time to get good and angry, and unlike the fire sign's brushfire or lightning-strike rages, Taurus can take a long time to cool down as well, and by the time she's done, there may be an awful lot of scorched earth. Still, remember that she is ruled by watery Venus and that dumping lots and lots of love on the problem can usually bring things down sooner. When she cries, which will not be often, it's the rain falling, and it's over. When she decides to push something down, she will do it if it kills her, which is not likely. That kind of strength is rare. Don't dismiss her earthiness as stony nonlife. Gaea is all about life, life of all kinds, even the kinds that you don't want around. That's why Uranus was so upset about her making giants and hundred-handed critters, but she didn't care. She had made them, and that was good enough.

The Taurus gift is the ability to be rooted, to be at home not only when you are at whatever place you hang your hat in, but anywhere you go. Rootedness is the ability to own, in turn, each square of sidewalk or road or floor or bare ground that you plant your feet on, with every step you take. When you're rooted, even in the midst of moving, it's very hard for you to be pushed down or thrown off. Ground and center, they call it, which just means that you are the ground and you are the center, no matter where you are.

Earth. Water. Sun. The recipe for life.

The Dioscuri
Sun in Gemini

According to Greek mythology, Leda, the queen of Sparta, was visited in her bed by the great god Zeus in the form of a swan, a creature of the air. She gave birth to two sets of twins, and both times one twin was the offspring of Zeus and therefore semidivine. The other twin was sired by her husband Tyndareus and was therefore fully human and mortal. One set of twins was male and named Castor and Pollux; the other set was female and named Clytemnestra and Helen. Although only Castor and Pollux were referred to as the Dioscuri—the children of gods—I count Helen and Clytemnestra also as Dioscuri. These two sets of twins exhibit all the terrible and wonderful qualities of Gemini. In fact, only a Geminian tale would have two sets of twins, anyway. Isn't that overkill?

The Dioscuri, however, are hardly the Bobbseys. Although Castor and Pollux are technically not full brothers, they are heartbound. One is mortal and the other immortal, but they are inseparable. However, they seem to mostly spend their time either adventuring or making mischief, sometimes both at the same time.

They go on adventures to rescue Helen from Theseus, who has kidnapped her; with Jason on the *Argo* to steal the Golden Fleece; and get into fights with neighbors over oxen and daughters. They never seem to settle down, and indeed settling down, at least mentally, feels like the worst thing that can happen to a Gemini. They also never seem to really suffer or get into trouble—it's as if the gods watch over them—until their very last adventure.

At this point, they are paying court to two daughters of a local king. Of course, two brothers so close could only love two sisters, which says a lot about the Gemini need for a multifaceted partner to assuage their potential boredom. The problem is that marriage inevitably means settling down and making commitments, and something in this volatile air sign instinctively knows that if he does this— becomes tied to the realm of Earth—his days of divine protection are over. He will have to take his karma and vegetables like everyone else. His time of being the puer—the eternal youth—will cease.

Another pair of brothers are paying court to the girls, and bad blood ensues. Battle comes, and Castor, the mortal twin, is struck dead. Pollux decides that he would rather die himself than live on without his brother, yet with his divine blood he will go to Olympus upon his death rather than Hades. He appeals to Zeus, who takes pity on him and decrees that the two brothers shall not be separated. They will spend half their time in Olympus and half in Hades. This suggests that part of successful integration of the Gemini Sun's twin selves is equal time in both twins' realms: part of the time on high Olympus with the gods and theories and imaginations, and part of the time down in the dark, instinctive realm where we all have to go from time to time. For Castor and Pollux to remain together, Pollux must willingly give up half his divine life to raise half his brother's life. Integration must be more important than whatever dark things it is that he fears. It must be remembered that Earth is halfway between the sky and the underworld, and to remain on Earth is to be balanced between them.

Their sisters, Helen and Clytemnestra, have an entirely different relationship. In Helen's case, her divine heritage means that she is astonishingly beautiful, while Clytemnestra is only average in that department. Helen is already set apart without even having to do anything. Her beauty is her power, shedding light on everyone it touches. She is so stunning, and becomes so desired, that her father actually allows her to choose her own suitor from the kings gathered around her in a panting crowd. She chooses Menelaus, the brother of the Achaean king Agamemnon, who is much older than her.

It is, however, passive power, unearned. This kind of empty charm with no substance or experience to it is another common trait of unevolved Geminis. They can be brilliant—Helen's name means "light"—but as this is a mental air sign, they can fall into the trap of keeping their intellect entirely separate from their emotions. Helen shines and everyone is impressed, but it's all superficial. And when you are superficial, you often become objectified, which is what happens. Paris, the prince of Troy, makes a deal with Aphrodite the love goddess to steal Helen, and she gets moved like a chess piece from one man to another. From being more than human she becomes less than human, a thing of brilliance to be possessed.

Part of Castor and Pollux's charmed life was that they were inseparable. When his twin selves are functioning as a team, Gemini works much better . . . but only as long as he lets the divine twin run the show. When they are separated, as eventually happens with Castor and Pollux, he suffers a deathly ordeal until he can make them truly equal in his psyche. When they are separated from the beginning, as with Helen and Clytemnestra who never get along, the suffering starts early. It is the mortal side, the feeling side, who does the suffering. Goddesslike Helen never seems to complain much about her changes in status. She is valued and fought over no matter where she is. Her face launched a thousand ships. No matter how the war turns out, she will still be a princess. She lives the good life, the from-the-neck-up life, while the feeling side is shut out.

And what happens to that feeling side? Clytemnestra's story is one of the great tragedies of mythology, and her brave struggle is ignored by those who later chronicle it. Seen as uglier than Helen and of less importance, she is casually married off at twelve by her distant father to a much older retainer. At thirteen, with a newborn babe in her arms, she is forced to watch while Agamemnon, as part of an ongoing feud, murders her husband. He then dashes out her baby's brains against the wall, throws her down on the bed and rapes her, and tells her that they are now married. When she fights him, she is locked up, and he begets four daughters and a son on her. Eventually she subsides, living in an apathetic coma and attempting to find happiness in motherhood.

Unlike Helen, whose passive beauty and charm give her some choices, Clytemnestra has none. She is used and abused and locked up, like the feeling side of a Gemini who has not yet integrated her twin selves. Whenever there is inequality in a Gemini Sun's psyche, the brilliant, divine day self wins out and the emotional, mortal night self loses. The Sun much prefers to shine through a divine light than a deathlike darkness. Clytemnestra is sacrificed so that Helen may be the admired princess.

Yet such a situation cannot go on forever, in the myth or in the psyche. Agamemnon goes off to the Trojan War, leaving what he thinks is a broken, docile wife to keep his kingdom in the meantime. Then, at the coast, the winds all fail and his fleet cannot move. One can sense the Gemini essence at work here in the fickle wind's refusal to come. It might symbolize the eventual failure of the cut-off mental processes, the air that suddenly deserts Gemini when he most needs it, leaving him beached and stranded. What does he do? The oracle tells Agamemnon that it is Artemis who is angry with him, and that he must sacrifice his oldest daughter Iphigenia on a funeral pyre to her. Artemis, protector of women, is in this book associated with the Sagittarius Moon, which stands exactly opposite to the Gemini Sun in both zodiacal and planetary energies. Although the sacrifice is a cruel thing, it triggers the situation to leap out of its comfortable chains.

Agamemnon does not hesitate for a moment. He sends for Clytemnestra, telling her that Iphigenia is to be married to Achilles, and she must be combed and perfumed and sent to the coast. When Gemini confronts the breakdown of his supposedly efficient splitting mechanism, his first thought is of what can be sacrificed to maintain it. Usually, this is something of value to his repressed feeling side that his thinking side discounts as expendable. Iphigenia is Clytemnestra's favorite daughter, the comfort to her harsh existence, but she figures that Achilles will be off fighting for some time and she will not be denied her daughter's company for long. When she discovers that her beloved daughter has been sacrificed so that Agamemnon can have his divine wind, she snaps.

As soon as his ships have left for Troy, she instigates a full-scale rebellion, abolishing the newer patriarchal laws and instigating the older matriarchal ones. She takes as her lover Agamemnon's hereditary enemy Aegisthus, a man who "like a woman would not go to war"; i.e., he is more interested in relationship than in action. She conducts wholesale executions of Agamemnon's loyal followers and gives women full rights with men. When Agamemnon finally returns after seven years, she rolls out the red carpet for him, draws him a bath, and then she and Aegisthus murder him in the tub. It's war and chaos, and the feeling side overthrows its chains and overwhelms the psyche. Gemini can find herself acting strangely, exploding at people, or even having a nervous breakdown. She swings completely over to the side of emotional reaction, and her values shift radically. This can go back and forth for some time. The repressed emotions, once they have surfaced, are hard to put back in the box—Clytemnestra would rather die than go back to being a timid wife.

The story does not have a happy ending. Agamemnon's son Orestes feels that he must avenge his dead father, and kills his mother and her lover. The Furies pursue him, as they torment all who are mother-slayers—just because you attempt to kill the irrational side doesn't mean that it goes away; rather, it comes back in an even more horrible form. He appeals to Olympus, and the gods are split down the middle. Finally the super-rational goddess Athena casts the vote in his favor, and the Furies are driven off . . . but at what cost? Helen goes back to her husband, but eventually becomes bored with him. She flees to Egypt, but while traveling in Rhodes she is caught by a group of women dressed as Furies, and they hang her as vengeance for all the men who died in the war over her.

This is the kind of persona division that put Gemini Marilyn Monroe into a deadly drug overdose. For Gemini Sun to fail in her integration process is to walk straight into chaos, madness, and death. For no other sign is it so easy to separate the thinking and feeling functions into tight containers, and for no other sign is it so important that they refrain from doing so. The only way out is the solution of Castor and Pollux—half of all time and energy spent in the mental world and half in the underworld of self-introspection—and for that, the twin selves must be allied, must not hate each other, must value each other as the most important thing in the world. If Gemini cannot do this, she will break down the middle. Yet from that integrity can grow true brilliance, deep and not superficial, with nourishing roots in the dark and limbs that spring toward the light. Even a drifting seed must put down roots eventually or it will die; without both light and darkness, so do we.

Demeter

Sun in Cancer

There are many mother goddesses, all over the world; they are all wrapped up with the comings and goings of birthing, suckling, nurturing, and generally bringing forth life. Mother is the first goddess, or at least the first one that we all experience. It will take a lot of technological and social change before we lose the initial infant awe of Mother, whom we come out of and without whom, in that crucial early time, we cannot survive. Cancer is the sign of Mother, even when its native is male; we all, male or female, come out of a woman, and we will all struggle with our relationship to her, and to all women, for the rest of our lives. Our struggles may differ drastically, but we will have them.

If we are placed into a position of nurturing ourselves, whether it is in relation to a child, a lover, a spouse, a friend, or an aging parent, we discover the struggles with the other side of that archetype. To be the nurturer is just as ambivalent as being the nurtured; to care deeply for someone and then watch them become independent of you—or die—can both fill your heart and rip it out of your chest. When the Sun is in Cancer, that ambivalent, beautiful relationship between caretaker and cared-for is highlighted by the Sun's light. It is the focal point of the native's sense of self.

Mother goddesses like Gaea or Erd or Mawu seem more identified with creation than with the deeply personal role of Mother. Their fecund wombs bring forth all sorts of life, and they rule over all that grows, whether it be wild or tame, animal or plant, great tree or small insect. Every form of life is sacred to them. The Cancer experience, however, is very different from Taurus's benevolent issuing forth of life. Cancer chooses one place to aim her nurturing, and promotes gross favoritism toward her chosen loved ones. To experience Cancer is to fall in love with *your* children, *your* lover, *your* project, *your* morals, and to clearly favor them and pay more attention to them than to the progeny of others. Cancer may be driven to nurture people to the point where she dishes soup to strangers in a shelter and gives kindly advice to coworkers, but she will turn aside at once if one of her own calls her. To be Cancer is to invest a great deal of love and effort in a very small basket.

Demeter, the ancient Greek goddess of the grain, is an example of this personal maternal instinct. She is the granddaughter of Gaea, but she is not goddess of all that grows. She concentrates solely on that which grows to the benefit of man: domestic crops. Wild plants and animals are worse than useless to her. She nourishes humanity with her gift, and does not give exemptions for squirrels, crows, and weeds. She also bears four distinct children in her lifetime, which she treats with very different sorts of love. Her mother-love is so personal that she cannot distance herself; Demeter lives her nurturing close up, with all the hardships this entails.

Her first child is Arion the talking horse. Not much is said about him, except that Poseidon cast his eye on her while she was a maiden bathing in the sea; she turned into a white mare to flee him through the tide, and he turned into a stallion and raped her. After that, she bore a pair of twins. One was a magical foal who could talk, which she named Arion; the other was a female child named Despoena. Unable to reconcile herself to their forced conception, she had them fostered out. Despoena became a goddess of deep mysteries, and Arion a traveling oracle. As for Demeter, she never dared go again near the ocean and hid for long years in a cave weeping with rage over her despoilment at Poseidon's hands. The symbol of Cancer is not a crab whose hard shell protects his inner self for nothing.

This reminds us of the truth that a nurturing nature is often taken advantage of by the unscrupulous or insensitive. This can cause deep wounds in anyone, but the sensitive Cancerian nature finds it especially difficult to heal. Cancers nurse grudges for a long time, as they cling to their memories both good and bad with the tenacity of a crab. Sometimes one cannot heal from a betrayal until one first begins to let go and forget, and this is a lesson Cancer will always find it hard to be resigned to. It is also interesting that her disastrous first attempt at childbearing produces children who are not entirely human and who are associated with mysterious cult activity. Cancer as Mother brings to the experience not only an immense depth of feeling and devotion, but also all the baggage of her emotional impressions and preconceptions; she can often respond to the child as she sees him through the haze of her past, rather than as he really is.

In order to bring her out of the cave, Zeus offers to marry her. Together they bear a third child, Persephone, on whom Demeter pins all her hopes of love. Her marriage with Zeus does not last, as he leaves her for Hera, but she hardly seems to notice. Persephone is the golden child, the laughing creature of beauty on whom Demeter can focus her entire attention. Finally, Mother Demeter has someone to love, someone who is completely dependent on her and cannot leave. She takes Persephone to an idyllic place, the fields at the foot of Mount Nysa, where she plays with the nymphet daughters of Oceanus and lives a picture-perfect, if slightly overprotected, idyll of childhood.

However, no childhood can be eternally perfect, regardless of the hopes of a Cancerian parent. As a young maiden, Persephone suddenly disappears. Demeter searches for her fruitlessly, becoming more and more frantic; finally Helios, the personification of the Sun, tells her that she has gone down to the underworld and is now in the clutches of Hades. Demeter flies to Olympus, where she faces down her former husband Zeus and demands that he force Hades to deliver Persephone back to her. Zeus refuses, pointing out that Hades is wealthy, powerful, and a good husband prospect, and Demeter flies into a rage.

Anger is different for Cancer-type people. While Aries may jump and strike, Taurus may bellow and charge, and Scorpio may lash out viciously, Cancer tends to internalize negative emotions and fall into a deep depression. This is the placement where the Moon rules the Sun, and eclipses it; emotion takes precedence over clear sight. All the water signs are far less concerned with what the facts are than with how they feel; facts are heartless and statistics offer them no love. After her initial anger, Demeter goes on a kind of total emotional strike. Nothing will grow, she tells Zeus, until my daughter is returned to me. She leaves Olympus in a wandering fog of despair, and behind her all the plowed ground becomes barren and infertile, and the people of Greece begin to starve.

Demeter's depression mirrors that of women suffering empty-nest syndrome, or of any man or woman who loses a lover or child. It also shows a truth about vulnerable Cancer—when they are overwhelmed by their feelings, it takes a long time for them to get any sense of objectivity. Demeter is so unhappy at her abandonment by the only person who loves her that she is willing to sacrifice the entire race of humanity in order to get Persephone back. Of course, during her wanderings she ends up nurturing again; she presents herself as a nanny to a local king and queen, and takes care of their baby son. The employment ends when the queen enters and panics at seeing Demeter placing the baby on the fire in order to make him immortal. Demeter, disgruntled that the mother does not want the gift of divinity for her son, reveals herself and leaves the palace. She does, however, teach the awed royal family to plow with paired oxen, and directs them to spread this knowledge over their country.

The Corn Goddess is not quiet in her mourning. She is dramatic, melodramatic even, making sweeping gestures of despair. May the whole world die with me, if I am to be plunged into darkness! This is often the response of a grief-stricken Cancerian, who will let things lapse rather than bravely go on as if nothing is wrong. Cancer is the sign closest to the heart of the feeling process; it is impossible for Cancer not to feel their feelings, and nearly impossible for her to conceal them utterly. Sometimes, when she is self-absorbed in her problems, she can lash out in irritation. In Demeter's story, a small boy mocks her as she trudges grey-cloaked from country to country, and she turns him into a lizard in a flash of rage, angered at his cold-bloodedness toward her obvious pain.

When Zeus finally gives in and fetches Persephone, there is a joyous reunion, but Demeter's happy home is not to be the way it was before. Persephone has pledged marriage to Hades by eating six pomegranate seeds, and is ready to become the queen of the underworld. In other words, she has grown up. Demeter is not happy with this, either; in some versions, after the reunion is over, she demands that Persephone be allowed to remain with her. Hades, on the other hand, also has a suit to press, and so Zeus decrees that Persephone shall spend half her time above ground with Demeter and half below with her husband. Persephone seems content with this equal division of her time and loyalties; there is no record of whether Demeter ever does.

There is, however, one small story of Demeter that seems to happen chronologically after the Persephone tale, and it is that she finds a mortal ploughman named Iasion, lies with him in the freshly plowed fields, and has by him a mortal child named Plutus, who spreads her cult throughout Europe. So it seems that even after the complete disruption of her happy home life, she manages to find some joy in living. The feeling principle of Cancer is strongly tied to people; people are her home and hearth and without them she would be adrift. Although she retreats into a shell periodically to replenish herself, a lonely Cancerian is a miserable Cancerian. Everyone must fight their way through old patterns and preconceived notions to come to a stand with the power of the nurturer, and learn both about holding on and about letting go.

cybele
Sun in Leo

When the Sun goes into Leo it is in its own sign, and it can shine through unclouded, with no other influences to get in its way. To have a Leo Sun is to experience the ultimate power of solar energy in its entirety, with no interference. It is about having your soul exposed completely to that life-giving golden light all the time.

You'd think that this would be nothing but a good thing, right? The problem is that sometimes it's useful to have a little something between you and the Sun. Like clothes. Or sunglasses. Or an ozone layer. If you really want to experience something like the full power of the Sun, go visit the Sahara desert at noon during the hot season. Even then, there will be an atmosphere between you and Sol; if you were to truly experience it without any protection, you'd simply be burnt to a crisp.

It's one of the unspoken dangers of being a Leo Sun. That solar warmth wants to shine through you, to use you as its conduit, and it's a seductive thing. If you're not careful, it can consume you utterly. That's when Leo goes down to its classic pitfalls of arrogance and egotism, all watery compassion and empathy burned away, believing that she is more than a flawed mortal like the rest of us. It's a hard game to shine and inspire and make others light up and yet not lose yourself in the Sun's demanding rays. After all, the Sun is the biggest thing in the solar system, and its call is the loudest, without exception. That's why the gods gave Leo a wild side.

Leo's symbol is the Lion, and in the ancient Near East, lions and lionesses were the totemic animal of the Magna Mater, the great goddess Cybele. She was shown as enthroned and dignified, in true Leonine fashion, her big cats flanking her throne like regal guardians. In one hand she holds her sacred drum, and in the other the lotus from which she pours forth the water of life. Her priests called her Lady of the Wild Things, and they preferred to eat wild game such as pheasant or hare rather than domesticated animals. Her rites were performed both in the great temples of the Magna Mater, called *metro'ons*, and in desolate places in the wilderness.

Cybele's high crown is shaped like a walled and turreted city, and she is the bringer and guardian of civilization. At the same time, she is also Lady of the Wild Things; her priests often worship her in the wilderness and eat wild game and foraged food. This dichotomy of wildness and civilization is the paradox at the heart of every Leo's existence. Leo almost always cultivates an aura of polished, urbane sophistication, and she likes to be the ruler of her own part of society. But beneath this veneer of civilization stalks a predator, still trailing the vines and creepers of the jungle, and when she is peeved she can suddenly revert to her animal side and lash out with her claws.

An example of this is found in her treatment of her son-lover, Attis. He is the classic golden boy, born of a virgin who ate a pomegranate from a magical fruit produced by the blood of a sacrificed hermaphrodite, Agdistis. When Attis is unfaithful to Cybele with Agdistis, the goddess vengefully turns her face from him, and there is no placating her except with his death. In one of the many versions of the myth, he castrates himself instantly, cutting off his own source of vitality, and bleeds to death. In another, she forces him to marry a mortal princess instead, and sends Agdistis to the wedding to drive everyone mad and cause Attis's self-castration and death.

Such is the strength of his contact with Cybele's life-giving warmth, however, that he does not die entirely but continues to live on as if in a coma. Cybele relents and encloses him in a glass coffin reminiscent of Snow White, and he becomes an object of reverence for the faithful. It is almost ghoulish, and reminds us that Leo is a fixed sign, and can hold on far too long and too possessively to a lover, a career, a child, or an image of herself. She needs to remember that wild part of her nature, the one who knows how to track down sources of water in the desert, who can bring her back to her own sources of inner wateriness so that she is not baked dry by the solar rays.

One of the great ambivalent blessings and pitfalls of Leo's solar warmth is her nature as the consummate performer. Associated with the fifth house of creativity, the Performer is a Leo archetype that can completely overshadow the life of an individual Leo Sun. All ancient religions had a tradition of music and dance, but this had a special place in Cybele's worship. Her festivals, and even her everyday veneration, were famed for their musical performances. Her main symbol was the tambourine—basically a frame drum, larger than our modern tambourines, with metal jingles around the edges. Another sacred tool was the cymbal; one of the rites was to eat bread from a drum and drink wine from a cymbal that was passed around. She was also credited with inventing the flute and the panpipes. Her followers lost themselves in hours of ecstatic dance to this music; in order to commune with Cybele, a large public performance had to occur.

The large public performance is also the preferred venue for communing with a Leo Sun, or at least that's what they believe on some level. Even if they have no musical or artistic talent at all, they will make their own life into a kind of dramatic (or melodramatic) masquerade. The shining solar persona that they don to impress others can become a permanent installation, rather like the classic mime who puts the mask on his face and then finds that it is stuck. At the worst, they can become so identified with that persona that they forget it is only an outer layer. No one gets to see them without their makeup and costume on, and thus they lock themselves into the trap of the star who is adored superficially by all but truly known by none. Living permanently in the archetype of the Performer can be a very lonely place.

The most likely reason that a Leo Sun might end up with the golden mask locked onto their heads is an underlying sense of low self-esteem. We must remember that so much light must have an equal amount of shadow, and Leo may use performance as a way to boost their ego. The irony is that the more you hide yourself from others in favor of the golden mask, the more you feel as if that hidden self is worthless and the lower your self-esteem gets. The very tool used to save the situation can actually make it worse.

The key lies in the fact that Leo is the sign of self-expression. To tell a Leo Sun never to perform, even if only for the tiny audience of the family circle, is an exercise in futility. They need to realize that the best performance is the one that actually shows the side of them that they find most vulnerable, polished and presented to the crowd with a sincere heart. It's a terrifying thing to do, and yet it is their destiny. It's the performance most likely to get them rejected, and yet if they find a way to make it work, it will be the only thing that truly gives them the love of self that they crave. They must be truly seen and loved for who they really are or it will all become a desperate charade.

The dark side of that cycle is, of course, that if they try to keep that charade up permanently, they will burn out. It is no accident that Lammas, the day on which the golden king of sun and grain is sacrificed, occurs while the Sun is in Leo. To take on the golden mask without surcease is to offer yourself up as a sacred king or queen, and to do that is to place yourself on the inevitable path of Cybele's partner, Attis. He is the other side of the Leo Sun, the golden boy who was born only to die so that others might live, again and again.

In this country, our sacred kings tend to be performers—John Lennon, Jim Morrison, Jimi Hendrix, Janis Joplin, Phil Ochs, Kurt Cobain, Tupac Shakur, Buddy Holly, Richie Valens, Elvis, and Jerry Garcia (a Leo Sun who died very close to Lammas). They sacrifice themselves to our greed for entertainment, to our need for that blazing solar warmth, and it consumes them. To be the sacred king or queen is to become more than mortal, larger than life, and the part of you that is human is locked away in a small, pitiful box where it beats vainly against the bars and becomes smaller and smaller in comparison to the image. The loss of self-esteem in such cases becomes a total loss of self, and the mortal side shrivels, weeps, and finally dies, taking the all-too-mortal body with it. To walk Attis's path is to die for the people . . . not as one of many, like a soldier or worker, but as the brilliant, special, one-of-a-kind sacrifice that reflects Leo's love of seeing themselves as unique. When the Performer seizes them, they would rather die than be just one of the masses.

A Leo's challenge is to learn to channel self-expression without being overcome by it. If there are no good places for a Leo to put that need for self-expression, it will come out in histrionics in her personal life. If the self-expression becomes central and paramount, it will consume her like a flame. She needs to keep in mind that Cybele's rituals took place around bonfires. The word *bonfire* comes originally from *bonefire*, because sacrifices were burnt in them. To be the bonfire is to be central, to be gazed upon, to be that which others gather around . . . and to be full of the burnt bones of sacrifices. The bigger the fire, the more bones are in it. Sometimes it's better to scale back and be a hearth fire for a while, warming only those who love and know you for who you are, who may only be able to give you small kindling, but who will not let you burn out completely when the ritual is over.

Hestia
Sun in Virgo

There are far fewer legends about Hestia, Greek goddess of the hearth, than there are about other Olympian gods, but that is not because she was less honored. Actually, she was one of the most frequently honored deities in her pantheon, as she was invoked every time the hearth was lit. At the center of every home sat Hestia, burning bright and giving out her light and warmth; without her, no food was cooked and no heat could help people survive the cold weather. On special feast days, the people of ancient Greece might go to the temples of the appropriate deity; they might also invoke them for certain occasional purposes under their various rulerships, but Hestia was invoked on a daily basis, and they were quite well aware that they were dependent upon her for their survival.

Hestia was literally the spirit of the home's center; her quiet, unassuming, unobtrusive presence was said to contain the peace of the household, and if she fled, chaos was soon to result. This kind of "dailyness," ordinariness, concern with sober, everyday, boring work, is one of the traits that Virgo is often ridiculed for today, yet it is what Hestia was honored for then. Hestia's face is never seen; she is represented only with a flame, and this also is sometimes the lot of the Virgos who make society tick, remaining behind the scenes, unseen, but without whom the whole mess would fall apart. Although everyone enjoys appreciation, Virgo has the ability to go on without praise or accolade or fame and not be terribly emotionally injured. Hestia did not need great parades; she knew that she would be invoked every day with the kindling of the new flame or the feeding of last night's embers into a renewed blaze.

She was not a goddess who liked change and adventure. She ruled the household and all its tasks under her different titles—Hestia Tamia, for instance, was the lady of the pantry, who inventoried the home's resources and saw that they were stored properly. Both she and the Cancerian Demeter were associated with food (not surprisingly, as Cancer rules the stomach and Virgo the intestines), but Demeter was goddess of the fields and the harvest, and as goddess of nourishment she brought the food into the houses and barns and storerooms, where it then had to be counted, preserved, and distributed—in other words, it passed into Hestia's realm. This kind of love of precision is for Virgo an act of worship. God is in the details, says Virgo, and she believes it. When she is unsatisfied, she often suffers from stomach pains or comes up with stringent diets, as if her food is no longer sacred and she is somehow trying to purify it.

The Virgo Sun does its detail work for two reasons. The first is that of the mathematician and the physicist, which, when all is said and done, is a kind of worship as well: worship done in honor and awe of the great ordering of the universe. The second reason is more prosaic: in order for everyone to have their share, everything must be carefully measured. In a perfect world, says Virgo—and make no mistake, a perfect world is her eventual spiritual aim—no one should go without due to mere sloppiness. If I cannot stop humans from being greedy and trying to take more than their share, at least I can do this: I can make sure that everything is in order so that we can be sure that malice, not incompetence, is to blame. When you find a Virgo who is nagging about apparently inconsequential things, you have found a Virgo whose drive to worthy service has been thwarted, and who desperately needs a Great Work to tend to.

The Greeks had a saying: "One must sacrifice to Hestia." It was a well-known euphemism, and what it actually meant was, "You have an obligation to help feed those guests who come to your table, and divide what food you have between you as best you can." Sacrificing to Hestia meant adding more water to the soup, cutting the bread finer, hauling out the extra carrots, doing whatever it takes to make sure that no one goes hungry. Like her opposite sign Pisces, a Virgo is driven to be of service to people, sometimes to humanity itself. A Pisces, however, does it because he is so empathic with the rest of humanity, so merged with them, that their pain fills him with compassion and he can do nothing else. A Virgo, on the other hand, does not merge well with anyone. She feels quite separate from the rest of the human race, sometimes even too much so. She does what she does because it needs doing and someone ought to do it, thank you very much. There is as much and perhaps even more honor in helping someone that you cannot empathize with, simply out of moral duty. It means that your aid is not subject to changeable emotional tides, for one thing.

Appropriate for the sign of the Virgin, Hestia is one of the three goddesses of Olympus who is sworn to eternal virginity. Her attitude is quite nunlike, and indeed she is a patron of those who seek a monastic life, especially those traditions that stress the sacredness of physical labor and the making of daily work into a discipline. Hestia is in sympathy with medieval nuns working in their potager and Shinto monks raking careful circles around the stones in their meditation gardens. She understands what a balm to the soul even hard, repetitive work may be when it is done with a sacred attitude. She also understands solitude, even while among a whole family of people, and that it can be a source of inner peace and not merely loneliness, and all of these are also Virgo secrets.

Of course, all that self-contained virgin energy is fine if you are going to become a monk or dedicate your life to a goal of service, but it gets a little tricky when it's time for close relationships with other human beings. Hestia prefers to keep other human beings at a distance, often ruthlessly—the Vestal Virgin priestesses in her temple in Rome were executed if they did not remain virginal—and so, it must be said, does Virgo. It isn't that Virgos don't enjoy sex per se, it's that they are uncomfortable with its necessary intimacy. A Virgo who is afraid of being psychologically invaded by sexual activity will often separate it from emotional love entirely. Unlike other signs who pull this trick and then turn it into casual sex, Virgo rarely does anything casually. Sex then becomes a job, either a tedious work of duty or a polished, accomplished masterpiece of physical ecstasy with which a Virgo dazzles, pleases, and serves a lover. Some people mistake the former for modesty and the latter for passion. However, a Virgo will not let you into her soul through her genitals until you have already made an entrance for yourself in other ways, such as being willing to do the dull daily work of a relationship, including negotiating who takes the car to the mechanic and exactly how much should be spent on cat food this month. Remember, for a Virgo, details are sacred. If you scoff at them, you lose her trust.

Although she never had any sort of a mate, the Olympian that Hestia was most frequently associated with was Hermes, the quicksilver god of travel. The oldest and youngest of the Olympian gods, they represented the tandem polarity of inside and outside, center and rim, hub and spokes. Hestia was the networker in the middle of things, and Hermes made his flights from her central hearth. She was the privacy of the home, and he was the community of the road. Although opposites, they were invoked regularly together in the same hymns, as if they were two sides of the same coin. Oh, yes, and speaking of coins . . . one point they had in common was the gift of inventory, Hermes through his patronage of merchants and Hestia through her rule of the storehouse. No merchant could do his work without knowing what he had and what he should charge for what amount. Again, we come back to the Virgoan work of accounting . . . Virgo, who is ruled by Mercury, the Roman name for Hermes.

Hestia has a deeply comforting and healing presence, in spite of her wish to keep her distance. She is the mistress of the home remedy, again in partnership with Hermes, who carries the healing caduceus. This is linked to yet another of Virgo's great mysteries: the one about being broken. The one that no one wants to hear. It goes like this: At some time in everyone's life, there will come a time when the universe will give you a burden too great to bear, and you will break. None of the other eleven signs really believe this one; they all have elaborate plans about how they will run away, or be too strong to break, or build a hard shell, or else they are just in denial about the whole thing. Virgo, on the other hand, has no illusions that sooner or later it will come to each of us. At that time, we must call on her power as the Great Repairer of the World and learn to pick ourselves up, fix ourselves as well as we can, and keep going, because there is still so much more Great Work yet to be done.

Dike
Sun in Libra

The sign of Libra exists in an eternal contradiction. As the Scales, Libra represents, forever, that which is difficult if not impossible to reconcile; the two truths that cannot both be true, yet are indeed so. Libra's job is not to come up with ultimate truths. Libra's job is to point out that even ultimate truths have contradictions. Other signs don't like this very much, especially the fixed ones. In fact, most people like the comfort of being able to know that some things, at least, are absolutes and cannot be contradicted.

Libra knows better. One of her fundamental paradoxes is that she is ruled by Venus, and therefore seeks harmony and peace while being the sign of Justice, which is usually not very peaceful. She is pulled in two directions forever by these opposing tides, and always will be. It is part of her cosmic job—seeing both sides, weighing, reweighing, doing a huge amount of disruptive work for the sake of eventual peace. Libra is charmed by appearances and is also driven to question them. Libra wants to be in relationship and yet is driven to argue with everyone. Libra idealizes love and analyzes its mystical foundations to death. Despite all the fluffy clouds, this is not an easy sign to live in.

The second wife of the great god Zeus, king of Olympus in ancient Greece, was Themis, the giver of social order. She had three daughters by him—the three Horae, or "hours," who were beautiful and graceful and represented the three seasons of the Grecian climate. The first was Eunomia, whose name means "rules"; Dike, whose name means "justice"; and Irene, whose name means "peace." They were also spring, summer/autumn, and winter, respectively. Of the three, the one who later broke away from her sisters and established herself separately was Dike, the goddess of justice, and she will be our Libran heroine here.

The word *horae* itself has many other word descendants, including hour, horology, whore, and the Persian angelic spirits, *houris*. The Horae are associated not only with the seasons but with all timekeeping and its study, as they symbolize all parts of the turning cycle. Priestesses would dance the "Dance of the Hours" in honor of the Horae, which survives in such unusual places as the Jewish *Hora*. As they exchanged their favors for temple offerings, they were ladies of the hour. It is not surprising that a sign ruled by Venus has links to her sacred prostitutes. Their later incarnations— the Greek hetaera, the Japanese geisha, and the courtesan of Renaissance Italy—were all educated, graceful women skilled in art, music, and good conversation. They were said to be experts in the art of gracious living that gives pleasure to civilization. Without that Libran aesthetic touch, our world of rules would be grey indeed.

What does it mean that such concepts as rules, peace, and justice are associated with the seasons of the turning year? It can imply that such principles are part of a natural cycle, such as the eternal turning of the solar climate, or it can suggest that moral concepts should be based on the observable laws of nature. These two possibilities alone can be seen as mutually exclusive and open to debate. The Sun lights up Libra's aesthetic side perhaps a little more than an argumentative Mars placement, but the urge to play devil's advocate to every side is still very much in evidence.

The Horae were originally seasonal deities who brought rain in the proper amounts to the proper times of year. They were associated especially with flowers and fruits, which shows a connection to the Venus-ruled goddess of beauty. The Horae are shown bedecking Hera's chariot with flowers and weaving garlands to protect the cradle of the infant Hermes. Thus their concerns are both with Venusian aesthetics and with the rules of society, as if laws and aesthetics were not mutually exclusive. Indeed, it is only in our culture that they are thought to be contradictory; in ancient Greece the presence of one was considered evidence of the other.

Dike is not just a beautiful flower-weaving maiden, however. In her later incarnations she stands alone without her sisters, sitting on a throne blindfolded with a sword in her hand. This is the Justice figure that we are more familiar with, the lady who coldly cuts the case down the middle. This face of Dike is just as relevant as the pretty maiden and gives us another clue to the Libran Sun. The dance of hours and seasons can also be the dance of karma, which brings us all what we deserve, step by step. All justice comes with time, and so Justice is bound up with Time. In the early days, human sacrifices were sometimes chosen with dice made from the pastern bones of hoofed animals, and thus referred to as "knuckle-bones." They were dedicated to (and named after) Dike, in the hopes that she would make sure the right person made the cut. Similarly, the handsome, charming Libran can suddenly pull back and go as cold as a sword on a winter day, saying, "That's not fair." Like Dike, they may change in an instant from a gracious host to a cool, dispassionate judge looking for the most effective person or thing to sacrifice.

As Aries represents the experience of "I," Libra represents "I and Thou," the balancing of not only two truths but two sets of needs. As such, it is the sign of one-on-one relating, and Libra-ruled people want very much to be in relationships with others. It's not so much like Cancer's need for family or Capricorn's for security or Scorpio's for deep bonding; Libra is simply driven to practice relationship skills, and can't do it alone. Without a partner to bounce off of, a Libra—and especially Libra Sun—can't finish her karmic lessons properly. It can be pretty humbling to realize that your karmic lessons rest on the wayward shoulders of other human beings, something that is sure to be bad for Libra's easily jangled nerves.

Libra is an air sign, and air likes to see things objectively, from a high-flying height. If you watch a Libra Sun calibrating her internal scales and look closely, it's extremely likely that the two sides of the discussion involve an air voice and a Venusian voice—one that wants to do the objectively right thing and one that wants to do the subjectively satisfying thing—the end result that seems right and the end result that feels right. The scales pull back and forth against each other until an equilibrium is found . . . or not. Sometimes the equilibrium is not the point. Sometimes the means are the end; the process is the important part. That's a Libran principle that more goal-oriented signs are profoundly uncomfortable with. (Remember that the symbol of air is the sword, which Justice holds.)

Dike finally gave up on humanity. After centuries of the injustice of man to man, she left her sisters and retreated to the top of a high mountain, swearing she would never come down until there was justice in the world. According to the legend, she's still there. This too is a Libra problem; sometimes the only way that a Libra Sun can get away from the constant disharmony of inconsistency and injustice is to retreat into a prettily decorated world of her own. After a while, she can also fall into the trap of believing that this is the real world, thus giving up justice for personal peace. With the removal of Dike from the equation, however, we are left with Peace and Rules, but no Justice. This is the kind of situation that creates dictatorships, and we should all be grateful that someone is saying, "But wait, let's look at the other side." Two Horae are not enough.

It's said that Justice is a whore, and not just because she was once one of the Horae. She takes no favorites and no man can woo her; she is available to all, for a price. Venus herself is the patron of sex workers, and her priestesses were sacred prostitutes. The idea that sex can be bought for money makes most people flinch, because we place sex above such things as physical objects and more menial services. On the other hand, we put money into religion, and sex can be just as great a spiritual experience, and doesn't the one who provides that experience deserve compensation? On the other hand, in our antisex society, how can we ever overcome the centuries of Christian teachings that sex is filthy enough to give sex workers real respect? On the other hand, would a sex workers' union, a true sacred band in service to Venus and the Horae, slowly change society's ideas about the difference between a whore and a housewife, and what justice they each deserve? This Libra Sun argument is brought to you by the element of air and the planet Venus. Thank you for playing.

shiva

Sun in Scorpio

The planet Pluto is referred to in whispers. When it transits over your Sun, astrologers shake their heads and warn you not to hold on to things too tightly or you might lose them in the bumpy ride ahead. When your child is born with Pluto on her Sun, they warn of a strong-willed troublemaker. And Scorpio, Pluto's patron sign, has the worst reputation in the zodiac. Just saying that you're a Scorpio to someone who knows barely anything about astrology makes them shudder or giggle, although they might not really know why. Scorpios themselves either exploit that reaction or are wholeheartedly tired of it. They have to live with the raging emotional intensity of Pluto blasting its nuclear energy through the Sun. They don't need others making warding-off gestures and running away.

In India, the three deities Brahma, Vishnu, and Shiva form a trinity that creates, sustains, and destroys all creation. Of the three, Shiva is the oldest and is actually integrated out of a much older tradition. He is known as the Destroyer, yet his destruction is a prelude to rebirth. First and foremost, Shiva destroys illusion, and as in esoteric Hindu thought the entire world of Maya/matter is actually an illusion, he is also its destroyer. This can be read as the Plutonian power of transformation and its ability to entirely destroy someone's "world," or at least world-view.

Shiva, like Scorpio, does nothing by half measures. This is the god of All or Nothing. In an opposite reaction to Libra's balancing act, Scorpio wallows in extremities and overcompensations. Scorpio is about the opposite of balance. In the Shiva invocation in *Hermaphrodeities* (Xlibris Press, 2001), Shiva cries, "I loathe halfway measures; when you are trying to find the right distance between the heat of the fire and the cold beyond it, you may know me as the solution which urges you to leap directly into the flames!" He spends centuries on top of mountains, doing yoga and meditating and working toward ultimate enlightenment, then comes down and flings himself into sex with his consort. One of his symbols is the giant lingam, and yet many of his followers are celibate or even castrated. He destroys without hesitation, and willingly throws himself beneath the feet of Kali to be himself destroyed in turn. He craves self-control, yet appears as a wild man with the River Ganga flowing from his long, wild hair. Libra might try to resolve such contradictions by moving to a middle ground, Gemini by suppressing one or the other by turns. Scorpio doesn't even try to resolve them. Contradictions are good for you. They build character. So does Pluto. What does not kill you, says Scorpio, makes you stronger.

One of the powers of transformation is the ability to take what is negative and find a way to transmute it into something positive; to find the wonder in the darkness, the utility in the castoff. This is a Scorpio gift, and true to form, they are fascinated (secretly or openly) with all things hidden, mysterious, and unacceptable. They upset the apple cart and lift the rug to see what is swept under it. Unlike Brahma and Vishnu, who were the patrons of people with status or wealth or social importance, Shiva claimed as his own the outcasts, the human beggars and untouchables, and nonhuman vampires and demons. He also honored those who rejected society for greater goals, such as hermits and ascetics. His holy place is the cremation ground, and his priests dance the *Tandava* with a skull held in each hand. Death is his friend and his tool, neither good nor evil.

However, this attraction to the dark side can go two ways: it can lead the Scorpion deeper into a morass of psychological muck, or it can spur him on to find a way to redeem it. When the great serpent

Vasuki threatened the world with his dripping poison fangs, it was Shiva who saved the fleeing mortals and gods. He drank the poison as fast as the serpent could produce it, until there was none left in Vasuki, and transmuted it into harmlessness with his own body. Shiva's throat was burnt blue from the ordeal, but the snake became harmless and gentled, and Shiva now wears Vasuki around his neck like a pet. There is something important about the Plutonian ability to use one's own experience of darkness as a way to heal others; when they pour out their inner poisons and you do not flinch, when you accept them without shock, when you show them how you survived and even grew stronger from your experience, you do Shiva's work.

Shiva's asceticism was such that when the beautiful goddess Parvati (see Venus in Virgo) fell in love with him, he ignored her. He sat on his mountain and concentrated on meditating; she danced erotic dances in front of him and got no reaction. Devastated, she went to the top of another mountain and meditated until she achieved a level of enlightenment close to his. When he suddenly became aware of her glowing spirit he fell in love, but even then he was plagued by Scorpionic suspicion. It can be excruciatingly hard for Scorpio individuals to trust anyone or anything, especially that which looks too good to be true. Sometimes, doing all that work in the dark makes you forget that the light is real, too. Taking on the form of a young, mortal Brahman, he distracted her from her meditations and tried to get her to give up this futile chasing after Shiva. She retorted that she would not give up until Shiva noticed her, and the god finally unbent and revealed himself to her. It is said that all the mountains trembled when they first lay together.

Shiva also shows the famous Scorpio temper. Unlike the noisy rages of a fire sign, a Scorpio will brood silently until the final straw, and then he will act quickly, brutally, and possibly still in silence. A Scorpio would rather slash your tires than bellow hysterically. Unevolved types often react to a perceived enemy with a lightning-quick slash of tongue or action, sometimes without much consideration as to whether the punishment is fair. In Shiva's myth, the god came back after an absence so long that he did not recognize his son Ganesha, nor did Ganesha recognize him. Shiva tried to force his way into the apartments where Parvati was bathing, and her protective son attempted to stop the stranger. Shiva flew into a rage and struck off Ganesha's head. After much weeping and recriminations from Parvati, Shiva remorsefully resurrected his son and gave him the head of an elephant.

People tend to forget that Scorpio is a water sign. They are deeply, intensely emotional; feelings well up in them like tidal waves and they cope as best they know how. Scorpios don't like to go with the flow like Pisces or Cancer; they try to impose control on that emotional chaos. Unevolved types attempt to control those around them; evolved types follow Shiva's path and work on self-control. Their forced-calm exterior often hides a great turbulence they restrain only with great willpower. To understand the lesson of control, which every Scorpio Sun will have to do, it is necessary to remember that magic is the will and the word. The word comes first. You speak the vow—"I will stop myself from flying into rages and hurting those I love"—and then you use will to implement it. Success increases your confidence, your personal power, and your faith in your own effectiveness, and the next time it will come easier. If you avoid taking vows, you never get a chance to build up your will and personal power. If you break those vows, you lose what you have gained. In time you learn an iron-hard faith in your will, and thus in your word. Shiva's word can destroy entire universes and re-create them anew.

One of the ways in which Shiva confuses people is that he is androgynous in an odd way. One of his titles is the Lord Who Is Half Woman. Many of his priests wear their hair in a distinctive manner—one side tied up in a woman's bun and one side hanging wild like Shiva's flowing locks—in order to represent inner harmony between their male and female sides. They either castrate themselves or are required to be married in order never to lose touch with the female principle. Shiva himself takes several goddesses as consorts, and has a different relationship with each of them. With Uma/Parvati, he acts closest to a real husband, including a sensual sex life. With the virginal Durga, he is a comrade in arms, slaying the demons of illusion. With Kali, who is a more powerful destroyer than he is, he submits himself humbly to accept the same treatment that he gives to others. (This is another crucial lesson for the Scorpio Sun; in order to keep from being mired in the delusion they criticize in others, they must have a Kali in their life.) His relationship with Shakti is more nebulous; she is at once an embodiment of all his consorts and also his own female side, with which he merges.

Scorpio is said to be the sign of sex, which is a great oversimplification. It can more accurately be summed up as the sign of deep psychological merging, which most fumbling humans use sex to achieve, with varying levels of success. Part of this attempt to merge is a matter of reaching for the *hieros gamos*, the internal sacred marriage of one's own male and female natures. As Ardhanarisvara, the hermaphroditic god/dess who is female on one side and male on the other, Shiva/Shakti shows hirself fully in touch with all internal aspects. We humans, of course, tend to project our currently less dominant side onto our lovers, echoing the symbolism of Shakti being both other and second self. When we finally learn that the idealized being we are chasing is actually within us, and learn also that no characteristic should be shunned simply because it does not belong to our social gender, we no longer need to be obsessed with people who apparently resemble that inner lover. Shiva/Shakti, the Lord Who Is Half Woman, is the evolved Scorpio response to the urge for deep connection; we cannot fully know another until we are whole within ourselves.

Ascetic and sensual, stern and demanding, avatar of self-control who gives up control to his consort, Shiva is intimately involved in

the life-and-death-and-life, gain-and-loss-and-gain cycle of existence. His path is never the easy one. Indeed, it may be the hardest
one of all—merciless, unstinting, sparing no one, including himself.
Yet the difficult path can be the most rewarding in the end, when
the more flighty types have all fallen away . . . rather like having the
Sun in Scorpio. It's not easy living with everything turned up to high
volume, but when the alternative is a dull, muted life, is that really
living? Scorpio doesn't think so, and neither does the Destroyer of
the Universe.

vainamoinen

Sun in Sagittarius

In the Finnish epic poem Kalevala, the unquestioned star of the pro-
ceedings is the hero Vainamoinen. He is the archetypal Finnish cul-
ture-hero, the deity to whom they pray when something needs to be
done. When a great famine overtook Finland, it is said that
Vainamoinen made the blueberries grow so huge that they fed all
the people; he is sometimes referred to in common speech as the
Blueberry God.

Vainamoinen is a hero-god, but he is a different sort of hero from
the Grecian or Celtic ideal of the warrior whose first skill is with
arms. Although he does fight at least one battle with the sword, it
seems to be his last resort. Vainamoinen is a wizard-bard, called the
"wisdom singer"; when in trouble, it is magic that he resorts to. He
is cunning and canny, and phenomenally perceptive. He sees what
others miss and acts wisely on the information that he gleans. He is
a strategist, not a sword-swinger.

There are other differences between him and other classical
heroes. For one thing, Vainamoinen is referred to as "Old Vainamoinen" throughout much of the Kalevala. We tend to think of
Sagittarius as being youthful and peppy, due to the proliferation of
pop astrology (and perhaps the sign's fiery vigor), but we forget that

it is one of the later transpersonal signs. In the archetypal round that posits the signs as the stages of life, Aries is the infant, Taurus the toddler, and Gemini the child. Cancer rules early adolescence and Leo is associated with the later teen years. Virgo, Libra, and Scorpio are adult phases having to do with work, marriage, and reproduction. By the time one gets to Sagittarius, the soul is well into middle age—not necessarily elderly, as old age starts with Capricorn, but middle age was considered old in ancient and medieval times. The Archer is no youth and, despite the fiery vigor, the Sagittarian essence has a more tempered quality to it than Aries and Leo.

Part of Vainamoinen's age, of course, is that he is kept for thirty years in the womb of his mother Ilmatar (Mercury in Cancer), who is unable to give birth until she has land to do it on. He grows to full adulthood inside her and becomes impatient and frustrated with his confinement. Starting with his feet, he forces his way out of her womb unaided and promptly falls into the ocean. One joke (which anyone who has raised a Sagittarian child will understand) claims that they tend to leave home early, occasionally as early as twelve or thirteen. The wanderlust in this Sun sign, even if ameliorated by other influences in the chart, tends to make Sagittarian teens chafe at the bit earlier and more intensely than children of other signs. To them, waiting until their eighteenth birthday may feel like a thirty-year gestation. I know an appalling number of Sagittarians who ran away from home in their mid to late teens, and almost none who were still living at home in their twenties.

Of course, the problem with forcing yourself out of the womb is that sometimes you fall into the ocean and nearly drown. Vaina-moinen is forced to swim, naked and freezing, for miles until he finds the nearest shore and washes up on it, offering prayers of gratitude for his very life. Then he promptly starts wandering again and never stops throughout his entire epic—ambling or hurtling from one adventure to the next. In the last chapter, he sails off into the sunset, promising to return someday. His gypsylike existence echoes the Sagittarian archetype of the eternal wanderer, always searching for the next beautiful horizon. When they are true to themselves, Sagittarians never stop journeying, if only mentally.

Vainamoinen is not lucky in love. He woos the daughter of Louhi, only to lose her to his friend Ilmarinen the smith. Other maidens, too, slip through his fingers. This may be a consequence of his archetype as the eternal wanderer; commitment is not something that comes easy to him (or to a Sagittarian) and so the permanent companion that he desires—or convinces himself that he desires—never quite appears. This is not an unfamiliar situation to many Sagittarians. Although they may have many lovers, they tend to keep some part of themselves aloof and unattached, as if they want an escape route should a greater adventure appear.

It may take them some growing up before they can make a commitment without their emotional fingers crossed, and part of that growing up requires a great deal of life experience. If they don't feel that they've had enough adventures, they won't be able to fully invest themselves in another human being. Sometimes they need to completely satiate themselves with the grubby side of the adventurous life before they can turn away from it. Vainamoinen is utterly unable to run away from a challenge when some harried local seeks his help; his travels take him to such extreme places as the land of the dead (which he escapes unharmed).

In Finnish mythology, all the heroes are sorcerer-heroes who defeat their enemies with magic powers. In order to gain these powers, they must learn the true name of whatever they wish to control. For instance, if you wanted to control the force of cold, you would go to the coldest place on earth and learn the true name of cold. It's a particularly Sagittarian form of heroism; it's based on what you know, not just how well you swing a sword. Learning it can go on for a lifetime—this is the sign of higher education—and involves lots of traveling.

Like all fire signs, arrogance is a major fault of Sagittarius, and Vainamoinen is no exception. His insight is excellent, but he cannot see all things, and he sometimes forgets this. He is full of helpful advice, which his companions ignore. Because he can perceive things that others cannot, he is convinced that he has the real skinny on how life should go, and he is upset when his views are not automatically accepted. More than anything, Sagittarius wants to be right. He wants to think of himself as holding the moral high ground even when his ethics are slippery, as clever Vainamoinen's often are. He will usually justify his slips to himself by saying that he can clearly see how these means justify a future end.

Sometimes he's right, in the sense that Sagittarius is often struck with prophetic moments (the keyword for this sign is "I see"), but that doesn't mean that he's always right or that he will be able to get his point across to others. Even when his analysis of the situation is correct, not everyone will believe him. Sagittarius sometimes feels like Cassandra, whose prophecies were never believed until it was too late. However, the truth of the matter is that people need to be left alone to make their own mistakes, and this infuriates Sagittarius. He cannot see why he shouldn't be able to interfere and help them avoid errors, and he keenly feels his lack of control in the situation.

At the end of the Kalevala, a radiant child is born to a beautiful virgin mother. All the bodies of the heavens declare that this child is the son of gods and that he is destined to rule the world. It is transparently the disguised figure of the Christ child, perhaps left over from a time when Finland was still pagan. The priest does not know whether to accept the child's claim or not, and calls in old Vainamoinen to scry the child's future. The old sorcerer-god recognizes the child's divinity, but prophetically realizes that his worship will nearly eradicate the pagan world of nature worship that Vainamoinen is a part of. Fearing for his country, his people, and his religion, he diplomatically suggests that the child should be killed.

The child remonstrates indignantly, saying that Vainamoinen is not pure and perfect and thus cannot judge him. His words imply that the sorcerer-god's time is over and his own is just beginning, and that Vainamoinen should accept his defeat gracefully. Impressed by his words, the priest accepts the child as ruler. The old minstrel-god does withdraw, but not gracefully. He sails off into the sunset in his magical boat, grumbling that he will return when people have enough sense to turn again to the "true religion."

It's a classic moment of an otherwise knowledgeable Sagittarius archetype going off in a huff because his wisdom is refused, waiting to enter again from stage left when everyone has had enough of disaster. Of course, he will be full of I-told-you-sos. The bluntness of this sign is legendary; Jupiter's rule of his tongue makes him worse than undiplomatic. Sagittarians secretly long for a world where radical honesty is the rule, and where one could say anything one wanted with no regard for anyone else's feelings. Since he has an excellent tolerance for receiving this ambivalent gift himself—unlike Aries or Leo or Scorpio, he really can take back what he dishes out, being a master at not taking things personally—he doesn't understand why anyone else ought to need him to curb his tongue. He'll do it, often skillfully, because he knows that it must be done in order for him to communicate his ideas. He won't enjoy it, though, and his respect for someone may secretly fall in inverse proportion to how much careful diplomacy they need and how little raw honesty they can take. His favorite playmate is someone who can verbally tussle him without taking it all so personally.

This concentration on raw honesty is part of his preoccupation with finding Truth. For him, there isn't just a whole lot of little truths, often contradictory; the very idea drives him mad. Somewhere, somehow, there has to be one great Truth that makes sense of all the others. It's one of the reasons why he falls prey to fanaticism, or at least rather pompous moralizing, so often. Vainamoinen's scathing preaching at Ilmarinen when he tries to make the golden wife is a good example of this. In his contempt for people's errors, he forgets the very real—and often emotionally nebulous— reasons why they make those errors in the first place, and thus his lectures tend to be rather unhelpful. It's a challenge for this fiery, intellectual sign to force himself to stop and consider such things as other people's irrational feelings and needs.

Vainamoinen's magic lies in the fact that he can figure out, through a combination of prophetic insight and sheer cleverness, exactly what has to be done to save the day. And if it's not something that he can do himself, he has an array of fascinating friends whose talents he can call upon to help him out. Although he is the unquestioned leader of the adventures—being the one with vision— he always has talented sidekicks whose powers aid and complement his own. He manages to get them going when they are reluctant by the sheer enthusiasm of his lust for life. In the end, this is the Sagittarian gift . . . to see the golden dream on the far horizon, to figure out the pathway there, to shoot for it, and to inspire others to do the same.

Hephaestus
Sun in Capricorn

Hephaestus, in ancient Greek mythology, was the unloved and unwanted son of Zeus and Hera, king and queen of the gods. In some versions of the myth, he is Hera's child alone; she is jealous of Zeus, who has created Athena out of his head (although he technically did it by swallowing his pregnant first wife Metis, transformed into a fly), and she tries to parthenogenically make a baby herself. When Hephaestus is born, he is disfigured with a clubfoot and a hunched spine, so she flings him off of Olympus to die. However, he stubbornly refuses to die, and this is the real secret of Capricorn. Ruled by Saturn, the planet of limitations, Capricorn children are born feeling as if there is some sort of restraint on them, even when they are healthy and well-formed. There's a sense of social awkwardness, of difficulty with expressing themselves openly, or a fear of being socially rejected if they do open up. Saturn's reserve is almost like a psychological crippling, mild or not-so-mild. On some level, they are painfully aware that they are not the easy golden children whom everyone will automatically love.

However, this outsider status does not necessarily crush them, because Capricorn is an earth sign and not easy to crush, and in this placement it is lit by the power of the Sun. Instead, they grit their teeth and decide that they will climb that mountain like the mountain goat that is their symbol, step by step, if it kills them. They will win their way to the top by skill and dedication if not innate charisma. One Capricorn woman I know says that her job strategy, in order to make up for her lack of social allure, is "I will make myself necessary."

Hephaestus, crippled and rejected outsider that he is, refuses to be so quickly cast away. He is determined to get back up that mountain of Olympus where the gods live, however he can do it. He is adopted and raised by two sea nymphs, but he still feels his rejection keenly. He learns the art of metalworking and smithery and soon becomes skilled at making all sorts of clever artifices. Smith-gods are generally associated with earth as they draw their material from the ground and also because they symbolize work. They are also associated, however, with fire. Hephaestus embodies this contradiction of a fiery planet—the Sun—in a hard-working earth sign. He toils endlessly to create his beautiful things, combining solar creativity with earthy persistence. His anger also smolders underground like the volcano that is his symbol.

The center of Earth is the closest place we have on this planet to the heat of the Sun; molten rock that burns white-hot. It is hidden under Earth's crust except for the places where it mounds up and leaks through; in a volcano like this, Hephaestus made his workshop. His intense emotions were channeled into his work, a typical

Capricorn strategy. With a job that they are passionate about or a job that will help them achieve a goal that they are passionate about, Capricorns can easily slip into workaholism. Although they can do any job if it furthers their goals, they do prefer a job where they actually get to build something, whether it's a machine or a company.

Hephaestus finally becomes skillful enough that he is able to build a golden throne, which he sends as a gift to Hera. As soon as she sits in it, golden shackles snap over her wrists and ankles, preventing her from moving. She is furious, especially as Hephaestus is the only one who can release her. The tables are turned now, and all must beseech the rejected smith-god for aid. In a Saturnian fit of pique, he refuses to come out of his workshop to free Hera. Let her stew a while, let her get a taste of what it is to be helpless, to pray for the goodwill of an unforgiving, distant figure.

It's the dark side of Capricorn. Being the loner and the outsider for too long can embitter him. Since he has difficulty with emotional release, he can let resentments pile up inside him until they explode, and then he frantically tries to control everyone else around him in an attempt to make up for his own loss of control. His tit-for-tat can become unreasonably cruel, especially if the pain of aching years is behind it. He can become rigid in his need, unbending and uncompassionate, and drive away the very love and appreciation that he secretly longs for.

Ares, god of war, was sent to drag Hephaestus from his cave in order to free Hera. The smith-god hid under the volcano and flung fiery brands at his brother, driving him away. Finally, the youngest child of Zeus, effeminate Dionysus, goes down to talk to him, a large jug of wine in hand. Dionysus is so obviously unaggressive that Hephaestus lets him in and accepts his wine. After a few hours of toasts the smith-god is falling-down drunk, although Dionysus is hardly tipsy (what, drink the wine-god under the table? Not likely). Dionysus convinces his half-brother that he should come up to Olympus and deal; loading the staggering, singing smith-god onto a donkey, he brings him up to face the immortals. Zeus is so impressed by his mystery son's ingenuity, courage, and stubbornness that he offers to make him one of their company if he will free his mother. Loosened up by wine, Hephaestus agrees and becomes one of the twelve vote-casting Olympians. It's a classic lesson of never underestimating the power of I'll Show *You*.

He is never fully accepted, however. Many of the other gods and demigods, all perfectly formed, snicker privately or even publicly at Hephaestus's stumbling, limping walk and imperfect body. Even though he has won his place through mastery and skill, he is still the only physically imperfect Olympian, and nothing he can do will change that in the eyes of gods such as Apollo, Ares, and Hermes. It's another battle for Capricorn to fight; even when people respect his skills, they may not like him as a person. He may often settle for respect rather than affection because he may think that this is all that he can get, and become even more closed within himself. Dignity, for the malformed and ridiculed god, is a rare and precious commodity, perhaps seen as the most valuable of all. No other sign so carefully guards its dignity or is so wounded without it.

When he crosses Zeus, however, he learns a Saturnian lesson in authority. He tries to defend his mother Hera when Zeus beats her, and the enraged king of the gods flings him off the mountain, almost killing him. This is the crossroads decision of Capricorn, who both feels for outsiders and underdogs (having been one himself) and desperately does not want to be one again. He can be put in the position of having to decide whether to defend people like him and be rejected, losing all that he has gained with hard work, or defend the status quo and submit to authority. Hephaestus, in terror of losing his position on Olympus, concedes to Zeus and is allowed to come back. From then on he preaches fatalistic submission to Zeus's will. Rather than criticize his choice, we should take this as an object lesson as to how devastatingly important social acceptance and respect is for a Capricorn, how much they risk when they rebel, and how much courage it takes for them to take the path of dangerous compassion rather than safe and useful conformity.

No matter how nonconformist the Capricorn Sun in question may act, there are some groups and forms of authority whom he will find it almost impossible not to obey. It's easier for him to wait, he tells himself, until he has enough power to be the authority himself, and then things will be different. Be patient, and work, and gather power and influence. The problem is that after twenty or thirty years of conforming, he may not be able to unbend when he actually has the power, and may merely repeat the cycle of conformism. Rebelling means reverting to the status of Lone Wolf and its attendant smoldering volcano of resentments. It's a choice that a Capricorn must make, again and again, on a daily basis. It is both his curse and that which makes him stronger.

Hephaestus was well revered, in his own way. He made hundreds of toys for the gods—Zeus's thunderbolts, the arrows of Apollo and Artemis, armor for Achilles and Hercules, Ariadne's diadem, and even the maiden Pandora herself. Like my Capricorn friend, he made himself necessary. The gods may have ridiculed him, but they were respectful when they came to his workshop, asking for some favor. In his skills lay his power, a lesson that a Capricorn learns well. He was worshipped by hundreds of smith cults around the Mediterranean, many of whom deliberately lamed their smiths, some say to prevent them from leaving.

In another Saturnian twist, when Aphrodite, the goddess of love, lands on the shores of Greece and every male god on Olympus vies for her hand, she chooses Hephaestus. There have been many theories as to why he is her choice, including him saying to her, "I would be a good husband for you. I work late." Her relationship with the crippled smith produces no offspring, and she has constant affairs with other gods, especially Ares, who fathers most of her children. Although Hephaestus starts out tolerant of her antics, he eventually flies into a jealous rage and rigs a trap to net the two lovers in public view in order to humiliate them. It backfires, however, as the Olympians find his cuckolded antics more amusing than the affair itself.

This is a blunt picture of a Capricorn's struggle with love and its attendant messiness. Capricorns are quite capable of deep, loyal love, but it is a rare Capricorn who can love openhanded, without trying to control what he loves. Capricorns have a tendency to marry or be attracted to warm Aphrodite types or partying Dionysus types, who are then expected to be the Capricorn's social interface for them—to find them friends, bring them to parties, introduce them to people, provide socializing when the solitary Capricorn is lonely, and make excuses for him when he wants to be alone with his work. Sometimes it works out, and sometimes the more outgoing partner rebels and tells them to go out and get some friends yourself, for god's sake.

As they age, Capricorn Suns loosen up and integrate the Aphrodite and Dionysus urges within themselves. It's as if Saturn, the god of time, gives them a gift for all that hard work in their youth. At this point, they may find that they no longer care about staying on that mountain no matter what the price. They may also realize that there are other mountains to climb, or burrow under, or pull down. They may even get around to scaling the mountains within themselves. After all, if you can get up an external mountain, you can get up an internal one. All the same tools and skills apply. It's one of those Capricorn lessons that no one else quite understands . . . but they ought to.

Athena

Sun in Aquarius

When the Sun, the planet of identity, moves into Aquarius, it enters again into the realm of air, of ideas and thought and the mind. Here

I have chosen the Greek goddess Athena to be the patron of this position, the goddess of wisdom of the Olympian pantheon.

Athena was, in her earliest incarnations, a weather goddess associated with storm and lightning. Her aegis, or great shield, in her earliest days represented the stormy night, and this is appropriate for an air sign like Aquarius. Although she eventually lost her meteorological associations, she still partakes of the air element's attributes; she is cool, clear, rational, objective, and works in the world of mind rather than body or mind or heart. She was born from her father's head, as he tricked her mother into turning into a fly and then swallowed her; she burst forth less like a baby and more like an idea, fully armed and ready to go.

Of all the signs, Aquarius is the one most uncomfortable with the physical world and the limitations of the body. It was probably an Aquarian who thought up the science-fiction idea of people's minds being translated into computers, where they could think forever without the difficulties of having to eat and sleep and be polite to annoying phone salesmen. It was an Aquarian computer genius who first told me about the drive to make a wrist computer that would be part secretary and part companion, not just reminding you when to take your medications but keeping you company when you were too annoyed with humanity, or they with you, to want to be part of their social species. For Aquarius, a body is at best an obstacle to be overcome, and at worst a nuisance to be cursed. Like Athena, they belong to the sky, not the earth.

Of course, Aquarians love to be revolutionaries. All Aquarians have ideals of how society ought to be and how people ought to behave and treat others, and they are quite willing to go to battle for those ideals, with pen and sword and garden hoe. Athena's dual roles as Wise Counselor and Battle Goddess, often wrongly seen as mutually exclusive, fit in perfectly with Aquarian aims. Aquarians come up with the far-thinking idea that no one else had the foresight to think of, write the book on it, and go to war for that ideal, whether it is lobbying in a suit or chaining oneself to a tree. When fighting in the service of humanity—even if she secretly thinks humanity itself is rather a bother—an Aquarius is ruthless and clear-eyed, her gaze on the goal and all her will behind the battle. Like Athena, the goddess of strategy, Aquarians can plan brilliantly and execute things that no one else would have thought of. Their spears are their intellect, their swords are their ideals, and their shields are their convictions. They intend to change the world, and they often do, to the chagrin of the slower people in it.

One of the most interesting things about Athena is that she is one of the only two cross-dressing gods in the Olympian pantheon, the other being Dionysus. Athena is shown either in full armor, which was a man's prerogative, or in a simple male chiton, such as would have been worn under armor. She is sometimes shown in a full woman's robe, but it is usually undecorated and concealing, and she tends to keep her helmet on. Her gender-bending goes even further than this, though; she says, "I am for the man in all things, save for marriage," and she means it. Everything a man does, she does, except for sex, which she has none of. However, she doesn't forswear all female arts; she is the patroness of weaving, a traditional female craft, and is traditionally attributed the gift of breathing creative life into craftwork.

In this way, she bridges male and female, an androgynous goddess, and this reflects the Aquarian mind. On some level, Aquarius gets quickly tired of the same old sex stereotypes and secretly (or not so secretly) longs for some kind of androgynous Utopia, where nobody has to choose their jobs on the basis of their genitals. Female Aquarians are particularly frustrated with traditional femininity, as they would generally prefer to be judged by their minds rather than their bodies, except for the few who are either entirely unaware that their bodies are getting them those perks or have coldly decided to use it as the tool that it is. The sexless androgyny of Athena perfectly reflects the Aquarian sensibilities of the sexless androgyny found in some works of science fiction. She also doesn't seem to care about whether the other gods on Olympus like or dislike her unusual gender arrangements; like every Aquarian, her individuality is more important to her than the opinions of others.

On the other hand, it is often true that androgynous, nonbreeding archetypes (and people) are also very creative in other ways, as if their dammed procreativity is forced into other channels. Athena as goddess of crafts—patron of architects, sculptors, fiber artists—echoes Aquarian creativity and inspiration. At the Panathenaeum, her yearly festival, arts and crafts of many different kinds were shown and judged in contests.

Athena also rewards the gender-crossing Tiresias, who in a spirit of exploration offered to be a test subject of the gods: agreeing to spend seven years as a woman after being raised a man, s/he was called before the Olympians to decide which gender had the greater pleasure during sex. When s/he confessed that women had it better in the matter of pure physical pleasure, Hera, the goddess of marriage, struck hir blind. Athena apparently could not undo the damage, but she stepped in and quietly gave Tiresias the gift of prophecy. Tiresias is a very Aquarian figure, with hir androgyny and willingness to experiment, and the gift of prophecy—of looking ahead into the future—is the ultimate Aquarian gift. Tiresias's enforced blindness to the now in favor of seeing the possible is also a stubbornly Aquarian trait.

Athena is a sworn virgin, but her virginity is very different from that of the other virgin goddesses. Artemis and Hestia both keep well away from the world of men; Artemis and her nymphs in the wild forest in protective bands, and Hestia in the monastic withdrawal of the honored elder. Athena, on the other hand, is not only unafraid of the company of men (or anyone else), she prefers men as her chosen companions. She seems to have no fear for the safety of her virginity, and every confidence in her ability to effortlessly protect it. In fact, the very idea that her virginity could be threatened seems impossible for her to conceive. No statue ever shows her naked. No sculptor would ever dare.

As an example of this certainty, Hephaestus, the blacksmith god, gets it into his head to ravish her. He does not even manage to get under her tunic; ejaculating against her leg is the best he can do in the split second before she irritably fends him off. The semen falls to the ground, where it becomes a baby, Erichthonius. Athena decides that abandoning the little mistake to die would be unfair, and she fosters him out to mortal parents. She does not raise the child herself, or even consider it. Neither Athena, nor Aquarius, is much known for parental nurturing.

This is typical of Aquarian flaws. It isn't that Aquarian types are necessarily sexless or prudes; virginity among the gods means something different than it does among modern mortals. Virginity, in myths, symbolizes a sort of emotional untouchability that cannot be breached, and this is something that many an Aquarian's lover has found frustrating. Some Aquarians are very sexually conventional and others are ready and willing to experiment with wild kinks, but regardless of the activity, the heart is often not connected to it. Sex can be for fun and pleasure, for marital duty, for friendly bonding, for making children, for putting a smile on the face of a partner, for good fierce exercise, but rarely is it about making love on a deep, soul-bonding level. The partner who instinctively seeks this from the Aquarian frequently has a feeling that something is missing, held back, unavailable. This can also extend to other romantic or deep friendship activities; there is always a certain detachment that can make an emotionally vulnerable partner feel like they are clawing thin air for a purchase.

The Sagittarian virginity of Artemis and the Virgo virginity of Hestia both hold back from male society because they know that they have something to lose. They see the breach of that boundary as a violation—of freedom on Artemis's part, and privacy on Hestia's. Athena, on the other hand, does not believe that she could lose, and that shows in the Aquarian nature. Aquarians are often blissfully unaware of their own untouchability; taking them to task for it often provokes bewilderment. "What do you mean, I'm not there during lovemaking (or a relationship discussion, or a shoulder-crying session)? Of course I was there! What are you talking about?" Not being aware that those depths can be breached makes one less vulnerable to it.

This makes it all the more dramatic when the wall of detachment is breached. When an Aquarian finds him- or herself in love (or hate), it takes them completely by surprise. It wasn't that they didn't expect to love or hate this person, it's that they didn't expect it to feel like this ("this" being, of course, intense and messy and uncontrollable). Generally, it makes them profoundly uncomfortable. They behave erratically and do things all out of proportion to the situation. Their normally objective judgment is thrown completely off. If they are moved to anger, they indulge in ten minutes of total scorched-earth rage and stagger off, refusing to believe that they actually did something that irrational, and then try to deny it or explain it away with a tortuous "rational" argument.

As an example of this, Athena's greatest love and loyalty seem to be for her father, Zeus. She is very much daddy's girl, and it is true that both male and female Aquarians have often preferred the stereotypically masculine world of logic, science, and numbers to the stereotypically feminine world of feelings and images. However, Athena seems entirely blind to Zeus's bad behavior and negative qualities; she simply chooses not to see them. When Arachne spitefully illustrates a tapestry with a long cartoon litany of Zeus's Most Stupid Stunts, she hits Athena's most painfully irrational button and the cool, detached goddess reacts with uncharacteristic fury, screaming and shredding the tapestry, changing the hapless Arachne into a spider, and stalking off in a huff. I'm sure that every god on Olympus would have paid to see that loss of control.

On her shield, her aegis, Athena wears the Gorgon head, the sight of which turns people to cold stone. Aquarians are often seen as lacking in human warmth and, as such, they make people around them feel distant and frozen as well. The Gorgon-eye of cold scientific inquiry can be pretty intimidating and does not encourage closeness and bonding. Like the other "human" signs, Gemini, Virgo, and Libra, Aquarians need to bring their human genius down to the level of the instinctual animal or it will never be taken seriously by more instinctual people, like the ones that hold the checkbook for funding their brilliant ideas, or the ones that they happen to be living with.

Above all else, however, Athena was the goddess of wisdom, with her owl symbol, and it is this that she is best remembered for. It is also likely that the best of Aquarian-type people are remembered the same way—for their insight, their foresight, and their visions of the future as it could ideally be.

DUMUZI
Sun in Pisces

Throughout many of the mythologies of the world, one figure stands out similarly in culture after culture. Usually male, he is known as Ing to the Norse, Tammuz to the Babylonians, Patecatl to the Aztecs, and Adonis to the Greeks. He is related to the twice-born Dionysus, the slain earth god Osiris, the Phrygian Attis, and he is the direct ancestor of the crucified Christ. In medieval days, he was celebrated in song as John Barleycorn. He is the sacrificed god, the one who dies so that all of us can go on living. In female form, he is the sacrificed maiden, like Persephone, Psyche, or Andromeda. He is the proud-standing grain that is cut down in its prime, beaten and crushed and baked in fire in order that we should be nourished. He is the animal led to the slaughter, the tree cut down to shelter us or warm us in flames, the vegetables we rip from the earth and eat raw and still living. He is the essence of Pisces, because the Piscean nature cannot be divorced from the concept of sacrifice.

We tend to think, today, of a sacrifice as being something worthless. In the days when sacrifices were offered up regularly, however, only the best would do for divine tribute; anything else would be an insult. Human beings who were sacrificed had to be perfect of body, high of rank, and beloved by others. To be the perfect sacrifice was, in its own way, to be the best. To give of yourself so that others might live was the greatest honor imaginable. To the Pisces Sun, this is still the truth on some level. It may be a truth that he fears, and some Pisceans can overcompensate in order to escape their urge to help others at their own expense. Afraid of giving away their souls, they lock them up. This is just as likely a manifestation as the Piscean Sun who loses too much of himself to the needs of others.

Neptune, the ruler of Pisces, blurs boundaries and merges individual consciousness with the greater whole. On a deeper level, Piscean self-sacrifice is part of the drive to obliterate one's separateness from the cosmos, and in doing so join with its essence. In many cultures, the dying and reborn king is associated with the harbingers of altered states; Ing is the beer god, Dionysus the wine god, Shiva the hemp god, Patecatl the mezcal god. Some sacrificed gods, like Odin who lives for a year as a woman, Ing whose living avatars rejoined the tribe as women if they survived ritual castration, and Attis whose priestesses were the transgendered *gallae*, blurred the boundaries between male and female. It is part of the larger shamanic pattern: in order to gain shamanic powers, one must first endure a major sacrifice and rebirth. In order to be the walker between worlds, one must step out of oneself and become someone or something else, repeatedly. It is impossible to achieve this with all the ordinary anchors of life that create a delineated personality, not this but that. The Pisces Sun often loses his boundaries or becomes confused around them. What is me and what is not me? Whose needs am I living my life around? To give up this constant danger is to give up the ability to meld with the cosmos. Individuality is sometimes at cross-purposes with higher consciousness.

Of all the sacrificial gods, the one we will concern ourselves with most directly is Dumuzi, the Sumerian consort of Inanna, queen of heaven. His first appearance in the myths is his arrival at the gates of the city to court Inanna; with their mutual blandishments full of agricultural overtones—hers about crops and his about livestock—it is clear that their wedding is a symbolic meeting of animal and vegetable production rituals. However, through the abstraction one gets a clear picture of a real courtship between two real personalities.

Dumuzi is a herder and owns no land, and this is at first seen as a hindrance to his marriageable worthiness. Although he is seen as a god of the natural earthy processes, he is in no way rooted. As a herder, he wanders from place to place. The fact that he owns no land is an important point in the understanding of Pisces, which is an ever-moving mutable sign. Although herding has always been a large part of the body-oriented cycle of food production, it belongs less to the well-planted field of the farmer or the woods and jungle of the hunter-gatherer. Herding belongs most often to the plains, the savannah, the steppe—the "endless sea of grass," wide and flat and hiding many small creatures. (Although the sacrificed god in general is also associated with grain and agricultural plants, he does not tend the grain as the Farmer archetype, he *is* the grain—the "sea of waving stalks.") Dumuzi the herder wanders aimlessly through this land-sea, following not his own whims but that of his animals, who know where the fresh fodder can be found. His possessions—his flocks and herds—are mobile, and can be taken away from him. His lack of landowning reflects the Piscean revulsion of property that ties you down. Ocean-fish Pisces secretly—or not so secretly—hates having possessions, hates the entire concept of possessions and of possessing.

In spite of his poverty, Dumuzi convinces Inanna that he is just as wealthy in his own way as any farmer. To Pisces, live wealth—your living ideas and dreams—are far superior to inanimate objects, just as Dumuzi rates his flocks and herds as better than jewels or palaces. Inanna concedes his point and agrees to marry him. It was said that their courtship lasted for years and their honeymoon even longer. Dumuzi might have been happy forever as Inanna's consort; Pisces has a tendency to be passive and accept the lead of a stronger-willed partner. However, Inanna herself (as is recounted in the Venus in Scorpio section) is dissatisfied with her life and seeks a deeper experience. She decides to visit her sister Ereshkigal in the Land of the Dead, even though it is likely that she will never return. Telling Dumuzi to wait for her, she sets off on her fateful journey.

From Dumuzi's perspective, when Inanna does not come back after the third day, she is lost forever. The Pisces Sun has a tendency to fatalism, and without the anchor of her presence, Dumuzi is unable to maintain his devotion and hope of her return. He drifts away from her orders, and when the desperate people offer him the throne in her stead, he takes it. There is no evidence that he actively pursues her throne; he simply allows the tide of circumstance to wash him onto it. Once ensconced, he is reluctant to give it up. When Inanna comes back from the Land of the Dead with her howling retinue of Ereshkigal's demons, her faithful handmaiden Ninshubur has run ahead to warn everyone. However, she fails to reach Dumuzi in time to tell him that the demons are waiting to capture anyone who is not glad to see her, and force them to take Inanna's place. She enters the royal palace in full glory, expecting to be greeted with love and wonder by her devoted consort. Instead, Dumuzi looks up from the throne he has just become used to and reacts with guilty annoyance. He knows she will be furious about his usurpation of her place and cannot hide his watery guilt in time. The demons attack him, shrieking in triumph. Dumuzi flees, barely escaping them, but they are close on his heels.

Being pursued by demons is often a familiar thing for the Pisces Sun. It is the hardest of all the solar placements; the ego-oriented

Sun does not like to be ruled by ego-destroying Neptune. The solar myth itself is often bound up with the dying and reborn king, and Pisces is the moment of death when the Sun is cast down from its height. Living a Neptunian life is not an easy thing, especially when one tries for worldly glory. The affinity for altered states can degrade into addictions or insanity, the lack of boundaries can lead to bad choices, and the empathy for others can deafen one to one's own needs. It is almost as if every Pisces Sun contains the seeds of his own self-immolation, which he sets in motion if he should become too wrapped up in earthly thrones and positions of worldly importance. Sooner or later, Neptune forces his hand. He may not understand, later, how it all came about.

At this point, the third player in this story comes forward. She is Geshtinanna, Dumuzi's twin sister, who is entirely devoted to him in a way that Inanna is not. The position of "twin sister" can be read, without much difficulty, as a sort of second self, another aspect of Dumuzi. Where he has failed in absolute devotion to another, she never flinches. He flees to her and she hides him willingly, and when the demons come, they alight on her and torture her hideously in order to gain information about his whereabouts. She never breaks—indeed, she bears her martyrdom with resolute defiance. If passivity is Pisces' greatest weakness, then passive resistance is his most effective weapon. Being a water sign, Pisces measures the worth of his cause in emotional terms, not intellectual or practical ones. It doesn't matter whether Dumuzi is worth being tortured for, nor that he has already betrayed Inanna. Geshtinanna loves him, and therefore she will do everything in her power to protect him.

In the end, her sacrifice is wasted; the demons find a friend of Dumuzi who proves more willing to betray him than she would ever be. The hapless Dumuzi is snatched up from his hiding place in the pigpen, among the swine who also wait to be slaughtered for our food, thus underlining even further his nature as a sacrificial beast. He is carried off to the Land of the Dead, where he will keep

Ereshkigal company. Here Geshtinanna steps in again with an act of utter devotion. She offers herself to Ereshkigal in his place, and the goddess of death agrees to a compromise: Dumuzi will spend half the year in the Land of the Dead with her and half the year above ground with her sister Inanna. Geshtinanna will take his place with Ereshkigal when he is gone. Thus she echoes the sacrificed-maiden myth of Persephone (Pluto in Pisces), who spends half the year with her death-god spouse and half with her earth-goddess mother.

Both Dumuzi and Geshtinanna reflect different sides of the Pisces archetype, which has little in the way of boundaries and no specific gender. It is significant that Geshtinanna does not really come into the myth, does not really come alive for us until she has a cause to sacrifice herself for. Her confidence in her ability to withstand torture comes not from any internal ego but from her deep love for her brother. In a way, the offering up of her soul is her way of being the best that she can be. Dumuzi, on the other hand, is an unwilling sacrifice, dragged to his death by the demons that swarm at his heels. Both embody the experience of the Pisces Sun. The difference between them is choice; he can choose the altar that he will lay down on and the knife that will take his heart or it will be chosen for him. In spite of its reputation for being soft and dreamy, Neptune is just as relentless as Pluto. Like water wearing away stone, it will erode the Pisces Sun's defenses until he faces the demons or walks down into the depths of his own free will. Only in impermanence is immortality, whispers Neptune. Only in dissolution is strength. Only in surrender is victory. It's Pisces wisdom, as old as the sea we crawled out of and the universe to which we will return.

The Moon

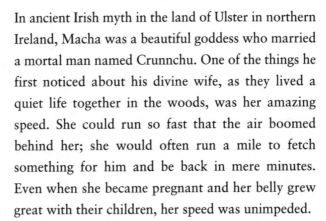

Macha

Moon in Aries

In ancient Irish myth in the land of Ulster in northern Ireland, Macha was a beautiful goddess who married a mortal man named Crunnchu. One of the things he first noticed about his divine wife, as they lived a quiet life together in the woods, was her amazing speed. She could run so fast that the air boomed behind her; she would often run a mile to fetch something for him and be back in mere minutes. Even when she became pregnant and her belly grew great with their children, her speed was unimpeded.

However, Crunnchu was a rather foolish man. In awe of his goddess-wife, he doted on her every wish, but when he would go out to the tavern in the evening, he would get drunk and brag about how wonderful she was. One day his loose tongue sparked a disaster: the king and his armed thugs, equally drunk, were sitting within earshot, and heard the luckless man boast about how his wife was faster than the best horses. The tipsy king demanded that he produce Macha the next day and force her to race against his fine-blooded stallions, or prove himself a liar. Crunnchu protested, but the king held firm, and finally he had to slink home and explain the situation to his pregnant wife.

Macha was angry, but she did not refuse; she would protect both his honor and her own, and she showed up for the race the next day, big belly and all. The king and his men laughed at her, but when the race began Macha set off at such a great speed that they were struck silent. She crossed the finish line ahead of the king's horses, fell to the ground, and delivered twin babies right there in the dirt. Struggling to her feet with a child in each arm, she then lay a curse on the king and all the men of Ulster, saying that peace would not come to their land for nine times nine generations. The men of Ulster would be weakened and laid waste, and the king and all his men should suffer birth pangs and menstrual cramps along with their women every month. Then she vanished with her babies and was never seen again in any tale.

The Aries Moon is, at heart, competitive. They can, and should, attempt to control this trait, especially when it leads them into obsessive conflict with loved ones, but something in them longs to pit themselves against others. At its worst this can become linked to a cycle of low self-worth, where they must continually compete in order to prove themselves worthy of their existence, but at its best it is a way to challenge them to further heights. They always run faster and push themselves harder when there is something to actually win; it's part of their nature and cannot be denied. The mature Aries Moon learns that the most worthy competitor is actually himself, and leaves off harassing his friends and family.

We notice from the myth that even though she is angry with her husband, Macha does not turn down the dangerous gamble. It's not even that she cares so much about her husband's honor—she does, after all, leave him afterwards—it's that she can't turn down the challenge. She is also fast, faster than anyone else, and this too is indicative of the emotional nature of the Aries Moon. She can go through five or six different feelings while others are still processing the first one. She flares up in terrible rages and is distracted again just as quickly. Her fancy darts from one person or idea or dream to the next, possibly too fast for commitment to be easy, and she can fall in and out of love with amazing rapidity.

Macha gives birth on the finish line, and this too is telling, as sometimes the competition is only the prelude to something big that the Aries Moon wants to take on. When one project seems too difficult or overwhelming, sometimes the Aries Moon will challenge herself with something else in order to use that victory to boost her confidence enough to take on the bigger challenge. However, in her rushing from victory to victory, she can leave loved ones behind in the dust; after her triumph, her husband never sees her again.

Macha may well consider him too weak to be worthy, another Aries Moon issue. Before they reach maturity, it seems that Aries Moon people end up with two sorts of lovers: weak, passive ones who let them have their way in everything and of whom they quickly become bored, or strong ones who stand up to them and with whom they are constantly fighting. Often it is the strong lover who leaves them, tired of the daily dinnertime battles, and they are hurt and confused. "Surely a few arguments don't mean that I don't love you, or that what we have isn't good enough, does it?" They will only be able to coexist with someone who understands and enjoys impersonal competition, unless they learn to keep their races internal and personal.

Like straightforward Macha, the Aries Moon is also honest and open at heart. There is no subterfuge with them, and they rarely have to sit around digging to figure out what they are feeling. If they are having a feeling, it is usually strong, and usually everyone else notices it too, unless there is a particularly placid or reserved ascendant. This means that they are pretty refreshing for people who have had to play too many games of "Guess what I feel!" Their emotional honesty is their greatest gift and their Achilles heel; it can be abused by craftier and less ethical people, but it also makes it easier for someone who is willing to admit their mistakes and ask forgiveness, as Aries Moon almost always gives it gladly and generously.

If they are abused and realize it, their anger can create lasting wounds, as seen in Macha's curse, which I do not believe (from the activity still going on in Ulster County, Ireland) has yet run out. They need friends and lovers who will be honest with them at all times and stand up to them when necessary; they are also usually willing to admit their mistakes when they are pointed out to them. The Moon in Aries is a warrior fighting for the right not to have their feelings declared unacceptable. This is emotional integrity we as a society desperately need.

Hathor
Moon in Taurus

In ancient Egypt, "cow-eyed" was a compliment to a woman of great beauty; it came from the "cow-eyed" goddess Hathor, sacred white cow, whose milk poured out into the starry night and became the Milky Way. Shown sometimes as a cow, sometimes as a cow-headed woman, and sometimes as a winged human woman, her symbol was the sun disk flanked by two horns. This symbolized the sun returning every night to Hathor's breast to sleep and arising every morning from her arms.

The Taurus Moon does indeed have restful arms and a comforting spirit to stabilize the wayward lunar energies. Just as the Sun is exalted in Aries, the Moon is exalted in Taurus, which means that she likes to be there, nestled in grounding earth energy and ruled by feminine Venus. A Taurus Moon is generally an emotionally stable person; certainly they can have as many emotional upsets as the next person, but they tend to take them slowly and not act impulsively on them, and often have them figured out and dealt with before they escape into action. This gives the illusion of being less emotional than others or perhaps more placid. You can yell at a Taurus Moon and they will just look at you for a minute, deciding whether or not it is worth spending their energy to respond in kind. They are hard to get a rise out of.

However, if you *want* to cause the bull to charge, threaten their home and family and comforts. Hathor was the protector of women and children; in her maternal aspect she nourished the world with her milk, and in her love-goddess aspect she ruled over marriage and women's beauty regimes. She favored a happy home with a happy family, and this is equally important to a Taurus Moon. The lunar-maternal and Venus-ruled love aspects of this placement make the prime directive one of being surrounded by affection and emotional harmony; if you imperil her carefully created hearth, she will bellow and charge at you, horns ready. Hathor is the "horned goddess," and she will defend her land to the end.

Taurus loves music, and the Moon placement here sometimes indicates musical ability; one of Hathor's symbols was a sacred sistrum, which she shook and danced with. She was proclaimed mistress of music and song and dance, and great musical performances were held in her honor. Even if the Taurus Moon in question can't carry a tune, they will respond strongly to music, and probably own (or would love to own) a really good sound system and a plethora of CDs and tapes, one for each possible mood. I've met Taurus Moon people who create "history tapes," putting together a series of songs for each important happening in their life—relationships, achievements, travels, friends, children. They can then play back the memories through the music.

Hathor was also associated with the dead; she is shown sympathetically giving them great care and succor on their way to the underworld. She was called the "Lady of the Sycamore," referring to a great sycamore tree at the edge of the underworld that marked her home; she would come out whenever Anubis passed by with dead souls and offer them bread and milk in welcome. This kind of nourishing of tired souls is a typical Taurus Moon response; her lunar nurturing sense is highly developed and easily touched, but her response tends to be something along the lines of offering a nourishing meal, a hot bath, a warm hug, and then some practical advice. After all, isn't this all anyone ever needs to make things better? She can be honestly bewildered at those for whom these earthy gifts are not enough, and hurt by those who reject her mothering as controlling.

If she has a fault, it is being too obsessed with her comforts. To Taurus, a rut is a nice, comfortable place that would be more trouble to climb out of than to stay in, so why leave? With a Moon placement here, this tends to create an emotional conservatism that does not like to take risks with the heart. The Taurus Moon prefers a sure thing, a good solid commitment, a lover who has already said "I love you" several times and who never looks shifty when you ask the question again. She will sometimes stay in a boring, unevolved relationship rather than risk heartbreak in the unknown waste of singles' bars; after all, if you're going to be emotionally untouched, you might as well do it comfortably in decent company. This concept might make a mutable sign scream and run, but fixed Taurus is her own hearth and makes her own decisions in her own time. Telling her how hidebound she is may actually make her dig her heels in further. Reminiscent of Hathor's role as goddess of the dead, a Taurus Moon can stay for a long time in an emotionally immobile state that might look like death to other, more volatile signs.

One of the gifts of Taurus is the ability to put down roots wherever she ends up, like a weed in a cow pasture. When you put down roots, you may get the rich manured area or the barren land, but it is your job to make do and cling on tenaciously, putting out side shoots, daughter-sprigs, and seed-children and eventually claiming the whole area for yourself. This gift of earthy rootedness comes through a Taurus Moon in their ability to make themselves at home in people's lives and to provide anchoring for others who may come along. The gifts of the placid cow goddess are not to be sneered at; remember that the very Sun rises from the warmth of her heart.

Thoth

Moon in Gemini

The Moon is the most emotional of planets, and Gemini is one of the least emotional signs. Lunar energy is not entirely comfortable here; one Gemini Moon individual characterized his emotional processes as "I Think (Gemini) plus I Feel (Moon) equals I Rationalize." Gemini is ruled by the trickster Mercury, not exactly a steady emotional barometer; one of the hallmarks of Gemini Moon people is that they are often out of touch with their feelings entirely for long periods of time.

For this lunar placement, I have chosen Thoth to represent the energy. Thoth, or Djehuti in his native tongue, is the Egyptian god of writing who invented the hieroglyphic alphabet and is the patron of scribes. He is apparently one of the very few lunar gods who is male; although he can be compassionate, he is most definitely not a lovey-dovey parental deity, and neither is he a lunar hag of bare trees and whistling winds and mysteries. Although I am not trying to imply that women are emotional and men are not, Thoth's masculine nature does suggest that he is not linked to female lunar cycles or stereotypically feminine emotional depths. To Thoth, the waxing and waning of the Moon is no mysterious thing; it is orderly, expected, and happens every month right on time.

Thoth was multitalented—scribe, doctor, scientist, magician, mathematician, astronomer, archivist, maker of calendars, inventor of wind and stringed musical instruments, patron of literature, grand vizier of Osiris. Most of these interests are associated with the element of air, from flutes to stargazing to writing to math, and Thoth's bird-headed form gives further weight to his association with the combination of air, Moon, and words that characterizes this placement.

Like Gemini, the jack-of-all-trades, he was the patron of nearly every kind of intellectual learning in Egypt, and the gods constantly called on him to help them with their troubles. Thoth aided in creation, inventing sound and words with his own voice, pronouncing the first magic word "Nun," creating incantations to aid Isis in bringing her dead husband temporarily back to life, performing the first mummification on Osiris's body, driving scorpion poison out of the body of the young Horus, and curing the wounds of both Horus and Set after their battle, refraining from taking sides and letting neither die. (Gemini often plays both sides; not out of fairness like Libra, but because it may still be uncertain where the winning side is going to lie.) For this apparent objectivity, he was chosen by the gods to decide which of them should be heir to Osiris's throne; forced to this choice, he voted for Horus and made an enemy of Set, whose life he had just saved.

Unlike spiritual systems such as Taoism, where innocent simplicity is valued and the common uneducated peasant is seen as the most wise of men, Egyptian society felt that the educated man set the example for the lower classes, and that wisdom could only be attained through great study and the accumulation of knowledge. Thoth has an almost Confucian aspect in this way; as the divine scribe, he was seen as the cornerstone of civilization in a world where education and knowledge leads to divine order. Like Ptah, who was the architect of the universe, Thoth was revered both for his cache of information and his skill in utilizing it. Gemini also feels this way, secretly or not so secretly. To Gemini, it's what you know, not what you sense or intuit, that sets you above the dull and ignorant crowd. Even mysterious lunar information, like feelings and intuition, can—*must*—somehow be contained within words or symbols that can be spoken, read, and passed on. The idea that there are some things that cannot be spoken, cannot be put into words, infuriates and terrifies a Gemini Moon.

Ruled by Mercury, Gemini is all about words and communication, and as such it is no accident that Thoth is the patron of all writers. He is the keeper of the divine libraries, the knower of all the names for everything. If it exists, he knows what to call it, and it is this power that a Gemini Moon holds to, desperately, obsessively. It is both his greatest gift and his greatest handicap. Knowing how to find words for things is a wonderful and terrible talent. It means that you can speak the unspeakable, give form to the nebulous, separate the assumed from the actual, and cut right through the bullshit. To Gemini is given the power to name, and to the Gemini Moon is given the power to name those things that most people have the greatest difficulty putting in words. They may do so through poetry or prose, the lyric phrase or the straightforward judgment, but they are always driven to look at the turbulent mass of the psychological underworld and call it into order with the magic of their words.

This talent can elicit many different reactions from the people who watch it happen. Some may be desperately grateful when a Gemini Moon gives words and form to the amorphous feelings that have been tormenting them. You can see this power in all the self-help and pop-psychology books on the market; whatever you may think of them personally, someone, somewhere, read one and said, "Yes! That's what it's like! That's what I've been trying to explain to people all along! Now I can make myself clear for once!"

At their best, Gemini Moons have this ability to speak for the psyche of humanity, being the storyteller for the world. Ruled by twinkling, light-tongued Mercury, they also have the gift of tongues, of language, not just the ordinary human languages created by cultural boundaries but the myriad forms of language that are more subtle. A Gemini Moon can figure out what a single person's "language" is, including their system of beliefs and world-view, and pitch their story with the right amount of imaginative slant to hit home. They can be masters of reaching an audience, translators of the human story from one human to the next.

Of course, not everyone wants to hear everything spoken out loud. Some people are far more comfortable when things are kept safely in the dark and nicely nebulous, as it's so much easier to manipulate other folks with that way. They won't be happy with this gift, and they will no doubt accuse the Gemini Moon person of deliberately trying to cause trouble. However, that's not their motivation. Unlike Scorpio, who is usually aware of the effect that naming has on others and either doesn't care or intended it that way—or Sagittarius, who simply blurts it out because it's there—Gemini Moons are doing all this naming for a very personal reason. They're trying to figure themselves out.

This is where it becomes a handicap to be overcome, as well as a gift to be gloried in. All too often, a Gemini Moon cannot distinguish his feelings until they have been named and spoken. If it can't be put into words, he can't work with it, understand it, trace it, or possibly even be aware of it. Without articulation, he is a helpless pawn of lunar tides he cannot control. When Thoth's gift fails, he is literally powerless; words are the dam and the plumbing and pumps that he uses to bring the water of emotion into his life, and without them he is simply swept away. To outside observers, Gemini Moon people may veer back and forth between being supremely rational to sublimely irrational; some may lean toward one side and some to the other, but each has both Twins within them.

In spite of his urbane, gentlemanly appearance, Thoth does have a cunning trickster side, which is illustrated in his only surviving set of major myths. The children of Ra, Shu and Tefnut, deities of the air and the dew respectively, had an incestuous union and created two more children, Geb and Nut, who promptly began making eyes at each other as soon as they were old enough. Troubled by the idea of continued incest, Ra ordered them separated; his decree stated that Shu should stand between them on every day of the calendar year. Shu forcibly separated them, lifting Nut up into the sky where she became the goddess of the heavens, her belly spangled with stars and only her toes and fingertips touching the earth. Geb he trampled underfoot, where he grew green with verdure and became the god of the earth, forever longing for his sister in vain. This went on for centuries.

Desperate, Nut appealed to Thoth for help and, like a crafty lawyer, Thoth found the loophole in the decree. He decided that what was needed was a few days that were not included in the calendar, and he went about finding them. In one version of the story he plays senet (a chesslike Egyptian game) with the nameless personification of the Moon, whose guardian he is, and wins enough light for five extra days not found on the calendar. During this time, the decree was not in force and the doomed lovers could meet, producing five children—Isis, Osiris, Horus the elder, Set, and Nephthys—who would rule the next generation of Egypt.

This story illustrates, again, that in this placement the Moon is ruled by trickster Mercury. Thoth is no fool-trickster like Coyote and, unlike Ellegua, is perfectly happy to uphold the civilized status quo, but he is also fully aware of how the system can be played so as to extract maximum benefits. Rather than rail against injustice, he will find a way to sneak justice by the authorities. Thoth illustrates Gemini duality in this way; he is both honorable and a cheat, both a supporter of the system and a subverter of it, both noble statesman and trickster, both fair and partial, both scientist and magician, and seems to have no qualms about these apparently mutually exclusive goals. F. Scott Fitzgerald wrote about how the mark of a really first-rate intelligence was the ability to hold two opposing ideas in your head and not go mad; the Moon in Gemini allows us to look at possibilities and ways of being that are multiple and often opposed to each other, and say simply, "Yes. Both." Are gods real, or merely archetypes? Is there one god, or many? Is magic real, or science? Is humanity, or life, sacred or profane? Ask Gemini Moons. They, like Thoth, know the answer.

KWAN YIN

Moon in Cancer

Throughout Asia, there are figures who stand for unconditional love and mercy. The most popular is Kwan Yin to the Chinese, Kwannon in Japan, and Avalokitesvara the bodhisattva of mercy in India. One of her Chinese titles is Sung-Tzu Niang-Niang, or the Lady Who Brings Children. She is shown as a tall, graceful woman, often holding a child cradled in her arms. She is draped in white and pale green, and is associated with the aquatic lotus. Her steed is a giant carp, on which she rides the waves.

Kwan Yin is a goddess of fertility, but not of the earth. She is specifically associated with human fertility, with the quickening of the womb and the blessing of children. Women pray to her regularly to make them pregnant. She is also a healer of illnesses, and so the lines to her temple at Miao Feng Shan were always long with sick or barren supplicants. Although she was considered at times to be a double with the goddess Pi-Hsia-Yuan-Chan, princess of the streaked clouds and daughter of the grand vizier of Lao-Tien-Yeh, Kwan Yin is almost entirely free of being embedded in the detailed Chinese hierarchy of royal gods. Kwan Yin was a peasant's goddess; her most fervent supporters were the great unwashed masses who begged for her respite from their miserable lives. She was also popular with women, who were mostly second-class citizens, and was the protector of children. Other gods may have guarded the favor of the privileged, but Kwan Yin was prayed to at the rudest hearthside. As such, she echoes the Cancer idea that the circle of home and family, not the outer world, is the most important place of all.

Cancer is ruled by the Moon, and here in its own sign it flows freely with no interference. It is also the most maternal of the Moon's placements; Cancer Moons are almost instinctive nurturers, who love to feed and cosset their loved ones, and hold the circle of family as sacred. If they have no children of their own—and they are likely to have children, if they can—they will fill that void with other people's children, or needy adults that they can aid. Cancer Moons can be found readily in the helping professions, dispensing Kwan Yin's graces. The early Hindus claimed that the first and most important kind of love was *karuna*, or mother-child love. Cancer Moons strongly want to give and receive this kind of intense, unconditional love. Unevolved ones will attempt to extract it with guilt; evolved ones will work hard to earn it. The Cancer Moon person closest to my heart once commented sagely that if one wanted to be loved, one had better learn how to be lovable.

Kwan Yin is the goddess of mercy, and mercy is not a rational quality. If the human race were entirely rational, thinking people, no one would ever get any mercy, nor would they expect or hope for any. When we beg for mercy, we are in effect saying, "Please overlook anything I might have done to get into this terrible place, and rescue me from this fate that I may or may not richly deserve." Mercy has nothing to do with justice. Justice is cold and impartial; mercy is based on the feeling rather than the thinking function and is intensely partial. Mercy, whether from human or divine sources, requires the undammed flow of emotion that Cancer represents. I feel for you, says the lunar principle doubly personified by this placement, and therefore I will help you.

There is a karmic aspect to mercy, however. Karma is the universe's rational response to human irrationality; when you issue someone else that get-out-of-jail-free card, you receive one back yourself from the universe, to be cashed in at some future date. People who have never been shown mercy often don't know how to give any; people who have bathed in its relieving waters before will be more likely to grant it in their turn. It is the gift that brings more good karma into the universe. It is part of why we don't kill our children or our loved ones when they anger us. Without this gift of feeling, so often belittled by the rational functions, the world would be a much crueler place.

Of course, part of having a clear channel of feeling is that it goes both ways. Cancer Moons can use the intensely partial gift of mercy in reverse, closing out those who are not their family or whom they do not value according to their extremely subjective standards. Kwan Yin was also appealed to for protection of the home; entire cities were said to see visions of her before battle, and they knew that they would win. The dark side of emotion is when the defense of one's loved ones becomes an attack on others. Kwan Yin is a protector of children; Cancer Moons can protect their own loved ones beyond all level of reason, even when they no longer deserve it, even when they are doing harm. Cancer Moons can also attempt to sacrifice the needs of others to protect their own loved ones, and that circle can include cherished ideas and beliefs as well as people.

Water conquers through surrender and absorption, like the Chinese people and like Cancer itself. When you strike water, it yields and then closes on your hand; it is unhurt and you are impotent. Even boiling it and turning it into steam merely culminates in its cooling, recongealing, and falling on your head as rain. We are three-quarters water the way that we are three-quarters emotion. Sometimes Cancer Moons seem to get themselves into situations where they are martyred to an extent that other signs would not tolerate, but those same people will often get through life untouched by other trials than their chosen martyrdom. Their need to love and be loved is not negotiable. It's not easy to face the fact that you cannot function alone, in a crab's shell. Yet it is through this opening of the ocean of feeling that we bring mercy into the world again and again.

BΛST

Moon in Leo

They say that all cats are inherently selfish, only interested in what you can do for them. They also say that if our cats could learn overnight to use can openers, we would all be dead in our beds before morning. They were reviled and burned in masses during the Middle Ages, and in modern days abandoned on the streets to be run over by cars. However, long ago in ancient Egypt, they were worshipped as sacred creatures, and every one of them still acts as if it ought to be so again. Just ask a cat owner. For that matter, just ask the parent or lover of someone with a Leo Moon.

In fact, most Leo Moons are not nearly as selfish as the average house cat, but they all crave being worshipped. Every one of them wants to be adored, even more than a Leo Sun or Venus, because the Moon is more emotionally dependent on it. A Leo Moon is more easily hurt than another Leo placement, for the same reasons. The domestic cat's ancestors may have been lions, and she herself does have teeth and claws, but she is no match for a crowd of humans with nets and large boots. By definition, the Leo Moon is the domestic version of this strong feline energy.

Bast herself was the patron goddess of the city of Bubastis. Once a year, travelers came from all over the land to see raucous parades, plays, and musical presentations. Appropriate for a goddess whose symbol is a musical instrument—the sistrum—Leo Moons love to be performers. However, they are less likely to have the actual musical or artistic talents of someone with the Sun or Jupiter in Leo; instead, their greatest talent is showing off. Leo Moons put on a wonderful performance of being whatever their audience wants, and since they truly put their hearts into it, the audience responds. When Bast shook her sistrum, she drove away evil spirits, and the Leo Moon may find that performing temporarily drives away the inner demons of low self-worth, neediness, and feeling unloved, which can sometimes underlie the Leo ego.

Bast was also the protector of children as well as cats, and Leo Moon people often have a childlike streak themselves, something naive and sunny and open, sometimes trusting and sometimes spiteful. Leo Moon's inner child gets to sit up front in the passenger seat instead of being relegated to the back seat, pointing out interesting sights and occasionally making a grab for the wheel. Playful as a kitten, Leo Moons need to be reminded that not all jokes are funny, and people's feelings can get hurt. Playing with another person as if they are an interesting mouse is not likely to get you the approval and adulation you crave, no matter how witty you are about it.

The Moon in Leo is symbolically the full moon, as if the Sun's reflected light shines on the lunar surface of the psyche. What this means is that all the things that are generally hidden about a Moon sign—all the emotions, the wild imaginings—are all out front. Leo Moons wear their hearts on their sleeves; they can't help it. This is not always a bad thing. It can mean that nothing ever gets relegated to the depths of their psyche for very long; living your emotions on the surface also means that you are living them where you, too, can actually see them and do something about them.

One of the things that Leo Moons have trouble with is letting go of idealized memories. In ancient Egypt, cats were mummified and laid to rest in small coffins of their own, preserved for eternity so that they might rejoin their masters in the Land Beyond. This may have been royal treatment once, but Leo Moons sometimes echo this tradition in an unhealthy way. Anything good that ever happened to them gets preserved in their memory, mummified in an idealized way that may or may not have any relationship to what actually occurred. This may be a cherished former love, a masterful performance, or some other "perfect" moment. They trot it out frequently to touch and fondle it, and it eventually becomes the ideal that nothing else can ever live up to, or that they can't live a full and happy life without, and so on. Sometimes these mummified little memories need to be given a decent burial so that Leo Moons can get on with their lives, but prying them out of their claws is not an easy thing.

Like any house cat, a Leo Moon secretly wants to be taken care of, to have someone else do the dishes and deal with the details. She may have a sense of her own "specialness," which can be based on real talent and worth, or just on ego. If it is the former, it can be used as a shield of optimism and conviction that will help her to keep going after disappointments; if the latter, life will deal her a reality ego-check sooner or later. After all, even Bast herself had a job; it was to shake her sistrum and drive away other people's demons, evil spirits, and blues. Take it as a lesson; shine that Sun right through the Moon.

Holda

Moon in Virgo

Virgo stands alone. When push comes to shove, Virgo is often as much about aloneness as Libra is about togetherness and Pisces is about oneness. She represents the experience of being aware of yourself, yet keeping that self apart from others so that it can be seen more clearly and improved. Although there are some self-improvements that can only be made in relation to others, Virgo is not particularly concerned with those. She wants to make herself better, cleaner, more effective, and she can't do that if she is all muddled up with other people.

The Moon, on the other hand, likes to be muddled up with others. Emotional and changeable, it is uncomfortable in the sign of the solitary Virgin. It isn't that people with Virgo Moons never marry, or have no feelings, or cannot make emotional connections with others; someone with a Virgo Moon can accomplish all these things.

It's just that they will have to work hard to get past a natural inclination to keep the innermost parts of themselves separate. Of course, Virgo is also all about work, so it's not impossible.

Part of this means, however, that it is more natural for them to show their love in less effusive ways that usually take the form of work. A Moon in Virgo will slave at the degrading job and bring home the paycheck uncomplainingly, clean the house till it shines, assiduously change the patient's bedpan, pay and account for all the bills perfectly . . . all so the ones they care about don't have to do it. Then they feel bewildered and unappreciated when they are accused of being cold and unfeeling. A Virgo Moon with a more sensitive or watery partner will faithfully attempt to take on roles and behaviors that the partner asks for, but it will be something that she must think about doing, not something that will ever come naturally.

For example, if the partner wants to be held rather than be given advice when upset, a Moon in Virgo can learn to do this, if the partner is clear and specific about the desired behavior, when it should be done, and how. (Yes, those details are necessary. How else is she to do it properly?) She is generally a quick study, and will do it dutifully. However, if the partner senses that it is being done out of love-and-duty rather than out of any spontaneous feeling on Moon in Virgo's part, he or she may become resentful and accusatory. Yet the partner in this situation will have missed the point; love is inextricably bound up with duty to a Virgo Moon, and there's no changing that. Duty, to them, can be a service to take on joyfully. To them, the deed that you work hard to accomplish is worth far more, both as a personal achievement and as a gift to another, than the one that arises easily and spontaneously.

The Norse goddess Holda, also known as Frau Holle, is a mysterious elder figure associated with cleaning, spinning, and the underworld. When the snow flies, it is said that she is shaking out her feather beds and pillows. She inspires women to clean their houses, often in a whirlwind of activity, and she can be invoked for aid in any domestic chore. She does not marry and keeps to herself unless dispensing wisdom and aid.

In the German tale of Frau Holle, a young maiden lives with her lazy, nasty mother and sister. The mother favors her sister and makes the maiden do all the household chores. This is a familiar tale for Moon in Virgo, who may get less favor than more showy or demonstrative types, and can be relegated to doing the work "because you're so good at it." The fact that she will generally acquiesce often adds to her being taken advantage of. At any rate, the maiden is told to go draw water from the well, but she accidentally drops the bucket in. With a Virgo fear of waste, she tries to climb over the edge and find it, but instead falls down the well, which opens at the other end into a strange underworld.

This is the land of Frau Holle, who is, after all, an earth goddess like earth-sign Virgo, and lives underground. As the maiden travels through this land, she meets various animals and people—dogs, pigs, cats, beggars—all of whom challenge or threaten her. For each one, she discerns that they are actually hungry or hurt or in some other discomfort, which she immediately remedies by giving them help or what food she has in her pockets. This trait shows the best of Moon in Virgo, which due to her Mercurial objectivity and Virginal reserve can often see beyond the hostility that might distract more sensitive souls and note the possible causes. She also selflessly attempts to help each creature, not so much out of compassion as out of realization that something needs to be done, and she has the ability to do it.

When she reaches Frau Holle's house, the old woman greets her with open arms and tells her, "Now you are my daughter." For her dutiful service and cleverness, she is granted a gift: with every word that she speaks, a gold coin will fall from her lips. The girl is then sent home to her family where she demonstrates the new talent by creating a pile of gold coins and assuring her family that they will never starve. This gift reminds us that Virgo is ruled by Mercury, the patron of words, and it suggests that discernment and service, when practiced together—and let's stress the word practice—can bring financial viability. In other words, the ability to discern what is wrong, even when the sufferer can't or won't tell you, and do something about it, can literally make one's words and deeds worth their weight in gold. That this practice brings Holda's favor is part of the Virgo Moon mystery.

On the other hand, Holda does not appreciate those who merely criticize rather than acting to help, which is the worst fault of a Virgo Moon. All Virgo positions are given to criticism, but with the emotional Moon in charge, the nagging and complaints can be aimed out of frustration and repressed resentment rather than an actual wish to help the situation. When the maiden tells her mother and sister about her adventure, they immediately decide that her sister has to get the gold-coin gift as well, and the mother tosses her down the well. Instead of aiding all the creatures that she meets, she tells them that they are lazy and she is not going to help them. Frau Holle, instead of treating her to a gift of golden words, curses her with an evil spell: for every nasty word she speaks, toads and poisonous snakes will fall from her lips.

Both sisters, and Frau Holle/Holda herself, are aspects of the Moon in Virgo, and the message is clear: merely criticizing rather than helping spreads poison, whereas pitching in breeds gold. It is a lesson for the work-oriented sign about endurance in the face of frustration. It may seem like a hard road for the Virgo Moon, always being the one to selflessly and quietly tackle the problem-solving, but it is the road to gold—gold words, gold relationships, gold knowledge, gold soul.

ISIS
Moon in Libra

Of all the Egyptian goddesses, Isis was the most revered. After partnering with her brother Osiris and becoming queen of Egypt, she set out to civilize humanity. She taught women to grind barley, spin flax, and weave cloth, but found that they were not in general faithful enough to their husbands to form stable and lasting families. To solve this problem, she instituted the custom of formal marriage commitment, transforming random liaisons into stable families. She felt that in order to bring up children properly, a woman must also be a wife.

This is one of the telling ideals of the Libra Moon. Libra is the sign of marriage, and when it colors the emotional Moon, the need to be part of a couple is a deep, driving compulsion. Every person with a Libra Moon desires to be partnered the way that a Cancer Moon desires to nurture and be nurtured. Venus holds their hearts hostage, and it is very difficult for them to adapt to life alone. For them, a good working partnership is the home base from which life should be launched. They will sacrifice a great deal to get and keep that partnership, sometimes going to ridiculous lengths.

This is the tragedy of Isis's story. The most terrible thing that can happen to a Libra Moon happens to her—she is widowed. Her beloved husband Osiris is slain by his brother Set. The first attempt Set makes is unsuccessful; nailing Osiris into a coffin, he throws him into the Nile where he washes out to sea. The coffin fetches up against a tamarisk tree where it is swallowed up by the magically growing tamarisk. Isis hunts along the shore until she finds the tree and frees Osiris.

The second time, however, there is no easy rescue. Set ambushes Osiris and cuts him into fourteen pieces, scattering them up and down the river. Isis patiently finds the pieces, reassembling Osiris bit by bit, but the phallus—the giver of life—had been devoured by a crab and he could not be fully reanimated. In marriage, a Libra Moon tends to be the one who picks up the pieces, makes the peace, and attempts to shore up and support both a failing relationship and a failing spouse. She tries so hard that it is a terrible disappointment to her when it all dies anyway in spite of her hard work.

Isis enlists the aid of Thoth, and together they bring Osiris alive just long enough to magically impregnate her with their son. He then dies permanently and goes to the underworld, where he becomes its king. This is probably the ultimate mythological attempt to keep a marriage going until the last possible moment, and in real life Libra Moons keep trying until it has been more than proved useless . . . or until they have a new partner in hand. This can be another lover, but occasionally it is an adult child whom they try to make into a surrogate partner. Their urge to twoness is so strong that it ends up being the way that they run all their relationships. It takes a strong and well-centered Libra Moon to keep a cordial distance from someone she cares about.

Isis gives birth to Horus and spends her time raising him and hiding from Set. She is a gentle, attentive mother, but at the same time that she gave him loving care, she trained him to become his father's avenger. This is one of the ambivalences of Isis; she was revered as a blessed mother who nurtured the dead souls of nobles like her own children, but at the same time there is a coldness to her dogged pursuit of justice for her husband. Likewise, the Venus influence of a Libra Moon can fool us into thinking that its gentle manners conceal an equally gentle heart. However, this is an air sign, and all air sign Moons are a little out of touch with their feelings. Libra is less so than Gemini or Aquarius because of the Venus influence, but she can still drift into her head and lose sight of the needs of others. Often, in her case, the problem is that her ideal of perfection for her mate and children doesn't match what is possible in reality. In Isis's case, she kept arranging for the ghost of Osiris to come forth and exhort young Horus to vengeance; using his dead father as her surrogate, she quietly molded him into a vehicle for her justice.

A Libra Moon parent will be a spouse first and a parent second. Part of what a Libra Moon seeks to give children is an example of solid partnership for them to use in the future; this is admirable but it can backfire if the children's needs always take second fiddle to the marriage or the attempts to find a new partner. No matter how much Isis loves Horus, he is still her tool, and she decides what he is going to be from birth onwards. It's a temptation for a Libra Moon to do this, assuming that organizing someone else's life is going to be a team effort and then being disappointed when her interference is not wanted. A Libra Moon tends to mentor the best chick in the lot, the one most likely to grow up into an eagle. Isis was one of the four Egyptian death goddesses who collected the souls of the newly dead, but she played favorites, only accepting the souls of deceased nobility. Pharaohs, not peasants, were her chosen people.

Libra Moons usually have excellent motivations—harmony, fairness, peace, balance. It's the means by which they achieve these ends that can border on the manipulative. Before her marriage to Osiris, Isis gains the magical words of Ra by less than ethical means. Ra was getting old, dribbling and half senile, but still refused to pass on his power. Isis set a poisonous snake to bite him, and then appeared and offered to cure him if he would give her the words of power. Desperate, he did so, and she became a powerful magician and put the ailing country to rights. Libra Moons often try to keep the peace through charm and subtle manipulation; they rationalize it by telling themselves that it's better this way. In the short term, it often is. In the long term, it's still mucking with the free will of others.

Isis's cult persisted for centuries; she was the most popular goddess in Egypt and her worship was only ended by the onslaught of Christianity. She brought harmony and fairness, romantic commitment and idealized mother love—all good Libra Moon qualities.

One of her symbols was the throne, the other the magic knot that bound together all that was separated. Libra's talent for togetherness can be, in the end, the gift that binds people together, that allows someone to look into the eyes of another and see a soul both different from and so much like theirs.

Hecate
Moon in Scorpio

Of all the goddess figures who were reviled in later years, whose faces and ways and visages were eventually combined into the figure of the old witch with her evil spells who had to be burned and hung, Hecate probably heads up the list. She is disturbingly unusual for a Moon goddess; not nurturing or kind or maternal, and yet she is unquestionably lunar. Underworld goddess, lady of the dark moon, and the waning crescent sliding through the clouds and bare November trees, she haunts the roads with her pack of moon-pale hounds. Crossroads are her sacred places and used to bear her triple visage. Sometimes she is an old hag, chanting over her cauldron; sometimes a cold, white woman who hunts you down across the midnight moors.

Although all deities have powers that we might call "magical," Hecate is specifically a goddess of sorcery and enchantment. I first met her as a teenager in *Macbeth*, as the queen of the witches who chant over their boiling pots. Those witches may have been old and ugly and creating some rather disgusting brew, but they seemed to be more on the ball than anyone else in the whole play, and I figured that if Hecate was their goddess, then she had to be interesting. Hecate oversaw all spells that had to do with controlling others, something that anyone with Scorpio dominant in their chart will secretly long for. People are fascinating to a Scorpio Moon; what makes them tick? How can I influence them? How can I keep them from influencing me?

With this in mind, she will bury her soul between layers of masks, careful not to reveal too much. Shrines of Hecate were set up at crossroads; they had a single woman's body but bore three faces on it. This represented the three faces of the Moon, but they can also show how a Scorpio Moon individual can hide behind different faces in order to conceal their turbulent feelings. It isn't that all Scorpio Moons are introverts, but all certainly have a lot more going on beneath the surface than they ever let on. The Moon likes growth, and Scorpio likes to throw things away, so there may be a lot of inner conflict about whether one should be expanding or contracting one's personality in the social space. I want to know more about people—yet I don't want them to know more about me, for my own self-protection. I can't get inside them without opening myself up. This sometimes creates the one-step-forward, two-steps-back way that the Scorpio Moon handles her intimacy issues.

Scorpio is the most emotionally intense of all the signs, and when the already emotional Moon is in this sign, it means a more or less permanent case of moodiness. Hecate may be a lunar goddess, but she is also an underworld goddess, passing back and forth between the depths and the night fields like a creature of caves who only comes out after dark. She never sees the sun's light, and in a sense neither does a Scorpio Moon. The dark depths of her psyche press upon her much closer than do those of other, more diurnal people, and she spends a lot of time brooding over them. On the other hand, Scorpio Moons can make very good counselors, playing the psychopomp role and aiding someone lost in their own underworld. She is not likely to be surprised or shocked by anything that the sufferer might say; she is familiar with the territory of darkness. She understands the kind of moodiness that veers between silent introversion and snarling rage like the baying of Hecate's hounds.

Part of this kind of depth-work is transformation, an important process for any planet in Scorpio. The rulership of Pluto gives Scorpio the urge to transform everything, including themselves, violently if necessary. As an underworld goddess, Hecate well understands the cycle of death and rebirth. She specialized in the kind of magic that we might consider necromantic: contacting and channeling the dead, asking their advice, gaining their protection, and persuading them to aid her power. The places that she haunted most frequently were crossroads, which symbolize choice, or places where crimes of passion had been committed, or criminals executed. This too is a Scorpio specialty; even if the Scorpio Moon person in question is as lawfully upright as possible, they may have a secret (or not so secret) fascination with the doings and deeds of those who are not. Death and darkness fascinates even the most timid Scorpios, because they sense in its forbidden power a deep truth about the nature of existence.

The other side of death is birth, and Hecate's other attribute was goddess of midwifery. Here she is linked to the Egyptian goddess Heqat, whose symbol was the frog as it resembled the fetus. These may have formed the inspiration for the hopping frogs and toads of the medieval witch. The fact that most midwifery among the poor was done by old granny-wives, the same sort of crone figure who might also sell magic charms to the peasants, inspired not only that witch figure but the mass execution of people who resembled it. Being shunned for your connection with the darkness when you are merely trying to break through to transformation and birth is something a Scorpio Moon will be quite familiar with.

Hecate, the intense and mysterious witch-goddess, rules the night and cannot be cast as a creature of the light; similarly, the Scorpio Moon cannot be made to be lighthearted and flighty about emotional issues. She takes things seriously, including her relationships, and she does not suffer fools at all. In time, she may work out all the roads to her underworld and so transform and rebirth her heart.

Artemis
Moon in Sagittarius

The Sagittarian Moon person has been characterized as having an elusive quality, like that of a wild and untrusting animal. Another astrologer once compared them to the deer in a local park, who can slowly, over time, bring themselves to feed from your hand, but when the hand appears in a glove, they bolt for the woods. The Sagittarian love of freedom, in the lunar placement, requires a certain amount of emotional space. Anything that seems to tie her down to one dream, one ideal, one relationship, creates a fight-or-flight response.

This lunar nature is evocative of the Greek goddess of the Moon, Artemis, archer and huntress, lady of the wild things. Independent and elusive as moonlight, she ran with the wild animals in the woods; her symbols are quail and doe and cypress. She is both the mistress and the embodiment of virgin forest, pure spring water, all that is untouched and uncontrolled by man. She was the special protectress of young girls between the ages of six and puberty; there is an echo of this youthfulness or yearning for the state of innocence in many Sagittarian Moon people.

Artemis is a sworn virgin, although in this denotation it means that she shares her life with no man. Instead she is the leader of a band of hunting nymphs; there is some evidence that she shares her sexual favors with them, but she is still separate and apart and there is no story where she shows anything more than a passing affair with a nymph. In fact, she banishes or kills any nymph who lies with a man, whether they weaken to seduction or are raped. Of all the virgin goddesses, Artemis is the most violent in defending her freedom and seems the most afraid of losing it; this is a common response in a wounded Sagittarian Moon, who can be suspicious of every lover as a potential jailer.

Artemis the archer symbolizes focus, as she aims her unerring bow, and her arrows are always true. She rules the kind of thought that has its eye constantly on the goal, even if that goal is merely the horizon. Like Sagittarius, she has no specific dwelling that is her home and her band of nymphs live a nomadic life, camping all over the forests of southern Europe. While the Moon is the most domestic of planets, under Sagittarius (the least domestic of signs) it becomes an internal rather than an external hearth—a "home is wherever I am" sort of attitude. The open road can often seem more homely, more familiar, than any enclosing building; like Artemis, she shoots her arrow of vision and follows its track. This can be toward an ideal of life or an ideal of relationship, either of which have the equal possibility of being a great adventure or an impossible dream.

The dark side of Artemis is that she is adamant and uncompromising, harsh in her idea of what is wrong and what is right, what can be tolerated and what cannot. She is the punisher of those who betray their oaths; it is Artemis who makes sure that Ariadne is left behind by her mortal paramour, Theseus, as she had earlier been sworn to Dionysus and he had a right to claim his bride. Her arrows fall swiftly, and she has no mercy. When Actaeon follows her into the forest and stumbles across her bathing naked in a pool, she changes him into a stag and lets his own hounds tear him to pieces. She represents the unmerciful side of nature, which encourages survival of the fittest and will let the weak die in order to strengthen the species.

There is a definite quality to this in the Sagittarian Moon, more so even than in the Sun in Sagittarius, as the Moon is more likely to be moved by irrational emotion than logic. Sagittarius is the sign of the religious fanatic, and the "religion" can be anything—Catholicism, Islam, Paganism, ecology, AA, vegetarianism, astrology, or the Republican Party. In fact, if the Sagittarian Moon has no spiritual or philosophical goal to pursue with that unerring focus, she will fritter her fanaticism away on petty, unyielding demands for the people around her to think and behave exactly as she says they should, because it is the Right Thing. Being right is very important to Sagittarius in general, and with a lunar placement, whatever she is doing has to feel emotionally right; because this Moon is in general rather distanced from the human feelings of others, she does not quite understand wholly that what is right for her may not be right for everyone else. Artemis holds everyone uncompromisingly to her own standards and slays them out of hand if they fail.

She also demands human sacrifices. When Agamemnon wants a wind to sail to Troy, he is told that he must sacrifice his eldest daughter on a pyre to Artemis. This triggers his wife into taking over the kingdom in his absence and murdering him when he returns. In some versions, Artemis substitutes a deer at the last minute and bears the maiden away to another country, where she becomes a priestess; either way, she is torn from her life and family for the goddess's purposes. For the Sagittarian Moon, when ensconced in the negative side of fanaticism, comforts are the first things to be sacrificed on the altar of belief, and if she can do it, why shouldn't everyone else? There is a kind of asceticism of principle with this placement and a certain lack of compassion. On the other hand, some people are driven to new heights and opened mentally to new breadths when confronted with this kind of challenge. There is certainly a lot of mental laziness in the world today; whatever else the Moon in Sagittarius is, she will not be a hypocrite.

Artemis is also a goddess associated with childbirth; although the Greeks had a separate goddess, Ilythiea, whose rule was only over childbirth and nothing else, she was the daughter of Hera and only gave her blessing to sanctified births within marriage. Artemis, who was the bastard daughter of Zeus by a nymph named Leto, has no such compunctions. Her aid extends itself to any woman in labor and pain, and a woman who dies in childbirth is said to be killed by Artemis out of mercy. The priestesses of the temple of Artemis were donated the clothing of women who died in this way. Her mother Leto gave birth to twins; Artemis was the firstborn, but Apollo was not born for nine more days of agony. Leto would have perished save that by the ninth day, Artemis was mature enough to aid her mother in delivering her brother.

This association with childbirth, and especially difficult childbirth, indicates the Sagittarian ability to midwife creative projects or new philosophies out of oneself or others. The Sagittarian Moon, with its combination of originality and conviction, can spark others to go on their own quests, leave behind their dull, bounded lives, and find their own hearts. Watching a Sagittarian Moon kick over the traces and run free can make others recognize their own chains.

frigga
Moon in Capricorn

In her great and beautiful hall Fensalir, the Hall of Fountains in Asgard, dwells the lovely and gracious Frigga, queen and consort of Odin. Honored matron and shrewd manager, she oversees not only her own hall and all its denizens but Odin's three halls as well, including Valhalla, with its vast and endless cadre of deceased warriors. Chief of the goddesses of the Aesir, she was held in high esteem by her husband Odin the All-Father, and she holds the title All-Mother to represent her status as ruler.

Although not strictly a lunar goddess—the Norse pantheon has a personified sun and moon, but no major deity holds its guardianship—Frigga does rule over the traditionally lunar domains of childbirth, family, and the hearth. However, she is not a cuddly mother goddess; like Capricorn, her maternal nature is more stately than comforting. She values competence and integrity and has no desire to keep any of her charges helpless and inept.

It is said of people with the Moon in Capricorn that they are too caught up in material things, that their emotions are too distant and subdued, that they had cold parents who wanted them to grow up too fast, and that they are at heart emotionally solitary people who do not come into the world with warm, open relationship skills. It is also true that the Norse were stoic people, and their All-Mother perhaps reflects this paradigm. Frigga does not feel sorry for herself, and neither does a healthy Capricorn Moon. For this Moon placement, if love does not come with respect, if affection does not come with clear boundaries, and if domesticity does not come with loyalty, then she doesn't want it. It's a tainted fruit, and she can do without it. She has, up until now; it was lonely, but she can go it again, on her own, for as long as it takes. A Capricorn Moon wants a destiny, a partner, a family, a life, a spirit that is not just comfortable but worthy, and she will work harder and do without longer than anyone else in order to keep from compromising herself.

It is said that to be able to get what you want is riches, but to be able to do without is power. Frigga understands this mystery, as does the Moon when it is in Capricorn. She lives a public life with her husband; she knows that he esteems her without the need for public displays of affection. He doesn't need her to be emotionally effusive at all times, as he knows that they are committed to each other for the long haul. Capricorn Moons like commitment. It makes them feel safe, and only in that safety can the crack open their layers of protective distance and reveal themselves.

The devotion of a Capricorn Moon can be shown in Frigga's attempts to protect her son, Baldur, from the destiny that has been laid upon him. She travels all over the earth and talks every mortal, giant, animal, and plant into refusing to harm him, except for one tiny mistletoe plant whom she judges too young to harm anyone. Loki the trickster makes a dart of it, places it into a blind man's hand, and arranges to have Baldur killed. Determined to save her child's life, Frigga again visits every mortal, giant, animal, and plant, begging them to weep for her son in the hopes that Hel will be moved to release him. She fails in her task, but her nature reflects the Capricorn Moon and its ability to go on, doggedly, with unfailing persistence, to aid a loved one.

Frigga's domestic efforts move in two spheres, the microcosmic and the macrocosmic. On one level, she is mistress of such homely domestic affairs as marriage, hearth and family, home-industry crafts, and household management. On a larger scale, she is a queen-consort, and a queen-consort who is much more than a royal brood mare or ornament. Frigga acts for Odin as a combination of First Lady and prime minister, helping him deal with his problems of rulership and managing the responsibilities of his divine halls. Her task is to bring *frith*—peace—to both the family hearth and the overarching community/tribe/kingdom. She shows that the same sort of power and knowledge used to run a household can also be used to run an organization, city, or nation.

Frigga's peace is not some sort of bells-and-harpstrings Libran idea of harmony; it is a matter of making sure that everything runs smoothly and gets done properly. She is a lady, and a competent one; she knows the right procedures and traditions and how to use those structures to make sure that everyone feels welcomed, acknowledged, and has no need to interrupt the flow of work. For Frigga, hospitality is an art more refined than teacup-tilting; she is part diplomat, part administrator, part business manager, and part contract attorney.

This last role is symbolized by her array of handmaidens, all of whom are demigoddesses with different roles. Among them are Syn, demigoddess of fair dealing, upon whose name contracts are promised, and Vara, who encourages businesspeople to keep their oaths. As marriage is also a contract and Frigga is in charge of it, another of her handmaidens is Lofn, who mediates between warring lovers. Other handmaidens offer such gifts as abundance, healing, and the ability to work.

This Capricorn ability to see all relationships as contracts to be negotiated, and conversely to see contracts as sacred oaths and vows, resonates in the goddess Frigga, All-Mother and queen. Reserved? When you finally earn my trust, you'll value it more. Distant? Such distance allows others the space in which to grow and flourish. Materialistic? Do not fail to remember, she says, that the first part of the word material is *mater*, Mother. We live here, in this world. Let's make the best of it.

mwuetsi
Moon in Aquarius

The Moon is, by its nature, emotional, illogical, and irrational. Aquarius, by its nature, is not any of these. It is ruled by Uranus, however, which is a pretty erratic planet. With Uranus ruling the hapless Moon, you get the intellectual idiosyncrasy overlaying the changeable emotions, and neither is quite in touch with each other except on the intuitive level. This combination can create an amazing, ingenious imagination, or it can become a scattered rebel, trying to change everyone else before he is fit to be any kind of a teacher or example of how to be and feel and think.

This tale is told among the Wahungwe Makoni tribe in Africa. It was said that the first being Maori the Creator made was Mwuetsi, the Moon Man. At first Mwuetsi lived at the bottom of a lake, far away from the Earth that Maori was slowly creating, but after a while Mwuetsi grew bored and longed to walk on the unfinished Earth. Maori warned him that if he went down to Earth, he could never come back, and as it was not yet finished, he would probably regret it.

Mwuetsi insisted that he would be a pioneer in the new world. Aquarian Moons are easily bored and don't tolerate being imprisoned in someone else's watery emotions for long. If there is a new and interesting place to go, they want to go there. Mwuetsi goes to Earth but finds it barren and unpeopled. He complains that there is no food, no plants or trees or animals, and Maori tells him that he has set foot on the path that will eventually kill him, when he could have stayed immortal forever. Mwuetsi cries up to Maori that he is lonely and Maori tells him it is because he has no tribe, people not yet being invented.

The lack of a tribe is a serious problem for the Aquarius Moon. One of the chief issues of Aquarius is how one does or does not fit in with the mass of people who are one's community. Does one rebel and stand out or band with them? Does one become an activist servant of humanity or a misanthropic outcast? An Aquarius Moon is capable of all of these reactions. Since the Moon, even in this airy, detached sign, rules the family, he is still driven to find that family, wherever it lies. No matter what kind of a rebel an individual Aquarian may be, he longs to be part of a tribe, the people who are different the same as he is. If that's an oxymoron, so be it; it's the Aquarian paradox. He can learn from the next part of the story: Maori tells Mwuetsi that if he wants his loneliness to cease, he must make the tribe himself.

Maori starts by making him a wife, Massasi the Morning Star. She is an innocent young maiden and is fairly ignorant of life. Mwuetsi does not want to become physically intimate with her, so he jumps over the fire, moistens his finger with ngona oil, and touches her belly. After this, she becomes magically pregnant and bears grasses, bushes, and trees—all the plants that they need to eat and shelter them—and they live contentedly for two years. Mwuetsi spends his time creating things like shovels and baskets and hoes and fish traps, and inventing agriculture. However, there is still no tribe.

Part of the difficulty in having an Aquarius Moon is that you need people and don't thrive without a group to be part of, yet you really aren't used to this whole emotional intimacy thing. The detached Aquarian nature resists bonding, symbolized by Mwuetsi's reluctance to couple with his wife normally. He would rather use fire (inspiration) and a single touch with magical oil (superficial connection) to create a relationship with her; actually getting down and making love might bring him too close to her in many ways. It might also bring up his fundamental discomfort with having a body, something that he cannot always control. So he lives this sterile marriage with her, and it does bring forth life, but only unmoving, nonspeaking life. It also inspires the imaginative creation of many useful projects, also a hallmark of the ingenious Aquarian Moon. But it cannot create true companionship.

Maori, on the other hand, sees what is going on and removes Massasi, and Mwuetsi mourns her loss terribly, weeping for eight days. Maori then creates a second wife for Mwuetsi, Morongo the Evening Star. She is nothing like Massasi, and she tells him so. When he wants to do his trick with the oil on his finger, she orders him to smear both their genitals with the oil, and then shows him how to make love to her properly. Finally able to make the intimate connection, Mwuetsi couples with her, and she bears livestock on the first day, cattle and deer on the second, and human children on the third. Mwuetsi now has a tribe, and he is happy. It's a utopia, a dream beloved of any Aquarian.

They live together in their idyllic peace for a while, and then he wants to couple with Morongo again. However, Maori sends a thunderstorm to stop him, telling him that if they do it again Mwuetsi will bring death into the world. Morongo convinces him to sneak into the hut with her and do it, and this time she brings forth all the predators of the world—lions, leopards, snakes, and scorpions. Mwuetsi is horrified and goes apart from her. Maori says, "I told you so." The airy, utopian-obsessed Aquarius doesn't like to think that there will always be difficulties in the world, and between human beings, that cannot be smoothed away logically. If only everyone would just be rational, he thinks, there would be world peace. When faced with the fact that no one is ever going to be rational all the time and that many will be irrational much of the time—to bring forth the leopards and scorpions of their pain and anger—he runs away feeling betrayed.

Mwuetsi then lives with his new tribe, the children born of himself and Morongo. He becomes their greatest king and innovator, their Aquarian leader. Instead of laying with Morongo, he lays with his descendants, the tribal women. This suggests that part of the Aquarian Moon strategy for dealing with the betrayal of the utopian dream is to dedicate oneself to the people, to humanity, to aid them as best one can. However, toward the end of his life, he gets the urge to visit his abandoned wife Morongo again—to make once again the deep and human connection. All the humanitarian aid in the world, and even the support of one's chosen community, does not satisfy the Moon if it has no place to put its need for strong emotional bonds, and this is a lesson the Aquarian Moon learns the hard way.

Morongo, in the meantime, has been living with a large poisonous serpent—in other words, with her resentment at having been abandoned for bringing forth things that the detached Mwuetsi found frightening and unsettling. He goes to her house as if nothing has happened between them—an open, straightforward Aquarius Moon is not always skilled at reading other people's subtexts—and asks to lie with her again. She tells him to go away, but he insists. During the act, the poisonous snake rears up and bites him, and he becomes ill but cannot die, being the immortal Moon Man. All the animals and plants sicken, the lakes dry up, and famine falls across the land. Many people of Mwuetsi's tribe die, and the remaining ones decide that the only thing to do is to kill both Mwuetsi and Morongo and send them back to Maori. They do this, and the land recovers. Thus Mwuetsi dies by the hand of his own people, the ones that he worked so hard to create.

An Aquarian Moon individual can be a great boon to his community with his imagination and innovation and his idealistic commitment to helping others. However, he can also start a great deal of trouble with his insensitivity to the needs of others, accidentally wounding more thin-skinned people and then being more impatient than empathetic with their pain. If he can learn how to deal with the lions and serpents of other people's fears, he can keep his place in the tribe, possibly even as its visionary leader. However, if he doesn't, sooner or later he will spread so many unintended problems that he will get himself banished from the very group he has invested himself in. Mwuetsi chose to come down to Earth and form a tribe, and in doing so he took upon himself the obligation to deal with all that it means to be human, even those things that are difficult or distasteful . . . like other people and their problems. It is important for every Aquarius Moon that they learn this lesson, or their dream of Tribe will die, again and again, by the hands of the ones they love.

Yemaya
Moon in Pisces

The sea is the source of all life, ever-changing and yet unchanging, fluctuating with the tides, giving forth life or sweeping away into death. It is the great salt bath that we all came out of, and it still runs in our veins with a rhythm like the tide. Even if we live landlocked and never see the sea, it has a hold on us. The Moon, too, holds us; every month it draws the fluid in our brains upwards and affects our moods. The combination—Moon and sea—is embodied in the astrological placement of the Moon in Pisces, and in the beautiful Afro-Caribbean lunar goddess Yemaya, orisha of the sea.

In European traditions, the Mother archetype usually centers around the earth; in the Yoruba tradition, the maternal instinct belongs to the sea. Yemaya was the sea mother of her people; nurturing, giving of herself, bringing life to the earth. She was the mother of many of the other orishas, including Shango, the god of fire, and Ogoun, the god of smithing and the hunt. She is also the keeper of dreams and the unconscious, the realms of Neptune, who rules the Moon in this placement.

Having a Pisces Moon means having an emotional nature that is wide open and oversensitive to the moods of others. Often, the problem may be that the Pisces Moon individual doesn't know if they are having their own feelings or those of the person that they are currently talking to, or living with, or thinking about. It is too easy to lose themselves in someone else's world-view, and because of this tide pulling them back and forth—what they feel, what others feel—emotional ambivalence is the hallmark of their existence. It is said that Yemaya can see herself in the faces of all women, and this kind of merging is both the gift and the trap of Pisces Moon.

At the summer solstice, which is Yemaya's day, hundreds of small altars of food, white wine, incense, and shells are laid out on the beach at low tide; by the end of the day they are entirely swept away. A Pisces Moon can often find herself so drowned in the turbulent emotional atmosphere of those around her that she must retreat or she will lose track of herself. The famous Pisces self-sacrifice often occurs because the individual is too caught up in someone else, or something else, to even remember that they have needs of their own, and they are important. People take advantage of her, and she gives until she is exhausted, telling herself that their happiness is enough.

In Catholic countries where the Afro-Caribbean religions were somewhat disapproved of by local religious authorities, practitioners used to camouflage their altars by making them into knickknack shelves piled with ordinary objects that were nonetheless sacred to one of the orishas. This has evolved into an aesthetic of unobtrusiveness, where altars are designed to be subtle. Yemaya altars, which are traditionally kept in the kitchen or perhaps the bathroom, are the easiest to hide; decorative piles of cups and bowls, or even a single bowl or wineglass of saltwater, can symbolize her oceanic nature. The prettiest camouflaged Yemaya altar that I have ever seen consisted of several blue soup bowls tilted petal-like out of another bowl, amid stacks of teacups of different heights. To the uninitiated, it was a bunch of crockery; to those who knew what to look for, it was a lotus floating on the water.

This kind of unobtrusiveness, of blending into the woodwork, is also typical of the Pisces Moon, who does not make a great show of herself. Because of this, she is often taken for granted by those around her. However, her empathy can make her an excellent counselor and healer; it can also push her spiritual nature to greater heights, assuming she does not become sucked into the tides of alcohol or drugs, or the even more treacherous drug of needing to please others.

Although she is the least easy of the orishas to offend, it is possible to anger her. As an example, a woman who was sworn to Yemaya in her youth met and married a Muslim man who demanded that she convert to Islam. She did so, but still kept an altar to Yemaya; after several years and a few children, he ordered her to get rid of it and formally renounce her oath to Yemaya. Out of love for him, she did so, and within six months they had become homeless and the authorities had taken their children. Yemaya had struck at their home and family, the areas of her expertise, and her retaliation seemed to be not only about the renunciation but the loss of self to another that precipitated it. Be careful, she says; if you cannot contain your love within boundaries, it will drain away and not be replenished. Even the sea has shores.

Yemaya understands sacrifice and how hard it is to say no to your loved ones. When her son Ogoun came to manhood, he was seized with a lust for his mother and routinely forced himself on Yemaya whenever they were alone together. She wept and protested, but was unable to bring herself to fend him off or reveal the abuse. He was, after all, her child, and she feared that he would be killed if the truth leaked. Finally, Ogoun was discovered and exposed by Ellegua the trickster. Yemaya sacrificed herself for her son's sins and knows the bitter fruit that this can bring. It seems that at some point in their lives, Pisces Moon people will find themselves in a relationship with a strong but dysfunctional person who simultaneously needs and resents them, and it will be all that they can do to break away from it.

Since it is ruled by Neptune, the Moon in this placement can be a carrier for idealistic fantasies and wild imaginations, sometimes to the extent that they find actual reality fairly depressing and live mentally in a world of their own. On the other hand, sometimes they can survive incredibly severe circumstances and come out of them emotionally undamaged, simply because they were too detached from reality to be touched by them. For someone so apparently fragile, a Pisces Moon can be awfully resilient. Like water, they flow around and away from difficulties. You never quite know which way they are going to float next; just when you think they are going to end up on the rocks, they manage to outlast everyone and still come through with their hearts intact.

Mercury

HORUS
Mercury in Aries

In a bright sky where it never rains, a falcon with keen eyes wheels over a land of burnt sand and fiery, indomitable heat. The falcon can see every move-

ment in the hot, shimmering sand, and when prey appears, he dives with a keen cry of triumph, scoops

up the hapless earthbound creature and flies away with it into the sun. Seeing a tableau like this on a regular basis created, in the ancient Egyptian mind,

the genesis of the Hawk God, who had many names and forms and histories. The youngest of them was

Horus, whose eye still appears as a symbol in many places. Horus was a hero-god in all of his incarna-

tions, usually shown as a hawk-headed man who had no fear of the fiery desert. His original name was

Har, which is onomatopoeic for the cry of a hawk.

There were actually two Horuses, the elder and

the younger. This came about when garbled Horus-tales from different areas of Egypt were reorganized

and written down. Right there we can get a taste of Mercury in Aries who, in his gifted, creative frenzy,

does not always check to make sure that his various garbled facts are straight, but may combine them

into the most exciting rather than the most accurate form. At any rate, when the late-era scribes were done with the stories, they had two Horuses who were father and uncle, and both took part in the same sweeping epic story.

Horus the elder, youngest son of Geb and Nut, and brother of Osiris, Isis, Set, and Nephthys, practically came out of the womb fighting with Set. The two of them stem from the old eternal conflict of Light God versus Dark God; in these older battles Horus emasculates Set and Set tears out both of Horus's eyes, flinging them up into the sky where they become the Sun and Moon. The protective Horus-eye amulet comes from this early worship.

Horus the younger was the posthumous son of Isis by the dead Osiris. After Set has cut Osiris into pieces and flung them into the swamps of the Nile, and Isis has carefully reassembled all but one of the bits and magically made them reanimate for a time, she conceives the infant Horus, giving birth prematurely to him on the island of Chemmis. Osiris, however, cannot stay mortal and must go to the underworld, where he becomes king, and Horus is raised alone by his mother. She is raising him for one purpose only: vengeance upon his uncle Set for the death of his father. As he grows, she encourages him to be warlike, and his uncle Horus teaches him the skills of warfare.

The young Horus was weak and sickly at birth, and during his childhood he was attacked by all manner of things—bitten by savage beasts, burnt, suffering from gastric pains, and finally stung by a scorpion whose poison was so deadly that Thoth had to cure him from the very door of death. The ghost of his father appeared to him periodically to exhort him to vengeance, and by the time he reaches his teens, he is a warrior steeped in vengeance.

Finally, the moment of truth comes; Horus brings suit against Set in front of a tribunal, claiming himself as Osiris's legitimate son and heir. Set argues against him but is thwarted by the judges who rule, of course, in Horus's favor. Desperate, Set refuses to give up the throne and the warrior boy raises an army and marches against Set. There is a terribly martial and no doubt exciting battle when Set wounds Horus the elder and is killed by Horus the younger. Vengeance over, Horus is crowned and sails off into the Nile sunset.

Mercury in Aries is a fast thinker and covers a lot of ground while others are still struggling with the first idea. Like a hawk, he sails from one broad subject to another, but like the prematurely born Horus, he tends to speak too soon with too little forethought. Often he doesn't know what he actually thinks until he works it out aloud. His speech can be fairly aggressive in its style; there is often a certain pattern of rapid-fire, staccato bursts of words, like a machine gun, and he is not above combatively interrupting. Mercury in Aries is not afraid of arguing and sometimes even enjoys it— what, Horus run in fear from a battle?—although he must resist the urge to make ordinary party talk into a debate or the more sensitive types will run from his brand of competitive conversation. Of course, one of the places that such a talent is really useful is in the practice of law, and one notices that Horus's battle against Set starts with a lawsuit, not a physical attack.

Another thing we can note from the myth is that Horus is one of the Divine Youths, and he has no living father, only a ghost whose legend he is steeped in and whose mysterious appearances no doubt only serve to heighten his idolization. There is something about Mercury in Aries that suggests the headstrong, uncurbed youth who was never given proper limits. He craves a code of honor, or a goal, which may be spawned from early fantasies of magical authority figures and have no actual relation to reality. Still, the world has few enough knights-errant that we need all we can get.

To Aries, the world is often all too black and white. There are the good guys and the bad guys, and the unimportant bystanders. He, of course, is one of the good guys, and if you attempt to slow down his course in any way, you must be one of the bad guys. Both Horuses, elder and younger, are permanent adversaries; it practically defines their nature. A Mercury in Aries person likes to think of himself as the righteous avenger, and without a clear enemy, he may start inventing one. Enemies that are nebulous, like "poverty" or "racism" or "boredom," infuriate him; you can't go after them with a sword or even break into their offices and beat on their desks. It is hard for him to understand that there is no one Big Bad Guy who can be vanquished and then everything will be better. It is even harder to get him to see the adversary's side of things.

One of the truly positive things about Mercury in Aries people, however, is their incredible mental optimism. Horus gets raised in exile, fatherless, with a heavy destiny; he is bitten and stung and burnt and comes down sick; he almost dies several times. This would crush a gloomier entity, but he comes out of it all healthy, spunky, and swinging. Mercury in Aries people are amazingly resilient; they are the last to succumb to depression and the first to recover from hardship and get back into the saddle with enthusiasm. They are fire and quicksilver, the bright, seeing eyes of a hawk in the air, hot with anger and ebullience and energy, crying to the horizon with a voice heard miles away.

Thor

Mercury in Taurus

Most gods of the sky and storm are capricious, volatile, fickle creatures. Among this erratic crowd, the Norse thunder god Thor stands out for his constancy and steadiness. The staunchly loyal eldest son of Odin, he never failed to defend those he called home and family. Red-haired and red-bearded, burly and muscular, he was considered both rude and noble, kind and brutal, and as courageous as they come. He was the most popular god of the Norse/Germanic tribes, bringer of thunder and storms.

Mercury is an airy planet, more at home in airy signs like Gemini or Aquarius than in down-to-earth Taurus. This placement is dismissed as giving a slow, plodding mind that falls easily into mental ruts. Although this is not necessarily untrue, it is a shameful trivialization of Taurean energy. One of Thor's strong points is that he insists that people keep their vows; he is invoked to watch over promises for that reason. He values commitment and frowns on those who treat their oaths frivolously. Mercury in Taurus can gift someone with a mental loyalty to a concept or idea or theory that enables them to pursue it doggedly long after everyone else has wandered off in boredom. The researcher with Mercury in Taurus will spend months comparing sources until he finds the information that is needed. The artist with this placement will spend hour after hour glued to his work, putting in one tiny detail after another. People who see it will oooh and aaah, and say things like, "I could never do that." For that moment, they see the value in Taurus's intellectual patience. Then they usually go back to admiring more mentally flashy types.

Mercury in Taurus rarely cares, however. He doesn't seek fame and recognition so much as he seeks comfort and security. What other people think of him is generally shrugged off. Where he does go overboard is on the smaller luxuries. The classic image is of Thor at the feast table, eating and drinking just a little too much. He doesn't need rarefied entertainments; he'd rather have the simple pleasures, and lots of them. Thor was a god of the common people; he was renowned as a warrior but stood more behind the peasant protecting his home from brigands with a homemade spear than the knight in armor. Norse peasants often named their children after Thor in order to place them under his protection. He was a patron of farmers; his chariot was drawn by goats, the livestock animal of the poor. He was the earthiest sky god in existence, seeing high up and down low at once. He was originally the personification of the rains that brought life-giving moisture to the earth.

It was not, however, that Thor was always a peaceful god. There was a side to him that inspired terror; the thunder was said to be the wheels of his great chariot rolling across the sky, and the lightning was his hammer Mjollnir being flung at whoever had earned his displeasure. His anger followed the Taurus pattern—long periods of peace punctuated by brief, violent episodes. He could absorb many wrongs, but when he was pushed too far, the bull charged and leveled everything in its path. This is a familiar state of affairs for Mercury in Taurus, who will patiently plod through muck every day, dark clouds quietly gathering in the distance, until the single moment when they reach an advanced state of Had It. Then they explode with enough force to terrify everyone around them, and shrapnel rains from the heavens. Afterwards, people say things like, "Where did that come from?" or "But he's such a quiet person."

The Taurus Mercury is not subtle. Thor's weapon is not the blade but the hammer. He has only three sorts of attacks: hit something hard once, hit it several times, or throw the hammer at it from a distance. Well, all right, maybe we could throw in "punch it with your fist" or "wrestle it bodily to the ground." This mental ability to persistently hammer something home can pay off in accomplishment, but it can also be too hard on the nerves of more sensitive types. He can also miss the fine print, and trickier types can run circles around him if he is not careful. In the myths, Loki the trickster is always getting the better of Thor until the red-bearded god catches on and decides merely to kill him on sight rather than listen to another word. Thor was often ridiculed in the Odinic texts for his awkward oafishness, but when you wanted something disposed of, you called him in to do the job.

Thor's hammer, the symbol of his personal force, was far more than just a weapon. It gave solemn consecration to private or public treaties, representing his word—which, as we have discussed, was unbreakable. Similarly, Mercury in Taurus is often the person whose word people somehow just trust. When they bother to speak, it is direct and to the point. They don't mince words or prevaricate; they will sit stubbornly silent rather than make tactful excuses. When they say that they will do something, you can usually count on it getting done—if not quickly, then with extreme thoroughness.

It is true that a Mercury in Taurus does not absorb new ideas easily. In fact, the mental rearrangement that new ideas stimulate can create a cognitive earthquake. Taurus would prefer to avoid such conflicts, and will stick to what he knows and is sure of; changing his mind is almost a painful process for him. In the areas where he is skilled and knowledgeable, however, he is stronger than most people. His victories tend to be many and small rather than singular and hugely impressive, but his tenacious efforts can add up to greatness in time.

During one of Thor's many adventures, a sorcerer challenges him to drain his magical drinking horn and lift his strange pet cat. Thor tries his best, but after a bellyful of mead barely manages to lower the level of the horn, and the cat is so heavy that he can only get one paw off the ground. The sorcerer confesses that it was all a trick; the horn's contents were the ocean waters and the cat was the Midgard Serpent. Although Thor himself felt that he had failed, he had actually lowered the ocean's level by a few inches, and his shaking of the sacred serpent had caused several earthquakes. "If I had known how strong you truly were," the sorcerer told him, "I would never have let you in." It is easy to underestimate slow, plodding Mercury in Taurus. It is also an incredibly foolish thing to do.

Hermes
Mercury in Gemini

The planet Mercury, smallest and fastest of all the lumps that circle our sun, whizzes around it like a fireball and is named for the god of speed. When it is in Gemini of the Twins, it is under its own rulership and nothing gets in its way. Pure Mercury pours out like lightning, unimpeded by any of the concerns of the other planets. To the Greeks, the Roman Mercury was named Hermes, and he was the messenger god of the Olympians. With wings on his sandals and his hat, he tore about barely touching the earth, traveling, talking, thinking, quicksilver and impossible to hold. Mercury in Gemini embodies this brilliant, untouchable force, the original Mercury namesake.

Hermes was the god of flocks and herds (only because he stole them from Apollo) and the protector of all travelers. Tall pillars surmounted by the sculpted heads of Hermes, called herms, stood at crossroads as travel charms. Since in ancient times commerce necessarily meant travel, he was the god of merchants and also of thieves. His tongue was glib and often embellished things, and this too is typical of Mercury in Gemini. After all, truth is really such a relative concept, isn't it? It's nearly impossible, irrational, foolish to try to reduce the human thought process to simple black-and-white concepts.

It has been pointed out, for example, that it is very difficult to get a true one-word answer to the question, "Have you been faithful?" First one must discern whether or not the questioner and questioned both have the same definition of the word. Do you mean sexually faithful? Emotionally? Does it count if there was no intercourse, but only alternative forms of sexuality? Kissing? Hugs? Flirting? Giving someone too much attention while neglecting your partner? How about fantasies? Does it count if I was unfaithful in my mind? If I fantasize about someone else while I am making love to you, is it infidelity? What about fidelity of the heart—if I am in love with them, but stay with you? You see, says Mercury in Gemini, I can't possibly answer that question with a yes or a no. And since I'm not stupid and I know you asked that question less for the informative value and more for reassurance, then the most useful thing that I can do for both of us is to come up with an answer that is at least half-true that will do the job of reassuring you. There. Will that shut you up?

If this seems cold, it's because in this detached air sign, everything comes from the head. A Mercury in Gemini can be brilliant and witty, but he is rarely interested in people's emotional issues; in fact, he would rather they didn't exist at all. Like a herm, he can sometimes end up a talking head, unattached to a feeling body. Like Hermes the Messenger, he can move so fast from topic to topic that ordinary conversationalists can never keep up. Even if they can keep up, they may get annoyed at his occasional superficiality. Hermes can fly all over the face of the earth, but the one direction he doesn't often move in is down. He can certainly do it, but it's not his favorite place.

The ancient Greeks saw the underworld of Hades, the realm of death, as a frightening realm. Not only was it well guarded by scary creatures such as Cerberus, the three-headed dog, but the paths inside were filled with lost souls moaning for aid; if you stopped to help them, they would drag you down and you would be lost. Hermes, the divine messenger, was the only god or mortal who could pass in and out of Hades at will, with no toll paid nor danger to his person. When the underworld is revisioned as the deeper world of our own and the collective unconscious, Hermes becomes the force that remains objective in the face of every psychological assault, guiding people in and out. Like Mercury in Gemini, Hermes is rather lacking in compassion, so the lost souls wailing on the path do not trouble him at all. He locks onto a goal and swiftly pursues it, and as such he can be invaluable as the psychopomp or therapist whose job it is to get someone out of a paralyzing crisis.

Where Mercury in Gemini falls down is when he has to actually spend time in his own underworld, rather than just whizzing in, rescuing someone, and whizzing back out. Mercury rules the nervous system, and this placement often gives a rather delicate set of "nerves" that act up whenever something boring or unpleasant or tedious or painful is coming down the rails. Tied to the tracks of his own emotions, a Mercury in Gemini can feel very out of his depth. In the human world, not the abstract one, logic does not rule, you can't run in a straight line, obstacles come up all the time, delays bog you down, and people say things like "I don't know" quite often. This is a serious drag for the god of speed, who would prefer that all processing sessions took less than twenty minutes and always stuck to the immediate point.

Logic and emotion have been compared to the black and white keys on the piano. Play only the white keys and they are plentiful and sound orderly, but you are limited to the key of C or maybe A minor. Play only the black keys and things sound weird and confusing with odd, unexplained jumps from note to note. In order for music to have real depth and breadth, both must be played together in one system. To a Mercury in Gemini, the black keys are often frightening and make him nervous. He doesn't know how to use them, and he would rather say many small, flat things than sing a great, complex symphony. On the other hand, he does live in the sign of duality, and one of the Geminian twins does know how to use those black keys. In fact, it's all he knows, and his light twin panics and consigns him to the basement rather often, where he calls lies up through a hole in the floor out of anger at his imprisonment.

This Gemini duality is how Hermes can be both the god of merchants and of thieves, of diplomats and of liars, psychopomp and avoidant. First one twin speaks, then the other. Eventually, if he's brave enough, he can learn to integrate the two of them and find himself speaking from a whole voice, touching the earth for more than a moment. After all, logic is a weapon that can be wielded by anyone, for any reason, if they try hard enough to justify themselves. It is not until a deeper feeling is added to it that it becomes truth.

Ilmatar

Mercury in Cancer

In the Kalevala, the tale of the old Finnish gods, the mother of the world is Ilmatar. She is the daughter of Ilma, the sky, and comes down to earth to rest on the waters. There is no land, and she is forced to float on the water for seven centuries. She is a virgin goddess and has never touched another being, but one night the sea lashes itself into a storm and she finds herself mysteriously with child, impregnated by the primordial waters.

When the sign of the mind goes into oceanic Cancer, the mind is flooded with emotion. In any Cancer placement, the feeling function overrides everything else, and most choices are made based on intuition and sentiment rather than logic or necessity. The thoughts may actually be lost in frequent and rhythmic tides of emotion, which may render the Cancer Mercury temporarily speechless. Intellectual Mercury isn't comfortable in incoherent Cancer, and the native may experience some of that Mercurial frustration in a constant battle to articulate those overwhelming feelings.

It is no accident that Ilmatar is an unsullied virgin; she represents the secret and unarticulated part of the Cancerian mind. Her untouched nature is due less to fear or paranoia (like Scorpio) or self-sufficiency (like Pisces); she probably longs for someone to touch that wordless part of her, but it may be that no one ever has. Her emotional storms leave her full to the brim with unborn thoughts and ideas, but it may take hours or weeks or months or years of waiting before she finds a way to release them. Water-sign Mercuries, in general, work better with poetic imagery and visually based word-pictures than with straightforward techspeak or contextless jargon. The way to free their tongues, and their creative powers, is to bring out the poet in them. Then the oceanic waters can gush forth in surprising bounty.

Ilmatar remains pregnant for years, unable to give birth. This is another characteristic of the possessive Cancer Mercury; when they get an idea in their heads, they hold onto it for ages. Their creative projects generally need a long gestation before manifesting, but when they finally come out they are often full-blown and ready to go, without as many of the intervening drafts as other, more hasty thought processes. This is also the sign that deals with the past, and the Cancerian Mercury makes an excellent historian. She can use her visualization abilities and her natural empathy to imagine realistically what it must have been like to live in a long-ago era. In some cases, she may prefer an idealized version of the past to actually living in the present, and may spend most of her free time fantasizing about it.

While Ilmatar floats, pregnant and uncomfortable, a teal flies down and builds a nest on her knee. The water bird is a succinct symbol for the airy Mercury in watery Cancer; the bird can fly anywhere, but her first wish and foremost concern is to build a nest, preferably on the warm and comforting knee of a mother goddess. Like the water bird, Mercury in Cancer's thoughts tend to revolve around an interior rather than an exploratory exterior scene, and the warm, comfortable nest is an important necessity for her. She thinks best at home, safe and uninterrupted, and may find a crowded environment entirely too distracting. The water bird lays her eggs—the gems of creativity—and they fall from Ilmatar's knee and hatch open. Out of them comes the Earth, Sun, Moon, and clouds. Now Ilmatar finally has something to work with, and she begins a long period of world-shaping. She forms promontories and caves, the shores and the ocean depths, the rocks and bays. In the entire story, however, she never strays far from the water's edge. Her feeling function never ceases to be paramount in how she shapes her world.

Ilmatar is pregnant with one more being, however—the hero Vainamoinen (Sun in Sagittarius). He lies in her womb for thirty years, but she shows no signs of giving birth. Finally growing impatient with her slowness, he forces his way out of her womb and falls into the ocean. A Mercury in Cancer does not like being pushed to think things through faster than is comfortable for her, and if someone tries to force her creative processes, she may well find the project distasteful and jettison it, as Vainamoinen found himself dumped into the sea.

The Cancer mind is sensitive and absorbent, picking up stimuli like a sponge. What she can understand instinctively or empathetically she will manifest much quicker; disembodied intellectual ideas take her longer to process. When she finally speaks, her clearly apparent conviction and depth of feeling make her a splendid orator, of the sort that moves people to tears. A Mercury in Cancer understands a truth that other people have a hard time swallowing: each person's truth is legitimate if only because it forms their worldview, and to understand it is to understand them. There is little point—to the Cancer Mercury, anyway—in ranking one sort of truth over another. If your truth does not touch someone else emotionally, they will reject it. If you reject their truth, they will reject you.

She knows this intimately, to the bottom of her ocean, and finds nothing unfair or illogical about it. It would behoove more frustrated logical types to take heed of her lesson, because in order to truly communicate your idea you must figure out what language the other person is speaking. A Mercury in Cancer may not know all the vocabulary in the English language, but she can be very adept in figuring out what people's emotional languages are and adapting quickly to them, including such things as tone of voice and body language. The ocean that lies within her can bring forth surprising secrets and skills, and even with her careful slowness she should not be underestimated.

Apollo
Mercury in Leo

In this placement, Mercury is ruled by the Sun in all its glory and egotism. Leo lights up the planet of words and communication with a spotlight, giving it a creative boost, as the Sun is the fountain of creativity. Without it, nothing grows and is created; without it, there is only coldness and death.

The ancient Greeks thought so as well. Apollo, the sun god of Olympus, brother of Artemis, drove the golden chariot of the sun across the sky every day. However, his job was much more complex than simply that of a glorified teamster. He was the god of music, who played skillfully on the lyre; he was a god of prophecy, who took over the old temple of Delphi; he was a god most of all of civilization. In his retinue were the nine Muses, who inspired people in the areas of song, dance, poetry, prose, comedy and tragedy, mime, history, and astronomy. Apollo was the prototype of the Renaissance man, whose cultured talents are many and varied.

Leo, as a sign, likes culture, or at least to be seen as cultured. Leo also likes attention, and Leo's ruler, the Sun, is immensely creative. It isn't unusual for planets in Leo to be personal muses for the individual chart, and Mercury in Leo puts both Apollo's magnetism and the gifts of the Muses squarely in the service of communication. A Leo Mercury is in an excellent position to communicate all sorts of wonderful and imaginative things to others, as long as he gets his head out of the clouds and stays down to earth enough so that he doesn't come across as patronizing or pompous.

Mercury in Leo has a warmth to his speaking that invites people in, makes them feel seen and heard, and sparks admiration. What a friendly fellow, what a gracious host, they think. Sometimes that warmth is genuine and sometimes it is entirely shallow and a mere mask to cover up the fact that he'd rather not be bothered with you, but only the most intuitive and observant people will ever be able to figure out which it is. Apollo shines out through his eyes and voice and casts a golden shaft of light onto the person basking in his attention, rather like one of those "inspirational" photographs of the single ray of light breaking through the clouds. You know, the kind that sell so well to the simple at heart? No one can say, "Thank you so much for shopping here. We really appreciate your business," or "I really enjoyed our date. I'll call you as soon as I get a chance," or "Sure, go ahead and help yourself" with as much sincere-sounding warmth as Mercury in Leo, even if he secretly hates you and desperately wants you gone.

For all that Apollo was gifted with words and music; for all that he could sing well and speak powerfully and charm the masses, he was an emotionally distant god. From his place high in the sky, he looked down on the "little people" and did not allow himself to become entangled in their problems and neuroses, imagining himself free of such things. Likewise, the Leo Mercury person can speak poetically about his various needs and drives, but somehow when the straight-up, forthright, no-frills I-need-help needs to be spoken, he chokes or loses it in a torrent of misdirection. It's hard for him to simply admit that he was wrong, or frightened, or irrational, or pathetic. Especially the pathetic part. He would rather die than be pitied.

The Leo Mercury person, for all his bright, friendly way with words, may not be taken as seriously at times as someone with more weight and sobriety. If he is still immature, he may hate and avoid conflict, like Apollo, who merely took to the sky whenever trouble threatened. Due to this kind of behavior, a Leo Mercury may be stuck with the Beautiful Youth archetype for a long time, being discounted as a lightweight. When you play the golden-haired favorite son or daughter for too long, you have a hard time breaking out of the archetype; no one is going to take you seriously as a leader when you haven't dug in and faced battle.

Yet that much light must have a similar amount of darkness, and one of Apollo's symbols is the wolf. As Apollo Lycaeon, he is the patron of werewolves, those who turn suddenly into ravening beasts, and once in a full moon this will also happen to the gracious Leo Mercury. Wolf-Apollo is almost always triggered by a public insult to his vanity, as when the satyr Marsyas outplays him on the flute and Apollo has him skinned alive out of pique. Similarly, it is wounded vanity that can suddenly turn a bright Mercury in Leo into a furious verbal razor, flaying the unfortunate who happened to set him off. The Sun can also strike blind with its rays like sharp darts, and Apollo was a deadly archer.

Beneath both the talent and the danger is a buried secret. Apollo's other symbols number among them the graceful swan, the serpent of Delphi, and the circling hawk. However, in ancient times before he was elevated to his position as god of the sun, he was a mere mouse god. Much covering up has been done of this fact, especially by scholars who idealized Apollonian values. On some level, Mercury in Leo people have a secret fear: that underneath all the shine and glow, there is only a frightened little mouse that will likely get stepped on if it raises its head. Since this is a Mercury placement, the fear may be around his ability to ask and actually receive, unless he lays on the charm as thickly as possible. This low self-esteem problem is the root of the wolf-rages as well.

There is only one solution to this problem. A Leo Mercury must learn to open up the door to the dark unconscious in himself and shine the light of his own words and reason down the flight of dark stairs, burning off the dust and gloom. For someone who seems outwardly to like himself as much as he does, it is often difficult to get him into serious critical self-analysis, but it is the most important thing he will ever do. The speaking ego, the "I," can only speak with authority and true inspiration if nothing is gnawing at its roots, trying to undermine it from beneath. Light cannot conceal shadow; it can only balance it, and this is Mercury in Leo's greatest task.

aesculapius
Mercury in Virgo

In ancient times, healing was a hit-or-miss activity. Medicine was a matter of trial and error, and was riddled with superstition cheek by jowl with empirical techniques. Germ theory was unknown, and doctors were as likely to believe a disease was engendered by a demon as by a physical condition. Even so, most cultures did not have a medical figure in their pantheons of gods; deities tended to wave their hands and miraculously cure someone. The implication was that if they actually had to resort to medicine, they weren't really divine. Perhaps that is why the only god of doctors, Aesculapius, was originally a mortal in his legend.

One of Apollo's many children by the mortal woman Coronis was a son, Aesculapius. He grew up tutored by the centaur Chiron and took to medicine like a duck to water. By his teens, he had surpassed his tutor and was seeking out cures from other men of medicine. At some point, he consulted with the goddess Athena herself, and she gave out the secrets of several medicinal plants of great potency. With this under his belt, he soon became the most renowned doctor of his age, and his cures were many and miraculous.

Although Virgo is ruled by Mercury, it has a very different feel to it in this practical earth sign than it does in Gemini. Virgo has a grounding effect on quicksilver Mercury, and this is, after all, the sign of the doctor. Virgo believes in precision and also in service. The healing careers are a place where he can put his love of meticulousness to work for the betterment of humanity. If he is of the sort that doesn't work well with people—and many Virgo Mercuries don't, as people are often too sloppy and emotional for them—he can throw himself into research and spend his days in front of a microscope, selflessly bettering humanity while not actually having to deal with them regularly.

A Virgo Mercury doesn't have opinions, he has facts. Lots of facts. Or, more accurately, he has only one opinion and that is that facts are more important than anything else. He can chew down and digest (remember, Virgo rules the intestines) vast columns of data that would terrify a Piscean. Numbers comfort rather than frighten him. Each project—and if he is a doctor that means each patient—is a problem to be solved, possibly with or without their aid or consent. He might admit that he is not wise enough to see the solution just yet, but he will never admit that there is no solution. To believe so would destroy his world-view of the universe as an essentially rational place.

However, Aesculapius's luck quickly came to an end. He had brought so many people back from the brink of death that Hades felt cheated and complained to the gods on Olympus. Hearing that the mortal doctor had actually extrapolated from Athena's wisdom to the point where he had begun to bring the dead back to life, Zeus was horrified. This upstart mortal had gone too far, and he was appropriating the powers of the gods. Zeus promptly struck Aesculapius down with a thunderbolt and killed him. Apollo was furious at the death of his exceptional son and rebelled against Zeus; he lost and was banished for a long time from Olympus. However, Apollo's rebellion did give Zeus cause for second thoughts, and he decided to deify Aesculapius and bring him up to Olympus rather than waste his talents as a corpse. Thus the mortal doctor became the god of doctors.

According to his myth, Aesculapius founds a temple dedicated to health and medicine, which spreads. He has several sons and daughters who all learn medicine, regardless of gender, showing that nerdiness is essentially egalitarian. They go on after he is gone, founding hospital-temples and making reputations for themselves. One of his aides is Telesphorus, who becomes the guardian spirit of convalescence. At his temples, the sick were put through a carefully detailed schedule of baths, fasting, and potions; the image of Aesculapius would appear to them and order their diagnosis and treatment.

If a Mercury in Virgo has one main fault, it is his ability to reduce his fellow humans to two-dimensional formulas and then be bewildered when they slip out of the boxes he has put them in. He also tends to lose touch with his own humanity and feeling side. In other words, if he forgets his own humble mortality, separates himself from the feeling masses by putting himself on a hypocritical pedestal of rationality, and starts to feel arrogant about his ability to think precisely, he can "die" emotionally. The only way to come back to life is to pay homage to the realm of Hades—the knowledge that there are mysteries that are beyond the ken of his finely honed intellect.

sarasvati
Mercury in Libra

The beautiful Hindu goddess of learning, Sarasvati, is partnered to the Creator god, Brahma, and as such is a very creative goddess herself. She is the patroness of learning, knowledge, and music, and the inventor of the Sanskrit alphabet. She is beautiful and graceful, a fine dancer and a learned scribe. Her realm cuts across both the arts and the more intellectual pursuits; she sees no division between them, and as such fits well with the energy of mental Mercury in civilized, gracious, beauty-loving Libra. In this placement, Mercury is ruled by Venus, and these individuals often have an artistic eye and an aesthetic bent. Sarasvati rides a peacock, the flashiest of all birds, and she is patron of artists as well as scholars.

Sarasvati is always at Brahma's side, as is fitting for a planet in the sign of marriage. Libra Mercuries may find that they do their creative work best as part of a team or at least that they are inspired by a partner. However, if Sarasvati has a fault, it is that she is too much Brahma's partner. Of her four arms, one holds the book of palm leaves that symbolizes learning, one holds the garland of harmony, one the drum of music, and one eternally holds a flower out to her husband. A Libra Mercury can spend a quarter or more of her creative judgment trying to decide whether her mate will like something she does or deferring to his advice. This goes for male Libra Mercuries as well, and even those without partners may find themselves obsessing about what a potential partner might think of their activities.

The famous Libra indecision, which can clog the Mercurial thinking process, is part and parcel with Libra's partner-oriented behavior. When it's not easy to make up your mind, sometimes it's a terrible temptation to just find a partner whose opinions you can use to break the mental deadlock. Of course, this can lead to losing your own individuality, and sooner or later the Libra Mercury will rebel, usually as soon as the beloved partner says something unfair. They may also be taken aback when their Libran, who just yesterday quietly submitted to their judgment, explodes today in a tirade against their injustice. A Libra Mercury needs to keep in mind that being her personal, infallible judge is too much of a burden for any one human being. We are all imperfect, and sooner or later her partner will show themselves to have feet of clay. They shouldn't be blamed for this, and she shouldn't expect otherwise.

The Libra Mercury mental processes seesaw back and forth, weighing each side, which is why this placement is useful not only for the artist but the lawyer. It takes a special kind of objectivity-at-will to be able to defend a guilty party for the sake of fairness. To the Libran Mercury, truth is shown by its aesthetic nature. Real truth, the Libra feels, should be evident because it is not ugly. Of course, much of truth is ugly, which puts a Libra into another tailspin. She adapts by one of two approaches: either floating on an airy cloud of denial about anything unbeautiful or learning to see an abstract beauty in justice, even when it is cruel. The former creates a Mercury individual who likes everything to go smoothly and nicely and is gracious in a cultured but shallow way, never looking below the surface. The latter can create someone who is an excellent mediator and lawyer, but who can seem cold due to their unwillingness to get emotionally involved with either side. This is an air sign, and with all its fluffy clouds, we tend to forget that. Venus's moistening quality does not change the essential coldness and clarity of a Libra Mercury. If she is less than clear on a subject, it is either willful blindness or indecision between two compelling sets of facts, not any confusion in her mental processes.

It is said that Sarasvati caused the great lord Brahma to grow five faces. The Hindu creator deity loved her at first sight for her great beauty. She danced a fast dance around him, trying to avoid his penetrating gaze, but everywhere that she moved, he grew another face to look at her. By the time she relented, he had five faces, one for each direction. This is a good metaphor for what a Libra Mercury can do to an unsuspecting subject. She uses her wit to charm him into "growing" directions of seeing other than his own—in other words, inducing in him a change of perspective. Because looking at things from both sides comes so naturally to her, she can help others to do the same.

The Morrigan
Mercury in Scorpio

Abundance and blight. Lush weather and foulness. Battle. Blood. The croaking of a raven. The Morrigan of old Ireland is not a pretty goddess. She is a triple goddess, but even her three faces have no mercy. Her virgin face, Badb, is a warrior of prowess, who can be found kneeling at riverbanks washing the clothes of those who are soon to die in battle. She was called upon for strength in battle, but it was just as likely that you would see her at your side before the enemy did you in. The mother, Ana, was the lady of abundance—abundant sunshine and storms as well, nine years of gloriously lush crops and then another nine of famine.

But her most common and well-known form was the crone Morrigan. No kind grey-haired grandmother this; she is pictured as big and bony, long grey hair whipping in the wild wind, limping, one-eyed, black-cloaked, stumbling about the countryside spewing blessings and curses equally through her crooked teeth. It was said that her tongue was a knife; she could cut a man to shreds or whip him into a frenzy. Anyone who has been on the receiving end of an angry Mercury in Scorpio knows what this is like. No other Mercury sign has such vitriolic command of the language when trying to wound. As Kipling wrote:

> Scientific vivisection of one nerve till it is raw,
> And the victim writhes in anguish,
> like the Jesuit with the squaw.

A wounded Mercury in Scorpio will turn to words before deeds when in need of vengeance and, like the Morrigan, they can be gallingly accurate in their ability to assess your sensitive spots and zoom in on them. Not all operate at the top of their lungs like the Morrigan, of course, but even the quiet ones can say the most venomous and stinging things in a sweetly polite tone of voice. They are keen mental detectives, and their favorite subject is people—how they tick, what pushes their buttons, and how to make them change. It's the ones who have learned the last lesson who are the most dangerous. No curses here; just speech that is carefully honed to exact a certain reaction from you. There are Scorpio Mercuries who bitch constantly, ones who live with a perpetually cynical tone of voice and whose sarcasm will slice your ego to ribbons (a friend once coined the word "scar-casm" for this kind of weapon) and, worst of all, ones whose speech is silky smooth, just the right kind of Iago-like persuasiveness to bend you to their will.

For, you see, the Morrigan is the keeper of the Words of Power. These were reputed to be words so powerful and magical that saying any one of them would cause the sky to darken or the sun to shine, to stop armies in their tracks or spur them on to certain victory. Scorpio Mercuries are keenly aware of the power of words. On a more positive note, they make keen and incisive writers and researchers, searching out hidden facts of the universe with Scorpio's dedicated, near obsessive love of uncovering mysteries. Many are found in the journalism field, or advertising, or scientific research. But their primary concern, when it comes down to communication, is to gauge the emotional effect that their words will have on an unsuspecting recipient. Being a water sign, they are familiar with emotional communication, but they usually try to school their words to gain a particular end—until the righteous anger hits them.

In many circles, bitching is just not seen as a desirable activity. Anger, screaming, and visible frustration are seen as a lack of self-control; evidence that something is wrong with you, not with the environment. Even among pagans, the goddesses one is enjoined to call on are serene and nurturing, gentle grandmother/therapists who can help all those poor wounded victims who need all those allowances made for their poor abused souls. They are not wild hags who can point a bony finger at you, speak a curse, and shrivel your courage like a withered fruit. The Morrigan, and her unforgiving glare and harsh, grating voice, is not welcome in their circles. And in denying her energy, we lose the ability to express and articulate those emotions that are not pretty, that eat us up inside while unspoken, that are the true measure of how free we really are. We also lose the ability to draw an emotional boundary and stand guard, defying others to cross it.

The symbols and harbingers of the Morrigan were crows and ravens, rooks and corbies, the blackbirds that feed on carrion, follow a battle, and fly before a storm. One of her titles was Stormcrow, which came to be a term for any bearer of bad tidings or earthshaking change. We dislike the image of these blackbirds flocking toward us, croaking their warnings, but how often do we ignore warnings that are not what we want to hear? How often do we shoo away the Morrigan's storm-crows—when we marry the lover who hit us on the third date, when we ignore those strange chest pains, when we dismiss our teenager's withdrawn and neurotic behavior as a mere stage? A Mercury in Scorpio has the gift of slicing through the glitter and fluff, through the layers of illusion and self-defense, to the naked and often ugly truth below. Morrigan's ravens perch on their shoulders, croaking warnings into their ears. Hear them. They are the measure of our own desperation.

Taliesin
Mercury in Sagittarius

The story of Taliesin starts with a small boy named Gwion Bach who is the foster child and scullery lad of the old goddess Cerridwen (see Saturn in Scorpio), a powerful enchantress with a magical cauldron of rebirth. He is employed to do chores, but his mistress resents him for being brighter and cleverer than her own son, who is slow and dull. She brews a potion in her cauldron for a year and a day, designed to give her boy the gift of clever speech. On the last day, she goes out to gather herbs and leaves, leaving Gwion Bach to stir the cauldron. He is instructed not to touch the potion, but somehow he manages to ingest three drops anyway. In one version of the myth, he does it accidentally; in another, he drinks them deliberately.

However it happens, he immediately realizes that he can hear the birds chirping outside the window—and that he can understand their speech. They are chattering about how the old woman is coming back to the cottage. It occurs to Gwion Bach that he has just ruined Cerridwen's year of hard work and that she is going to be furious with him. Exercising his newfound powers, he turns himself into a rabbit and runs for his life. The powerful goddess turns into a hound and pursues him. He turns into a fish and she follows as an otter; he turns into a sparrow and she follows as a hawk; he turns into a grain of wheat on a farmer's threshing floor, and she becomes a hen and eats him.

At some point later, Cerridwen finds that she is pregnant and realizes that it must be Gwion Bach, magically surviving in her body as a fetus. She gives birth to him, but does not wish to keep him. Instead she sets him afloat on the ocean and he gets caught in a fisherman's weir. He is rescued by the local lord, a man named Elphin, who is amazed to hear an infant speak clearly and fluently. He names the child Taliesin, or "bright brow," and raises him as his own. By the time he reaches puberty, Taliesin is already a great bard and magician and has learned untold amounts of lore.

When Mercury passes into Sagittarius, the sign of mind expansion and travel, it exhibits a certain amount of precocity. Individuals with this placement think and talk fast, and their minds seem to go in several directions at once, a phenomenon a friend once referred to as "tangent brain." As children, they are often the "walking encyclopedias," interested in widely varying subjects, chewing down knowledge like popcorn at a movie. Whether or not they actually digest it thoroughly is debatable, however. This placement goes for breadth rather than depth, covering as much ground as possible.

Sagittarius the Gypsy loves to learn about and experience other cultures; they have an affinity for seeing things through the eyes of different people and go native fast when placed into a new world. Taliesin's instant ability to shift his shape in order to hide and blend in reflects this talent. Of course, he is pursued by a goddess of death and catharsis, who does not stop until she has caught him and forced him to undergo a transformative rebirthing. This is where the freedom-loving Gypsy is ambushed by the other Sagittarian quality: the urge to higher spirituality. This is the sign of religion, after all. The more interesting facts and perspectives a Mercury in Sagittarius collects, the more he is dogged by a sneaking feeling that there is more than just this. The desire to gather knowledge and experience for its own sake is transformed into a drive to find all the pieces of the big puzzle. He becomes convinced that everything is connected, and if he just absorbs enough bits, the great pattern will resolve itself in his head and he will know and understand the greater meaning. The experience of shifting his world-view turns him from the path of Scholar to that of Shaman.

When Taliesin is thirteen, his beloved foster father Elphin is imprisoned by his liege lord Maelgwn over a petty insult. The boy-magician travels to the court of Maelgwn, who is holding a bardic competition. He is not allowed to enter because of his youth, so he stands to one side as all the eminent bards enter and casts a magic spell on them. He puts his fingers to his lips and burbles them, making a *blerwm-blerwm* noise, and when the bards open their mouths, only that sound comes out. Lord Maelgwn is furious and strikes the chief bard; this snaps him out of it and he whirls and points at Taliesin, accusing him of laying the hex.

The boy-magician now stands forth; when Maelgwn asks his name, he launches into a long litany claiming to have been many things in many eras in the past. "I carried the banner before Alexander; I know the names of the stars from the North to the South!" he cries. "I was in the Ark with Noah and Alpha . . . I obtained my inspiration from the cauldron of Cerridwen . . . I have been instructed in the whole system of the universe; I shall be till the day of judgment on the face of Earth." He claims that he is both immortal and also quite old, having seen all of history. Generations of scholars have tried to decipher these rantings, assuming that they must be hidden clues to an esoteric system of mythic knowledge. For the purposes of the myth, however, they simply illustrate the complete self-confident audacity of a teenager who stands in front of the king whose court he has disrupted and claims to be eternal and all-wise.

It is a Sagittarian sort of audacity; although all the fire signs are audacious, their ego sits in different areas. Aries wants to be first and strongest; Leo wants to be on top and in power. Sagittarius, on the other hand, wants to be Right. To this sign, your power is in what you know, not who you are or what you do. Therefore, what a Mercury in Sagittarius knows has to be bigger, better, broader, and most of all more true than what anyone else knows. The search for truth thus becomes paramount to this placement, but the fiery intellectual ego involved sometimes has a habit of stopping too soon and declaring that truth has been found. An optimistic Sagittarius desperately wants this to be the case, and so he declares that this is it and then is required to defend his newfound truth to others. If he is not careful, this can bring him over to the negative side of Sagittarius: the Fanatic. Although Taliesin's ego is more benevolent, he still comes across as an enfant terrible who is defending his version of the truth with a long resume of implausible and mysterious credentials.

In the myth, of course, a great wind comes up and shakes King Maelgwn's castle, and he is suitably impressed and chastised by this arcanely powerful child. Fearing divine retribution, he releases Taliesin's foster father and offers the boy a place at court. Taliesin grows in size, wisdom, and talent until he has a run-in with a hostile druid also living at court who gets him banished. He sails off in a coracle into the sunset to explore strange lands across the sea—an appropriate ending for the travel-loving Sagittarian Gypsy archetype—but as he leaves the shore, he casts a curse on the druid, turning him into a standing stone forced eternally to stare out to sea. The verbal outbursts of a Sagittarian Mercury can be both surprisingly vicious and surprisingly powerful, as they use truth as their ammunition whenever possible. If you are at home with truth, you are more able to use it as a weapon in verbal combat.

Taliesin's song, which details shapechanging into such forms as a red deer, a sword, a bull, an iron in a fire, a raven, a fox, a swift, a squirrel, a boar, a frog, a crow, an eagle, a shield, a harp string, and a tree, illustrates how the Sagittarian Mercury ought to be going about his search for truth. First he has to let go of the concept that there is one truth that will be the same for all; then he must learn to see the world through as many contrasting eyes as possible. Each different viewpoint contains a small piece of the puzzle, but none has the whole picture, and collecting all the pieces is beyond our human ability to accomplish. Of course, that doesn't mean that one should stop trying, only that to search for truth and wisdom is to constantly be reminded, to the end of one's days, that there is still an awe-inspiring amount of truth left to discover.

ptah

Mercury in Capricorn

There is a lot of disagreement over the origins of the ancient Egyptian god Ptah, architect of the universe. Some say that he grew out of a couple of earlier earth and vegetation gods named Tenen and Seker. Others claim that he was originally a famous mortal architect who designed many temples and possibly the pyramids, and was deified after his death, and thus is shown as a mummy with only the head and hands exposed. The world may never know which is true, but both origins could be considered useful to discuss his relationship to Mercury in the sign of Capricorn.

Mercury likes to be in this earth sign; he and Saturn do generally get along and the strict Saturnian rays tend to give him stability and structure. Mercury in Capricorn gives him the mind of a planner, someone able to think carefully several steps ahead and then carry out those plans. It also gives the ability to explain the plans in a sensible and well-reasoned way that most people can understand. Mercury in Capricorn tends to sound logical and astute even when they have no idea what they're talking about. It's a gift.

Ptah was the master builder and master architect of Egypt. He was worshipped at Memphis, and his hands hold the *djed* or symbolic staff of stability. Although several gods were credited with fashioning the world, Ptah was given his own version wherein he carefully designed the earth like a good architect, laying out the plans and blueprints not only for the land itself but for all its inhabitants. He was the patron of all architects, builders, and masons, as well as minor craftsmen such as stonecutters, woodcutters, smiths, and smelters of metal. His high priest was always a functioning architect and bore a title very similar to the one given to master builders of medieval cathedrals.

As an earth sign, Capricorn is tied to the sensory body and what it can do; this is not a Mercury that is easily intuitive unless there are other lunar or Neptunian aspects. Like Ptah who grew out of a vegetation god, an earthy Capricorn likes to work with his hands and mind together on practical, efficient constructions. Like Ptah who was once human, he may be personally humble, letting his creations speak for him. Even if he craves social acceptance, he may hold back that knowledge and patiently work toward the pinnacle of his career. A Capricorn Mercury without career goals is a very unhappy person, because he has no way to get the respect he needs.

There is one drawback to Saturn's influence over the mind and that is symbolized by the fact that Ptah is a mummy, an animate dead body. A Mercury in Capricorn is very prone to depression, pessimism, and being out of touch with emotions. You can tell the Mercury in Capricorn person who has let Saturn entirely overcome him by his flat, lifeless tone of voice. All the precise equations in the world can't be applied to a brooding cloud of depression that hangs a grey pall over everything. Ptah is long dead, but a living person must recall the needs of his living body and spirit and not just live within the lines of his future plans. Some joys need to be experienced now, not at some future date when everything is done, earned, and taken care of.

Ptah has another side, one seen only occasionally; he is sometimes shown in the aspect of a deformed dwarf with twisted legs and a huge head. Far more pathetic than the robust Bes, he wears his head shaved except for a sidelock, the emblem of the child. This may seem entirely out of line with the dignified Master Architect, but in this form he protects against wild animals, accidents, and other dangers. This figure is everything that Capricorn fears—to be a clumsy, awkward laughingstock, treated with no more respect than a child—and this very bogeyman lives and breathes in the mind of every Capricorn-ruled person. That's what drives them, why they try so hard to earn respect, why they long for social acclaim even if they outwardly pooh-pooh it. Yet Ptah shows his socially awkward side on occasion, because he is sure enough in the respect he has gained. It's a lesson for a Mercury in Capricorn to ponder as he creates the next imposing speech about his many lordly plans.

Quetzalcoatl
Mercury in Aquarius

Few deities have elicited more fantastical theories than the Toltec/ Aztec god of wisdom and knowledge, Quetzalcoatl the Feathered Serpent. In a land where all people were brown-skinned and beard-less, he was somehow pictured as white and heavily bearded. The conquistador Hernán Cortés was able to use this myth to his advan-tage, claiming to be Quetzalcoatl and thus able to vanquish the Aztec people. Since then, hundreds of scholars have wondered whether there is an echo, in Quetzalcoatl's unusual appearance, of an ancient European come to the shores of Mexico and worshipped as a god for his peculiar knowledge.

There is also the fact that there were two Quetzalcoatls. The strange god came first, one of a pair of rival deities brought by the conquering Toltecs. He was a god of learning, and his priesthood were scholars and scientific types. He invented many crafts and eso-teric forms of knowledge, giving freely of his ingenuity to make life better for his people. He created a mythical utopia in an area referred to as Tula, where corn was always tall, pumpkins grew huge, cotton came in many colors, and birds with precious feathers sang in all the trees. In this happy realm, no one had more hard labor than they could manage easily, and no one ever starved. Quetzalcoatl was known as the god of the air, and long after his worship had declined in favor of the brutal Tezcatlipoca, god of the smoking mirror, he was the patron of merchants, craftsmen, and especially jewelers.

The second Quetzalcoatl was an actual human king of Teotihuacan who named himself after the god who was his patron. He ruled wisely and well, and tried to discourage human sacrifice among his people, attempting to substitute the burning of copal as a god-offering instead of human hearts. He invented the art of feather-crafting and spread it among his people, and encouraged crafts such as metalworking and architecture. The indignant priests of Tezcatlipoca eventually forced him into exile, and he supposedly made a great ship and sailed away, saying that he would return in the year of Ce Acatl, the One Reed. It was indeed in this year that Cortés and his people landed on the Mexican coast, to the everlasting regret of the Aztec people. It is yet another of the quirky, coincidental mysteries surrounding this deity, which may be less about coincidence and more about synchronicity.

Every individual with Mercury in Aquarius, regardless of how scientific—and this placement is especially good for the scientific intellect—harbors a secret desire to create a utopian world or at least contribute to the making of one. No matter how dry and rational they claim to be, no matter how many statistics they can pull up to prove their theories, their secret goal is to better the world in the way they think it ought to be bettered, to work toward the dream of Tula. They are reformers, or occasionally counter-reformers, at heart; they like to see themselves as the intellectual hero who develops the information that will save the world and selflessly distributes it among the less fortunate. Both Quetzalcoatl legends, the mythical god and the mythic man, are bound up in the Aquarian ideal of the wisdom-hero, right down to his sailing off into the sunset and promising to return someday.

The Feathered Serpent himself is strangely reminiscent of winged Mercury and his serpent-twined caduceus, flying through the air. As god of the air, Quetzalcoatl flies high and takes an objective view of things; like the snake, he is cold-blooded. One of the hallmarks of a Mercury in Aquarius is a cool refusal to care what other people think of his ideas or projects. Those who denigrate him obviously either don't understand yet or are merely stupid. He is completely immune to public opinion. This is the most independent mind in the zodiac, but his reserve and psychological autonomy can come across as cold-blooded and callous.

Although Aquarius is a volatile and fast-moving sign, ruled by lightning-strike Uranus, we tend to forget that it is also a fixed sign. One of the characteristics of a fixed Mercury is that he has very definite opinions that he finds difficult to change or at least does not generally care to do so. A Mercury in Aquarius betrays his fixed nature by his tendency to cast himself as the good guy and whoever holds an opposing opinion as the bad guy. We find this black-and-white emotional thinking clearly in evidence with the worship of Quetzalcoatl, who was frequently set up as the white hat to Tezcatlipoca's black hat. Of course, Tezcatlipoca does make a pretty impressive bad guy, what with all those hundreds of still-beating human hearts that he required to be ripped out of the chests of his sacrificial victims, and his legions of warlike Toltecs with filed, pointy teeth. Still, a Mercury in Aquarius has a bad habit of seeing his opponents as every bit as black as the Smoking Mirror, even if all they did was disagree with his right to mount videocams in the lobby of his apartment building for reasons of tracking down who might have stolen his bicycle.

What does it mean to be half bird and half snake? Certainly there is the idea of lifting oneself, and eventually others, from a life of belly-crawling to the freedom of flight. There is also the problem of moving between wild flights of brilliance to cold, staring focus. A Mercury in Aquarius can do both and comes up with truly creative solutions to problems. He just needs to remember to keep his heart attached to his head. The Feathered Serpent's namesake, after all, tried to banish human sacrifice. In his honor, every Mercury in Aquarius should swear to keep from sacrificing the human needs of themselves and others, and the wisdom-hero will return, good as his word, in each of their souls.

orpheus
Mercury in Pisces

The planet of words in the sign of the Poet? When Neptune rules Mercury, the result can be an amazing fountain of verbal imagery or a confused and inarticulate mumble. This is the home of the flight of fantasy, the place where logic gets left behind and intuition rules. Mercury in Pisces people live half in and half out of Never-Never-Land, where misty dreams all come true. They tend to think in images rather than in sentences and be visual rather than auditory or kinesthetic learners. This placement gives an appreciation of art and music, but generally as a haven and an escape rather than as a performance. An example is a talented Mercury in Pisces musician friend who is incredibly talented and yet hates performing; his music is for the balm of his soul alone.

The singer Orpheus, a half-divine figure who was the son of one of the Muses and the god of dreams, was said to have such a beautiful voice that he could charm anyone or anything if he managed to get it to listen. He was one of a band of heroes who went about doing brave deeds, and on his journeys he used his music for great feats. He pulled the ship *Argo* down off a beach where it was stranded, he lulled the guardian dragon of the Golden Fleece, he quieted the moving rocks of the ocean that threatened to crush them all. Beasts came running to hear his songs, and even trees would attempt to follow him. However, his great career ended in sorrow. His wife, Eurydice, whom he loved passionately, was bitten by a poisonous snake and died. Orpheus was grief-stricken but swore that he would bring her soul back from the underworld if it was at all possible. Thus began one of the greatest underworld-journey tales of all time.

Orpheus descended to the underworld to beg Hades to return his wife. On his way down, he was threatened by Cerberus, the three-headed dog who was guardian of Hades, and by various souls of the dead, but he lulled them all with his lyre and song and thus passed by. The underworld journey, in any myth, is the journey to the dark places of the experience of being human. Underworlds are always divided into many regions, and this is not inappropriate: there is the part of the underworld that is our own fears and demons; the part that is the collective unconscious; the part that is linked to something even greater. A Mercury in Pisces is so impressionable, like a vibrating string, that the mind and moods can be somewhat fragile. He is prone to fears and depressions simply from having to deal with the uncaring world of matter and unpleasant people. If he does not have enough creative outlets, he may find himself a regular resident there, as he cannot "sing" his way through the traps. And if, as Orpheus does, he loses the thing most precious to him, in which he has set all his emotional hopes, he will be driven there by anguish.

However, Orpheus starts out with success. He comes before the thrones of Hades and Persephone and plays for them, singing about their own love and how it grew in that cold place underground. He begs for Eurydice's life, and Hades is so moved that he agrees to make an exception for her. She will be allowed to return with him to the upper world, but there is one catch. She will follow behind Orpheus, but he must not look back to see if she is there until they have both left the gates of the underworld and walked a good distance ahead. In other words, he must trust the word of the lord of the dead, and the worth of his own talent, and good luck.

In doing this, Hades sees straight into Orpheus and nails his weakest spot. Up until now, he has succeeded largely because of his ability to charm people and things into doing what he wants. Up until now, he has been able to assure himself of some measure of control. Indeed, his assault on the underworld shows that he longs to have control over death itself. A Mercury in Pisces can be passionate and imaginative and loving, but he is not innocent. As the last sign, there is much that Pisces knows, and suspects, and believes, and some of it is not true. Ruled by Neptune, it is his destiny to attempt to embrace oneness with the universe, even if only in some small way. Part of this is the ability to trust in the universe, and in the word of the gods, or the grace of God, or however you would prefer to put it. Hades, as lord of the dead, has a word as final as death itself. Death is not capricious or fickle; that is a subjective human way to see it. The reality of death is an inevitable part of the cycle, something that will always come. If Death says that you have a chance at a rebirth, then by all the gods you should take it and not look back.

Yet Orpheus fails at this one test. He had almost reached the gates of Hades when he could not help looking back, just to make sure that Hades had not lied and that Eurydice was actually following him. He saw her—for one second, before she was blown, crying in anguish, back into the underworld, and he realized that he had just forfeited his last chance. He had failed to trust in the universe, and he paid the price.

Weeping, he fled along the river Hebrus, and there he met with a band of bloodthirsty Maenads, Dionysus's drug-crazed women, who hallucinated that he was an animal and tore him to pieces. His head was thrown into the river, where it sang mournfully as it floated. Orpheus, being the child of two immortals, cannot die so easily. He was fished out and installed at the temple at Lesbos, where his head gave forth prophetic oracles until it eventually died.

Orpheus, having shown that he does not trust his own destiny, is sent to death a harder way, one which is not under his control and robs him of his power to act upon anything. He is dismembered, like the shamanic experience the world over. This is often the way these stories happen, in or out of real life; if you blow the easy, willing path, you get the harder one, whether you like it or not. In order to be a divine channel for his inspired words and music, he has to learn to ride the wave of giving up control to the deeper power. To drive this home, the universe takes away all his limbs and he is reduced to a talking head—a very appropriate metaphor for Mercury.

However, after all this pain, he has the ability to prophesy. He has become a cult object, and he inspires the Orphic cult of regeneration and rebirth. This is the real lesson for Mercury in Pisces people—that part of learning to dance with the universe is about being an object of hope and inspiration for others. Having been helpless, having endured loss, having been through death and dismemberment, Orpheus is now in a position to give compassionate counsel to others. He can even extrapolate their dooms through knowledge of his own mistakes, and that is why a mature and experienced Mercury in Pisces is a voice to move others, whether in speech, song, or writing. It is their place as voice of the gods.

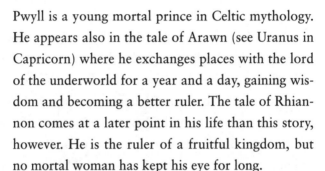

♀ venus

Rhiannon
Venus in Aries

Pwyll is a young mortal prince in Celtic mythology. He appears also in the tale of Arawn (see Uranus in Capricorn) where he exchanges places with the lord of the underworld for a year and a day, gaining wisdom and becoming a better ruler. The tale of Rhiannon comes at a later point in his life than this story, however. He is the ruler of a fruitful kingdom, but no mortal woman has kept his eye for long.

One morning, Pwyll sees a beautiful young woman on a white horse emerge from out of an ancestral mound. Pwyll attempts to catch her by riding his horse as fast as possible, but the faster he pursues, the farther ahead she seems to get, even though her horse does not seem to be moving any quicker than a leisurely trot. Finally she disappears out of sight, and he is heartbroken. The next day, however, she reappears again out of the mound. Pwyll tries again to catch her and again fails. The third day he borrows a faster horse, to no avail. After a week of this, he is frustrated and finally gives up and calls out to her to stop. She wheels her horse and stops, and he approaches her; at this point, she coyly tells him that it would have been better for him if he had called out for her to stop several days ago.

Rhiannon's behavior is a good example of the Martial Aries spirit when it is transformed by Venus. Aries is competitive even in love, and Venus in Aries has a tendency to set little tests for her lovers, to send them off on quests and inspire them to great deeds. This is not done out of Scorpionic suspicion or Aquarian whimsy. A Venus in Aries is plagued by conflicting urges. She wants to be taken and subdued by her lover, but she'll be damned if she'll submit to any-one but the best, and her tests are a way of checking out her future conqueror's mettle. Male or female, a Venus in Aries often indulges in a Red Sonya-like courtship rite—"The only one who can have me is the one who can best me in battle!" Except that battle, in most cases, is likely to be a battle of wits and wills. If you really want me, she says, you'll work for it. Rhiannon is in love with Pwyll. She con-fesses immediately that she has seen him from afar and fallen in love, and her daily rides were a way to attract his attention, but she will not turn her head to look at him until he gives up pursuing and begs her to stop.

Once they connect, however, she tells him a tale that inspires him to anger. Rhiannon is not a mortal woman; she belongs to a race of immortals that lives under the hill, and her father has promised her to another suitor. This piques her independent spirit, and she asks Pwyll to help her escape from her father's kingdom and humiliate her bridegroom-to-be. A Venus in Aries doesn't like to be told what to do when it comes to her love affairs and tends to rebel against those who would judge or control her. However, she also tends to be impetuously angry. She says and does things in the heat of the moment that she may regret later. She may also, with Venusian per-suasion and Martial passion, be able to attract champions who are easily convinced to take up her cause and run with it, sometimes further than she might expect.

Having set the eager and lovestruck Pwyll to this mission, Rhian-non returns home. While her father and fiancé are having a feast to celebrate the joining of their families, Pwyll and his men burst in on the feast and claim Rhiannon. Knowing that Rhiannon wants to see her fiancé humiliated, he puts the man in a sack, and he and his men kick the sack around the room until the poor man is half dead. At this point Rhiannon's father cries out and begs for his guest's life, and tells Rhiannon to be gone from his court forever. She leaves with Pwyll in a state of dishonor and banishment, and they are married in his mortal kingdom. In declaring her independence, a Venus in Aries can create an epic, overblown struggle that defies not only the wishes of those around her but of the entire social order.

However, after her impulsive cruelty, Rhiannon reaps a terrible harvest. As sorry as a Venus in Aries is after the harsh words have been flung and the angry deeds finished, mere apologies are not usually enough to assuage the feelings of others. Her plan to take vengeance on her fiancé and father for their attempt to control her has gone entirely too far, and it is she, the instigator, who will pay. On the night that she bears her first child, her abused former fiancé sends a terrible monster to climb in the window and steal the baby. Her maidservants, terrified that they will be blamed for the missing babe, smear her with blood and accuse her of being a child murderer. Pwyll manages to avoid making the accusation public, but the same thing happens again with her second babe, and her third.

At this point, Pwyll himself suspects her of killing their children, but he cannot bear to execute her. Instead, she is sentenced to a lesser fate: she must sit outside the palace in a little hut, telling her story to every traveler who comes by and offering to bear them and their goods on her back to and from the palace. This goes on for six years. Rhiannon is a horse goddess, one of the free and fiery horse goddesses of European legend such as Rigantona and Epona and the Cailleach, but her sentence reflects the other side of being a horse: the fate of the beast of burden. It is a hard lesson for any Mars-ruled sign: bad deeds done in the heat of anger cannot be merely apologized away—"Oh, I didn't really mean for it to happen, just forget about it"—because they destroy trust and the hope of future relationship, symbolized by the missing children. It is altogether too easy for her to gain the undeserved reputation of someone far crueler than her basically honest and impetuous Aries nature makes her—to be, in fact, wrongly smeared with blood. The only way to undo these mistakes is long, hard, patient work, as well as the need to tell her story, over and over, until someone believes her.

At the same time that Rhiannon's children are going missing, newborn foals are also being stolen from the stables of neighboring noblemen. The monster set loose by Rhiannon's actions is completely out of control. The night that Rhiannon's third child is stolen, a nobleman interrupts the creature attempting to nab a foal from his stables and kills the monster. In its knapsack he discovers a beautiful infant and he and his wife decide to raise it themselves. Six years later, they hear the tale of Rhiannon and her stolen children and recognize their son's true origin. They return the child to Pwyll along with the tale of the creature, and Rhiannon is exonerated and reinstated in his affections.

Years later, Pwyll is killed in a battle, and Rhiannon is remarried to the wise sea god Manawyddan. This may suggest a slow transformation in time for the Aries Venus, going from the sort of person who is most attracted to the impetuous warrior to the sort who values the older, wiser, cooler head. Yet the deeds of Rhiannon's past follow her. Her former fiancé, still desiring vengeance, sets a trap for her and her family. All are accidentally transported to a different time, and her children are trapped in a strange palace. Rhiannon bravely goes in after them, demonstrating Aries courage, and between her bravery and Manawyddan's cunning, they manage to defeat the enemy and convince him to leave them alone forever.

It's hard for the watery, feminine Venus to function well in fiery, masculine Aries. At its best, it can be a union of the two forces within one person—sort of an internal hieros gamos—that brings balance. At worst it can make someone intensely combative toward those they love, putting competition ahead of love, and often losing those relationships in the process. It is also important for a Venus in Aries to claim her own power instead of manipulating others to act out her aggression for her while she sits back claiming to be innocent. She is possessed of great courage and stamina and can go harder and further for her loved ones than anyone else—if she remembers that they are never the enemy. Even when they become the opponent—for example, when they confront her with an argument—she must treat them as an honored opponent whose respect one hopes to keep and whose friendship one wishes to maintain. Regardless of her fiery nature, she must learn that love is the one place where a scorched-earth policy is never the right move.

oshun

Venus in Taurus

Oshun is the love goddess in the Afro-Caribbean Yoruba-descended tradition, and she is considered the youngest of the orishas, or deities. She is also prayed to for wealth. This combination of love and money may seem overly pecuniary to some, but to a Venus in Taurus it is the very recipe for happiness. A full larder, bed, and bank account fulfill the basic background needs of this earthy, sensual placement, and although more airy signs may look down upon her values, she does not envy them their theatrics.

That doesn't mean that a Venus in Taurus always creates a cud-chewing blob. On the contrary, Venus is in her own rulership in Taurus, and Venus likes the good life. Like the beautiful Oshun, whose charm was unmatched among her people, Venus in Taurus people radiate an earthy charisma that invites others to touch them. They are physical people who love to cuddle and adore soft textures, such as silk and velvet, and have a strong artistic or musical sense. This is also the sign of the Farmer, so the most spiritually uplifting thing that a Venus in Taurus can do may be to grow a beautiful garden.

Oshun's favorite color is yellow and gold, the color of ancient wealth and the sun. Her favorite offering is gold jewelry, and her favorite drink is brandy, especially honey brandy. She loves sweet things, especially honey and fruits such as peaches, oranges, and mangoes. She symbolizes all the sweetness and succulence in life, and thus must be offered sweets in trade. Taurus understands this situation well. The sorts of things that a Venus in Taurus likes, unfortunately, must usually be bought with money. She thrives on gourmet food, a secure and lovely home, fine objects (especially art), good music, and a sensuous lover. She is not completely consumed by status or showing off to the neighbors; a Venus in Taurus cares little who sees her lifestyle and who doesn't. She is often self-indulgent about treating herself to the things she loves. More than any other sign, Taurus knows how to do that for herself.

She also knows that she deserves it, a philosophy that may delude others. A Venus in Taurus has a firm grip on the concept of universal abundance. She believes in the idea that there really is more than enough to go around and that the universe will come up with your share, if you just ask it. She will often live this philosophy by sharing generously with others, and she finds that the more she shares, the more the universe sends her. Unless there are severe astrological complications, a Venus in Taurus is confident in the universe and her place in it.

Although a Venus in Taurus is very good at commitment—too good, some might say—she sometimes has an Achilles heel for exciting people who aren't nearly as dedicated as she is. If she's not careful, she might find herself being the "ground" to a flighty, restless spirit who will romance her one minute, expect to be mothered by her the next, and treat her like an obstacle the minute after that. If she is already married to them, it may seem like a better deal to stay and take the frustration than to leave, as she hates divorce and breakups and can patiently endure a bad situation for much longer than a more changeable sign. Oshun had an affair with the fiery Shango, but it did not last; he may have been too volatile for her tastes.

She may also find herself in loco parentis to a less mature soul, who is dependent on her to lend them money and dig them out of whatever foolishness they may have fallen into. Unlike a Venus in Cancer, being a parent to her lover is not her first choice; she likes to take care of people, but she prefers the solid support of an equal. Still, due to her endurance and her unwillingness to change quickly, a childish lover can take advantage of her for a long time. Of course, unlike a more fragile sign, they will be unable to break her, and when she has finally had enough and leaves, the game will be over for good.

There is another side to Oshun than charm and gold. One of her symbols is the peacock, but the other is the vulture. There is a legend that in her youth, Oshun volunteered for a hideous duty that all the other orishas shied from, and they openly doubted her ability to do the job. She accomplished it at great personal risk by taking the form of a peacock. She flew a long way to give a message, but in the process her beautiful Venus-bright feathers were burnt off and she returned as an ugly vulture. On an even deeper level than the steadfast loyalty and willingness to sturdily face hardship that this tale suggests, there is the fact that the ugly vulture is the one who cleans up and recycles things. Without carrion eaters, the world would be a disgusting place indeed.

A Venus in Taurus is not fragile and not repelled by the difficult jobs that need to be done. She loves beauty, but she understands the sacrifices that need to be made to maintain it. Whether this takes the form of slaving over a kitchen floor, or slaving over art in a garret, or slaving over the needs of a relationship or family, she is in for the long, long haul. With that kind of willpower, it's no wonder that she knows everything will eventually turn to gold.

Eros

Venus in Gemini

In these modern times, the name of Cupid, the Roman name for Eros, brings forth a bunch of chubby little winged babies flying around on Valentine's Day cards. These are also sometimes called cherubs, in a confusion with the Hebrew angelic spirits referred to as cherubim, which were actually giant monsters made of multiple wings and eyes. Eros was personified in ancient Greece as a youthful boy, slender and handsome; in the Renaissance, portrayals of him as a winged toddler came into vogue.

Either way, there is one thing that both presentations of Eros have in common; they are both less than adult. This is telling, especially when we are talking about Venus in Gemini. Ruled by Mercury in this placement, Venus is often like the archetypal butterfly, flitting from one place to the next. Eros, too, is always in flight, which is appropriate for this air sign. A Venus in Gemini never seems to "touch earth" in the sense of making commitments or admitting to one's own earthly weaknesses, or being willing to climb the mountain of work and success, romantic or otherwise. A Venus in Gemini wants to be able to fly all the way up and land quickly, without all that work of step-by-step climbing involved. Then, when he does land, he finds that the treasures that slower folk find are not there for him. This is one of the great but difficult lessons of the earth.

Eros is the son of Aphrodite and Ares, Love and War, and as if in tribute to his parentage, he likes to create romantic trouble. This is not unusual for the Gemini Venus, who will sometimes start arguments with his friends and lovers just for the fun and mental challenge of it. Eros is a mischief maker, going about shooting people randomly with his love arrows, which is the sort of thing that Gemini, ruled by one of the two trickster planets, would find hilarious.

Until it happens to him, that is. When Eros finally gets his own, he shows himself every bit the dithering idiot as everyone he ever shot. In the tale of Eros and Psyche, Eros sees Psyche chained to a rock as a human sacrifice, carelessly wounds himself with one of his own arrows, and then falls madly in love with the beautiful mortal girl. He swoops down and rescues her from this fate, which is a good beginning, but after that it all begins to go terribly wrong. Eros is not a hero type; he doesn't know how to make the triumphant entrance with the adoring girl on his arm and make it work. He immediately begins to mentally sabotage himself and the situation.

A string of excuses as to why he shouldn't be doing this runs through his mind. She's only a mortal; I can't possibly marry her. (In a Venus in Gemini's mind, read this as: I thought she was perfect from a distance, but up close it is revealed to me that she actually has flaws! Oh no!) Everyone will laugh at us up on Olympus. What will Mother say? She'll be furious. (Read: I'll have to grow up and stand up to her and the other authority figures.) Hmmm, maybe I can find a way to have my cake and eat it too . . . Here the Gemini tendency to scheming and plotting kicks in. A Venus in Gemini is not above the sort of romantic shenanigans that are the stuff of Shakespeare's comedies; he may keep more than one lover on a string, trying his best to keep each of them unaware of the other, or he may lead a double life with two different sets of lovers and identities. If he is bisexual, his double life may reflect that, with a heterosexual lover for camouflage and secret liaisons at the gay bar. Honesty in relationships does not come naturally to him; it has to be learned, often the hard way.

Psyche means "soul," and Eros has just discovered that love is really about touching souls. She's come closer to getting under his skin than anyone else ever has before. With his airy nature, he hasn't been checking in on what goes on below the neck with any regularity. The truth is, he's panicking. He has a sudden vision of his wings being clipped, and so in his desperation he tries to control her instead, and her access to information—a true Gemini strategy.

He carries her away in a dark cloud to a beautiful palace, where he installs her; the servants are all sworn to silence and the only communication she has is with him. He comes to her only by night, so she can't see his face, can't truly know him. They are married in darkness, and he woos her with nighttime lovemaking and romantic tales. The foolish thing is that he actually expects to be able to carry off this charade indefinitely. It does not occur to him that others might think this arrangement strange and make their opinions known, or that Psyche might get curious and find a backbone. This is a Venus in Gemini at his worst; he often marries someone quickly while still on his best behavior. He is afraid to let them in under the glitz and glamour for fear that they will finally get to see what he's like inside, and be disappointed. Sometimes they aren't, and he only fears that they will be.

What happens next, of course, surprises no one but Eros. Psyche's sisters come to visit and are horrified by the way she passively accepts this total lack of information. What do you mean, they cry, you've never seen his face? How can you live like this? Their visit becomes a wakeup call for her. Both in myth and in fact, the innocent partner of a Venus in Gemini lover can remain in the dark for years. A real-life Eros and Psyche situation that I saw starred a woman whose husband convinced her that he had a part-time job as a secret undercover agent for the DEA that required him to dress as a woman to bust drug lords, when in fact he was just a closet cross-dresser. For four years, she dutifully helped him with his makeup and dresses, because if he didn't pass perfectly, "his life might be in danger," and sent him off to what turned out to be the local bars. It took the discovery of friends to expose the situation for what it was.

And, of course, when she lights the candle and discovers him, he panics again and flees out a window. Being discovered generally gives Venus in Gemini the flight response. However, Aphrodite, the force of love, steps in and puts Psyche through a series of tests that make her a stronger person, and eventually she is elevated to immortal status. As an immortal, she can face Eros down and demand his honesty; surprisingly enough, he gives it. With her persistence, she has won love; when he finally accepts her and lets her inside, he gains soul. It is a good bargain, and one which every Gemini Venus should study hard.

Mariamne
Venus in Cancer

For a thousand years, the name of the goddess worshipped all over Europe was Mary, the mother of God. She was not considered a goddess consciously, but she was revered with a fervor that made up for the loss of all the other goddesses. In many ways, the Virgin Mary (and various saints) absorbed the qualities of many other goddesses into themselves. However, Mary herself did have a particular character, rather than simply being an all-woman figure. She was maternal, loving, and the giver of mercy, much like Kwan Yin in the Orient. In her most famous pose, she held her child to her lovingly. The term *madonna*, or "my lady," became after a while synonymous with mother-child love.

Mary herself is the namesake—or perhaps the disguised incarnation—of a far older goddess, who was called by such variations as Mariamne, Marian, Maria, Myrrha, Myrta, Miriam, Mariham, Marratu, Mari-Anna, and Aphrodite-Mari. The same family of words produced the Latin term for the sea, *mare*; in every one of these incarnations, she was essentially the Sea Mother. Even in medieval times, Mary wore the blue robes and pearl necklace of her ancient form, and it is like this that she can be seen in a thousand small garden shrines today. The original word for her name was *Marah*, translated as "bitter" but actually closer in meaning to "briny," the saltwater of the sea and human tears.

There is something very poignant in the connection between seawater and tears, especially as the name of a goddess who became the European Lady of Mercy. The Marine Mother is a comforter, a consoler, a serene nurturer. Like Kwan Yin, she aids those in need; legends abound as to how the Virgin Mary gave miraculous aid to the poor and suffering. Millions preferred to cry out to her than to the more ascetic Christ and his remote father in times of real need. She was one of the domestic deities, at home as much in a rude peasant hut as in the huge cathedrals dedicated to her graciousness. To this day, she is still one of the most invoked goddesses in the world.

Yet in spite of her maternal associations, she was also identified with Aphrodite the Love Goddess. As she later ended up as a sexless Virgin Mother, this may seem contradictory, but it is reflective of the inherent contradictions of watery Venus in Cancer. When Aphrodite's planet Venus manifests in the sign of moon and water and mothering, the Sea Mother stretches out her loving arms and gathers you in. Cancer taps into the concept of *karuna*, the mother-love that the Hindus believed was the primal love upon which all other love is based. Although that may be debatable, in the case of Venus in Cancer it is absolutely true. The ability to give and receive adult love with a partner—Venus's task—is completely dependent on the individual's ability to master the giving of karuna.

What this means in practical terms is that their early experience of parent-child affection is the yardstick by which all other love is measured, and it can be hard to change. A Venus in Cancer loves to be needed and to provide a nurturing space to protect and comfort her loved ones. Similarly, she wants someone to provide the same for her when she needs it—which may be often, as she is sensitive and easily hurt. The dark side of a Venus in Cancer is that in some cases she is actually more comfortable when those she loves are needy supplicants, praying for mercy at her feet like medieval peasants in front of Mary's statue, to be gathered graciously into her warm arms.

Since a large part of her ability to feel desired is based around feeling needed—and this goes for male Cancer Venuses as well—she can be too generous, giving too much of herself away whenever she is faced with need. Unlike Pisces, she is not martyring herself to the universe like a bodhisattva. She is responding with heart-wrenching empathy to some poor soul's need, often with inappropriate intensity. One medieval legend tells of how a starving beggar prayed before the gilded statue of the Virgin Mary, and she miraculously gave him one of her gold shoes. The beggar was arrested for stealing the shoe by skeptical citizens, but as he was paraded back past her statue, another miracle occurred and she gave him the second shoe. The townsfolk released him in wonder, but the bishop locked up the golden shoes "lest the Virgin again be tempted to bestow them upon some penniless beggar who prays for her aid." Sometimes, like the bishop and the Virgin, a Venus in Cancer can end up in a second sort of relationship. This one might be with a disciplined Saturn-type who keeps track of her generous urges and quietly prevents her from giving away the whole store.

Sexually, she can blow hot and cold. When she feels needed and loved and secure, her sexual appetite can be as all-devouring as the sea; when she feels unsafe, she is as untouchable as the Virgin Mary. She swings back and forth between Virgin and Harlot, Mary and Aphrodite-Mari. Her lovemaking is excruciatingly context-dependent; her feelings, not her partner or her desires or her body, determine who will be in charge of her genitals at any given time. In the end, though, sex is a means to an end for her, not an act by and for itself. It is either a way to give nurturance or a way to get reassurance and emotional connection, or both. To say that she has a hard time separating sex and love is an understatement. It is more true that she cannot really conceive that they could ever be separated.

A Venus in Cancer loves as a response to being needed and loved, in that order. If there isn't even real love coming back her way, she'll settle for need. She will love regardless of merit; it doesn't matter what the rest of the world thinks of you as long as you make her feel needed and give her an outlet for her nurturing. Her emotions are as vast as the ocean, like the Sea Mother she represents. Their ebb and flow is not guided by human events, but by her own inner rhythm. Sometimes they can drown her in their intensity. Unlike when noisier signs go down, a Cancer emotionally drowning can be quiet, almost unnoticed; this is because a Venus in Cancer is not one of the more verbal Venus placements. It's hard for her to turn that great flow and crush of torrential feeling into a compressed squirt of words. She'd rather communicate with an embrace, or a gift, or another show of love. When she opens her mouth to speak, her feelings, like a tidal wave of seawater, may rise up in her throat and choke her.

It's the reason she strives for peace and serenity in her immediate environment. She senses that home is the only sphere she can have that kind of control over, so she concentrates on home. In a serene and peaceful context, the tidal wave can come out in slow rivers, little by little. It will not be backed by a storm made of all the briny tears she ever swallowed. The irony in her karmic lesson is that although she may initially create her safe space in order to comfort and protect others, its ultimate purpose must be her own comfort and protection. That includes protection from the people she's comforting, who may drain her of her emotional resources. At some point, she must shift from Mariamne to the distant Virgin Mary up on the pedestal for her own preservation, so that when she becomes the Sea Mother again her channels will run free. She must battle guilt in order to do this, and the cries of others in need. Her own rhythm of love is that of the tide—in, out, in, out. Like breathing. Like water, she will slip through your fingers if you try to nail her to one point on the shore. Like the tide, she will come back again, inevitably; let her ride her waves of feeling and trust them to return her safely home.

Ishtar

Venus in Leo

Although Ishtar and Inanna are both considered to be the same goddess, or variants on the same goddess, their cultural placements make them subtly different. Both were associated with Venus as Goddesses of the Morning and Evening Star. The later Ishtar has Inanna's history but a different focus. Inanna (see Venus in Scorpio) was queen of heaven and mistress of the storehouse, a goddess of the starry heavens and the fertility of the earth. In Babylonia, Ishtar's position as lady of love and war was more pronounced. She was shown as mighty in battle, driving a chariot pulled by seven lions and lionesses. Priestesses of Ishtar were also sacred prostitutes called *qadishtu*, and her temples were holy brothels. In her guise as the Morning Star, or the Star of Lamentation, she sowed strife and discord among people, and as the Evening Star she brought them together with love.

Ishtar was known as the courtesan of the gods who had mastered all the sexual arts, and all the gods lusted after her. "Courtesan" does not imply a two-dollar whore, and her priestesses were not low-class hookers either. Ishtar's world was similar to that of the upper-class Greek *hetaera*, or the smoothly trained Japanese geisha, or the Renaissance courtesan who was skilled in music, diplomacy, and languages. She has both ultimate class and irresistible sex appeal, and everyone respects her for the former quality and madly desires her for the latter. It's the ultimate fantasy of Venus in Leo, who wants to be both queen and sex goddess.

In one of her myths, Ishtar faces down Enki the inventor god (see Mars in Aquarius), who has created all the magic *me* (ritual spells) that rule humans and run society. It's a moment of opposites as Leo's charm faces down Aquarius's inventiveness, and Mars and Venus face off in a challenge. Leonine Ishtar ends up winning hands down as she gets Enki very drunk and then charms him into willingly giving up all the *me* to her. After she leaves and he sobers up, however, he changes his mind and wants them back. He sends wave after wave of armies against her as she crosses the ocean, but she and her warrior maidservant Ninshubur drive them all away with their valiant combat, foiling his plans. She sails in triumph into the harbor of her city, where a great parade of people applaud her returning laden with so much power.

This one image—Ishtar returning after a great and perilous adventure and everyone giving her mass adulation—is the secret dream of every Venus in Leo. She is no delicate fluff of a Venus; she knows how to fight, and she is willing to brave dangers untold—as long as she is sure that she will get a parade of admirers if she accomplishes the deed. She will go to great sacrificial lengths for her lovers, but they had better be prepared to lavish appreciation on her. She is a star, and their job is to be her biggest fan. If they can remember that, she will do anything for them. Her generosity is as dramatic and extravagant as her love; the goddess Ishtar is shown on her statuary as holding her breasts in a gesture of offering, symbolizing overflowing abundance.

Ishtar's retaliation to Gilgamesh reminds us that she is also the goddess of war. She finds the warrior-hero, newly come from victory, to be quite desirable, and offers her favors. It is more than just an offer of a roll in the hay; Ishtar's offering of her favors indicates that he would be given rulership over the land by mating with her. As the ruling priestess who symbolizes the earth, her bed was the blessing on each new king. Gilgamesh, however, is more involved with his warrior-partner Enkidu than with any woman, and rejects her. Not only does he turn down her favors, he does it in a particularly nasty way, recounting all the lovers that she has wooed and then had killed or imprisoned.

The goddess of love and war is infuriated by his words. Not only does he reject her sexually—which is bad enough to a Venus in Leo type—he rejects ruling at her side. He turns down the kingship of the land if it means being her consort. Since Venus in Leo thinks of herself as a status symbol in some sense, or at least as coming with a whole lot of perks, this is a slap in the face. His recounting of the unpleasant past affairs rubs salt in the wound. Ishtar is deeply insulted and goes to her father Anu, complaining that Gilgamesh should be punished for insulting her.

Anu sends a great bull to kill him, but Enkidu slays the bull to protect Gilgamesh. He also flings its bloody hide at Ishtar where she stands on the walls with her priestesses, calling out that this will be her next time if she tries any more tricks. From this point on, it is war between them, but Enkidu is only a wild man while Ishtar is a goddess. He is struck with an illness and dies, and Gilgamesh wanders weeping into the wilderness on a quest for a way to bring him back.

This is the dark side of a Venus in Leo, and it has to do with her wounded ego. Although she will never admit it, she is terribly vulnerable to the perceptions of others when it comes to her own desirability. Without an audience, a performer is nothing, and without positive reinforcement, a Venus in Leo finds it difficult to keep from sinking into a morass of self-doubt. In a sense, she needs someone to believe in her, to believe her into a beautiful, glamorous, strong, mesmerizing person, which she will then become on the strength of their belief. When they reject and insult her, she reflects their contempt back to them almost instinctively. They have created her as the virago and she will play the part because that's what she does. Nothing is too terrible for them when she is in this mood.

If she can realize her reflective nature and armor herself against those who would create her as something she would rather not be, she can begin the task of self-creation, which is what Leo is about anyway. When the Sun's light shines through the planet of love, it can create a charismatic glow from within that attracts everyone, right or wrong. A Venus in Leo needs to understand that she is desirable, no matter what others say or do not say, no matter what her reflection looks like in their eyes. When she can value herself as herself, instead of all the trappings and kingdoms that come with her, she will be even more beautiful and desirable in the eyes of others, and less likely to take their rejections personally. Ishtar's abundance will flow through her, and her pride will be not only in her status but in herself.

parvati
Venus in Virgo

In the mythology of India, the consort of Shiva takes on many different forms. As Uma, she is the maiden of innocence; as Durga, she is the virgin warrior; as Kali, she destroys and rebirths him. These faces are as much different goddesses as the same goddess; whether or not they are facets or separate gems is irrelevant to their power. However, the face that is the most loved and called upon—the goddess, in fact, that has the only real and loving relationship with Shiva the Destroyer—is Parvati. She alone is called wife, not consort or warrior. She alone truly reaches out to him with love.

Parvati is an earthy goddess, fond of dancing and the pleasures of the body. We tend to forget, in our dismissive attempts to see Virgo as only an ashtray-emptying neurosis, that it is actually an earth sign. However, it is ruled by Mercury, the airy, shapeshifting, all-in-your-mind energy, which continually tries to pull her focus away from the body-conscious earth energy. That's why, when Virgo deals with the body at all, it's from a mechanic's perspective, tinkering with its health and well-being and what to put into it in order to make it run better. It's a hard place for an earth sign to be in: wanting to connect with the earth urges, yet constantly being distracted by a continuous stream of mental chatter. If it's hard just to make Virgo sit comfortably with her ruler, Mercury, imagine what soft, watery Venus thinks about having to channel herself through this prickly spot.

According to the myth, Parvati fell in love with Shiva while he was up on his mountain, doing his ascetic best to ignore the entire world. She tried every trick in the book to distract him and show him her feelings—singing, talking, begging, pleading—up to and including doing a sensual naked dance in front of him. He ignored it all, ensconced in his quest for enlightenment. Parvati the beautiful was stymied for the first time; that which she wanted the most was unobtainable with her usual skills. This is a pretty clear parable for what happens to Venus when she tries to function in ascetic Virgo. Her normal open and receptive flow is dammed up; she becomes repressed and laconic, cut to pieces by the million sharp edges of this sign's discriminatory nature.

The story of Parvati gives a good clue as to the only way out of this quandary. The goddess decided that she was going to win her love, no matter what it took. So Parvati the beautiful, earthy goddess of fertility, sexy Venusian dancer, went up to the top of a mountain that faced Shiva's hermitage. There she put aside her fancy clothing, wrapped herself in a simple shroud, sat cross-legged on the bare rock, and began to meditate. She sat there for a full year, meditating and seeking enlightenment just as Shiva did, until the brilliance of her mind and spirit penetrating the universe became so clear and bright that even he could not ignore it. And Shiva the Mahadeva gazed upon this powerful mind and spirit that had come so far in its quest for oneness with the universe, and he was awed and fell completely in love. He begged her to marry him, and Parvati achieved that which she had longed for.

Venus in Virgo craves discipline in love. This does not mean some kind of sadomasochistic sex play, or emotional masochism, although it sometimes will manifest that way. It means that she needs to see love as a kind of sacred work, one that you must plug away at with a long and steady discipline. It isn't that Venus in Virgo doesn't value love; she does, but to her, the thing that you have to work and struggle for is so much more valuable and satisfying than the one that is merely tossed freely to you, like an unwanted throwaway. She's willing to keep working at it, too; she will keep trying to polish and perfect her relationships, and her ability to love, for as long as the other person is willing to hold out.

Part of the key to understanding Virgo is to study the meaning of the word "discipline," especially in its noun form. A discipline is a precise system of self-improvement that one follows in exactly the same way, over and over, until one becomes skilled at it and betters oneself in some way. There is an implication that one may never be finished, per se, with this discipline, and that's all right. The problem is that we are not, as a society, taught how to love. There is very little in the way of a manual or rule book or, yes, a discipline, to show us how to do it. Those who admit to wanting such a thing are generally denigrated by the majority of people who think that love should just come perfectly and spontaneously. It's why relationship counseling has such a stigma attached to it.

This makes a Venus in Virgo crazy. She wants to be good at love, but no one gives her the manual to study and practice, or even suggests that there might be such a thing. If she asks for help, she's scorned as being unromantic or unfeeling. If she wants to be told, step by step, logically and rationally and consistently, what to do, she's rejected for dullness and lack of spontaneity. Her best skill—analytical criticism—is often at its worst in the super-irrational arena of love, where a less thinking-oriented (or simply hurt and fearful) partner can see every word as a scalpel of pain.

This can make a Venus in Virgo withdraw again, like Parvati to her mountain, to search for an answer within herself. Periodic withdrawal is necessary for the mental health of any planet in the sign of the Virgin, as it gives them a chance to work on themselves in privacy. Virgo understands the concept of being a worthy prize; that is, that you must be a worthy offering in order to get anything worthwhile back in return for your gift of self. Love and intimacy does not come easy to her, and she can turn away in frustration if there seems to be no way out by any clear rules that she can discern.

Withdrawal itself can also cause problems, as Parvati's continuing story tells us. She and Shiva were married happily for a long time, but they were often apart for various journeys and quests. Once, when Shiva arrived home after a long absence, eager for his bride, he was unable to see her. She was taking a relaxing bath and ordered her son Ganesha to turn away all interruptions. In his rage at being excluded, Shiva cut off Ganesha's head. He repented a moment later and gave Ganesha the head of a wise elephant, but the tale shows how a Venus in Virgo's withdrawal from intimacy can be seen by loved ones as abandonment and can spark anger and resentment. The sharp, cutting words that often fly in such a situation can be pretty hard on the family bystanders, too.

In the end, this is the sign of service and sacred work. If a Venus in Virgo can see love as a sacred work, with emphasis on the sacred, she can overcome her own obstacles and learn to polish her ability to love. She must work out a discipline of loving and stick to it. It may be necessary to talk to others who have done the same thing and learn from them. Parvati, after all, did not invent the process of meditation by which she won Shiva. She had the resource of hundreds of years of mystics to fall back on. The discipline of learning to be in relationship to others is not a new thing, and there are those who have already trodden that road who may have words of wisdom.

She must also have a partner who understands the "love as sacred work" concept, with emphasis on the work part, who is not averse to using their relationship as a discipline of self-improvement and a constant, persistent process. They must not see loving struggle as a flaw, or careful planning as a killjoy, or negotiated equal sacrifice as loss of self. Only in such a dedicated, egalitarian, communicative relationship can the purity of a Venus in Virgo's path be reached. Only when each partner understands what it is to be

Virgin—to be one-in-yourself—can the hand be extended between two isolated mountaintops in a connection of ultimate intimacy.

Aphrodite
Venus in Libra

When in Libra, Venus is in its own sign, as close as possible to a single energy; of all the signs, it seems that Libra carries the Venus energy best, or at least most similarly to the original Venus, called by the Greeks Aphrodite, Foam-Born, Lady of Love and Beauty. Born from the severed genitals of Uranus, flung into the sea—disembodied phallus immersed in nameless oceanic womb—she sprang full-blown from the waves and was carried to shore in a giant pearled shell, as was immortalized forever in the Botticelli painting.

Aphrodite, therefore, is the daughter of sky and sea, and her symbols reflect this: the dove and the scallop shell. The planet Venus has a watery, emotional quality to it (even though its physical manifestation is actually blazing hot and dry), and Libra is an air sign; both meet in the beauty of Aphrodite. People with Venus in Libra have this talent; somehow even if their clothes are old hand-me-downs, they look remarkably well-put-together; even if their rooms are cluttered with junk, it somehow all looks interesting, as if it was artistically arranged, which it probably was. Even if they are stockbrokers or fast-food fryers, some part of them will love art or music, and they may well do it on the side.

Aphrodite herself is not the most decisive of goddesses, however, and Libra, the balancing scales, is not the most decisive of signs. Aphrodite cannot choose between lovers, or perhaps she does not bother. Her sacred moments are sunrise and sunset, when the two opposing poles of day and night meet; this is reflected in Libra's ability to see both sides of things. Aphrodite brings people together, builds bridges, crosses boundaries, and forms bonds; her greatest talent is that of synthesis, bringing the opposites onto a single road.

Aphrodite is the goddess not only of love but of beauty, and of all the signs, Libra is the most concerned with aesthetics and appearances. Ideally, in a Libra world, everything would look good, be pleasing to the senses, and have a certain elegant charm. Libra craves aesthetic beauty like some of the other signs crave security or stimulation. It doesn't matter what system of aesthetics the Libra in question clings to; every one may have a highly individualistic idea of what constitutes beauty, but whatever it is, they will yearn for it and demand it. Wherever they go, they will work at shaping their environment in their favorite aesthetic; the Libra Venus who lives in a spartan undecorated room, or worse still, in an off-the-rack space decorated by someone else in someone else's taste, is depressed and miserable and has given up on living.

However, this craving for beauty can be Libra's biggest downfall as well. When everything must be beautiful according to her personal system, she can lay this standard on her lovers as well, and reject them for not being attractive or elegant or polished or sophisticated enough. When she is manifesting her shadow, she seems to pick her partners and friends by how well they suit her decor, or match her style, or go with her wardrobe, or decorate her arm. This can quickly devolve into shallowness of the pettiest sort; the friend or lover who gains a few pounds, or gets a terrible haircut against Libra's ever-so-tasteful advice, or joins an unacceptable group is surgically removed from Libra's perfect life with all the coldness of any air sign.

Libra has a love-hate relationship with conflict; she will go back and forth between avoiding it obsessively (it gives her headaches and flusters her and is so unattractive) and actively seeking it out (it just isn't fair that they're doing this, and they need a good talking-to), which makes her appear flighty or hypocritical. What is driving her, however, is Aphrodite's need to bring opposites together. No matter how hard she tries to make her world perfect and aesthetically homogeneous, the balancing of her inner scales will force her like a magnet into contact with people and ideas that are her opposite, making sure that the Venus gift is not wasted.

Keep in mind that Aphrodite's main lovers were not like her at all; Ares was the violent god of war, and dour, brooding Hephaestus was the ugly, crippled smith-god. Her relationship with them kindled the birth of Fear, Terror, and Harmony with Ares, and inspired Hephaestus to new heights of creative work. It is the work of Venus in Libra: create your system of beauty, and then force yourself into a clash of mind and heart with its opposite, and somehow integrate the two. This then changes the system enough so that its opposite is now something entirely different, and so the cycle repeats again. Mind and heart. Sky and sea. Beauty and love. The cycle of stars and tides. Peace and conflict. Only from this balance can true harmony grow.

Inanna
Venus in Scorpio

Inanna was the Sumerian queen of heaven. She was goddess of the Morning and Evening Star—i.e., Venus—and also lady of the storehouse, queen of fertility and war, and goddess of love. Although Ishtar and Inanna are considered to be culturally variant versions of the same goddess, I have chosen to separate them in this book, and use Ishtar to symbolize those parts of these twin goddesses' natures which are Leonine, and Inanna to represent those that are Scorpionic. The central story of Inanna's myth is her journey down to and back from the underworld, and it is the Venus in Scorpio story because Venus in Scorpio is never satisfied with anything but the deepest experience.

Scorpio is well known as the "paranoid" sign, always looking under things for the hidden agendas, secret resentments, and dangerous manipulations she is certain she will find. Part of this certainty, this compulsion, is Scorpio's karmic assignment to seek the depths, whatever the cost. Nothing shallow or surface-level contents her. She must find the deeper meaning, the bare bones of truth hidden under the emotional layers, or stagnate into depression. A Venus in Libra seeks harmony, but a Venus in Scorpio wants to overturn the apple cart and look for the wormy, rotten one. She does not expect to find a golden one, because she is very sensitive and easily hurt and disappointed, so it is always a surprise to her when one appears.

In love, the success of this kind of seeking depends a great deal on the cooperation of one's partner. If they are dishonest, she will find out and go into paroxysms of rage. If they cannot stand up to her and meet her fears straightforwardly, she will suspect them of all sorts of unfounded sins, and either make accusations or build up resentments that leak out in other areas. If they are emotionally reserved, she will fling herself against their wall until she is let in or permanently rebuffed, because what she wants is the deep bonding experience and the only way she knows how to seek it is to probe and keep probing until some half-wished-for door opens. A Venus in Scorpio, when all is said and done, wants to bond on the soul level, to become not only one flesh but one soul as well.

In the myth of Inanna, the Queen of Heaven hears that her sister, Ereshkigal, the goddess of the dead, has lost her husband. She hears Ereshkigal through the ground, weeping, and decides to visit her, leaving her lover Dumuzi in charge. She sets Dumuzi's sister Ninshubur at the gate of the underworld with orders to go for help if she does not return in three days, and descends. She is greeted by seven gates, each of whom has a guardian, and they require her to be stripped of all her jewels and garments before she can enter the realm of Ereshkigal. This is part of a Venus in Scorpio's path; although she would like to strip away all the illusions and defenses of others, as a fixed sign she often finds it hard to give up her own. Part of learning to trust, and truly going into the depths with someone else, means that you both have to get naked. One person doesn't get to be clothed and look down on the other partner's vulnerability. That's not a relationship, that's a lab rat under a microscope. However, fate usually intervenes and forces that stripping down in a Venus in Scorpio sooner or later, ready or not.

Inanna comes before Ereshkigal naked, and Ereshkigal scorns her, openly jealous that Inanna has a spouse while she, her bereaved sister, does not. There is some question about Inanna's motivation in coming down to see Ereshkigal: comfort, catharsis, or gloating? This, too, is not inappropriate; a Venus in Scorpio often deals with many layers of motivations that must be sifted through, and she rarely shows all her reasons up front. Piercing Inanna with the eye of death, Ereshkigal paralyzes her and hangs her on the wall above her throne from several meathooks. There Inanna reaches the point that has been called the *katabasis*, the bottom of the pit, the point from which there can only be a rebirth. She will not come out of this ordeal unchanged, and neither will her marriage. In a sense, part of having Venus in Scorpio is the constant urge to go down to the bottom of the pit and back up again, over and over, until it is a familiar place that has no more power over you. This is part of the Scorpio process, and it may involve facing bad patterns inherited from childhood that are played out over and over in a relationship until the tape finally snaps and ceases to run. This kind of relationship-as-depth-therapy requires a patient and committed partner who is willing to take these underworld journeys with a Venus in Scorpio, and who has the backbone and honesty to appreciate the process.

Meanwhile, Ninshubur waits three days and then runs back to the gods, telling them that Inanna has been captured. They know that Ereshkigal is unlikely to hear an appeal from any of them, so they cleverly create two messengers who are neither wholly male nor female and send them down to her. Seeing the sad Ereshkigal, they weep for her and give her their sympathy, and she is so moved by them that she allows Inanna to go free—on one condition.

Everyone she meets must be glad to see her come back, and the first person who is not glad to see her must take her place. At this point, it becomes obvious that Ereshkigal knows something that Inanna has not yet faced.

Inanna emerges from the underworld, renewed and triumphant, back from the dead . . . and escorted by a cloud of chittering underworld demons. Ninshubur runs ahead of her, warning everyone to act as if they are glad to see her, but she does not reach Inanna's palace before the Queen of Heaven and her demon entourage. There disaster awaits. As soon as it had become clear that Inanna was trapped in the underworld and unlikely to return, Dumuzi had set himself up to rule in her place. He was so busy glorying in his new position that he had not bothered to take part in the rescue effort and thus did not know about her return. When she barges through the door, he is taken aback and unable to hide his disappointment. The demons leap on him and carry him off to Ereshkigal, who has now managed to turn the tables on her sister.

At this point, the worst has happened. Inanna has been stripped of the last of her illusions: that Dumuzi is all-devoted and that there is no resentment on his part about being her subject and consort. She is furious with him. She also still loves him and wants him back. This state of affairs is not unusual for a Venus in Scorpio. Having seen the dark places within herself, she is more able to accept imperfection in others. Love and hate are often inextricably linked for her, and she moves back and forth between them more freely than other signs. It is the intensity of her feelings for someone that is important. For her, love is not the opposite of hate, nor vice versa, but both are the opposite of indifference.

Ninshubur unselfishly offers to take Dumuzi's place for half the year, and so Inanna shares him with her sister from then on. This can symbolize a Venus in Scorpio's longing to be with a partner who will accept both the light and the dark within her; who will marry all of her, including the less socially acceptable parts. It also illustrates how the chronic trips to the underworld that a Venus in Scorpio is driven to take can shake up the hidden anger and resentments in a relationship, allowing a chance for a new rebirth to a higher level of honesty. For this is the sign of transformation in relationship, and all who venture near had best hang on for the ride.

Krishna
Venus in Sagittarius

Vishnu the Preserver, greatest of the Hindu's widespread pantheon, had many incarnations, mostly as real or mystical animals, in order to experience what it was like to be alive in many forms. His most famous incarnation, though, was Krishna, a mortal man. Krishna was the grandson of a king who had been told he would be killed by his grandchild, so Krishna's parents sent him off to be raised in secret with a band of peasant cowherds. He grew up both of the upper and the lower classes, equally comfortable with both, and thus is called upon by members of all classes and castes for protection and enlightenment.

Astrologically, when Venus goes into the freedom-loving sign of Sagittarius, she finds things a little more difficult than when she is in more watery or earthy signs. A Sagittarius's fiery nature and seeker's soul is uncomfortable with many of the deeper emotions, which he sees as getting in the way of his quest for knowledge. He needs the freedom to experience the world, and that means the freedom to experience lots of people, carnally as well as conversationally. He romanticizes love and believes in it with all the strength of Galahad searching for the Holy Grail, but what he considers love may not bear any relation to the everyday fighting over the coffee that most lovers have to wade through in order to achieve anything deeper.

As a young man, Krishna began to work various miracles that showed him to be the incarnation of a god. He also took up with a band of *gopis*, or shepherdesses, and became lovers with every one of them. This was not considered wrong, as he informed them that they could achieve spiritual salvation through sexual relations with him. He charmed every woman with his magic, proving himself the greatest lover that she had ever had. It is said that he created the illusion of many Krishnas at once, so that each of the women thought they were with the real Krishna at any given time.

The average person with Venus in Sagittarius would probably love to be able to pull off that trick. This is the Venus placement most likely to have difficulty settling down into long-term monogamy, and he will prefer to play the field, or have multiple lovers at once, for as long as he can get away with it. An unevolved Venus in Sagittarius lover will charm a potential conquest with a tale of soulmates and destiny; he may even believe it at the time. He may also try to live double or triple or quadruple lives, where he can be a different lover to each of his paramours, mimicking Krishna's magical multiplying. More evolved individuals with this placement will understand that just because you are destined to be attracted to someone does not mean that this person is fairy-tale marriage material. Sometimes you come into a relationship to learn about yourself, and it may not last. Of course, a lover may not enjoy being told this on the first date.

Sagittarius is symbolized by the centaur archer, who is half human and half animal, unlike the other signs that have either human or animal emblems. Much of the Sagittarian pursuit of knowledge is actually a quest for that fine line that separates the two, if indeed such a thing exists. If he attempts to shortchange either his animal or his human nature, he will become unwhole and fall. This goes doubly so in the purview of a Venusian, where he is constantly prone to separate lust and love into two compartments, never to sully each others' complexities.

The way in which he must bridge the two is not by forcing them together, because his intellect and experience will just deny it. Instead, he has to bring them both into the practice of his spirituality, and then bridge them with that spiritual practice. Venus in the sign of religion suggests that for him, both love and lust are ultimately supposed to be vehicles for expanding his religious faith, whatever that may be. After all, Krishna was not an ordinary man, he was the incarnation of a greater being who was temporarily on earth to learn about such things as love and lust in order to further his understanding. He would not have gone to all that trouble if he did not have great respect for them. When a Venus in Sagittarius awakes to his true path, he will realize that the above description applies to all of us.

Some religious traditions, of course, are a better fit with the exploration of sacred sexuality than others. Here again a Venus in Sagittarius has to make the hard decision between instinctive animal and thinking human. If the faith that raised you is insufficient for your needs, you have two choices: stay and change it, or leave and go wandering for something better suited to you. Both are equally difficult, equally challenging, and equally valuable. One is the choice of Sagittarius the Priest and the other the choice of Sagittarius the Wanderer. Whichever he chooses as his outward practice, his inward faith must bring both the physical animal body and the thinking human mind together in equality within his sexuality. Part of the reason for the rampant dishonesty in modern Krishna cults is that they have cut off the physical, hedonistic, sexual aspect of Krishna, claiming that his love is only a spiritual entity. Without the balance between the two, his nature and that of his worshippers descends into delusion.

The evolved Venus in Sagittarius puts honesty in relationships first, before anything else, even if it is going to hurt himself or his lover. He may find a way to accept monogamy with the right person, but if he cannot, he would prefer to remain unattached rather than make a promise that he could not keep. The modern practice of polyamory—open, above-board, negotiated nonmonogamy—can often be an ethical alternative, as it allows him to have variety and a certain amount of freedom while not requiring dishonesty. At any rate, he needs a partner who can keep up with his radical honesty and will refrain from game-playing; as soon as he feels that he is being manipulated, the Wanderer will be out the door, unlikely to return.

At the end of Krishna's myth, he dies from an arrow shot by a hunter that strikes him in the soles of his feet, his only mortal place. This recalls the Sagittarian tendency to attempt to get away from boring earthly agendas that might tie down his restless spirit. In the sign of the Wanderer, he moves so fast across the landscape that the soles of his feet are the only part of him that are in contact with the earth. As such, they are where he is most vulnerable. The arrow of truth flies both ways, and sooner or later it will bring him down to earth with a thud. He may finally realize that the love he wanted is too idealized to exist, or that the way he is going about things is miserably unsatisfying. We may all be gods in our own way, but we are here as mortals for a reason, and we must find happiness here first. For a Venus in Sagittarius, the compromise is between principle and love, and sometimes the only way to resolve that dilemma is with either new principles, new love, or both at the same time.

freyja
Venus in Capricorn

Of all the Norse gods who lived in the worlds surrounding Midgard, the most beautiful of all was Freyja of the golden hair. Sister of Frey, god of the fields, she was not only a goddess of love but of fertility as well. Folks prayed to her to make their livestock go into heat and conceive; unlike the urbanized Aphrodite, she was a love goddess whose first worshipper was the farmer.

The Norse had several groups of gods; sky deities like Odin and Frigga and Thor were Aesir, the gods of the warrior class, but Freyja was the foremost deity of the Vanir, the farming-class gods whose mastery lay in the work of agriculture and earth magic. Like earthy Capricorn, her skills of love were at the service of those who needed practical help. Freyja is also a mistress of the kind of shamanic craft called *seidhr*, which includes skills in prophecy, clairvoyance, and what might today be called channeling. Her magic was powerful, and Odin himself apprenticed to her in order to learn it.

According to the old Norse myths, Odin and his brothers Vili and Ve first met the Vanir on a journey into new lands. They were accosted by an old woman who called herself Gullveig and asked them for gold as a toll to pass through her country. Angered, they threw flaming brands at her, and she burned like a torch but did not seem to be harmed. Laughing, she put the flames out and declared war on them. The old woman turned out to be Freyja in disguise, who had come to see these new warriors and test their courtesy—a test they failed.

The Aesir fought the Vanir for a long time in a terrible war, until a truce was called and hostages were exchanged to live in good faith at each others' halls. Eager to avail himself of her knowledge of magic, Odin requested that one of the Vanir hostages be Freyja, and so she came to live at Asgard. When she came, Odin gave her great honor and made her his partner in the work of rescuing the souls of those doughty warriors who die in battle. He gave her a hall of her own, Sessrumnir, and half of the fighting souls went to it rather than to Valhalla, including all those warriors who were women. She led a troop of magical swan-maidens, the Valkyries, who swept across a battlefield seeking the bravest of the brave.

A Venus in Capricorn thinks a lot about security and old age. She can't help it. Financial security and old age are ruled by Saturn, who rules loving Venus with an iron hand in this placement. One of the first questions that she will ask herself, even if only unconsciously, is, "Will this person make me feel secure? Will they be there for me when I am old and decrepit?" If the answer is no, she will be vaguely unhappy even if she loves the partner dearly. These internal needs are symbolized by Gullveig, the old woman who asks for gold, but the story also shows a Venus in Capricorn's need to test the worth of potential suitors. As well as financial and emotional security, she has a secret (or not so secret) fetish for a lover of high status and public worth.

Her association with the harboring of dead souls also reflects Saturn, which has a great deal to do with death. However, she does not just go about collecting any random dead souls; that is Hel's job. Only the cream of the crop are chosen by Freyja; Sessrumnir is a high-status hall. A man or woman with Venus in Capricorn may settle for an "ordinary" lover, if they are faithful and provide emotional security, but secretly they are drawn to the idea of a hero or heroine, someone who is publicly lauded, who has value and status in the eyes of the world. Sometimes they may play Pygmalion and attempt to make a hero or heroine out of someone with potential but little ambition, but they will often become disinterested if their "project" shows no signs of achieving any success.

One of the myths about Freyja that perfectly illustrates a Venus in Capricorn and her willingness to measure sex and love in terms of its practical value involves the necklace Brisingamen. This was made of gold filigree by four dwarven brothers, all of whom were skilled smiths and had worked together for months on the piece of jewelry. It was said to be the most beautiful and valuable thing that had ever been made of metal, and Freyja took one look and decided that she had to have it. The price, it turned out, was simple; the four dwarves took one look at Freyja and agreed that Brisingamen ought to adorn her neck . . . if she would spend four nights, one with each brother, pleasuring them sexually. Freyja agreed without hesitation and four nights later left with Brisingamen about her swanlike throat. Others spoke of the incident with ridicule or disapproval but she ignored them, secure in the knowledge that she, not they, had gotten the greater prize.

As anyone with Venus in Capricorn would understand, this was not a matter of Freyja merely being loose with her favors. The dwarves were offering her a thing of great value, their most precious treasure, and she was offering them something of equally great value in exchange. Paying for Brisingamen with sex did not cheapen her so much as it showed how much she and her body were worth—the most precious golden artifact ever made. A Venus in Capricorn does, on some level, feel as though her love can be measured in material worth, and usually, if her self-esteem is not damaged, she believes that it is worth a great deal indeed. One of the classic archetypes of Venus in Capricorn is the high-priced courtesan, for whom men are willing to pay huge amounts in order to enjoy them for a single night . . . because they are worth it.

In Norse society, it was very important for a man who sought a bride to pay for her with a magnificent bride-price; the higher the bride-price, the more honor done to the bride. This may seem to us today as if the woman was merely property to be purchased, but the actual mindset was very different from this. Women in ancient pagan Norse society had a good deal of freedom; they were not chattel and could divorce their husbands simply by packing up and moving out. Rather, the bride-price reflected an attitude about material objects: they were thought to have a great deal of good luck or fortune, especially if they were valuable, highly useful gifts from esteemed friends and relatives, and even more so if they were heirlooms handed down through the family; this gave them extra luck with every succeeding generation. The house itself had a class of fortune, of which the hearth, the woman's place, was the center.

A bride—who would come with a houseful of inherited and gifted goods, and who would be the domestic priestess who would tend the hearth—was in herself the greatest source of good luck a man could hope to have. Should she choose to leave him, he would lose not only her company and her household goods but a great deal of good fortune as well. He had to show how much he valued her by passing on gifts to her family, gifts that would help to dower other brides in future generations.

This attitude is one of the mysteries of Freyja, goddess of love, and of a Venus in Capricorn: if you believe that your love and attention is worth a great deal, then you must expect a great deal in return, because you will be more than just a bed warmer, conversationalist, and dishwasher to your partner. You will be a source of good fortune, a living good-luck charm, a supportive hand who will aid them in their climb to the top of their achievements, and who expects the same in turn. In order to feel valued, a Venus in Capricorn needs to have this kind of mutual support of goals, both ones achieved as partners and those achieved separately. She will be frustrated by a vague, goal-less partner, because her greatest gift will be wasted on such a person, and she will be unable to make them understand how important it is for them to help her achieve her own long climb to the top of the mountain.

ganymede
Venus in Aquarius

One day, the great king of the gods, Zeus, decided that he needed a new cupbearer. His original cupbearer had been his daughter Hebe, goddess of health, but she had just been given to the newly deified Hercules as a prize bride and was no longer available for the position. Looking around the mortal world, Zeus suddenly spotted a youth so beautiful that every one of his bisexual instincts was triggered at once, and he decided that this youth must be his new cupbearer, and more besides. He changed himself into a great eagle and swooped down from the sky, catching up Ganymede and bringing him back to Olympus, where he immortalized him.

Anyone who has studied ancient Greece will know that it is practically a cliché that it was socially acceptable for older, upper-class men to take young male lovers in the same way that they took female ones. Such relationships were celebrated in literature and even vaunted by some to be superior to male-female relationships, as they were between two people of the same upbringing and expectations. Heterosexual marriage was said to be more difficult, as the couple must communicate across a vast gulf of cultural difference. On one level, this myth is simply a way of showing Zeus in that social role; on another, it illustrates the idea, quite familiar to any Venus in Aquarius, that traditional marriage and family is not the only way, nor even the most positive way, for everyone to run their relationships.

This does not mean that a Venus in Aquarius is any more likely to be gay or bisexual than a Venus in any other sign. What it does mean is that a Venus in Aquarius is not satisfied with the same old heterosexual game. You know the one . . . boy meets girl, girl has to wait shyly for boy to get his act together and make the first move. He has to brave all the rejection, and she has to flirt desperately yet never be seen as too assertive. This goes on all through the courtship. If he's angry at her, he can threaten to leave her or date one of her best friends, who will of course throw over a friendship at a chance to be with him. If she's angry with him, she will withhold sex in order to punish him, because it's assumed that men need sex and women don't, and therefore it's her only power over him. Then they get married, and he wants her to stay looking young and sexy even after popping out three kids, which she of course is so much better at taking care of, and she expects him to get that promotion and keep going out to work every day and still be emotionally involved with the family at the end of the day. If he decides to relocate, she must give up her job; if she decides to quit her job and stay home, he is obligated to support her. They are both equals in playing the jealousy game over who looked too hard at that attractive person over there. Eventually, their lives resemble a sitcom.

You know. That dance. The one that far too many people are doing.

A Venus in Aquarius thinks that this is useless and ridiculous and not even romantic. He doesn't see the point in playing any game except his own, and his own starts with the rule "We are friends first." He means that, too. One of his good points is that he will not throw away a friendship for a lover. In fact, a friendship with seniority comes first, and he will expect his lover to understand this. He will also expect them to divest themselves of any attachment they may have to the aforementioned heterosexual dance, and he will also expect them to learn to keep a certain emotional distance, just as he does. A Venus in Aquarius is one of the least likely signs to see the ideal of settling down and having children as romantic; it is no accident that Ganymede does not involve himself in procreative relationships. He wants his partner to be his best friend and confidant, but he also wants freedom to do his own things, without dealing with clingy insecurities. When his chosen partner doesn't share these values or is unable to live up to his expectations, he distances himself and quickly leaves.

While a Venus in Aquarius may know what it is that he *doesn't* want, he may not be clear on what he does want a relationship to look like. Or, more likely, he knows exactly what he wants . . . and it doesn't resemble anything he's going to get out of a mere mortal, or even two or three mere mortals. In a way, the story of Ganymede's rise to Olympus is the dream of a Venus in Aquarius— to be swept off the lowly earth with all the whiners, raised up into the air (this is an air sign), and brought to a high place where you can have a relationship with a divine being.

The eagle has symbolized such things in the past as objectivity and the fly-high-see-far mode of being, or a message from divinity. A Venus in Aquarius would prefer that others share their views on how relationships should be; he may have an idealized view about how their partnership is going to be different from all the rest, not so unevolved or jealous or dishonest. Of course, with a partner who shares his values, they might just achieve that. It might be a gay or lesbian or bisexual arrangement where they combat bigotry together; it might be a polyamorous relationship where they commit to more honesty and communication than the average "sitcom marriage" can stand; it might be simple, monogamous heterosexuality, but with a commitment to be absolutely equal and never, never fall into the old gender roles. This last one might be the hardest challenge of all and the most worthy of real respect when and if it actually occurs. Whatever the situation, a Venus in Aquarius will not be happy unless his love life is also taking on social mores in a way that matches his politics.

Ganymede was originally an early Greek god of the rain that falls from heaven; later Hellenic myths morphed him into an honored mortal. He is Zeus's cupbearer and brings him the divine nectar and ambrosia that sustains the gods and gives them immortality. In a sense, he takes on the same role as the goddess Iduna does for the Norse gods—that of being the giver of immortality. A Venus in Aquarius understands immortality in relationships, but sees it in a very different way than that of, say, Taurus or Cancer or Scorpio. For them, immortality in love means that you cleave to each other, never leave, and are buried together in one grave.

For a Venus in Aquarius, the longevity of the affair has little to do with it. Instead, he asks: Did it serve as an example of social change? Did others watch you combat the system of stereotypes and become moved to do the same? Did it change the world, outside of just the two of you? And, most importantly, even if it didn't last very long, did you both part friends? Because lovers may come and go, but good friends truly last forever. This is the kind of immortality that a Venus in Aquarius means, and it is based not on the intimate internal but on the greater, external possibility. This is the cup that Ganymede holds out, and the challenge that he gives to all. His cup is neither sweet nor bitter; it is clear and refreshing as the high winds, and it promises the mysteries of going from earthbound, tradition-bound mortal to a being who knows how to fly.

oba

Venus in Pisces

Shango is the great fire-and-thunder god of the Afro-Caribbean Yoruba religion, and he is an assertive, masculine character with a great love for ladies. He has been lovers with Oshun many times, but she knew better than to marry him. His first wife, however, was named Oba. She was utterly unlike him, being quiet, retiring, and devoted. Other than that, she did not seem particularly interesting or remarkable at first.

This is not an unusual situation for the self-effacing placement of Venus in Pisces. For these people, being part of a couple is far more important even than the Libra urge to twoness. For them, it is more about oneness (as it always is where Neptune is involved); that is, oneness created by merging with the partner and his or her needs and wishes. Venus in Pisces people never sacrifice themselves grudgingly; they do it gladly. It fulfills them. They love to be able to anticipate a lover's needs and often have to be prodded to keep some part of themselves independent and assertive.

For years Shango dallied with various lovers, but always came home to Oba, and she was content. However, one day havoc came home in the form of Oya, the volatile and fiery goddess of the weather and the cemetery. She was the wife of Ogoun at that time, and Shango had met her while ordering spear points from Ogoun's forge. Oya was chafing under the lack of attention from her workaholic husband and handsome Shango immediately drew her eye. Before Ogoun realized what was happening, she had left him in order to be with the fire god; there was a terrible chase through the woods, and much flinging of sorcery, but in the end Oya had escaped and come home to Shango's house. He installed her immediately as his wife, as such a proud and powerful creature could not be a mere dalliance.

Oba was terribly intimidated by Oya, and Oya was annoyed with the shy and timorous Oba, who had the position of senior wife. Oba was also greatly hurt by the fact that Shango rarely came to her bed any more, as he was captivated by the fascinating wind goddess. She did not, however, reveal her worries to Shango. This reflects Piscean experience; as a water sign, Pisces is not comfortable with confrontation and in fact will do anything to avoid it. The more forthright signs find this sort of thing unbelievable—"Why didn't you just say something!"—but if it can be smoothed over without getting a loved one angry, she will try it. A Venus in Pisces has deeply felt emotions and is empathetic to the point where it can seem natural to her that a lover must have what they want, even if it pains her. Their pain is more real to her, sometimes, than her own is.

At any rate, Oya noticed that her co-wife was glooming about and asked if anything was wrong. Oba confided that she was terrified Shango had lost interest in her and would eventually cast her out. Oya, lady of wind and rain, was as capricious as the weather, and something of a trickster; she decided to play an evil joke on the far-too-good Oba. She told Oba that if she cut off her ear, chopped it up into a stew, cooked it, served it to Shango, and made sure that he ate it, he would be hers forever and never stray from home again. Oba, desperate to keep her beloved husband and her place, did as she suggested, cutting off her ear and cooking it up into a stew.

Oba's sacrifice is grotesque on many levels; not only is it a mutilation, but it is done as part of an underhanded love spell. For Venus in Pisces people, the line between sacrifice and manipulation is very fine, and they sometimes pass back and forth over it. Being a martyr can have a great deal of power in terms of the guilt factor; this may be a reason over and above simple jealousy that Oya wanted to get rid of Oba. The problem with saintly people is that they make everyone else feel less saintly in comparison, and they often trigger the strange human urge to martyr them. A Venus in Pisces may try to gently manipulate a lover into doing something, especially if it means that she can avoid a confrontation. Unlike Libra who is driven to argue, Pisces would rather indulge in a small amount of dishonesty to keep the peace than have total honesty with bickering.

Venus in Pisces people can also sacrifice to the point where they cut off pieces of themselves in order to be whatever their partners prefer. Oba's sacrifice of her ear suggests that she was discarding her ability to hear what was really going on in favor of eternal emotional security. It takes a strong individual with this placement to maintain good boundaries and stand up to those she loves. It may take years of practicing on her part even to get to the point where she can willingly enter an argument without fear of loss and abandonment.

In the myth, Shango is served the stew and eats it unwittingly, but at the end of dinner he notices Oba's bandaged head and asks her what has happened. At this point she breaks down, comes clean, and confesses everything from her insecurity to Oya's suggestion to her own mutilation. Shango is horrified and repulsed by Oba's act, but he is also furious at Oya. He throws her out of his house and repudiates her for her cruelty, and she is brought up before the other gods for judgment. In some versions of the story, Oba is also ejected by a disgusted Shango; in others she stays on as his wife. This may suggest that when a partner discovers how much their Venus in Pisces lover has been constricting themselves, or hiding themselves, or not being fully open and honest in the name of "peace," they may leave in disgust or stay to try and work things out. Either way, the story warns, things cannot go on as they have been.

In the final part of Oba's myth, the gods pass judgment on Oya for her nasty trick on her co-wife. Oya is the lady of the cemetery, keeper of the dead. The gods decree that she must share this office with Oba; everything above ground is Oya's, but everything below ground is Oba's. This part of the story rings strangely like Persephone becoming queen of the shades below the earth after finding her way out of passivity. It is not an uncommon theme for Neptunian heroes and heroines to pass from submissive self-sacrificer to mystical communer with the ancestors and the shades; apparently there is some psychological link between being the sacrifice and the ruler of those who have also been sacrificed. A Venus in Pisces excels at being a counselor, bringing lost souls back from the dark places where she herself has been. Oba goes from being the victim to being the one to whom millions look for their protection. Why stop at oneness with only a single person when you can have it with the entirety of the earth?

♂ Mars

Ares
Mars in Aries

Where is the line between action and aggression?
Aries doesn't know and doesn't care. Is it true that
every act of creation is an act of violence, forcing
your will onto a resisting world? Of course it is, says
Aries. So what? Should you seek out struggles or
wait for them to find you? Why sit around and wait
for anything, says Aries. Go for it! When it is acti-
vated by its ruler, Mars, you get a double helping of
that fiery Martial energy. The ability to *do* becomes a
compulsion to *do something*, anything, preferably
something big and fast and energetic.

Ares, the Greek god of war, was the son of Zeus
and Hera, but he did not get along well with either
parent. His impulsive aggression caused his mother to
shun him as unrefined, and he continually fought with
his father over every small thing in his life. Their
biggest arguments seemed to revolve around Ares'
constant interfering with mortals and their battles.
Zeus preferred the gods to meddle in the mortal world
only when it would do him and his Olympian crowd
some good. Ares, a creature of emotion and strong
passions, would jump in wherever he thought that one
side might need his help, like a sort of divine vigilante
looking for fights to take part in. Who he chose to
help was generally a spur-of-the-moment, subjective

decision, not based on any thoughtful consideration, and might just as easily be the wrong side. Ares was not a strategist. In fact, it seemed sometimes as if it didn't matter much to him who the "right" side was; he just needed to be fighting someone, for something.

As a child, his tutor was Priapus, the god with the giant phallus. People talk about Mars (the Roman name for Ares, appropriate for this most Martial of Mars placements) as being merely a drive to action, but it is also the drive to sexuality, the instinct that scientists call "mounting behavior," the urge to seek out and get oneself some sexual satisfaction. Mars in Aries people, regardless of gender, may be considered too aggressive in the arena of flirting and suggestion; they don't notice sexual subtexts very well and are too impatient for a long, drawn-out, come-here-go-away romantic courtship. They want to know, now, whether you find them interesting enough to bother, so they can either get down to brass tacks or stop wasting their time and move on. In the Libran arena of lowered eyelashes and suppressed giggles, their straightforward honesty can seem as socially unacceptable as Priapus walking in with his three-foot penis erect and in full view.

Before Priapus taught him the arts of warfare, however, he first taught Ares how to dance. Early tribal war gods are often associated with dancing, just as young male warriors in tribal societies dance wildly as a way to attract mates and gear themselves up to fight. Dancing can also symbolize the kind of resilient fancy footwork that Aries learns to do as he tumbles from one dangerous situation into another. A mature Mars in Aries has learned to roll with the punches, never lay sprawled despairing in the dirt, get up and face the fear again, or at least move on to the next problem with confidence. His momentum carries him through. Dancing is the best preparation for fighting, both physical and mental. It keeps you supple and resilient and allows you to duck.

The god of war was both dearly beloved and reviled, venerated and hated. Ares is the embodiment of the aggressive forward push, something that we generally want to appear in a blast of competence and fearlessness when we need it and to conveniently disappear afterwards, waiting on our command. Ares was called upon with great pleadings when the citadel needed defending, and the rest of the time he was dismissed as an impetuous brute. The problem is that it's not so easy to put that genie back into the bottle to be ignored until it's needed next. People with Mars in Aries or a strong Martial chart often become the social scapegoats for people who like to pretend that they themselves have perfect control of their Mars urges and don't need or use them much anymore. They are the ones sent to the front lines and considered expendable—"Let them do the fighting, they're better at it, and they were annoying anyway."

This is the original Adrenaline Placement. Mars in Aries people need active stimulation, preferably with some struggle involved. It's when they can't get the positive sort of self-challenging struggle, the personal test of their courage, that they start picking fights with others. People roll their eyes at Mars-ruled "adrenaline junkies" who jump out of airplanes or race cars or climb mountains with their fingernails, but these are actually people who have discovered a useful way to channel that energy. Perhaps it's not useful to the rest of the world, but pitting oneself against the limits of one's own body and endurance is an excellent way to build up the kind of courage that Aries craves. It's also a much better alternative than starting fights. A pugnacious, chip-on-the-shoulder Mars in Aries is either bored or suffering from low self-esteem through lack of positive challenges. It's as if no matter how hard he tries to live the quiet life, the Powers That Be push him toward physical challenges of some kind. If he's not consciously working with these urges, it can leak out as warlike behavior.

Ares interfered most when the mortals being injured were children of his. Although he is derided as being an immature hothead, pugnacious to a fault—"a graduate of the Han Solo School of Action Without Thought," to quote a friend of mine—he was the only Olympian deity to routinely step in whenever mortal children of his were in danger. The other gods often ignored their mortal offspring; not Ares. He even defied Zeus's command to stay out of the Trojan War when a son of his was killed in the fighting. This kind of willingness to protect loved ones, or the weak and innocent, is the best quality of a Mars in Aries. It recalls that the Roman version of Ares, for whom the planet Mars is named, was much less of a youthful hothead and more of a seasoned protector of cities, the defender of those who called upon him. After all, what's the point of building up all that courage if you're not going to use it to champion those who need help?

The lover of Ares was Aphrodite, just as Mars and Venus complement and are drawn to each other. Indeed, this is the way that the intense, overreactive Mars in Aries placement can be calmed down and controlled—not through Saturnian discipline, which will only provoke rebellion, but by the Venusian touch. He needs to learn deeply, emotionally, that even the people he fights with are not demons but humans who are worthy of compassion. He needs to understand love, and what it means not only to defend those whom you love, but to defend their rights as well . . . against yourself and your own anger, if necessary. He needs to learn how to apologize and to atone, and if possible to think first before jumping and striking . . . or at least to feel first, in order to know how the other person is feeling and thus short-circuit the destructive urge.

Ares's children with Aphrodite were Deimos and Phobos (Fear and Terror) and Eros and Harmonia (Falling In Love and Harmony). A Mars in Aries, like his namesake, can go either way. He can reap fear and terror, or love and harmony. It's the choice between being the destructive force or the hero, and the world can use all the heroes that it can get.

ılmαɾinen

Mars in Taurus

In the Kalevala, the poetic myth cycle of the Finnish people, Ilmarinen the smith is the most singularly talented figure of all. The other heroes can do magic and swing swords, but Ilmarinen can build almost anything. His forge brings forth sorcerous items of great beauty and power. If there is something that needs to be made or fixed, he can usually take care of it. Part craftsman, part alchemist, he works day and night when the creative fever is on him.

When Mars goes into Taurus, the driving force of accomplishment is centered firmly in the element of earth. Not infrequently, however, there is a strongly aesthetic side to the industrious nature. The Venus rulership injects an element of longing for beauty, and creative people with this aspect often spend their time making beautiful things or at least making the money to be able to buy beautiful things. Ilmarinen's tireless creativity masks a secret need for luxury and comfort that becomes evident in his treatment of the women— the Venus aspects—in his life.

Ilmarinen's friend and adventuring companion Vainamoinen (Sun in Sagittarius) at one point asks him to make a vague magical item called a sampo. This creation, while never fully described, apparently is some sort of lidded container that brings forth inexhaustible wealth. It is the required bride-price of the fair eldest daughter of Louhi, queen of Pohjola, whom Vainamoinen wishes to wed. The good-natured Ilmarinen agrees to make the sampo for his friend, and after many tries he manages to come up with the precious box. He presents the sampo to Louhi, and she is so impressed with his talents that she gives her daughter to the talented smith instead of the wandering minstrel.

This is a Mars in Taurus dream come true. Taurus believes in reward through hard work, and with the energy of Mars behind it, this placement is not afraid of putting shoulder to wheel and pushing. It is a combination with a terrific amount of steady drive. Mars in Taurus people can work from the moment they wake up to the moment they drop at the end of the day, and they can keep it up, day after day, long after everyone else has fallen by the wayside or wandered off in disgust. Unlike cynical Capricorn, however, this Mars placement is ruled by Venus, so these people do (secretly or not so secretly) expect to eventually win wealth, comfort, luxury, and love through their efforts.

The first three things on this list are quite achievable; Ilmarinen does have the skill and talent to create the sampo, which brings forth wealth of all kinds. This Mars placement can often assure at least a comfortable income and modest luxury, if not much more. The problem is with the last item. Love, he finds, is not so easily won in the same way one gets money or resources. Ilmarinen finds, to his dismay, that the beautiful maiden who has been summarily handed over like a prize does not want him. All the way home on their sleigh, she weeps and complains and says that she would rather be anything else in the world than his bride. Ilmarinen keeps driving because he is stubborn and does not like to be swerved from his path (a Taurus trait) but he tears his beard in despair with every word she utters.

When his wife arrives at their home, no amount of gold showered upon her can make her any happier with the situation. Ilmarinen is at a loss, but his mother intervenes, treating the girl with caring and telling everyone how proud she is of her new daughter-in-law. Her nurturing wins the girl over when Ilmarinen's materialism does not, a trick that a Taurus Mars had best learn if he wishes to get anywhere with a potential partner.

Unfortunately, the honeymoon is short-lived. The smith takes on a slave in order to make his household more affluent, but the youth turns out to be a sly, sullen traitor. When the young wife is rude to him, he lures a bear to the house and watches while it devours her. This is one of the pitfalls of Mars in Taurus—the need for affluence can literally devour the softer aspects of a relationship. It all stems from a deep need for security, which earthy Taurus translates into financial rather than emotional security, mistaking one for the other.

This materialism and need for security can strongly affect his choice of partners. Mars in Taurus sees a relationship as an investment, and they prefer them to be like any other investment they might make—stable, long-lasting, likely to pay off big in the future, and a safe bet. If they can see financial potential in your future, that's even more attractive, although not entirely necessary. They tend to end up with people who have more money or resources than they do, although they may overtake them once they have a firm base to stand on. When a Mars in Taurus is really hurt romantically, he can give up on love entirely for a while, perhaps seeking a "kept" position as a housewife or househusband, a mistress or gigolo or other paid sexual companion, or an arranged marriage. He can stubbornly marry for money or position and consider himself lucky . . . until his Venus-ruled nature seizes him from below by making him fall madly in love with someone, usually in such a way that fulfilling the affair will wreck his carefully built security.

After Ilmarinen's wife is killed, he builds a maiden out of silver and gold, with hair of copper thread. His minions work night and day at his forge to create this living piece of alchemy, but when she is created she is a disappointment. She does not love, and she has no warmth; he tries to breathe life and warmth into her by wrapping her in blankets and bringing her close to the fire, but to no avail. Once settled into a bloodlessly secure relationship bound in silver and gold, a Mars in Taurus may attempt to breathe some actual love and affection into it. Since he's stubborn and often has low emotional expectations, this can go on for a long time, trying diligently to win the love of the person that he married for unlovely reasons. This often ends in disillusionment, however; Ilmarinen finally gives up and brings the golden wife to his friend Vainamoinen, who lectures him interminably on the love of gold and how it will not warm him.

He then goes back to his wife's family, asking for their second daughter's hand to replace that of his dead wife. They are appalled, and refuse. He becomes angry and seizes the girl, carrying her off. The girl weeps and cries, and this time his mother is not available to win her over, so he turns her into a mewing seagull and lets her fly away. It's another lesson in not letting your appetites run away from you, a lesson that needs to be driven home to a Mars in Taurus. Generally these folks move slowly and deliberately, but once in a while they fly into a fury and do rash things that they later regret. These are usually related to their prodigious appetites for all that they hold valuable, and they resent being hindered in what they see as their rightful climb to the lifestyle they prefer.

In the final episodes of the Kalevala, the sorceress Louhi steals the sun and moon and locks them inside a mountain. For once, even Vainamoinen the Wise is stymied. Ilmarinen decides that he will forge a new sun and moon, but his creations—like the golden maiden—fall short. They do not shine with their own light, and he ends up downcast. Just when you might think that he will end up the pathetic failure to be moralized about once again, the sorceress Louhi drops by his forge in the guise of an eagle. She asks what he is forging, and in the heat of his frustration he says it will be a collar to bind the evil Louhi by the neck to a great rock by the sea forever. The force of his will comes through in his voice, and Louhi becomes terrified. She immediately flies back to the mountain and releases the sun and moon.

A Taurus Mars has a will to be reckoned with, and this can be sensed by other people with lesser wills. Sometimes it means that they draw weaker folk to them who want to be protected, and sometimes it means that they can ward off predators by simply digging in their heels and saying, "No, I will not move." One rather slight woman that I know with Mars in Taurus, when menaced by a neighbor wanting to extort money, looked him in the eye and said bluntly, "I've had so many bad things happen to me that there's nothing you could possibly do to me that hasn't already been done. So get the hell out of my way." He moved. When faced with the fire of Mars behind Taurean bedrock, so would anyone.

Marduk
Mars in Gemini

Warrior gods fight battle after battle, down throughout the myths of human history, and yet the only thing we know about who won or who lost comes directly from who wrote it all down afterward. In a sense, the saying that the pen is mightier than the sword is quite true. Today, after thousands of years, all we know about the battle of Marduk and Tiamat, and how Marduk came to rule, comes from the words written by his priests. By writing down his victory, they made it true, whether it happened that way or not. Tiamat was struck down by Marduk's sword, but she was truly put to death by his scribes.

Mars in Gemini understands that words are a powerful weapon, far more permanent than any mere club or cannon, because they can keep cutting long after the hand that wrote them is dead. In the Tarot, the suit of Swords or Knives represents the element of air, acknowledging the fact that it is the mind that cuts things into small pieces by analysis. From a watery point of view, however, analysis is dissection and that which is dissected usually dies. From Gemini's airy point of view, you can't explain something adequately to someone else until you have taken it apart and seen what makes it tick.

Mars the Warrior in the mental sign of Gemini becomes a living embodiment of the blade, a knife incarnate. The knife can be a verbal rapier in a duel of wits, or a scalpel to prod things out of curiosity, or a butcher's cleaver hacking away the nebulous, the vague, or simply that which is unwanted to the spin he wants to put on things. The war between Marduk and his grandmother Tiamat (see Neptune in Pisces) may be merely a myth about change and re-creation, or it may be the echo of an ancient coup, the powers of the old matriarchy against the onslaught of the newer generation. We will never know, because Marduk's scribe-warriors did such a good job.

In the actual Babylonian myth, Marduk is one of the younger generation of gods, which is appropriate to youth-loving Gemini. Not only that, but he is not even the eldest (and most favored by the elders) son. He is a disaffected and ignored younger son, wanting an inheritance that is being given to the older and steadier children. The archetypal story of Mars in eternal-youth Gemini often becomes Youth And Energy Trumps Age And Stodginess, at least for the first part of their lives. There is something eternally youthful about any Gemini placement, but with Mars behind it, the sign manifests more as exuberant, aggressive youthfulness than as shy playfulness.

Tiamat's major complaint with her younger offspring is that they are noisy, and this too is a Mars in Gemini trait. They may give forth a constant stream of chatter, and even the ones who are quiet can easily be prodded into long, talkative lectures or rants. Marduk also has Gemini's canniness; when Tiamat's disaffected younger children approach him and ask him to overthrow their parents before they are destroyed out of pique, he extracts a promise from them that they will invest him with supreme authority should he actually win. Unlike the intellectual magician Enki or the wind god Anu, both of whom have failed to stop their ancestors, Marduk is first and foremost a warrior deity, and he plans to be a ruler.

Driving off Tiamat's armies, he slays both her and her consort. His chief weapon is the hurricane; his chariot is a violent tempest; he controls the winds. Anyone who thinks that Gemini is merely a playful, breezy air sign has never engaged one in a war of words. It can feel very much like being hit with a hurricane, especially with the driving energy of Mars behind it. The enemy is battered and buffeted by winds from all sides, until they are beaten down into hopelessness. Thus Tiamat, the dragon of the ethereal, is defeated.

Marduk then takes his blade—the cutting edge of analysis and cold, objective thought—and cuts Tiamat up into pieces. As with anything, once the force of primal generative chaos is cut into pieces and exposed for display, it is dead. This is the job of a Mars in Gemini; he cuts things to pieces and makes other things out of them. For him, the death of dissection is a prelude to creation—arranging things as he pleases. For some Gemini Mars individuals, this manifests as imagination or brilliant mental creativity; for others, it manifests as the ability to edit their own reality until it may bear no resemblance to what is actually happening. One negative trait of this placement is the stories that change, subtly, little by little, until they have become completely slanted in favor of the teller and may no longer have much to do with the truth.

Out of Tiamat's body, the ruins of the old regime, Marduk creates the heavens and earth. Her body is split "like a fish"; half is raised up and half lain underfoot. From the blood of her slain consort, Marduk creates the first humans. Then, seeing that they need laws and instructions to live by, he creates the Tablets of Fate, rules and words by which they can order their lives. For a Mars in Gemini, destruction is the prelude to creativity. In his world, the intellect always triumphs over the body and heart and soul.

However, the real world is not so simple, and Marduk's rule is not secure. First the Tablets of Fate are stolen by the storm bird Zu, another aspect of Mars in Gemini. The storm bird represents Mars's wrath. Gemini, in general, doesn't like anger. He tends to repress it, putting it aside with a quip and a jest, until it builds up inside him and then explodes. When this happens, his vaunted intellect—the Tablets of Fate—go out the window. Desperately, he advertises for a hero, even offering his kingship to anyone who can get the tablets back. Suddenly, all the other gods have something better to do, and he is forced to struggle with the storm bird himself in order to regain them. In a sense, the stormy, watery feelings that he slew in Tiamat have come back to haunt him. A Mars in Gemini must eventually come to a peaceful reckoning with that part of himself, or it will crop up again and again in new guises, each one harder to kill.

Then the worst comes. By this time, Marduk is no longer the victorious younger son. He is now the patriarch himself, and there is a new generation of disaffected youngsters who would like to remove his stodgy self from the throne. They conspire against their elders and send demons to steal the moon's light, which would be a weapon against emotionally repressed fire-and-air Marduk. The war god manages to defeat them, barely, but he is stunned at their conspiracy. Everyone gets older, and the problem with identifying constantly with the youth is that sooner or later actual youths start to disown you, and you have to face your own aging. A Mars in Gemini hates to admit that he has overcome the elder conqueror only to become the elder conqueror; he has to face the fact that the more you struggle for the top, the more likely it is that you will be called upon to embody things you did not expect.

Marduk's story ends there, but a Mars in Gemini has to live his story to the bitter end. In midlife, he needs to turn his formidable intellect to dissecting his own inner nature, even if it feels like a form of suicide, or self-death. If he does not come to terms with his vague, nebulous side before the youngsters reject him and rebel, he will have nowhere left to stand and be in for a hell of a midlife crisis. The hardest battle of all is the one against yourself, but it is here that the war god's path inevitably takes him. To be a real victor, one must not slay things in contempt for their natures but rather view them as honorable opponents, which requires some understanding of them and their reasons. If the re-creation of reality is not to become delusion, reality itself must not be dismissed but appreciated, even in all its flaws.

frey
Mars in Cancer

One of the most telling things about Frey, the Norse god of fertility, is that he is a warrior who has no sword. He starts out with a magical sword whose power was that it would practically wield itself, and with good judgment as well. Yet when he saw the beautiful giantess Gerdr, he loved her so much that he would do anything to get her, and he ended up trading his sword to her father for her hand in marriage, even though it meant that he would be unarmed at Ragnarok.

What does it mean to be a warrior without a sword? For one thing, Mars is in its fall in Cancer. The Martian urge to rush forward is constrained, made cautious, forced into a sideways crabwalk. On some level, the Cancerian Mars warrior knows that he is not as well armed as the other Mars placements, and he rarely lets himself get in the line of fire. The missing sword can symbolize the open aggression that Cancer finds too painful to manifest, or since swords and knives are often associated with air, it can symbolize a lack of clean, cutting objectivity. This is, after all, a water sign. Although Frey was most associated with the earth, he was also a son of the sea god Njord.

Sideways action, sometimes bordering on the manipulative, is the most natural one for him. When Frey fell in love with Gerdr, he did not approach her himself (shyness is often the bane of a water sign Mars). He sent his servant Skirnir to convince her, and Skirnir made a mess of things by threatening Gerdr and angering her father. Frey had to come out and negotiate in order to save things, and it is said that they had a happy marriage. The important point, however, is that Frey gave away that sword for love. This is a clue to the Mars in Cancer nature, which is the most empathic of all the Mars placements. It even tops Mars in Pisces in this regard, as the Piscean Mars may be more self-absorbed in Neptunian fantasies. To be the warrior who is open to the world's pain is a hard thing indeed. It means that you only fight when you absolutely have to: in the defense of what and whom you love and value. It also means that you are motivated by feelings, by what you love and hate. This is the most fiercely loving Mars of all.

Where Mars in Cancer comes into his own is in the domestic sphere, and this is where Frey was most honored. He was one of the Vanir, the agricultural "farmers' gods," not the upper-class warrior deities of the Aesir. He was the god of fruitfulness, fertility of the soil and livestock animals, and of course fertility among humans. He was the only god in the pantheon who could be prayed to for the gift of children. In the spring, a hole was dug in the earth and food placed in it as an offering to Frey. He gave the rain that made the crops grow and filled the larders; he was the god most closely associated with food (with the possible exception of the beer god Ing) in the pantheon.

There is a strong desire in a Mars in Cancer to protect their nurturing supply, whether that be their food, their safety, or their family. Like Frey, having peace, prosperity, children, and nourishment is his idea of a proper goal, and if he expands this goal to the outside sphere it will be an attempt to bring these gifts to others, bettering their lives.

Frey owned a magical ship named Skidbladnir, made for him by the dwarves. It could sail on the land, the sea, or through the air. It could grow large enough to hold many passengers and then shrink to fit into his pocket. Any Cancer will understand the importance of having a lifestyle that fits well with both large things and small; a Mars in Cancer often tends to run a business like a family, or vice versa. The extroverted outer world ought to feel like a bigger version of the introverted interior world, he thinks, and he is often shocked when the small rules don't fit the big picture.

To truly understand the ambivalent destiny of Mars in Cancer, one must realize that Frey was a hostage. When the Aesir and Vanir fought each other to a standstill, hostages were exchanged in order to keep the peace. Frey, his sister Freya, and his father Njord were sent to Asgard to meet the treaty demands. The idea of a homebody god like Frey being forced to leave home and live his life with strangers, especially sky gods who did not even value the things that he did, must have been incredibly painful. This often plays itself out in the life of a Cancer Mars. All too often, the home life that he strives for is strangely confining or unsatisfying. Perhaps the workload involved in sustaining and protecting his home is so great that it ceases to hold any joy for him, or he may end up surrounded by warring family members whom he is too nonconfrontational to oppose for any length of time.

Frey made his home—when he was not required to be in Asgard—in Alfheim, the faeryland of the Light Elves. A Cancer Mars can create a world in their head where everything is cozy and warm and safe, and then try to make it real. If they succeed, all is well; if they fail, they may keep going day after day by living in a state of constant denial, pretending that they are still in Faeryland while things crumble around them in reality.

However, one of Frey's gifts is the ability to free captives, and sooner or later a Cancer Mars will finally decide that he has had enough, and he will flee. He may also stand and fight, but first he is likely to attempt to get others to fight for him, like Frey whose chariot was pulled by two huge, bristling boars. Using the tusks and might of others feels safer to him than a direct engagement. It's why there are more successful generals than successful foot soldiers with Mars in Cancer; it's easier to send out someone else to do the actual fighting, to sacrifice them for love of country and homeland. We tend to forget that Frey was a sacrificial god, and men were sacrificed in his honor. To him, as to a Mars in Cancer, you ought to be willing to die for what you believe in . . . or, for less-evolved types, what he believes in.

All water sign Mars placements benefit from an understanding of deep psychology and its ability to untangle their mysterious and semiconscious urges. For a Mars in Cancer it is especially important, as he needs to decipher his ambivalent feelings about home and family, the feelings that unconsciously get him into those awful domestic arrangements. Idealizing the peaceful, prosperous home while being a hostage to the turmoil of others can take a toll on the warrior-for-love. A Mars in Cancer needs to learn that in order to create Faeryland in reality, you must first acknowledge that you are not actually in it, and then you can start to analyze the steps necessary to bring some of its energy into the world. Then, when it is strong enough, you will not have to defend it from all comers any longer; its serene and loving energy will spread out to affect everyone who touches it.

sekhmet
Mars in Leo

In this placement, Mars the Warrior combines with the solar force of Leo the Lion, and this can be an overwhelming combination of fire and sun, explosion and brilliance. It can light the sky, bring down the walls, or blow everything to pieces. Here we honor the Egyptian lioness goddess Sekhmet, whose name means "powerful." Fierce and gracious, regal and deadly, she was usually shown as a lioness-headed woman sitting on a throne. The Egyptians tried to marry her to Ptah the architect god, but she did not take well to the marriage and was generally worshipped separately. Her son was the warrior god Nefertum, who carried a curved saber and was said to have discovered how to carry coals in hollow reeds, thus bringing portable fire to the human race.

The great sun god Ra ruled the land of Egypt for many years, and when he grew old and withered, there was talk among his people of putting him down and choosing another god to replace him. Enraged, he brought forth a lioness goddess and sent her to savage his people. However, his plan worked too well; she tore through so many of them that he feared the human race would be exterminated and begged her to stop. She laughed at her erstwhile creator and refused, saying that she was not yet sated with blood. "By my life," she told him, "when I slay men my heart rejoices," and she continued the carnage.

Ra then came up with an idea to stop her by guile, since no force could stand against her. He had the frightened peasants brew up a vast quantity of beer and dye it red with pomegranate juice. This he placed in seven thousand jugs, which he placed at strategic points across the battlefield. Thinking that they were actually jars of blood, Sekhmet drank them all and became so intoxicated that she passed out, and the people were saved. From that time on, Ra decreed that on the date of her massacre, the twelfth day of the first month of winter, every priestess of the Sun should brew jugs of red pomegranate beer in order to placate her. This day was said to be unlucky and hostile, and according to Egyptian tradition, one should avoid seeing a mouse at this time.

Mars in Leo is an aggressive placement with a great love for showmanship—and yes, she has a temper. She has the potential to be a great warrior, fighting tirelessly for a cause, but first she has to learn that righteous rage is not the emotion to carry you into battle. Not only is it exhausting and hard to keep up—although a Mars in Leo will run with it further than most people—it also impairs your judgment, making you vulnerable to being tricked by the more cool-headed strategists, as Sekhmet indeed was. Mars in Leo people also require regular payment for their fighting, unlike a Mars in Aries who will do it just to prove that he can—and it has to be in the coin of appreciation, and preferably adulation. Compliments are like paychecks to them; well-earned and vital to survival.

When they are in love with you, a Mars in Leo person will shower you with gifts, usually in a public setting where it would look ungracious for you to refuse. They are not above the dramatic public proposal, either; to be fair, it's only partially social blackmail and mostly that they just want an audience for this moment of glory. Mars in Leo people expect to be noticed, and feel put out when they aren't. It is not enough for them just to win and be first in the door; they must be seen to have won. A Mars in Aries may be content with being the head of the parade; a Mars in Leo needs the adulation of the crowd as well. This need comes out in the kind of overkill that inspires Sekhmet's bloodbath. It was not enough for her to merely do the job that Ra had assigned her; she was determined to make a name for herself forever, even if it was a name of fear.

This need to be seen comes out of a Mars in Leo with all the melodrama of a silent movie star. When she is in love, the whole world needs to hear how wonderful her beloved is. When she is wounded by her lover, she raises the roof with her hysterical scenes and everyone gets to find out, loudly, how she has been betrayed. When she is angry, she may sometimes vent it on inaccurate targets in her need to have people fully understand her mood. Sudden rages, sudden tears, and sudden smiles, unheralded and often unexplained to others, are her hallmark. When she is embarrassed or unprepared, she flees. Like Sekhmet, she can get drunk on her own forward momentum and needs distractions to be able to stop herself.

The Queen of Beasts is powerful and dangerous and finds it difficult to bow to the will of others, including other planets in the chart, and she may try to run over the needs of not only those around her but of the person who has this placement. Mars in Leo people must pay tribute to this fiery goddess within, but never let her rule completely, or they may alienate everyone with their pushiness. Properly kept in check with a combination of common sense and appreciation, however, Mars in Leo can be an enthusiastic protector and a source of divine warmth.

Brigid
Mars in Virgo

Mars is a fiery, aggressive planet that is most at home in other fire signs. When it is placed in an earth sign—Taurus, Virgo, or Capricorn—it becomes all about work. The drive of Mars gets channeled into practical areas, and in Virgo it is the love of detail work. These are the editors and correctors of life's faults, the ones who go through thousands of possible errors in order to make a project as fault-free and perfect as possible. Lest this be disparaged, please recall that sometimes an error can be a hole in a HazMat suit or a couple of loose tiles on the side of a space shuttle. In order to get through this kind of mind-numbing work, you need the fire of Mars behind it.

Fire and earth. The Irish goddess Brigid was the maiden of fire, but not wildfire. She was warrior, smith, healer, and poet. In her smith guise, she is where fire meets iron, forging metal from the ground. She also has patronage of other crafts, such as fiber arts and jewelry. For Brigid, it is not just about competence—although one can certainly ask her for that—so much as it is about how a craftsman puts a piece of soul into his work. Soul into work . . . fire into earth. The hammer and the anvil. True competence is more than just making something properly, although Virgo is all about proper. Things made by true craftsmen draw the eye, invite the touch, and make you want to admire their elegance, even if they are just simple tools. There is something about them, you tell yourself as you explore them with your earth sense—touch—that is hard to explain. It makes them more than inanimate objects. It gives them something that could be called a soul, and it can be recognized even by someone who does not understand their use.

Brigid is a warrior, and we must not forget that this supposedly most humble of Mars placements is quite capable of fighting just as hard as any other Mars, and with more skill than many. To find her weapon, we must look to the rulership of the placement. Virgo is ruled by Mercury, which gives a touch of air to the fire-earth combination, and here we notice that one of Brigid's gifts is that of poetry. She supposedly invented all the Celtic alphabets, including the Ogham writing, and inspires bards and writers. It is also true that the sword of Mars in Virgo is verbal or written criticism, often pungent. All Virgo signs like to critique, but when it is Mars on the other end of the pen, you can be sliced to ribbons almost as thoroughly as a Scorpio placement. The difference is that Scorpio strikes to wound, while Virgo actually firmly believes that this is all for your own good and that you should be thankful for such attentive correction. She is often taken aback when people are not appreciative of her efforts to perfect them, using methods she would never ask anyone to use if she was not willing to use them herself. The hidden truth is that a Mars in Virgo isn't really modest at all. (What, Mars modest? Not in any sign, sorry.) She just acts that way because she feels that there's no point in calling undue attention to yourself, but in reality she believes that she really does know best and that others should listen to her if they really want to improve themselves.

Brigid is also a healer, skilled in the arts of earthly herbs and their use, reminding us that Virgo is also the sign of the doctor. A Mars in Virgo can give a drive toward the active, practical processes of healing, whether that is herbalism or allopathic medicine or apothecary work or the medical and scientific research that creates new treatments. It is an area where the careful observation of detail can make the difference between life and death, and also where Mars can pit herself against a real, unmistakable enemy: disease of the body. A good doctor needs to be partly a warrior, because it's the only way to keep from giving up when all seems hopeless and ugly, as disease often can be. If Mars in Virgo has a flaw here, it's that Virgo detachment can allow Mars to run rampant over the patient, forgetting that the "battleground" here is a living human being with their own needs and opinions. Compassion is fairly foreign to this sign, being more a quality of Virgo's opposite, Pisces, and she may need some reminding of the humanity of those she seeks to heal. They may not, in fact, actually want to be healed, and having to accept that opinion even when she thinks it ridiculous is an important trial for her. Sometimes people are just going to resist your help, and you can't run after them.

The bravery of a Mars in Virgo manifests itself in humble but still courageous ways. This is the placement that will keep going quietly when other Mars placements give up and scream in frustration. In a sense, a Mars in Virgo expects to meet difficulty, and so is not surprised when she does. Often, she uses her gift for detail and Mercurial ingenuity to solve the problem rather than flinging herself at it repeatedly until it moves or she is defeated. She is a patient untier of knots, as shown by the legend of her Christianized form, St. Brigid.

St. Brigid is an abbess, and although some people may be jarred by the transition of pagan goddess to nun, it is important to remember that abbesses often had more power, both socially and over their own groups, than any other women in medieval society. To this day, in Kildare, there is a shrine to Brigid where women (monastic and otherwise) keep a flame burning at all times in her honor. This sacred discipline has the feel of the Roman vestal virgins, related to Hestia's Virgo energy in the other fiery planet, the Sun. There is also a definite monastic feel to the sign of the Virgin, both in her concentration on work as a sacred discipline and her ability—more than any other sign—to be one-in-herself without being lonely. This is not to say that no Virgo-oriented person ever gets lonely, but they tend to be much more innately skilled at aloneness, and even require it periodically for their own spiritual development.

At any rate, St. Brigid asked the local lord for some land to build an abbey. He wasn't keen on giving any up, and so told her rather derisively that she could have as much land as she could surround with the edges of her black woolen nun's cloak. A Mars in Virgo has a tendency to take things literally, and St. Brigid decided to do just that. All day she unraveled the threads of her cloak and tied them together into one long string, and all night she unrolled it until it surrounded many acres of land. The next morning, the embarrassed lord grudgingly granted her petition, as his colleagues were applauding Brigid's ingenuity, determination, and persistence. Those three words translate into Mercury, Mars, and Earth, and they sum up the long, trudging road of this archetype of sacred work.

Arthur
Mars in Libra

There are those who believe that there was actually a King Arthur or someone of that nature, a British chieftain who fought a losing battle against the Saxons long ago. I am not interested in arguing the point. The Arthur that we know, the one who lives in mediums as diverse as Malory's *Le Morte D'Arthur* to Marion Zimmer Bradley's *The Mists of Avalon* to Disney's cartoons, is a legend, a true myth. He wears fourteenth-century armor and fights by thirteenth-century rules. He is the embodiment of the Age of Chivalry, which happened long after any British chieftain would have died out.

This Arthur belongs to the league of Hercules and Orpheus, the magical hero-god-king, not the realm of history, and it is in this guise that we place him among their ranks. The central fact of Arthur's reign is that he rules a country divided into warring parts, all of which he attempts to bring together not by force of arms but by diplomacy. To do this, he recruits as many warriors as he can and imprints upon them the code of chivalry. From the moment of their knighting, they would be expected to behave in a noble and gentle manner, even while hacking the heads off of their enemies.

A Mars in Libra is the embodiment of the chivalrous warrior. Like Arthur and his knights, he fights for justice rather than for greed or blind callousness. He has a cause that must be weighed thoroughly on his internal scales before he will take up a sword in its behalf. The code of chivalry reads like the Libra Mars value system—honor, graciousness, loyalty, courtesy, righteousness. "Not might makes right, might *for* right!" cries Arthur in the Broadway musical *Camelot*. The Arthurian knight uses diplomacy first or at least tries to dissuade and warn his adversary before charging him. He never stabs from behind and always gives the other man a fair chance. In his mind, winning by unjust means is as bad as losing.

He also holds women in high esteem, a reminder that in this placement, Mars is ruled by feminine Venus. Unlike the opposite placement, when the Aries Venus is overrun by the Martial energy, here the planet of love is in control, and she places velvet reins on her knight. The Libran Mars is motivated by an ideal, a vision, a quest for what is most beautiful and desirable. He can be the archetypal knight on the white horse pursuing the Holy Grail, gallant toward all the women in his life, carrying the favor of one special female whom he puts on a pedestal and worships as his inspiration. If the lady (or lord) in question fails to live up to his ideals, he rejects them and seeks another.

Like Arthur, romance is often the Libra warrior's downfall. His search for perfection can grate on a partner to the point where they seek the imperfect arms of another, as Guinevere ended up doing. They may also be defeated by lack of conviction; all that diplomacy may seem like prevarication and fatal indecision to the warring parties that they try to hold off. Arthur inherited a kingdom torn by religious differences; the older pagan faith was clashing with the newer, more aggressively spreading Christian religion and it was his job to keep the peace. He called himself a good Christian knight, but kept a pagan wizard by his side as an advisor; he married a Christian woman but had an affair with his pagan sister. By the end, not only was there no peace, but neither side trusted him due to his unwillingness to take any side at any time.

His worst mistake, of course, was to disinherit his illegitimate son Mordred, raised by his pagan priestess mother and aunt. Because he was not the child of a Christian legal marriage, Arthur felt that endorsing Mordred as an heir would lose him the support of his Christian knights, and so he refused to claim him. The rejected Mordred raised an army and eventually defeated Arthur, causing his death in battle. He died knowing that his hesitant attempt at compromise between two warring forces had failed. "Neither good Christian, nor good pagan, nor good husband to me!" bewails his wife in *The Mists of Avalon.*

A Mars in Libra does not like to take sides unless he is sure that it is the side of Justice and Right. Once he has actually committed to a side, however, he is an implacable fighter, fueled by his certainty that he is doing the Right Thing. He will use diplomacy until it fails, and then will be surprisingly forceful. For those who doubt the Venus-ruled temper, remember that every Libra placement is at heart an argumentative lawyer. Sometimes it even seems as if he argues for the sake of arguing.

He will also have to learn that you can't always impose peace from the top down. It is very difficult to force others to behave well or do good, and it is almost impossible to force them to want to do good. Sometimes you just cannot get people to move your way, whether you wheedle them or push them. A Mars in Libra doesn't understand why people have to behave badly. This is an air sign, and this warrior is more in touch with his principles than his feelings. I can restrain myself, he thinks, so why can't they? If they could only be made to try harder, I'm sure they'd see it my way.

The white knight may find it difficult to comprehend people's earthier or more emotional motivations and why it is so difficult for those people to transcend them. He needs to learn that he is more effective as an example than as an agent of forceful change. One of the qualities of chivalry was the attempt to civilize the mounted, well-armed, and brutal thugs that passed for knights in medieval

Europe. Many were illiterate, few had manners, and most did not respect women at all. After the chivalrous Arthurian tales of the troubadors, suddenly these thugs were being encouraged to read poetry, dance, sing, engage in polite banter, love from afar rather than drag the woman off by her hair, and fight fairly in battle. This is the ultimate goal of a Mars in Libra; by being the chivalrous warrior, and winning, he sets an example to the other Mars placements that being strong is not synonymous with being coarse and brutal. His mere presence, when he is at his best, is what makes others want to behave better. He becomes the avatar of chivalry, and he will inspire those who cluster around him to new heights, new goals, and the occasional Holy Grail of conquering love.

cuchulain
Mars in Scorpio

In Celtic mythology, Cuchulain is the greatest of all the hero-gods. Like other divine heroes, his tale is less that of a deity as a human whose magical gifts set him apart from others. He is the nephew of Conchobar, the king of Ulster, by an unknown father who may be the god Lugh. He is originally named Setanta, earning his name in his first great battle, where he kills the great Hound of Culann that protected the borders of Ulster. Realizing that he has left the kingdom short of a great protector, he offers to take the Hound's place as guardian of the lands and is renamed *Cu-Chulainn* or Culann's Hound, the name of his slain prey. This shows that he takes part in the ancestral bond between hunter and hunted, where the prey's spirit enters into its conqueror after death.

Mars in Scorpio understands death, being ruled by Pluto, and he respects a worthy fallen opponent more than most others. However, this does not stop him from attacking and conquering them. There is something of Pluto's implacability about Mars in Scorpio. He is not the big brawny boasting warrior—Cuchulain, by all accounts, was a small youth whom one would not have expected to be so physically powerful. He was handsome, with spots of blue, crimson, green, and yellow on his cheeks (probably magical tattoos) and hair that shaded from clear yellow to red (probably from the Celtic custom of dyeing hair in streaks with urine). Like Mars in Scorpio, he seems an unlikely foe at first, and then he leaps into the fray and downs fifty opponents.

This Mars placement tends to be silent and act rather than speak, but his actions can be extreme. When he decides on an enemy, nothing will do but that it must be entirely destroyed and obliterated. Scorpio loathes halfway measures, and he often lacks compassion and mercy. When Mars in Scorpio does actually get angry enough to lose his iron control, all hell breaks loose. He will do devastating things that horrified onlookers may characterize as complete overkill, and he may lose his sense of perspective—and even morality—when he is seized by this frenzied wrath.

Of all the famous warriors of mythology, Cuchulain is renowned for one thing above all else: his berserker battle-rage. Although he normally fought like an ordinary if highly skilled warrior, when he became angry he underwent a horrible transformation. First he quivered all over, and then his body began to twist backwards. His knees and shins shifted themselves to the back, as did the frontal sinews of his neck, where they protruded out like lumps. One eye receded back into his head, and the other bulged out upon his cheek. His mouth widened until it met his ears, and sparks flew out of it. His heart pounded as loud as a great metal drum, and his locks stood up on end, with a spark of flame at the end of every hair. A great horn jutted out of his forehead, and a vast spurt of black blood jetted up from his skull, where it spread out like a cloud of dark gloom over the battlefield.

Many astrology books mutter ominously about how Mars in Scorpio is prone to violence. A more accurate truth might be that Mars in Scorpio is attracted to violence, although they may not be the one who is actually assaultive. Sometimes this sign manifests as the attacker, sometimes as the one needling someone into attacking, sometimes as the one who is drawn to violent people out of fascination. Whichever version you get, it becomes clear that this placement does much better when he has an actual cause toward which to focus his violent energies. Without a goal to hurl himself against, his intensity turns inward on himself or explodes out at others. If a Mars in Aries goes into battle in a kind of glee, a Mars in Scorpio goes in with a kind of teeth-gritted, fight-to-the-death determination that smokes with barely repressed anger.

It was part of Cuchulain's birth prophecy that he should be the greatest warrior in all of Ireland and yet should have a short life. Sometimes Mars in Scorpio acts as if this is true for him, taking risks to his survival that would scare off other signs. He has a tendency to live as if death doesn't matter, and with Pluto ruling this planet, that may feel true for him. Pluto sees death as just part of a cycle, and the Scorpionic warrior would rather die than find himself in an intolerable situation. Often this placement bestows not only a lack of fear with regard to death, but a great fascination with it as well. This is the person who forges into the plague-ridden area to help others or takes the possibly fatal hallucinogenic drug, just to show that nothing can conquer him.

Indeed, it's as if he's secretly looking for something that can conquer him, and if he survives it, it becomes an ideal of great respect. The Mars in Scorpio person will only follow someone who has proven that they can outfight and outlast him. He will test all potential leaders with constant challenges and love them only if they can slap him down. If they fail to subdue him, he no longer respects them. The primitive dynamic of the alpha who rules by sheer power is strong in him. The test may be physical (can they beat him up?) or mental (can they browbeat him into submission?) or even moral (can they hold stronger and more unswervingly to some code of honor than he himself?), depending on the value system of the individual in question. It's almost as if, in spite of his formidable will, he secretly (that Scorpio word again) fears that his inner monster will get out of hand, and he'd better have a stronger person around to keep it in check.

When Cuchulain falls in love with Emer, the daughter of Forgall the Wily, he is sent off to hone his skills on Scatha's island in order to be worthy of her hand. Scatha is a martial goddess who teaches combat skills; to even approach her isle one must undergo a dangerous obstacle course, ending in a huge leap over a deep river. After a year of learning combat from her skilled teachings, Cuchulain returns and requests Emer's hand again. Forgall, intimidated by this alarming suitor, refuses him again. After Scatha's training, however, he is powerful enough that he merely kidnaps her and runs away. This is one of the Mars in Scorpio faults; if you betray or wrong him, or go back on your word, he may feel that honorable behavior no longer applies to you and that you are fair game for any sort of revenge. Before he can learn compassion, he must first embrace a code of honor and understand that dishonorable behavior, even as a means to an end or directed toward someone who may deserve it, belittles one's own spirit.

Cuchulain's downfall comes through his own pride. He meets a strange woman who propositions him; when he rudely refuses and threatens to kill her, she reveals that she is the Morrigan, the Irish goddess of battle and death (see Mercury in Scorpio). She tells him that she has owned him since his birth, and that he should do her honor by becoming her lover. When he responds yet more rudely, certain of his own power, she says that she will take away the ungrateful life that she has given him. They meet later to fight, and Cuchulain temporarily overpowers her, but she comes back in another incarnation—the sorceress Maeve, who swears to destroy Cuchulain.

Cuchulain is bound by a number of geases—odd taboos that he must obey or lose his power. In Celtic myth, the greater the power, the more numerous and difficult the geases. This can reflect a Mars in Scorpio's addiction to doing things the hard way, loading himself down with extra challenges. It can also reflect the weird fears that may assail him from the watery depths of his unconscious; being a water sign ruled by the planet of the mysterious dark void, he has plenty of these. At any rate, Maeve and her band of hired sorceresses set deliberate traps for him that are geared to every one of his geases, forcing him to violate them all. His power is diminished and his enemies conquer him at last, although he fights defiantly to his last breath.

Cuchulain dies because he has failed to fully acknowledge that he has no power over death and that he must give some gratitude to the Powers that sustain him. So much of Mars in Scorpio's time is spent attempting to be independent that he often forgets how interdependent we all are and how that cannot be escaped. He also fails to properly appreciate Lady Death and her place in the world; after all that time spent ending other people's lives, when Death comes along and offers deeper knowledge of what he has been handing out blindly, he rejects her. This is crucial for a Scorpio Mars, who is fascinated with death. However, he needs to learn death's place in the cycle of life on a deep spiritual level in order to properly respect it. If he has no respect for death, then she will come, in one form or another, to teach it to him directly.

shango
Mars in Sagittarius

Fire. It leaps and dances and reaches for the sky. It comes down from the sky as lightning, which was perhaps where our ancestors first gained its use. It warms us, perhaps even allows us to survive . . . and it eats things, if we let it. That's why anger is associated with fire. That's also why warriors are associated with fire. They can kill to protect and defend, or they can kill for less honorable reasons. They carry a two-edged sword, or in Shango's case, a double-bladed stone axe. Mars, the red planet of warriors, has fiery energy, and Mars in any fire sign has the double-edged gift of righteous rage to deal with.

Shango is the Afro-Caribbean Yoruba *orisha*, or deity, of fire. His colors are red and white, and he loves offerings of beer and spicy food. (Actually, it's rare to meet someone with Mars in Sagittarius who doesn't like beer and spicy food.) One of his sacred animals is the horse, which strikes sparks from its hooves when it runs. Like Mars in Sagittarius, Shango is at heart an impulsive person who prefers to work fast, run fast, and act on the first things that he feels. Sometimes this is genius intuition, sometimes it is disaster. He is straightforward and not very diplomatic, and prefers to get right to the point without frills, also a Sagittarian trait.

According to the myth of Shango, the orisha started out as a mortal king. He was a great ruler who won many battles, wooed many women, and was loved for his strength of personality. After his death, when he became a divinity, he slowly grew in popularity until he was one of the most prominent of all the orishas. Even today, he is exceedingly popular with young men, athletes, and anyone who likes to bet on sports teams. Altars of red and white beer cans and spicy corn chips are built to him during the Super Bowl.

Shango originally held the powers of Ifa, the prophetic oracle, but he traded them to Orunmila for the ability to dance. Sagittarius is associated with psychic gifts such as "flash" precognition or short-term prophecy, but they have a terrible time with Cassandra complexes—only being believed when their advice is not followed and being discounted when it is followed and the disaster fails to appear—and they can often suppress or discount their ability to look ahead. Other things, especially with the Mars in Sagittarius placement, are much more interesting to them, like dancing. Shango's love of dancing is not only about a fun and sexy pastime—which Mars in Sagittarius, with his direct approach to courtship, adores—but it is also an athletic discipline. This is often a very physical Mars with a good deal of athletic ability if the rest of the chart does not block it. Dancing was traditionally a form of training for warriors, creating flexibility and agility. Warriors often danced before battle in primitive cultures, both in order to work themselves into a frenzy and to loosen their muscles. They danced afterward as well, telling the story of their triumphs and losses, impressing the watching women in the process.

One of the wonderful things about the tales of the orishas is that they all seem to be reformed sinners. All have committed some great sin in the past that they have repented of and learned better, and perhaps paid a great penance for committing. In many of these cases, the penance was self-inflicted, as the orishas learned that these actions were not worthy of them. In Shango's case, during his tenure of mortality, the god of fire frequently started brawls with others, friends and foes alike. Anything that angered him was worthy of instant combat, and he was all too easily angered by any perceived injustice or insult. Too often his fists and axe flew to defend some idea or principle, and since he was a great warrior, he usually won—at least the physical battle.

One of the problems of a fiery Mars is the ability to control one's anger and channel it properly. For a Mars in Aries, the anger is deeply personal, from perceived insult to one's person; for a Mars in Leo, anger comes from lack of being appreciated. A Mars in Sagittarius is different in that for him, the insult is to his ideas, his principles, and his dreams of how the world could be. There is a streak of the fanatic in every placement of Sagittarius, and Mars in particular tends to turn the warrior into the crusader. He must make sure that the crusader's sword does not mow people down unjustly; in the blinding light of righteous rage, smaller concerns are often missed and trampled underfoot.

Shango's reign came to an end when his best friend, someone who had been with him from the beginning and who was one of the few who dared to disagree with him, began a quarrel over some minor point. Shango lost his temper, attacked his friend, and killed him. Standing over the body, the rage cleared from his mind and he realized that he had lost all control over himself and his life; he had murdered the one person who had given him the gift of honesty, the gift that every Sagittarian values most when all is said and done. He realized that his honor was broken entirely, and that only one thing could atone for his deed. Bowed with grief, he did that thing; he hanged himself from a tree, ending his life.

His people were all too frightened by his deed—or disapproving of his murder—to cut down his body, so it was Oshun the goddess of love, occasionally the lover of Shango, who cut him down and dressed his body. The orishas then held a council and decided that Shango's instant atonement for the murder he had committed had washed the blood from his hands and restored his honor; they resurrected him and made him one of them, giving him the gift of fire. His tale is of the fall of hubris, and it is a good one for a Mars in Sagittarius to remember. It is possible, when one is sure that one is in the right, to attempt to force others to believe as you do, and it never works. Even if you are sure that they are wrong, you must at least try to understand the motivations behind that belief before you attempt to change them, even by the most diplomatic methods. And no one—no one—ever truly changed their mind by being attacked.

For a warrior to be something other than a mere thug, he needs a code of honor to restrain his ardor and guide his judgment. Part of honor is honesty, not only with others but with oneself, which a Mars in Sagittarius needs to learn. Another part is having something to fight for that you believe in, which he already instinctively knows. Each of these places limits on the other, making sure that one can reach one's dreams without crushing underfoot the needs of others. Fire, after all, is dangerous. It is also the sustainer of life. Perhaps that's true of anything worth having at all.

Ogoun
Mars in Capricorn

In the Afro-Caribbean Yoruba faith that spread, with imported African slaves, all over the Americas, Ogoun is the Hunter and the Smith. Earthy and practical, he nonetheless is a man of action. Work is his prime motivating force, and he never stops. Dour and uncompromising, he glares up from his hammering at the anvil to see you, to see through you, to find what mortal annoyance is now taking up his time, and to either dismiss you or give you a curt but terrifyingly accurate answer. It is all you will get, and it had better be enough.

Ogoun is the patron of all metalworkers, from the ancient forge to the modern factory, including all machinery. As all metal weapons are also under his patronage, his followers place knives, guns, hammers, and power drills on his altar. His altar in a worshipper's home is often the toolbench, piled high with metal objects, or the gun cabinet. As a hunter, he prefers four-legged meat as an offering; he is an unapologetic carnivore, and his favorite drink is gin.

As the god of the jungle, happiest among the trees, Ogoun is solidly planted in the element of earth. His sacred colors are green and black, like foliage and soil, and his number is four, like the stable square. At one time Ogoun was persuaded to come out of his lone jungle workshop and administrate things as king of all the people, and he agreed. For centuries he ruled fairly if grimly, but eventually he became tired of the demands of mortals and abandoned the throne, returning to his life of solitude and work. This is often a Capricorn problem; on the one hand, Capricorn's nature is solitary at heart, but on the other Capricorn's ambition forces him into the public arena. The price of becoming the head honcho is often a loss of precious privacy, and this can contribute to Capricorn's dourness, arrogance, and insensitivity. Ogoun, of course, had the sense to leave and go back to his retreat before he became unbearable.

Another area of Ogoun's patronage is the police and the military; the men and women that he protects are not lone warriors but soldiers willing to stand in lines and wear identical uniforms, not the heroes on a quest but the guardians of the people. He is especially fond of police officers, as they combine the archetype of the uniformed soldier with that of the hunter; one makes offerings to Ogoun to avert their gaze. In this, he shows the Capricornian value placed on protecting the status quo and regulating society. As king, Ogoun specialized in creating just laws and a strong army; good organization is his goal. His translation of Mars energy works in a structured, government-approved group for the good of all society; there will be no running off on wild solo actions from which you might never return. It's just not practical.

However, Ogoun has a darker, more violent history, symbolized by the leopard form he takes on to hunt. As a youth, Ogoun was seized with a desire for his mother Yemaya and began to rape her on a regular basis; his Mars energy began by expressing itself in violence. When Ellegua discovered and exposed him, and Shango brought charges against him to Obatala, Ogoun confessed immediately; he might be violent and secretive, but he had a basic honesty to his nature that argued against undignified excuses and side-stepping. Obatala asked him to choose his own punishment, and Ogoun did not spare himself. Realizing that his sexuality was out of control, he willingly took on a curse of eternal workaholism; from that time on, Ogoun would work continually and never stop, directing his Mars energy into creating things rather than destroying them. To this day, however, women who are menstruating are discouraged from presenting themselves to Ogoun's altar, as his leopard nature might still be triggered at the scent of blood and he might attack them.

Ogoun combines in himself Capricorn's work ethic and the warrior qualities of Mars; like those with Mars in Capricorn, he has a violent streak based on a Saturn-ruled lack of compassion for others. It can get out of hand if it is not consciously directed toward more constructive activities, something that the Mars in Capricorn individual has to figure out for himself. Structure and work, gifts of the Saturn rulership, change the power of this Mars placement from potential brutality to potential creativity. Since Ogoun's self-induced ascetic punishment, he has been austerely upright. His integrity is as hard and uncompromising as the iron that he pounds; he is the patron of disciplined soldiers and police officers, not of thugs. He takes action in the name of justice; he both understands the black heart of the sociopath and fights against it.

A Mars in Capricorn understands this deal—eternal vigilance earns eternal redemption, inner demons need to be worked to the surface with time and effort. The planet of fiery Mars and the sign of hard Saturn meet between the blacksmith's hammer and anvil; you are forged in fire and pounded with unceasing blows, and you either break beneath the force or are tempered into steel.

Enki

Mars in Aquarius

In ancient Sumer and Babylonia, Enki was known as the Organizer of Creation, Magician, Master of Ritual and Incantation, Mediator Between Gods and Men. He was the god of wisdom and knowledge, whom even the other gods consulted when they needed troubleshooting of one kind or another. His name meant "lord of the clay," a reference both to the earth and to the river clay that was dug out to press cuneiform letters into. One of his epithets was *Ningiku*, which translates to "he whom nothing escapes," as he was Lord of the Sacred All-Seeing Eye. His priests channeled his wisdom through their mouths, much as today's Aquarian Age mystics still do.

In Babylon, he was called Ea, which means House of Divine Waters. He was not, however, a marine god, nor one of lakes and rivers. The particular kind of water that Enki/Ea ruled was not physical water but the Apsu, the ethereal waters that surrounded Earth in Sumerian myth. The world floated on these waters, which bounded it in a manner vaguely reminiscent of the Norse Midgard Serpent. Like Aquarius, the Water Bearer who carries the water of divine wisdom in his jug, Enki's intelligence and creativity poured itself out onto the world and nourished it.

His main job was that of inventor god, but Enki does not invent people or nature or things so much as he invents ideas. Specifically, he created the *me*, which are ritual spells used to make a particular activity possible/sacred/blessed/competent/fortunate. They are partly rules for the socially appropriate method of doing something and partly charms for its success. There are *me* for everything under the sun; *me* for the working of religious duties, rulership, crafts, warfare, diplomacy, architecture, birthing, and dying. The final *me* is the most important: the *me* for making decisions, without which none of the other ones are useful.

Like Enki whose genius invented all the rules of society, a Mars in Aquarius likes to think that he, too, is a genius and that his ideas for how society should be run are far superior to how they are actually run. He has many opinions on that, too. Whether he is the rebel or the reformer or the counter-reformer, he prides himself on being able to think outside the box, come up with the creative solution that no one has found yet, and save the day with ingenuity. He moves fast and thinks fast and hates being tied down to one place or system or idea. Sometimes he can be the intuitive virtuoso that points out the flaw and invents the solution on the spot, the whiz kid of concepts. (Enki is the one who figures out how to get someone past Ereshkigal when Inanna is held captive; since she will resent and slay both men and women, he creates two people who are both and neither.) He continually searches for the perfect master plan—the *me*, if you will, for fixing everything. Some Aquarian Mars people are suckers for the get-rich-quick scheme for this reason.

All his intellectual tinkering, however, has an eventual goal of changing things. Any plan to change the world is irresistible to a Mars in Aquarius, which places the warrior planet in the sign of innovation. His ideas, which with a little prodding can become ideals, are worth fighting for in his mind, perhaps violently. Those who disagree with him are merely wrong, shortsighted, and can be ignored or rolled over if necessary. This is not a diplomatic placement; Uranian lightning does not make Mars any more thoughtful and may actually make him less so.

Enki is, by nature, a random and arbitrary god. He gives all the *me* to Ishtar in a drunken fit of generosity, and as soon as he sobers up he decides to take them all back—by force if necessary. Showing Martial rage, he sends army after army of interesting creatures to attack her, birds and fish and strange hairy monsters. Her faithful female servant fends them off, but each time the attack is renewed until she reaches land and he can no longer chase her.

Enki's actions often don't make any sense except to him, which is something that the loved ones of an Aquarian Mars can relate to. He can become so caught up in what he believes to be true or right or at least worth trying that he forgets other people have feelings and thoughts and values that are radically different from his. It also fails to occur to him that those opinions might have as much value as his own, that they might actually teach him something. Another thing he might forget is to apprise bewildered people of why he is doing what he is doing, even if it will waste his fast-flying time.

One myth of Enki tells that he mated with a goddess named Ninhursag, and then with her (and his) daughter, and then with their granddaughter. Ninhursag stole the semen from her granddaughter's thighs and used it to fertilize the ground. Eight plants sprang up, but Enki realized where they had come from and ate them. Ninhursag cursed him and the plants promptly made him ill. This parable does not imply that Mars in Aquarius is more likely than any other sign to commit incest; the myth is much more subtle than that. It does imply that like Enki, he can go on to a newer idea or cause or project or passion, and then a newer and newer one, perhaps without finishing or valuing the first one. It also implies that he can see himself so strongly as the idea whiz kid that he finds anyone else's creations threatening, especially if their discoveries came out of his. This can create quite a few interpersonal problems. In the myth, Ninhursag fertilizes herself with the last of the stolen semen and gives birth to eight gods, each of which heals a part of his body. If a Mars in Aquarius can see other people's use of his ideas as a natural evolution, if he can keep from being proprietary and let them go as one might let children go, he can keep his relationship with others, the universe, and himself whole and healthy.

psyche
Mars in Pisces

If Mars is the principle of action, then Pisces is the most difficult position for a Mars placement. It is the most passive of the Mars signs and often has difficulty getting started, but the myth of Psyche can outline a game plan for the maturation of a Mars in Pisces.

Psyche was a princess of ancient Greece, thought to be so beautiful that she was compared to Aphrodite herself. The goddess, enraged, demanded that Psyche be sacrificed, tied to a rock and devoured by a monster. To this Psyche submitted without any noticeable struggle. Mars in Pisces people are often passive, molding themselves to the idealized image, and the wishes, of others.

Once chained to the rock awaiting her fate, however, Psyche was sighted by Eros, the son of Aphrodite and the god of love. He fell instantly in love with her and, saving her from the monster, spirited her away to his high castle. They were married in darkness, and Psyche never saw her bridegroom's face. Knowing that his mother would be enraged by his marriage to a mortal, he told Psyche that he would only visit her at night and that she must never look upon him in the daytime. To this, again, she submitted passively. But then her sisters came to visit her and voiced serious doubts about this strange husband who never showed his face. "What if he is a terrible monster?" they asked. Often it takes the worried or skeptical voices of a close confidante to awaken a Mars in Pisces out of the dreamy self-enclosed passivity that has blinded them to the fact that they are living in an intolerable situation.

So Psyche crept into Eros' bedroom and held a lit candle over his face. Unfortunately, as she marveled at the handsome god, a drop of wax fell from the candle and woke him. Seeing that his wife had broken her promise, he flew angrily out the window. When a Pisces type gets into a relationship where their giving natures and natural unaggressiveness is taken advantage of by an inconsiderate mate, they often let things slide for a long time before taking any action to defend themselves. Then, on the day they finally rebel, the partner is shocked out of their complacency and reacts through defensive violence or abandonment.

Weeping, Psyche fled the palace, only to be found by Aphrodite, who offered her a challenge. In order to prove that she was worthy of marriage to a god, she must complete four near-impossible tasks. Then, and only then, she would be united with Eros. Distraught, Psyche agreed. For the first task, she was required to sort an enormous pile of seeds and kernels into smaller piles of each type of grain. Despairing, she was about to give up when a train of tiny ants came to her aid and did the job. These ants represent the process of mental sorting and organization, of getting one's priorities straight. In order for a Mars in Pisces to mature, they must first decide what it is that they value, what they can do without, and what they want for the future, in order of importance. Then they must outline the steps needed to achieve these goals and follow them with uncharacteristic antlike patience. In this way, the watery nature of Pisces learns something of the patience of earth.

For the second task, Psyche was required to rescue some fleece from a flock of huge rams who fought together daily in a meadow, charging about and battering their horns together. Knowing she would be crushed if she entered the field, Psyche waited until they had left for the evening and then pulled the strands of fleece off of the bushes that the rams had brushed against. A Mars in Pisces is often not cut out for the arena of conflict that we see in corporate and public life; the gladiatorial challenges of ambition and politics bruise them, and they must learn to stand aside and wait for the right moment to seize what they need without entering into head-banging conflicts. For this they need strategy and cleverness. In this case, water is learning how to handle situations where fire signs have set the rules and have all the advantages.

For the third task, she was instructed to fetch a flask of water from a rushing river at the bottom of a gorge so steep that no mortal could climb it. This time an eagle came to her aid, swooping down and scooping the water from the dangerous waves. The eagle represents objectivity, the ability to fly high and see far, to plan ahead to the next horizon, to get a clearer and more distanced view of emotional problems. This is an important lesson for a Mars in Pisces, who as a water sign tends to get mired in their own emotional conflicts, as well as that of others. Here the elemental nature of air has something to teach watery Pisces.

For the final and most difficult task, Psyche had to descend into the underworld to borrow Persephone's beauty box for Aphrodite. The kind of beauty inherent to Persephone is different from the kind of beauty associated with Aphrodite, and with Psyche as well. The ability to charm, to beckon, to seduce, and to bring joy to the body, senses, and imagination is the golden gift of Aphrodite to humanity. But Persephone, the queen of the underworld, has a different kind of beauty. It is the beauty of soul, of experience, of the serenity born of long struggle with one's own personal underworld, the dark and ghost-ridden place within each of us. A Mars in Pisces must eventually make this journey into the depths, to meet Persephone, as Psyche did, at the center of the underworld.

To make the task even more difficult, Psyche was told that at each turn of her journey, she would meet pitiful lost souls who would beg her to stop and help them. However, if she paused on her journey, she would be lost with them, and so she must turn away from their plaintive cries. This is perhaps the most difficult task of all for compassionate, empathetic Pisces. Their instinct is to offer help even at the expense of their own emotional energy and boundaries. Learning to say no to friends, co-workers, mates, parents, and obligations, especially when the cries seem especially helpless, is a hard lesson, but an important one if they wish to be able to make that underworld journey undistracted. The ghosts can also be the internal ghosts on the way down; a Mars in Pisces has to learn not to become obsessed with one fear, one problem, or one difficulty at the expense of the deeper experience.

When she had completed her tasks, Psyche was reunited with Eros, but this time as a goddess; Aphrodite granted her immortality. Only when a Mars in Pisces has matured and can form their own boundaries, centered around themselves instead of the mate, guru, or dream that they desire, fear, and expect to solve their problems for them, can they have a truly equal relationship. Psyche's reuniting with Eros can also be seen internally, as the feminine Pisces energy seeking a masculine active principle but needing to mature to the point where she is comfortable with herself before she can become one with her masculine self, yin and yang within, decisive and gentle, firm and compassionate, with beauty of both outer and inner worlds.

4   Jupiter

zeus

Jupiter in Aries

Aries is the first of the signs, the harbinger of beginnings, the fresh start, the enthusiastic child. Aries is also the warrior, pushing his way through the battle, sword in hand and shielded by his ideals. He wants to be first to look on the new land, pass the gateway, brave the storm. He is courage against all odds. He is the explorer who will not let fear or pain or discomfort stop him from his path. He rushes across the paths of others, sweeping all before him in his Mars-ruled warrior's instinct.

Long ago, the people that we now call the Indo-Europeans rolled across Europe in waves of settlers, each wave a few centuries apart. They were numerous and their technology was greater than that of the sparsely settled peoples whose land they moved in on. The first waves were wagon-peoples, agricultural, in great wains drawn by oxen; they settled in among the natives and intermarried. Then, later, the second waves began to come through, and they had changed from their earlier relatives. Adopting the horse culture, they lived and fought from the backs of their steeds, and their philosophy was Take and Go. Every one was a skilled fighter—more skilled than the agricultural people that they invaded, who were quickly subjugated in terror.

When the dust had cleared, the horse-culture warriors had set themselves up as the masters and upper caste in the new society, where their profession would be the most honored; where the ability to kill would be more valued than the ability to grow; where courage was the foremost virtue and peace was scorned as a coward's way. These Mars-like invaders brought with them their chief god, called by many different names, all meaning "father." He was Zeus, Zu, Zagreus, Dis Pater, Jove, Dyaus Pitar, eventually Ju-piter, king of the warriors. He was not a god of the earth. He was fire and wind, rain that fertilized the passive ground and the blazing thunderbolt that smote it in his fury. He lived in the heights, where man could not touch him but only gaze upward in awe. As the sky, he covered all creation with his power and could thus be worshipped anywhere. To pray to him, warriors plunged the points of their swords into the earth, symbolic of the thunderbolt, and knelt before the blade that was his symbol. He was the first of the great warrior-gods, and he made his way into the pantheon of every subjugated culture, usually taking one of the chief goddesses to wife, often whether she was agreeable or not.

The Grecian king of the gods, Zeus, is a clear incarnation of this original warrior's deity, perhaps the most clear and obvious. He is a regal ruler with a cosmopolitan civilization around him, but under the thin veneer of his sophistication he is still a barbarian. Like the horseback ancestors who brought him, he rules with an iron hand and no one gainsays him without peril. He throws fits of temper that often end up in impulsive cruelty, only some of which he is sorry for later. He will try to take any woman of lower rank that he sees and wants, even through her anguish and that of his fidelity-obsessed wife. His vengeance is terrible and his patronage a blessing. At his right side stands his son Ares, the incarnation of the soldier, and at his left is his daughter Athena, strategist and wise counselor. In other words, he is the perfect archetype of the Indo-European warrior-king.

With this kind of larger-than-life characterization and power, it is no wonder that one of his names was applied to the planet of all things large and abundant. Wherever Jupiter is astrologically, nothing is done by half measures. The gifts of Jupiter are accompanied by an urge to use those gifts as often as possible in as big a way as you can manage. He can, if you let him, take over your life, just as the horseback invaders took over all of Europe and half of Asia.

This kind of enormous scheme, the glorious Take Over The World plan, is a good example of the kind of colossal ideal that an individual with Jupiter in Aries can dream up. After all, who would believe that a bunch of guys with horses and swords could subjugate so many other peoples? If we didn't have evidence that it had happened, we would never believe it. Yet a Jupiter in Aries dreams that big. His dreams may not be of the military conquest of lands or peoples; they may be of great business success or great scientific achievements, or perhaps just climbing Mount Everest alone, but they will be Big, whatever they are.

Unlike Sagittarius, he may not even be particularly interested in what is on top of the mountain or beyond the horizon. He does it because he wants to prove that he can do it; each adventure is as much a personal test of his own mettle as an adventurous journey. When the project is done and things are calm and peaceful, then he must move on to the next thing or be bored. A bored Jupiter in Aries is a dangerous thing, because in his dissatisfaction and ennui he can start violating other people's rights for his own entertainment, like Zeus—anything to create some excitement on straitlaced Olympus.

Whatever his dream, you can be sure that in its final incarnation—in his mind, at least—he will be at the head of the parade, running the show, being the leader that all others look up to. Zeus was actually not the best of all possible rulers, as he had many faults, but somehow most of his people still loved him and those that didn't felt that he was too powerful to unseat. This, too, is often how others see the Jupiter in Aries person; some love him for his quality of faith in himself and his vision, and others are intimidated by his relentless energy, at least usually enough to get out of his way.

Jupiter is the guardian of faith, and a Jupiter in Aries must have faith in this dream of conquering something, even if it is only his own fears and smallnesses. Like Zeus, he is extravagant and expects to win. His vision of the world is often brighter, cleaner, and less complicated than the reality, and he is often shattered when he realizes the gap between the two. And, like Zeus, rage is usually his first reaction to the world's betrayal of his dreams. That's when the thunderbolts start flying.

Yet in the older mythology, those thunderbolts were thought to stimulate life in the earth and water, and scientists now speculate that the first microbes of actual life may well have come about through the electricity of lightning rippling through the primordial waters, so this ancient belief may not have been simply an empty myth. It's the sort of story that would enchant Jupiter in Aries. After all, his sign rules the kiss of first life, the one that wakes the sleeping princess, and isn't that the way all good hero-stories should end?

ganesha
Jupiter in Taurus

If the elephant had to be classed under a sign, it would be Taurus. Immense, strong, and intelligent, they travel in protective family groups and stay with wounded or dying members. Male and female elephants are referred to as "bulls" and "cows," and they are descended from some kind of herd animals that did time in an aquatic environment. We think of elephants as silent, but recent studies have shown that they are quite talkative. The pitch of their voices, however, is so deep as to be mostly below the hearing threshold of mere humans. Like Taureans, they actually have a lot to say, but we don't notice it and so assume that they are silent and dull. In India, they were the symbol of wisdom and the most beloved god.

The mythical explanation for Ganesha's elephant head was that he tried to keep his volatile father Shiva out of his mother's bedroom, and the angry destroyer god—who had been gone so long that son and sire did not recognize each other—blew off his head in a fit of rage. When Parvati wailed that he had beheaded his own son, Shiva promised him the head of the first creature that came along. It happened to be an elephant, and thus Ganesha gained both a new head and a source of elephantine wisdom.

He is prayed to not just for wisdom, however, but for prosperity. Ganesha is a god of wealth, luxury, comfort, and good home cooking—all the things on a Taurus wish list. Like every Jupiterian god, he gives generously and openhandedly. By far the vast majority of offerings made to him are for money; he understands why it's so needful and finds ways to let it come into people's hands. People with this placement often have a little bit of Ganesha's magic; they may not be rich, but when they need the cash flow, it magically appears, if only enough to keep them for another day. This is the placement of money luck, but it only works if they are equally generous with outgo. The Taurus Jupiter who hoards his wealth will find that no more of it mysteriously shows up. The planet of bounty expects you to aid him in his work if you want the handout. Ganesha carries an alms-bowl in one of his four arms, showing that he expects as much generosity from his supplicants as he himself gives them.

Jupiter is also the sign of overdoing things, and Ganesha, true to his Taurus nature, is a glutton. His belly is huge and fat, symbolizing abundance, and he prefers to be offered huge amounts of food by his devotees. One day, when he had gorged himself on offerings so heavily that he could hardly walk, he decided to take a ride on his rat in order to stir up his digestion. A large snake slid across their path, and the rat reared and tossed him off. Ganesha hit the ground so hard that his belly burst open. In order to repair the damage, he seized the snake and wrapped it around his belly like a truss. The moon laughed at the sight, and in a fit of bull-like rage Ganesha hurled one of his tusks at it, wounding it so badly that it still shrinks in pain every month.

However, this was a rare outbreak of violence; for the most part Ganesha is gentle, calm, and loving. He likes people, and people like him. Jupiter in Taurus people often have this knack for appearing friendly and personable to members of all classes. Often they move in and out of many different social circles, unobtrusive but valued for their affable natures. The people in these different circles may not have any idea how solvent these natives actually are; they can pass as comfortably well-off or humble working-class as they choose.

Ganesha's tusk also doubles as a writing pen; he is said to have written the Mahabharata with a tusk dipped in ink. He is the patron of literature and also the protector of children. Taurus is possessive, and no one messes with his family members. With the Jupiter influence, his protective nature can come out with an abundance of zeal, which is probably how Ganesha got his head blown off. His mother didn't need to be protected from his father, but in his Jupiterian self-confidence and Taurean possessiveness he thought that he could stand up to the forces of destruction and win.

A Jupiter in Taurus can also endow one with a wealth of common sense and the ability to see through the complexities to the shortest route. In another tale of Ganesha, the gods all gathered on their magical animals for a race around the world. Everyone laughed at the fat elephant-headed god who was riding a rat, symbol of canny practicality and survival. The rule was that whoever crossed the finish line first would be the most revered of the gods. After the signal was given, the other divinities flew or raced around the earth; Ganesha considered the situation, rode his rat a few feet behind the finish line and crossed it. At the other gods' wrath, he pointed out that the rule only specified that one must cross the finish line first, not that one had to go around the world beforehand. The other gods had to admit that he had found the loophole, and from that time on Ganesha was the most beloved of all gods.

Ganesha's association with money is such that he is the all-time favorite god of shopkeepers and businessmen in India. His shrines are kept in banks to keep them solvent, and if a bank in town fails, all the shops turn their Ganesha figures to the wall for a day in mourning. We westerners often have a strange attitude toward wealth: we all want it, but we don't like to admit that we want it. Those of us that have it want to show it off, but feel guilty about it. People who gain more wealth and rise in class tend to drop their poorer friends. We don't understand that wealth is for spreading around, that the true measure of one's monetary status is how much you can give away to others and still remain solvent. It's a lesson that we desperately need to learn from Ganesha, the god of resourcefulness and plain old good cheer.

Lemminkainen
Jupiter in Gemini

In the Kalevala, the Finnish myth cycle, one of the most fascinating figures is the mischievous hero-god Lemminkainen. Born amid many islands, his wise old mother raises him in strength and perfection of both body and mind. With her magical charms, she makes sure that he has the gifts of war, magic, scholarly learning, and the hunt. By the time he is grown, he has become a notable hero. But he has a streak of the mischievous trickster in him; he is still more Till Eulenspeigel (the German folktale trickster) than Hercules.

First of all, this is a hero with two names—Ahti and Lemminkainen. Somewhat confusingly, he is referred to by either name in what seems a random order. Which is his true name? Well, why should he settle for only one true name? It's not uncommon for

Jupiter in Gemini to have two names, or two identities, or even two lives. With Jupiterian luck, he often manages to pull it off far longer than anyone else might. He might even have more than one lover, who may or may not be aware of each others' presence.

This is Lemminkainen's first downfall: he likes the women altogether too much, and he flits from one to the next without thinking of their feelings. Finally, however, he sets his sights on one particular girl: the beautiful virgin Kyllikki. She is of a higher station than he, and she has turned down every suitor who can come for her, including the sons of the Sun and Moon and North Star. This is another Jupiter in Gemini problem: if you want him to stop messing around and focus on wanting one thing very badly, just make it unattainable. The more he's told that he can't have it, the more he wants it.

When he arrives at the maiden's house, he is in such a hurry that he manages to overturn his chariot in her yard. A Jupiter in Gemini has the gift of speed, and he likes to do everything fast—think fast, talk fast, make fast decisions. Sometimes his speed is an asset and sometimes it means that he can miss details or make poor choices. However, he usually has the gift of words and charm and the gift of a clever mind, and he generally uses these to get him out of trouble time and time again. This is Lemminkainen's power as well: at first all the handmaidens of his paramour's household mock him, but within a month they are all charmed and smitten by his words and talents.

Kyllikki, however, is unmoved. Finally Lemminkainen, in a burst of impetuousness, snatches her and carries her off in his chariot. She weeps and pleads to be returned, but he woos her with sweet words and tells her everything that he will give her, and she finally falls under his spell and agrees to marry him. It's the kind of thing that only a sweet-talking Jupiter in Gemini could pull off without terrible repercussions. As a last request, she makes him promise to give up his raiding for loot, and he makes her promise not to go to public dances where she could flirt with other men. His mother praises him for bringing home such a beautiful and high-ranking wife, and for the moment all is well.

However, Kyllikki becomes bored simply waiting on her clever husband and goes off to the public dances after all. Lemminkainen flies into a fury and announces that he is going off to raid the wizards of Lapland. Both his wife and his mother plead with him not to go, as they feel that even with all his skills, he is no match for Lappish wizards. He refuses to listen and charges off in his chariot. He finds a castle full of wizards and slays them all with his Words of Power.

Like many placements where Mercury is involved—including this case, when Mercury rules Jupiter—words have a special power to the individual. A Jupiter in Gemini is clever with words and symbols; he usually has a good memory and is proud of his cleverness. Lemminkainen slays his foes not merely with a sword, but with chanted and sung magical spells. However, he spares one old blind shepherd, whom he mocks and sends away. The old man swears vengeance on him and stumbles off.

Lemminkainen now decides that he will take himself another wife to replace his imperfect Kyllikki, and he demands that the queen of the fortress give him her eldest daughter. She refuses, saying that the girl can only be won by a suitor who slays the wild moose of the Laplands. Undaunted, the hero has a smith make him a pair of magical snowshoes and sets off on the adventure. The wild and magical moose, however, proves too great a prey; it smashes his snowshoes, javelins, and arrows, and bounds away. Chagrined, Lemminkainen prays to the gods of the forest and the hunt, and they aid him in catching the moose. When he brings it back to the queen, she tells him that her daughter can only be won by the man who captures for her a horse of fire that lives in the mountains. This task, too, he completes, and she sends him on a third one—to bring back the black swan that swims the river on the border of Tuonela, the Land of the Dead.

This time the great hero is foiled. As he kneels beside the river to shoot the swan, he is shot in turn by the old blind shepherd, who has prayed to the gods of the dead for vengeance. His body falls into the river and is chopped to pieces by the son of the death god Tuoni.

Jupiter is in its detriment in Gemini, and as such this placement enacts the myth of the fall from hubris again and again, until the lesson is finally learned. He is driven to test Jupiter's lucky invulnerability, pushing it to its very limit, until he falls from grace in some large and dramatic way. Jupiter and Mercury endow this trickster with the ability to skate out from under responsibility for his actions in a small and limited way; he has a certain amount of karmic credit, as it were. He can sweet-talk his way out of scrapes and seems to be untouchable . . . for a while. It's never enough for him. He is continually driven to go too far and exhaust that credit, and see all his schemes fall down around his ears. It's as if the gods give him the gift of plenty of rope, knowing that he will not be able to resist hanging himself at least a few times.

Lemminkainen can best the airy powers of words, the earthy power of the wild moose, and the fiery horse. The river of death, however, is his nemesis. Not only is this fiery planet in the airy sign at a loss when it comes to matters of watery emotion, he thinks that he can avoid death—or its symbolic manifestation, karma—indefinitely. It's not unusual for his fall to be triggered by some sudden emotional crisis born of his own denial. The crisis can be his own or that of someone that he has carelessly wronged. Either way, he is plunged into the roiling river of death and dies there—but not forever.

The watery, emotional part of Lemminkainen's existence is symbolized by his wife and his old mother, both of whom he treats alternately with wheedling and with contempt. In the end, however, it is his mother who saves him. She rushes to the northlands so fast that hills are leveled in her path, and she entreats the queen of

Pohjola to tell her where her son has gone. The queen at first puts her off with excuses, but the wise old woman accuses her of lying and finally gets the story out of her. Lemminkainen's mother asks the trees, the pathways, and the Moon if they have seen her son, but they all refuse to help. The Sun finally takes pity on her and tells her that his body lies in many pieces in the river of Tuonela.

Going to Ilmarinen, the world's greatest smith (Mars in Taurus), she begs him to make her a magical rake with which she can fish all the pieces of her son out of the river. The rake, made by the earthy, practical smith, symbolizes the slow process of dredging up from the depths all the things that the fleet-footed Jupiter in Gemini has repressed, and that have finally caused his downfall. It is deathly slow and unpleasant work, but the mother—the internal force of nurturing and emotion—manages to recover all the lost parts. She joins them all together and prays to the goddesses of healing to revive him. His heart begins to beat again, but he is in pain and cannot hear or speak.

His mother sends a bee to get honey from a magical tree and places it in his mouth to heal his wounds. This reminds us that a Jupiter in Gemini does not like to admit that he is dependent on others in his life, as we all are, for the sweetness of love. He would prefer to charm it out of them and still feel as if he is in control. In order to be healed, he must accept that love while he is still helpless. In order to restore his sight, his mother sends the bee to another source of magical honey, this one on an island guarded by fire; the honey must be snatched from the kettles of the people there. This restores his sight, reminding us that a Jupiter in Gemini must learn to see what others are willing to go through for him and to truly appreciate that.

To restore his speech, his mother sends the bee to the hardest place of all—he must get honey from the orchards of Ukko, the heavenly creator. The bee protests that he cannot fly to heaven on such tiny wings, but the mother pleads with him, and he tries and succeeds. This is perhaps the most difficult kind of love for a Jupiter in Gemini to connect with—the love of the divine powers. In order for his magical speech to be anything other than empty, shallow, manipulative chatter, he must connect with the love of a divine power and let it flow through him. Jupiter is the sign of religion, and the intellectual focus of Gemini can distract the native into a morass of petty everyday details, unable to see the bigger spiritual picture.

With the touch of the divine honey, Lemminkainen is restored. He mopes about having failed his quest, but his mother reminds him that he has a wife at home who loves him and a mother who was willing to go to the Land of the Dead for him. He agrees to come home and live a peaceful life, finally gaining the wisdom for which he had to die and be reborn.

Nzambi

Jupiter in Cancer

Among the Bakongo people of the Congo in Africa, the earth mother goddess found in almost every culture is named Nzambi. She is the giver of both great generosity and punishing famine, depending on whether or not she feels someone is worthy. One of her favorite tricks was to take on the shape of an old beggar woman and go from house to house, pleading for food. Those who gave her scraps would receive a small amount of money in the near future, and those who brought her in and gave her a meal by the fire were rewarded with great wealth. Those who turned her away were sent famine and poverty, taking away what they would not share.

Jupiter is exalted in Cancer, and this position often brings wealth and prosperity that were not necessarily earned, usually through family or partners. This is the classic position of inheriting or marrying into money so that one will be "taken care of." This is not to say that the Jupiter in Cancer individual necessarily plans for this, but it often just seems to happen to them. Whatever other forms of wealth they earn, the family circle will usually be there for them to fall back on.

This placement often suggests a happy childhood with loving parents and a love of children—although Jupiter's tendency to overdo things may make her overprotective and suffocating. Like all Cancerian planets, she loves to take care of other people and to be taken care of in turn; mutual nurturing is her idea of the best possible relationship. She loves to give advice to people, even to strangers. Like Nzambi, she can go from home to home among her acquaintances, judging the people who live there and deciding whether they need help or a good scolding. This can make her well loved by some and disliked by others.

Like Jupiter in Cancer, Nzambi's lessons emphasize the rule of hospitality, of extending the resources of the family circle into the world outside. When the planet of gifts goes into the sign of the home, it focuses on both the receiving of gifts into the household and on giving charity from that charmed circle. Although we have developed a cultural bias against the word "charity," its original meaning stems from *charis*, or grace. To do largesse in the right way, both the giver and the receiver must be gracious. The giver must not have a secret agenda of obligation, and the recipient must accept the gift quietly, without criticism or overt show. It is the grease that makes Jupiter's gift-giving action work without snarling everyone up in hurt feelings.

In one of Nzambi's legends, she is approached by a crab, the symbol of Cancer. The crab has no limbs, and asks her for legs. She grants him a pair, but he wants another, and another. Finally, after he sports more legs than most other creatures, he asks for a head as well. Nzambi agrees, but says that he will receive his head in a few days. The crab invites everyone to be present at the receiving of his head, which he turns into a big ceremony. When Nzambi arrives, he is strutting about arrogantly, moving sideways instead of forwards so as to show off all his extra legs.

The Earth Mother becomes disgusted with his arrogance and pride, and informs him that she will not be giving him a head after all; she sentences him to scuttle sideways forever. Crab is so humiliated that he hides under a rock, which he has done ever since. Nzambi's lesson is more than just disapproval of overweening pride; she is angry that he has flouted the greatest tenet of the giver-recipient relationship: the lion's share of the attention must go to the giver.

This may sound unfair, but it is crucial to understanding the actions of Jupiter in any sign, and especially in the sign that rules food, growth, and nutrition. The applause must go to the giver, not the receiver, because that applause—and that feeling of having positively affected the universe—is what induces people to give in the first place. Without the positive stimulus of the recipient's smile of pleased surprise, no one would bother, and this would be a miserly and constrictive world.

Cancer understands miserliness and constriction; the negative aspect of any Cancer placement is the crab in her hard shell, nipping anyone who gets close. Cancer also understands that the solution to this lies in the emotions: it must be overwhelmingly emotionally positive to be a giver, or no one will be moved to do it. The receiver should bow out of the spotlight; if she wants it, she had better become a giver in turn. Jupiter is royalty, and royalty is noble due to their ability to be generous. If you want to wear the crown, you have to hold out the open hand. It's how Jupiter breeds more givers. The Earth Mother can only do so much, after all; we have to pick up the slack ourselves sometimes, and it is part of her task to teach us how.

Amaterasu Omikami
Jupiter in Leo

In many cultures, the Sun is male while the Moon is female. Not so in Japan, where the life-giving force of the Sun is considered un-equivocally female. Her name is Amaterasu Omikami—the latter part of her name meaning Great Spirit of Nature—and she was born from the creator god Izanagi and his dead wife Izanami. When Izanagi fled from his wife's burial house, he washed his face to clean off the stench of her corpse, and from his right eye was born the Sun, Amaterasu, and from his left eye the Moon, Tsuki-Yomi. Amaterasu is the ancestor of the Imperial family of Japan, and she dresses like a Shinto priestess, as she is the first of all priests. As the Sun, she is the life-giving force that spreads across the sky and gives vitality to all things.

Leo is the sign of the Sun, and Jupiter in Leo is, in a sense, the biggest Sun of all. Jupiter in Leo gives the gift of performance, the ability to project both solar warmth and solar power. Someone with this placement is born knowing how to command others and, in many cases, make them want to obey. They can also pull off a good deal of charm and self-confidence; few Leo Jupiters have as much trouble with low self-esteem that other signs (or even other Leo planets) may struggle with. It's the faith-based Jupiter gift: in Leo, it is quite literally unlimited faith in oneself and one's own power.

Amaterasu is the first and foremost god in the Japanese pantheon (Leo does not tolerate being anything but the central figure very well), but she is not omniscient. In Japanese myth, there has long been an estrangement between heaven and earth. It is not easy for the gods to see what goes on down among humans . . . or at least the heavenly gods. Minor domestic gods such as the Seven Lucky Ones tend to live among us and aid us with our problems, and thus they are more invoked by the common people on a daily basis. The heavenly gods, however, must rely on reports from the lower gods and thus are more removed and difficult to engage. As the one on the top of the hierarchy, Amaterasu is the most difficult of all to reach.

This can also be a problem with a Jupiter in Leo. One of the dirty little secrets about people with this placement is that they secretly (or not so secretly) think they are superior to the great mass of people. This belief can help them survive the greatest indignities with their self-esteem intact; e.g., "What do I care about their opinion? They're just ignorant peasants. Screw 'em." It can also keep them from really connecting with anyone they consider to be beneath them. They can go blithely along for quite a while without noticing that people are seething or resentful about something they've said or done.

The best thing that a Leo Jupiter can probably do with this attitude is to transform it into one of noblesse oblige—the idea that if you're really so superior, then you have to be a model of behavior to everyone else and that means no unworthy displays of arrogance. They must learn that you catch more flies with honey than with demands, as it were. Their lesson is summed up by the story of an exiled noble father and son; when the son lamented that they were now poverty-stricken and had no servants to care for them, the father told him, "Act nobly, son. The servants will come."

In the end, even if she does not aspire to leadership (which is rare with this placement), a Jupiter in Leo needs to learn that, if nothing else, the "peasants" are her audience. The appreciation that she craves (and hates to admit to craving) will not come if she's alienated them enough that they throw rotten fruit instead of applause. A Jupiter in Leo is perfectly capable of channeling Amaterasu's open, sunny warmth, if she can put aside any feelings of annoyance and contempt that she may have. Applause is terribly important to a Jupiter in Leo. Throughout Japanese history, the common man's way of reverencing Amaterasu is to greet the sunrise with clapping hands. They know, instinctively, that she needs applause.

She is a born performer, even if she has no musical or acting talent per se. Her life will be a dramatic opera, complete with song cues. Her feelings will be displayed lavishly if she feels that they are performance-worthy and discreetly hidden if they are embarrassing. In a sense, she is always on stage, like the sun in the sky, except when she is hidden from view. When she's not feeling well, she will simply disappear rather than be less than her powerful best in front of the audience. Of course, being with someone who is always performing can be hard on her lovers and friends. It takes a patient, loving partner with a good sense of humor to put up with being a perpetual audience for a Jupiterian diva.

A Jupiter in Leo can also be extremely generous to those she loves. It's about largesse: rulers should always give what they can to their followers. Jupiter in Leo instinctively understands what anthropologists call the "Big Man" model of leadership: you are a leader because you can throw the best parties, entertain the most people, and create spectacles that take the peasants' minds off of their daily grind. Similarly, your wealth is measured by how much you can give away, not how much you can hoard. To a Jupiter in Leo, even wealth squandered on fripperies is fine, as long as the fripperies are shown off for the entertainment of others. Leo is also a sign of creativity, being associated with the creative fifth house, and Jupiter in Leo can indicate great creative gifts. Among her other tasks, Amaterasu wove the clothes for the other gods, and weaving ceremonial robes has been a task of Shinto priestesses ever since. They were probably splendid and ornate. A Jupiter in Leo is a lily-gilder, leaning toward the side of pageantry rather than simplicity, but whatever she does will shine.

Susanoo, the wild storm god and the younger brother of Amaterasu, became angry with his sister over a litter of people that they had created to populate Earth. He decided to play a nasty joke on his dignified sister; he skinned a horse and threw the corpse at high speed through the roof of her house. Amaterasu was sitting with her weavers and working; when the corpse came flying through the roof, it made such a mess that one of the weaving-women was accidentally impaled on a distaff and died.

At this point, Amaterasu did the typical Leo thing and retreated to a deep cave. When a Leo planet is offended or embarrassed, she hides and nurses her wounded dignity until such time as she feels ready to return to public view. She doesn't want whispers and giggles or, all gods forbid, pity. She'll sulk in her cave until the situation has either blown over or she can convince herself that she doesn't care. With Jupiter in this sign, a sulk is likely to be as dramatic and prolonged as everything else that she does. However, when Amaterasu retreated to a dark cave and wouldn't come out, the world was plunged into darkness and cold, and all the people lamented. (This is rather what a Jupiter in Leo fantasizes will happen when they flounce off.) The gods convened a meeting and figured out a plan to lure her out of her cave.

Their plan can be read as spot-on advice as to how to handle a sulking Leo planet. They decorated a tree with a giant mirror facing the cave's entrance and festooned it also with strings of jewels and bright streamers. Then the goddess Ama-no-Uzume got up on an overturned washtub and started a striptease. By the time she got naked, the gods were making such a ruckus with their cheering and laughing that Amaterasu could not help but be curious as to what was drawing such attention. (All cats are curious, and that includes any Leonine planet.) She called out to them, asking what was going on, and Ama-no-Uzume retorted that she wasn't needed any more, that they had found an even more beautiful and powerful goddess to give life to the earth. This, of course, roused her curiosity even further—what, someone better than me?!—and she emerged from the cave to see this goddess.

Amaterasu came face to face with her own reflection in the mirror and stopped, charmed for an instant to see her own face. A Leo never tires of seeing herself reflected in the eyes of others; it's the perfect bait. It's also the way in which she learns more about herself. Mirrors of any kind are tools of self-knowledge, and a Jupiter in Leo knows on some level that self-knowledge must come before self-expression. The gods ran up to Amaterasu while she was still struck with her own reflection and dragged her out of the cave, stretching a rope across it so that she could not return. By doing this, they let her know how important she was to them, and how valued, and what lengths they would go to in order to keep her with them. She thrived on this appreciation and promised always to stay with them. It's a bargain that a Leo Jupiter could never refuse.

osein

Jupiter in Virgo

As we discussed in the Sun in Virgo chapter, one of the great secret lessons of Virgo is acceptance of the inevitability of being broken and the capacity to fix oneself as best one can, get up, and keep moving. The planet Jupiter is the great gift of the cosmos, and as such Jupiter in Virgo blesses its recipients of a gift that seems modest and unassuming (two more Virgo words), yet is actually a great wonder. It is the gift of the ability to fix oneself, no matter how broken you are under the wheels of the world.

I had a conversation once with a friend about what the single most important advantage modern humans have in keeping their population up to the point of endangering all the other creatures on the earth. She felt that it was modern food production methods. I felt that it was modern medicine. If we read accounts of the high percent of the population that died young from illness before the last century, we are struck by what a disease-free world we now live in. Part of the reason that we are so horrified by AIDS and Ebola is because we are so many centuries removed from the time of small-pox, yellow fever, and the black plague. Our medicine is what keeps us powerful as a species; we are the only species that *can* fix ourselves, especially when it comes to injuries and serious disease, and that is the real way in which we are now thwarting evolution.

The Afro-Caribbean orisha Osein is the guardian of the wild healing herbs. These are not the plants that grow serenely, bred and rebred for purity, in people's gardens. These are the wild plants that our ancestors collected for millennia uncounted, the green chemicals that were the centerpiece of their meager medical knowledge. These plants often cannot be grown in greenhouse or potted conditions, so the only way to get them is to search the wild. Today, many of these plants are endangered from overharvesting, and it is illegal to pick them. (One example is the lady's slipper that grows in my back yard; if people knew that it had a secret use in treating a common and annoying ailment of this technological society, no law in the world could protect it from being hunted into extinction.) We may think of the ancient times as being an era of unlimited resources, but it seems that overharvesting was a problem then as well, because it is the central fact of the myth of Osein.

Osein is a hard worker, placing and maintaining all the wild medicinal plants; this reflects another gift of Jupiter in Virgo—the ability to work hard and steadily at a job that would make others despair. Apparently, people had been taking too many of the healing herbs that Osein lovingly tended in the forests and jungles. They did not properly appreciate these plants, and they did not do any offerings to them, or to their keeper, when they used the plants to save lives. Osein grew annoyed, feeling that his hard work was taken for granted (a common Virgo problem) and worried that soon his herbs would all vanish. He decided that enough was enough, and hid all the healing herbs in a pot. He then took the pot and climbed to the top of the tallest tree, where he built a nest and stayed, hidden from everyone.

Things quickly became serious for the tribal peoples. They began to die like flies, having no new supplies of the healing plants to help them. They appealed to the other orishas, who searched the forest for Osein and finally found his hiding place. The orishas begged him to come down, but he refused. They tried to shoot him down, but could not hit him among the leaves. Finally Ogoun (Mars in Capricorn) mixed together a gunpowder bomb and blew up the tree. Osein was blown through the air, and the healing plants scattered all over the world, where they are to be found today. Their unlucky keeper, however, had his arms and legs blown off.

Virgo is a sign of Jupiter's detriment, and this tale does have an unpleasant twist. Expansive Jupiter is uncomfortable in quiet, detail-oriented Virgo, and that planetary frustration can appear as an overblown expansion of some of the negative Virgo traits—criticism and cynicism. Osein's holier-than-thou "none for you" attitude may even be justified, but it is not appreciated by the desperate masses. Similarly, the individual with Jupiter in Virgo is generally a practical sort, ruled by rational Mercury, who cannot understand why people won't just be sensible. Because this is the planet of overabundance, his punishment is often far out of proportion to his crime.

He may be able to overcome his attitudes toward the rest of humanity, or perhaps he may choose not to. Either way, he still has one magical gift left. In the tale of Osein, there are two endings, depending on who tells the story. In one tale, he grows his arms and legs back little by little, until he is whole again and takes up his job. In another version, he finds that he no longer needs arms and legs, developing the ability to float through the air and move things with the power of his mind. No matter how cruel life is to a Jupiter in Virgo, he can always find the strength to heal and repair his psyche, either by rebuilding it in stages or finding an entirely new way to compensate for the problem.

This may seem like an unimpressive gift from a secondhand faery godmother, but those who find their minds and souls wounded and ripped from traumatic experiences may well wish that they had it. Jupiter in Virgo people don't trumpet their neediness to the world;

they quietly bring themselves back up to working capacity and then go back to work. If Osein's gift was not so important to our survival, we would not try so hard to steal it, as we always do.

Hera
Jupiter in Libra

Directly across the sky from Jupiter in Aries is Jupiter in Libra. They oppose each other, but an opposition is not necessarily a bad thing. Sometimes, when someone opposes you, it can be as an opposite partner whose differences complement yours and to whom you are drawn in the way that opposites attract. Sometimes an opposition can be objective, pointing out where you've gone wrong. Sometimes, of course, it can be an adversary, someone who stands for everything that you are not.

Aries starts every sentence with *I*; in fact, Aries is the original *I*, the archetypal ego. Libra, its opposite, is very aware of being its opposite, an awareness that Aries generally does not share. Libra thinks in terms of we, of itself in relation to others. Together, they are the I-Thou polarity of the zodiac.

Whenever anyone thinks of Hera, or Juno as her Roman version was named, what's the first thing that they think of? Of course, that she is Zeus's wife. Very few people ever stop to think about the fact that she was not always Zeus's wife, that once she was an incarnation of the Great Goddess of southern Europe. However, the way that Hera differentiated herself from the vague Great Goddess archetype is that she got married, and in doing so she created her own archetypal niche in the world. We can argue whether the marriage was forced or tricked or willing; we can dispute whether the marriage tale most appropriate is the Hellenic legend of Zeus as a shivering swallow or the sociohistorical theory of the sky god taking on the chief goddess as his spouse for reasons of legitimacy, but in the end it all comes down to this: Hera got married.

And after this crowning achievement, she became the goddess of marriage. To her was given the territory of marital commitment and fidelity, and blessing the long-term relationship. As Juno, she had many titles, all organized around the wedding: Juno Pronuba arranged marriages, Juno Moneta advised couples, Juno Domiduca escorted the new couple over the threshold, Juno Nuxia anointed the lintels of the door, Juno Cinxia unknotted the girdles on the wedding night, Juno Ossipago protected pregnant wives, Juno Sospita oversaw delivery, and Juno Rumina brought in the milk supply. Hera's gift, and this is the gift of Jupiter in Libra as well, is the gift of relationships. A Jupiter in Libra wants to be in relationship and knows how to commit to it. She has skills of diplomacy and hospitality that make people feel welcome, listened to, heard, and believed in. She has Jupiterian faith in the ability of every relationship to survive, and it is very hard for her when they don't, whether it is her marriage, or best friend, or children.

Of course, there is such a thing as too much togetherness. Jupiter does tend to overdo things, and when it is ruled by Venus, being in relationship can be the only thing that a person lives for. Here we have the battered wife who will not leave her husband; the man who stalks his ex-lover because he cannot imagine life without her; the people staring into their glasses at singles' bars, desperately hoping that the next person to come along will be The One who will give their empty lives meaning and make everything better. The myth that people come in pairs like shoes and socks is strong in our culture, and those who do not fit the mold often find themselves a subject of scorn, both from others and themselves. People with Jupiter in Libra can find that their great gift for being in relationship has become a great obsession if it is not fulfilled in some way; as with all Jupiterian gifts that are not used, there is a vague sense that one's life is being wasted.

Hera is an ambivalent figure. On the one hand, she gives happiness in marriage and the ability to commit with a whole heart. She gives harmony and stability to relationships and helps people find their places on the social continuum. On the other hand, her own marriage with Zeus is a study in frustration and abuse; he is often overbearing, demanding, and selfish, and she spends a good deal of her time fighting with him and plotting against him. This, too, is a Libra trait; although we think of Libra as peace and harmony, it is also the sign of justice, and when she feels herself betrayed beyond all means, she strikes back at the unfairness. Libra is the sign of the diplomat, and someone with Jupiter in Libra can go a long time in a relationship that is unsatisfactory, desperately trying to even the scales with soft words and friendly, Venus-ruled methods. Sooner or later, though, if these fail to work, she will balance the scales by any means necessary, including becoming the opposition and trotting out the other Libran weapon: the full-scale argument. With Jupiter behind it, those arguments can become dramatic and explosive, like Hera and Zeus's clash of the Titans.

What Hera wants is fairness—she's given her vows of fidelity and she wants the same thing in return—and knowing exactly where she is on the social scale, which is also a Libran issue. Her husband's constant infidelities are unfair and shake her feelings about her place, her status, and her worth in his eyes. When confronted with this injustice, she will not remain silent and take the misuse. Libra may be the sign of the Lover, but it is also the sign of the Lawyer, and a Jupiter in Libra is always ambivalently torn between submission for the sake of the peace and conflict for the sake of justice. She knows intimately that there is no right answer, only a choice of agonies.

There is one more face of Juno and that is Juno Lucina, the Light Bearer. This is the aspect that was the still, small voice inside every woman; a man's was called his genius, a woman's her juno. This voice is the intuitive force that lights up the dark morass of confusion, and this too is a Libra gift. The planet of faith in the sign of balance gives an underlying belief in the fairness of the universe, even when all seems at its worst. It is said that when Hera could bear things no more, she would leave Zeus and go to a fountain of immortality, where she would bathe in its waters and be made young again. Perhaps the greatest gift of Jupiter in Libra is that faith—that no matter what happens to your dealings with other humans, you will always be given the grace to begin again.

Ariadne
Jupiter in Scorpio

People tend to be afraid of Scorpio. Not so much Scorpio people, but Scorpio energy. It has such a bad reputation that Scorpio people tend to continually get comments like, "But I would never have thought you were a Scorpio, you're so . . ." (nice, or kind, or not obviously a serial killer). What gives them the shivers is that Plutonian transformation stuff, even if they don't realize it as the source of their fear. The truth is, of course, that we all have Scorpio in our charts, even if only as an empty intercepted house, and we all have Pluto in there somewhere, and we all have an eighth house, and we all have Pluto transits, and most of us will have a planet progress into Scorpio at some point in our lives, or form a relationship with someone who has planets in Scorpio, or whose composite chart has a Scorpio planet. It's inevitable that we will have to deal with it at some point, so we should stop whining and just deal with it.

Why is it so frightening? Because Pluto is about transformation of your internal parts as well as your external ones. Transformation hurts, and deep introspection is uncomfortable. It's like exercising a part of your body that hasn't been stretched in a long time or healing after surgery (a Scorpio-ruled phenomenon). It's going to hurt and be uncomfortable, and you'll be better afterward. Because we're lazy, we resist deep psychological and spiritual introspection, and we prefer, paradoxically, to wait until something drags us down there "against our will." We call this catharsis, and we come up shaking and weeping, and changed. We are glad to have done it, but we hope that we will never have to do it again. And, of course, we will.

Having Jupiter in Scorpio is like having a gift for catharsis or even a compulsion toward it. A Jupiter in Scorpio will spend a lot more time down there in the underworld than most people, and she'll have something of an easier time of it. Although we are all of us mostly powerless down there, a Jupiter in Scorpio has been given certain tools that aid her in enduring the flaying terror of the Mysteries—patience, faith in one's personal power, fascination with alternate states of mind, and an ability to see them as transcendent rather than merely frightening or entertaining. They are given, as it were, a thread to guide through the labyrinth.

In ancient Crete, Ariadne was the goddess of the labyrinth, the winding path of mind and soul that circles inward to the center point and out again. The Greeks wrote about her later as if she was merely a Greek maiden, the daughter of King Minos, but her divine nature shines out through the cracks. She had been promised to Dionysus, the god of wine and shamanic altered states, in her childhood. However, by the time she was an adult, she forgot this and fell in love with a mortal man, Theseus. She aided him in entering the labyrinth by giving him a ball of thread that he used to find his way in, kill the flesh-eating, monstrous Minotaur, and get safely out.

They eloped together, she forsaking all of Crete for him, but the gods intervened. Ariadne was promised to Dionysus, and she must not lower herself to be married only to a mortal man, however heroic. Artemis, the goddess who sees to it that people keep their promises, intervened and informed Theseus that Ariadne was a goddess and thus off limits to him. He promptly abandoned her on the island of Naxos and sailed away.

This part of the story—the grieving, the mourning, the abandonment—is all too familiar to us. Usually we undertake the journey to the underworld, willing or unwilling, for the wrong reasons. Instead of going down willingly like Inanna, because it is time to do so, because the old patterns are worn and a general housecleaning must be done, we do it because some external situation is pressing on us. Not infrequently it has to do with a bad romantic situation—an abusive or distant lover, a bad affair, a marriage gone wrong. It's not unusual to use lovers as tools and motivations for catharsis; we learn a great deal about ourselves from who we are when we're with new people. It might also be another sort of love—a distant, idealized dream that has fallen irretrievably through our fingers or a shattering of an idyllic, romanticized life. Ariadne's infatuation with a mortal man is her downfall, inevitable and expected. He is beneath her, not because he is so much a lowly creature, but because in order to be with him she must make herself smaller. The great hero Theseus would never put up with a goddess as a partner; he will persist in preferring a relationship more on his own level, with a mere mortal woman.

Ariadne's downfall is realized when she is abandoned on Naxos after her initial triumphant escape from Crete. If a Jupiter in Scorpio has a flaw, it is a kind of spiritual arrogance. Because she can get in and out of the labyrinth more easily than most, because her catharses leave her stronger rather than killing her, she can come to believe that she can beat the labyrinth, to become its mistress every time. This can manifest in the idea of invulnerability to the slings and arrows of the world; it is clearly demonstrated in Jupiter in Scorpio types like Napoleon Bonaparte. In arrogance, a Jupiter in Scorpio forgets that mastery of the self is an ongoing process that must never cease. As soon as you think you're done with all that pain and nastiness—that there's nothing the universe can throw at you to make you flinch—the universe will think something up just to prove you wrong. After all, the reward for a job well done is, of course, a harder job.

The key is a certain humility, which isn't easy for any Jupiter placement, much less intense Scorpio. Ariadne, Goddess of the

Labyrinth, is reduced to a wailing girl on the shore of an isolated island. It is she who has done this to herself by allowing obsession with a lesser lover to pull her away from her own divine nature. Her escape from Naxos, from the labyrinth, was like an adolescent attempt to flee those duties that are hers by Fate—being a guide to those who go down and arise. If a Jupiter in Scorpio forgets her humility in the face of personal triumphs, she will be forcibly reminded of it. If she climbs high enough that she can no longer see the underworld below, she will topple, and the higher the climb, the greater the fall.

However, this is a Jupiter placement, not a Saturn one. The story usually has a happy ending, because the humiliation is merely a prelude to the sacred marriage. In the myth, Dionysus appears with his train of Maenads on the shore of Naxos, and he takes Ariadne to wife, rescuing her. The two of them create a mystery religion that is outlined in images in the Villa of the Mysteries in Pompeii. Her escape from being the underworld guide was an attempted escape from her own soul, her self, and her destiny, and like all such attempts it was doomed to failure. Once she accepts that this is a part of her, she is rewarded by her sacred marriage to Dionysus. The shamanic god of wine and drugs also refers to a Jupiter in Scorpio's other area of excess: the pursuit of transcendence through chemically altered states. It's almost inevitable that a Jupiter in Scorpio will experiment with these things, if only as another tool in her underworld journeys, but it should be done carefully and not excessively. Addiction only readies one for another fall.

It may help her to remember that the circle isn't complete until she can use her experiences to extend aid to others. Her role as guide to the underworld, mistress of the labyrinth, means that she has skills and information that others will need. Rather than being contemptuous of their weaknesses, she should make herself into a resource for others. Scorpio is associated with the eighth house, which rules other people's resources, and a Jupiter in Scorpio does best when she can find a way to help others struggling on the dark paths. It might be in one of the counseling professions or perhaps just as a friend who gives sound advice or a shoulder to cry on. If nothing else, it will keep her humble. The grandiosity of Jupiter's arrogance can be ameliorated by thinking of oneself, at least occasionally, as a public utility created by the gods. Even in suspicious, retiring Scorpio, Jupiter still means generosity. Like a spider who pulls the thread from her own body, she will find that Ariadne's threads of guidance never run out and that the gift of transformation can create a web of bonds to hold her up when she falls.

Agni
Jupiter in Sagittarius

Jupiter, a fiery planet, is at home in its rulership of fiery Sagittarius. This is the one sign where his luck and good fortune can flow most freely, and it is not uncommon to find people with this Jupiter placement either making it easily and successfully on their own—at least financially—or having the sort of situation where others magically show up to provide for them. It can make someone incredibly lucky, which can either help them achieve great goals almost effortlessly or it can make them too soft to achieve anything that offers a challenge. The rest of the chart and the willpower of the individual will tip the scales one way or another.

Agni is the Hindu god of fire, both the hearth fire that aids humanity and the lightning strike, earthly and heavenly fire. He is pictured as wild-haired, with sharp golden teeth and a swift tongue, his face smeared with butter or ghee. These were often poured into the fire as offerings; thus he is greased with them. Part of the symbolism of this grease is a plea to allow the worshipper to "slide by" in everyday affairs, as a type of good fortune that Agni brings. Likewise, Jupiter in Sagittarius can give this ability to somehow be magically missed by most of the missiles that splatter the rest of us. The teeth and tongue are symbolic of the tongues of fire that eat up anything they are given, reminiscent of the Sagittarian tendency to blunt verbal takedowns, summing up the situation with undiplomatic, even brutal causticity.

One of Agni's attributes is that he likes almost everyone. He constantly travels from building to building in people's hearth fires, and it is said that there is no home where he is not at home, no hearth that he despises. He is welcome everywhere, or at least everywhere that uses some form of fire to heat themselves and cook their food. This is a classic Sagittarian gift; Cancers may balk at being pried out of their homes, but Sagittarius gladly travels all over the place. He goes to foreign countries and goes native fast, especially with Jupiter there to aid him. Like Agni, he can find a way to feel at home almost anywhere he visits, yet no place has a monopoly on his attention. People with Jupiter in Sagittarius often have a long list of friends of all stripes and forms who will put them up on a moment's notice, no matter where in the world they wander.

They tend to leave early, too. Agni's fiery nature is hard on parents. It is said that as soon as he was born, he realized that his parents could not support him and promptly devoured them. This is an anthropomorphization of Fire that consumes the two dead sticks whose rubbing it is produced from. It can also be an accurate description of Jupiter in Sagittarius children who can't wait to get out of the home and away onto their own personal quest. The pairing of this sort of child with a clinging parent is a recipe for pain, and the resentful child may explode frequently with fiery resentment. They tend to get along better when fostered out frequently to other families, friends, or apprenticeship positions. As an adult deity, Agni is a generous mediator who brings luck and fortune, and forgives people for sins committed during hotheaded moments. Similarly, the adult Jupiter in Sagittarius is generous to a fault and willing to forgive people several times for their problems, as long as no one tries to rein in their enthusiasm and wanderlust.

However, having the easy life and slipping through the thorns can create its own kind of fault, and that is known as hypocrisy. Jupiter in Sagittarius people usually have a religious or spiritual bent, although it doesn't have to be an organized religion. They love to give spiritual advice and can get pretty bombastic about it. In fact, the sermonizing on others' faults is a perfect example of a Sagittarian Jupiter who is terrified of challenge, of running out of luck, and who has hemmed themselves in with fear. The pontificating is a coverup for their own trepidation and cowardice. What they really need to be doing is getting on with their own spiritual quest, which both draws and terrifies them.

What is this spiritual quest? In a word, truth. When you get used to the easy life, truth isn't terribly appealing. In fact, it's hard, and a Jupiter in Sagittarius often isn't used to hard. Yet this is the ultimate gift of Agni, of fire. Fire has always been associated with truth in some way, in many cultures, as it burns away the outsides of things and shows their true insides. In the Norse rune system, the rune of fire, Ken, implies truth. Agni, too, thousands of miles away but heir to the same system of Indo-European mythology, is about truth.

One story about Agni tells of Bhrigu the storm god, who fell in love with a young woman and abducted her away from her demon lover, hiding her in a cave and marrying her against her will. Her lover raised a great search for her, but Bhrigu confided in no one but his friend Agni. The fire god, after much thought, revealed the abducted woman's whereabouts to her demon lover and she was rescued. Bhrigu was furious and cursed Agni, saying that he should be cursed forever as "the one who eats all things." The fire god pointed out to his friend that he had only been telling the truth, that liars were cast into the deepest of hells, and that withholding information about wrongdoing is the same as lying about it.

This last point is especially important. We as human beings do tend to keep our mouths shut if the wrongdoing going on in front of us doesn't directly affect us, and this kind of blase callousness allows wrongs to go on. For evil to flourish, they say, good men need only do nothing. When a Jupiter in Sagittarius is doing his spiritual duty—as truthsayer, whistleblower, the child that points out the emperor's lack of clothing—he is much less liked. He may lose those friendships that require loyalty over honesty. Agni goes on to say to Bhrigu that he too can hurl curses, but he chooses to control his anger, and that he is the mouth of the gods that receives all sacrifices, and so must only tell the truth. Bhrigu is abashed and ashamed, and withdraws his curse. He instead blesses Agni, saying that he does indeed purify all things.

Not all the people who receive Agni's gift are going to change their tunes as thoroughly as Bhrigu. In fact, most will be much less receptive. However, this is the whole point of Jupiter's luck. It was given for a reason, says the big planet of faith. If it is not used for taking risks around truthsaying, the Jupiter in Sagittarius native will find it slowly slipping away. He must indeed find himself becoming the mouth of the gods, giving forth truth at his own risk of safety. If fire is contained in too small a space—physical or spiritual or moral—it goes out.

orunmila

Jupiter in Capricorn

Jupiter is the planet of luck, but when he flies into Saturn's sign, which is the exact opposite of luck, his gifts are less about blind fortune and more about gifts that allow one to exploit one's opportunities. Unlike Saturn in Sagittarius, where Saturn can get sidetracked into Jovian quests for Truth and Right, with this placement Jupiter has to play by Saturn's rules. Saturn's first rule, of course, is Thou Shalt Work. Jupiter's corollary, when in Capricorn, is this: Yes, thou shalt work. But thou shalt do it skillfully, and profitably, and above all joyously, and reap the benefits of truly Jupiterian abundance and prosperity.

To have this kind of material success, one has to have more than just the ability to work hard. It is necessary to have a large amount of really accurate foresight, which is part reasoning and extrapolation and part plain intuition. If one were to sum up the true gift of this mixed Jupiter-Saturn placement, it would be called practical prophecy.

The Yoruba orisha Orunmila is the keeper of the Ifa, the oracle worked with a painted board and a bag of cowrie shells. Ifa is not a process that one can learn in a single day; followers of Orunmila study for several years under the instruction of a master. Orunmila is quiet and studious, and expects his prophets to work hard and not grow too fat on the adulation of others. To him, divination is something that is accomplished by the polished skill of the diviner, not merely some airy-fairy communion with the universe. In some legends he is one of the first divine beings who helped to create the world; in others he was once a mortal man who was befriended by Ellegua and Shango and made immortal through his worthiness and their regard. This echoes the rags-to-riches story that often accompanies this astrological placement.

Orunmila knows a thing of value when he sees one. One of his titles is Agboniregun, meaning Hunter of the Medicine for Good Fortune. When the powerful orisha Odu walks into town, complete with magical birds given to her by the Creator, Orunmila decides on the spot to marry her. He makes impressive offerings to her and to the earth, and she favors him and agrees to his offer of marriage. This is a good example of Jupiter in Capricorn canniness, which bestows the talent of knowing a good thing when you see one and being able to figure out how to earn it.

This placement does tend toward workaholism, but for different reasons than other workaholic placements. Saturn in Virgo or Capricorn will plod along at a job for year after year out of duty, or to distract themselves from the complexities of their lives, or because the work itself is a kind of spiritual discipline. Jupiter's gift to this Saturn-ruled sign is more often a specific kind of work that the individual can fall in love with. These are the people who work eighty hours a week and come out blissful, because they are so enthused about their career paths. Jupiter blesses them with the ability to find work that they can really sink themselves into emotionally, sometimes with as much or more satisfaction than they would get from relationships with actual people.

The problem with being married to one's work, of course, is that she can be a much more all-consuming wife than any mortal woman. Orunmila's wife, Odu, was so jealous that she demanded no other woman should ever study the Ifa oracle—and thus get too close to her husband. So Orunmila has no female followers, for they would court Odu's wrath. It's hard to tear yourself away from something you love, and this is especially true for a Jupiter in Capricorn if his work is "divine" in some way—i.e., it is taken up with making a positive impact on humanity. Jupiter gives him superior stamina in working those eighty-hour weeks, but sooner or later he needs to have an affair with the rest of life.

A Jupiter in Capricorn can become so identified with his work that he ends up that way in everyone else's mind as well—no more than "the plumber" or "the accountant" or "the family lawyer." People become very dependent on his competence, which he enjoys and takes pride in. They may cease to think of him as a person with a full range of feelings and consider him more a fixture that can be called upon in need. This means that if he changes careers or simply decides to go elsewhere, his personal community can react angrily, as if the rug was being swept out from under them. He needs to make sure that he has a few good friends who will see him as a person and to whom his career means nothing. It will keep him anchored to his own humanity and keep his individuality from being eaten by his work.

Orunmila eventually grew tired of the gods forever coming to him and asking him to cast Ifa over any little thing. He felt as if no one really valued him for himself, but only for his work. Saddened and angry, he told his wife to spread a rumor that he was terminally ill and on his deathbed. Sure enough, each of the other orishas came to call on him before his death. Odu refused to let them see Orunmila, and while she served them tea and spoke with them, Orunmila hid behind a curtain and listened. Every one of them eventually got around to slyly asking who Orunmila had chosen to inherit his sacred Ifa board, which glumly confirmed in Orunmila's heart that he was not loved for himself.

Finally Ellegua (see Uranus in Gemini) the trickster orisha came to visit, and he pleaded with Odu to see the supposedly dying Orunmila. When she mentioned the board, he dismissed it and instead stressed that he wanted to see his friend one more time before he died. Orunmila was so touched that he stepped out from behind the curtain and explained the ruse. He offered Ellegua the board, saying that he was going to travel far away out of dejection, but Ellegua said that if he was given the board he would never use it; he would only keep it as a memorial to Orunmila, and thus there would be no more prophecy. Orunmila was thus convinced to stay on as the Ifa oracle.

Another set of keywords for Jupiter in Capricorn, at its best, might be destined success. Of course, having a destiny does not mean that one will necessarily fulfill it. The individual with this placement has the free will to turn aside from this path, and he may do so if other planets predominate in the chart. If he decides to go this road, however, all he needs to do is ask the universe to send him the right work, and it will come. Buckminster Fuller scorned the career taken up solely for its material gain; he said, "Do what you love and the money will come." There is no better advice anywhere for this child of the Divine Giver and the Holy Taker.

ꜰoꜰtunɑ

Jupiter in Aquarius

Throughout the Middle Ages, the goddess who was most frequently worshipped in Europe was the Virgin Mary, calm, comforting, and maternal, the Goddess of the Catholic Church. However, one other goddess was also revered and invoked, and she provided just the spark to push the world into its new age of exploration and risk-taking. No temples were built to her, unless one counts gambling dens and brothels, but men called on her before great undertakings and prayed for her blessings. Her name was often upon their lips, in anticipation or joy or curses. Her name was Fortuna.

She had originally been a Roman goddess, older even than the Greek deities that they subsumed. Her statue was always kept in the bedchamber of Roman emperors, and it was said that anyone who had extraordinary luck "had a Fortuna." While on a boat in a great storm, Julius Caesar reportedly told the pilot not to bother worrying, for his ship carried Caesar's Fortuna. Indeed, she was revered by sailors both during the Roman period and the Renaissance, and they prayed to her for her aid in avoiding storms, returning alive, and having profitable commerce from the journey.

Fortuna was hailed as a weather goddess, weather being one of the most unpredictable elements in a possible disaster. She could bring sunny skies or throw thunderbolts with the best of them, revealing the Aquarian rulerships of lightning and electricity and its air-ruled sky nature. Most people tend to think of Aquarius, since it is a fixed sign, as some kind of inert gas like helium, but we forget that its ruler is the bringer of storms, like Fortuna. She was often shown whirling in midair or spinning in the center of her great wheel. Capricious and inconstant, she favored opportunists, but could easily bring a man up with one hand and cast him down with the other.

Uranian-like chaos permeated her character and legends; men scrambled to find ways to please her fickle spirit, unpredictable as a storm at sea, and yet her favor could be immense, truly Jupiterian in scope. One of her symbols was a ship's rudder, which suggested keeping to the path; another was a cornucopia. Her home was said to be on an island, where she lived in a great castle that was majestic and grandiose on one side and fallen into ruins on the other. With Aquarian equality, she held out her hands equally to the denizens of palaces and hovels.

"Luck, if you've ever been a lady to begin with, Luck be a lady tonight!" goes the song, and indeed there is a great deal of doubt as to whether she was ever a lady. Aquarius is the sign of the people, the proletarian class, in opposition to Leo the nobility, and the only realm in which Fortuna is Queen of the World Turned Upside Down. The fife-and-drum corps of the defeated royalist British army, by the way, played that song when they went to surrender to the low-born kingless American troops in 1781 at the end of the Revolutionary War. Fortuna approves of revolutions and so does Jupiter in Aquarius, because they are Big Change. Of course, revolutions are often messy and bloody and turn out nothing like what their instigators expect, but this too is par for the course with Jupiter ruled by Uranus.

In fact, one of the most common ways for Fortune to be portrayed was as a whore. This is partly to symbolize the capricious way she gave out her favors and partly because the whore was the lowest woman in society at that time. Elaborate rituals were set up by her would-be petitioners, with four men representing the figures in her wheel and Fortune herself always played by a sex worker or other woman "of loose morals." No virgin she, but then Aquarius has always been in favor of equality between the genders, including their morals. Four hundred years later, Jupiter in Aquarius in 1962 would start the era of birth control and the sexual revolution.

Fortuna's wheel also serves as a symbol of her Aquarian talent for social change. Traditionally, there are four figures on it: a king enthroned at the top, a beggar at the bottom who is crushed beneath the wheel, and two figures on either side who are either rising in the world or falling from social grace. The Goddess of Luck, in spite of her chameleon gaze, tends to like to mix it up with those who have been in one place for far too long and who need a good shaking up. The Jupiter in Aquarius individual tends to find their luck in change; staying too long in one place or doing only one thing finds them abandoned by Fortuna. They are also drawn to the world turned upside down; strong aspects to this placement often indicate that they were born to socially unusual parents, perhaps into an obscure subculture where being a social outcast was as familiar as breakfast.

Called equally by the names Bona Fortuna and Mala Fortuna, the Goddess of the Wheel did not seem to care how many bodies were left in her wake, so long as evolution did its dance. She believes firmly in survival of the fittest. However, we humans need to buffer the world a little from her capriciousness, for the sake of kindness—a lesson a Jupiter in Aquarius, often ready to tear down any flag and stomp on it on principle, needs to learn. Storms are wonderful things to behold from a distance, but sometimes their actual visits may not be what you expect, and that goes double for Fortuna.

obatala

Jupiter in Pisces

"Great White King, Great White Queen . . ." With these words, the Afro-Caribbean Yoruba orisha Obatala is summoned and praised. Obatala is the Divine Creator of this tribal belief; Obatala created man from clay every day and baked them in a kiln every night. Since Obatala experimented with glazes and baking times, various batches of humans came out in different colors. Obatala is both male and female in turn, appearing as either; however, it is said that Obatala appears to you in the sex of the parent whose nurturing you lack for the most. Obatala appears much more often as a father figure than a mother figure. Readers are invited to make up their own minds as to what that means.

Obatala is the sage of the orishas, wise and compassionate and fair and gentle. Obatala always speaks softly and is respected for great wisdom; all the other orishas come to Obatala when a wrong-doing has been done and the culprit needs to be judged. The "white" in Obatala's title does not refer to race; Obatala is usually shown as an androgynous African elder. It refers instead to Oba-tala's favorite place, the tops of mountains. The only place where a blanket of snow falls in Africa is on the tops of the highest moun-tains, and Obatala chooses these as home, separated from the world below yet watching it from afar. Obatala's symbol is a pure white cloth spread on the ground like snow; those who are appointed as judges often sit on such a cloth in order to show that they are putting themselves in Obatala's place as compassionate, objective observers.

One of Obatala's gifts is that of healing, not just of the body but of the spirit as well. Pisces is the sign opposite to Virgo, the doctor who specializes in healing the mechanics of living; Pisces heals the wounds that are harder to see and correct. Bodies heal in weeks or months, but wounded psyches can limp on for a long time, festering and burning and becoming more and more set in their own poisons. Part of having Jupiter in Pisces is having a pull toward healing oth-ers, especially in therapeutic fields. As Pisces is the last and most undifferentiated sign in the zodiac, it gives the ability to identify with a wide variety of people, mirroring Obatala's ability to become male or female at will. One Piscean said to me, "I'm just like every-one else, only more so." This identification talent allows a listener to offer that most important of therapeutic tools: unconditional, positive regard. It gives a measure of visible compassion that people want to trust, want to open themselves to.

However, in order to heal, especially from a complex Pisces perspective where nothing is done the easy way, you must first heal yourself. This is where the double-edged sword of any planetary placement, even Jupiter, comes in. Another possible manifestation of Jupiter in Pisces is to lose oneself to that undifferentiation. Jupiter in Pisces people can have such poor boundaries that they can lose their own desires in those of their loved ones, or social messages. They may get to a point where they literally do not know what it is that they actually want, as opposed to what others think they ought to have to do or be. In order to get to a place of sympathetic identification that does not get so involved with others that the self is lost, Jupiter in Pisces has to do long periods of self-examination, preferably alone. Their own wounds must be healed first, lest they merge with the wounds of others.

With the planet of excess ruled by the planet of dreams, drugs, and delusions, this can also be a prime placement for either falling into a fantasy life of denial or getting sucked into addictive behaviors or substances that are a distraction from the real internal work that needs to be done. It is especially hard when the people that a Jupiter in Pisces loves so dearly—and identifies with so strongly— are quarreling or unhappy. Obatala fell into this trap, too; seeing how all those carefully created humans fought and harmed each other, Obatala took to drinking palm wine. As time went on, the palm wine became a regular habit. It began to interfere with Obatala's judgment, but the other orishas were too polite—or too much in denial—to point it out.

Unfortunately, one night Obatala made a batch of humans while completely soused. Tossing them into the kiln, Obatala staggered off to bed, only to awake the next morning to a terrible sight. The alcohol-induced humans were terribly deformed, but since they had been fired, their shapes were hereby added to the pool of humanity.

Birth defects had been invented, and they spread throughout the human race. Obatala was horrified at the results of this drunken creativity and swore off alcohol forever. To this day, you may put gin on Ogoun's altar, or beer on Shango's, or white wine on Yemaya's, or red wine on Oya's, or rum on Ellegua's, or brandy on Oshun's, but Obatala will only accept pure white milk or coconut milk. To place booze on the altar of a recovering alcoholic is the ultimate insult.

The Obatala archetype is the one who has made mistakes and learned from them, and in that bounty of compassion for fellow sinners can lend a hand to help them up as well. To live this experience is to be humbled, and humbled so much that even when you are lifted up and acclaimed, you never forget how very human you are. A Jupiter in Pisces knows that no matter how much love you give away, there is always more in the inexhaustible well.

♄ saturn

TYᚱ
Saturn in Aries

Ruled by Mars, Aries is often seen as the quintessen-tial warrior of the zodiac. It is also seen as the Child archetype, but when it is laid over Saturn, the planet

of the Old Man, the Child grows up and matures whether he wants to or not. The Warrior, on the other hand, is always an ambivalent creature. His

boundless energy can erupt onto the wrong people; his protective nature can be set to protecting only his own interests; he can wreak more destruction than

good. At his worst, he can eat the world. This is what happened to Fenris, the great wolf who creates the defining moment of the story of Tyr.

Tyr is one of the Norse warrior gods. Unlike Thor, who is hail-fellow-well-met and enjoys a good horn of mead and a long story, Tyr is stern and unyielding

and Saturnian. Also unlike Thor, who was beloved by farmers and the lower ranks of the warriors, Tyr is an aristocrats' god. As a deity of the upper classes,

the officers, he understands what it is to have responsibility for the fates of many others, and this seems to weigh on him heavily. He is a strategist, the

one who moves the pieces around on the chessboard rather than the man on the front lines with the

sword. His nature is characterized by dour Saturnian reticence, yet no one doubts his bravery.

Fenris was one of the sons of Loki, the trickster god who was first welcomed and then betrayed by Odin the Aesir. Odin has Fenris's mother, Angrboda, killed out of fear of the powerful children she was bearing, of whom Fenris the Great Wolf is one. Loki strikes back in covert trickster ways, but not so Fenris. He rises up in wrath and starts tearing a strip of destruction across the countryside, eating everything and everyone in his path. He is so strong in his wrath that no one can stop him—the epitome of Mars gone wrong, an angry force of rage and vengeance and holy fury.

This is the dark, unevolved side of a Saturn in Aries, who often feels so out of control and powerless that he will attack first instead of waiting to defend himself. "Get the bastards before they get you" may be his motto. The kind of open trust that is often the hallmark of Aries the Child is blocked by Saturn, and he trusts no one easily and possibly no one at all. He may assume that everyone is out to get him, and thus his overreactive jump-and-strike approach to any perceived threat. He is no strategist, as he cannot see far enough beyond himself and his anger to think ahead. His only recourse is blind lashing out in the dark, and he rarely understands what kind of pain he causes.

The Great Wolf lives within every person with Saturn in Aries. Sometimes he may overcompensate, becoming passive and overly timid, but this is just his desperate way to restrain the Wolf that he fears. He gives up all power, because he has given all his power to the Wolf and left none for himself. Inevitably, the chains fail and the Wolf leaps out. Fenris was so strong that no chain could hold him, so the Aesir forged a special chain made of six impossible things—the roots of a mountain, the beard of a woman, the sensitivity of a bear, the spittle of a bird, the footfall of a cat, and the breath of a fish.

Besides being merely a cunning list of absurdities, these items all have subtle meanings. Fishes' breath is water, the quality of soft yielding emotion that Fenris has lost touch with. The footfall of a cat can be heard, if you listen closely in silence; it is the quality of stillness and paying attention to what most overlook. Birds don't drool, but they do drink; the "spittle of a bird" suggests that which replenishes a throat thirsty for song and music. The sensitivity, or "nerves" in the original, of a bear recalls the berserkers, men who went into battle wearing the skins of bears, in such a terrible rage that they could feel no pain. This reflects the experiences of Fenris and suggests that the "bear" needs to feel his pain and therefore that of others, developing empathy. The beard of a woman connotes androgyny, the balancing of male and female natures. The roots of a mountain allude to the deep parts of the earth, the dark places underneath everything else where sullen things rot and fester, driving the enraged Wolf out into the open air—dark places that need to be exposed to light. Taken metaphorically, the elements of the magical "chain" become a recipe for stopping the Wolf with a series of little, inconsequential, gentle things.

However, the chain still has to be bound onto the Wolf. Fenris was justly suspicious of the gods who surrounded him and asked, as if in fun, whether he could break this chain that they had made. He smelled a trick—a Saturn in Aries is always untrusting—and demanded that one of the gods place their hand in his mouth while the chain was fastened around him, just in case. It is here that Tyr steps up and offers to do the deed. Surely he must have known that the worst would happen, that he would lose his hand, but it is worth it to him to stop Fenris's destruction. This is the kind of courage that a Saturn in Aries needs to tap into, and it is borne from that evolved Martial quality referred to as honor.

Honor is a word that has been used to mean many ambivalent things, such as ego or pride, but in its purest sense it means that you walk your talk, that there is no contradiction between what you practice and what you preach. It means that you are not afraid to give your word and that you keep it even when that may mean sacrifice, discomfort, and pain. When you live with honor, your word has more weight and more power. Tyr alone had the courage to make this terrible sacrifice, and thus it was that Fenris believed him. The Great Wolf was bound, and indeed he did bite off Tyr's hand. Yet from then on men invoked Tyr when they made bargains or gave their word; his name had become a word of power that created honor out of nothing.

The final step in restraining the Wolf within is always a painful one. Tyr loses a hand, which limits his ability to do, and a Saturn in Aries often has to turn to an arduous and self-limiting discipline in order to redeem himself and his anger. Saturn is the planet of limits, and he explains patiently to us that sometimes limits are not a bad thing, even when they feel like chains or a handicap. Sometimes they are the boundary between unfettered destruction and everyone else's life. Honor is a handicap. By voluntarily giving up your option to break your word and skate off when times get tough, you doom yourself to a lifetime of striving to keep that word, a lifetime of limits and chains. You also become a more powerful being, whose name is synonymous with *fairness* and *honesty*. Is it worth it? For a Saturn in Aries, there is no such question. It is the only way out of hell.

saturn

Saturn in Taurus

When the Romans conquered Greece and amalgamated their gods together, it was the Grecian archetypes and personalities that triumphed over the original Roman gods, to the point where it is very difficult to know anything about the primal Italian deities. One of the exceptions, however, was Saturn; the Romans identified him with Zeus's father Cronos, but the association was tenuous at best, and the original Saturn-figure was more clearly visible under the Grecian overlay. This may well be because Saturn, unlike Cronos, was the god of farmers. This may not mean much today, but in ancient times that meant that it was Saturn who 90 percent of the Italian populace were praying to on a regular basis, not Jupiter or Juno or Mars.

Farming is an activity where you spend a lot of time trying to gain control over a system that will always outmatch you. No matter how hard you try, something will always go wrong, and at best you can attempt a rate of more successes than failures. The weather is impossible to predict, especially months in advance when you are planting a particular crop, and diseases can strike plants and animals out of nowhere. Failure in this uncertain profession generally comes with death by starvation. If you work extra hard, are highly organized, and build in as many fail-safes as you can, maybe you'll make it with some surplus. Or maybe not. To live by agriculture is to know just how little power you have over the earth.

Taurus is perhaps the most earthy of the earth signs; ruled by watery Venus, it has the connotations of fertility and stability, bedrock and fertile soil above it, great-grandfather trees that bear rich fruits, nourishment at the end of steady work. It is associated with farmers and gardeners. Yet the things that Taurus wants—security, comfort, perhaps a little luxury—rarely resemble the actual experience of farming, which features a lot of work under uncertain conditions for chancy rewards, and is unlikely except in rare conditions to foster a luxurious lifestyle. It looks less like the idealized country of fertile Venus and more like, well, Saturn's territory.

One of Saturn's titles was Saturn Stertutius, the Lord of Manure. Yes, that's right, he was the god of manure. These days people tend to think of manure as something unwanted or disgusting, but to anyone who grows crops, it's "brown gold." Saturn was also associated with riches and abundance, and particularly with keeping it. A great statue of Saturn was kept under the Roman state treasury, and its hands were bound with strips of woolen cloth and its feet set in chains in order to keep Saturn, and thus the money, near at hand. This keeping of resources is often a real problem for people with

Saturn in Taurus; money flows out of their hands like water unless they struggle hard to budget like misers. Poverty for long periods of time is often the rule for them, and yet when they have money they often do not know how to use it to make more—they spend their "manure" and then it's gone. Some are hugely invested in making as much money as possible; others are hugely invested in how unimportant money is to them. None of them has a noncommittal attitude toward it; the chains of Saturn hold them too closely. He and his abundance, or lack of it, shape their lives.

One of the great talents of Taurus is the ability to sustain rootedness. This is the quality of being able to put down roots in a place, to extend yourself and your energy throughout that place, to make it your own. In order to farm, for example, you must not only have land of your own, but you must have it under your hands for several years while you work and improve it. Yet all too often individuals with Saturn in Taurus seem unable to reach this state of rootedness. They move restlessly from place to place, wanting to settle down except that nowhere seems "right." It's not the places that are wrong. It's that they can't find the roots within themselves to put down. They want to be rooted—every placement of Taurus wants to be rooted—but it keeps eluding them.

This is the pattern of Saturn in Taurus, Lord of Farming—the insistent desire for stability accompanied by constant instability. Permanence, says Saturn, must be paid for with hard work. You must earn it, and re-earn it, and never cease to earn it. You must never take it for granted even for a single year, or you will lose it. It is the lesson of the farmer—every year you search the sky with your eyes worriedly for rain or lack of it, run out and cover delicate plants in the wake of spring frosts, till in or replant crops that didn't make it, and never waste a thing. The only parts of this life that are stable are the seasons—that spring follows winter, and summer follows spring. Saturn in Taurus people need to look further up the chain of existence for the permanence that they so desire—to the rhythms of the earth and nature, of the cosmos. This will reassure them that some things do not change, at least in their lifetimes, no matter how chaotic their microcosmic lives may be. If they can learn to absorb some of that rhythm, perhaps apply it consciously to their lives in a pattern of personal ritual, or prayer, or other regular activities, then they might be able to bring it into their lives in the form of simple, natural order. And after all, when all the manure is cleared away, that's what Taurus really wants.

LOKI

Saturn in Gemini

The story of Loki is one of the most tragic in Norse mythology. Originally a fire deity, he grew from a minor figure to the Aesir's Public Enemy Number One. He became the archetype of the Dark Trickster, the thief and liar who is not just a mischievous clown but a dangerous and unpredictable enemy. In the later tales, he is not one of the Aesir but a particularly powerful Jotun, or giant, whom Odin befriends and later swears blood brotherhood with. As Odin's blood brother, Loki is welcome in Asgard and does many favors for the various gods of that realm.

Loki is a classic Gemini figure. He is constantly complimented for his cleverness and his ability to disguise himself in a multitude of shapes. He has the smoothest tongue in the Nine Worlds; he can talk anyone into anything. When the warrior-heroes fail at something—for example, when Thor's hammer is stolen—it is Loki who is called upon to save the day with a clever scheme. He even uses his quick tongue to convince ultramasculine Thor to cross-dress on at least one occasion. Also, in true Geminian fashion, Loki also has two simultaneous—and very different—wives. When he becomes Odin's blood brother and earns a residence in Asgard, Odin offered him a woman of the Aesir—Sigyn—for a wife. It didn't seem to matter that he already had a Jotun wife; that sort of thing didn't bother the Norse as much. Sigyn seemed to be a quiet, unassuming, childlike sort of girl who idolized Loki and was devoted to him.

Loki's Jotun wife, Angrboda, whose name means "hag of the iron wood," was a completely different creature. Tall, muscled, and terrifyingly strong, she is an independent-minded giantess/demigoddess and a powerful sorceress. In one myth where she appears under another name, she pulls a stranded ship into the water with her own strength when a team of men and horses could not budge it. Her children are as awesome as she is: Hel, the goddess of death (see Pluto in Virgo); Fenris, a great and terrifying wolf, and Iormundgand, a serpent so large that her coils encircle the world.

Odin and the Aesir are dismayed and unnerved by Loki and Angrboda's brood and immediately move to neutralize them. Fenris goes on a killing spree and is tricked by Tyr (see Saturn in Aries) into being bound with an unbreakable chain and is locked permanently in an underground cave. Iormundgand is forced to swallow her own tail, so that she can only remain in an eternal circle around Midgard. Hel, whose birth was prophesied as that of the most powerful witch in the world, cannot be disposed of in this way. Odin presents her with a truce: he will give her the frigid realm of Niflheim for her own and the rights to the souls of all who die a "straw death," a death other than on the battlefield. In return, she is banished from Midgard and agrees not to trouble Asgard. Then Odin decides that Angrboda herself must die before she spawns any more formidable children that might threaten the power base of the Aesir. Inviting her to a feast, he kills her and burns her body.

Loki finds her ashen heart and realizes that his blood brother has betrayed him. In that moment, he swears that he will have revenge on Odin and all the Aesir. Since they have slain his beloved woman and shown themselves to be false and greedy, he will dedicate himself to their downfall. From this moment on, all his wiles are directed toward undermining the grip of the Aesir on Midgard. From the point of view of the Aesir, he becomes entirely evil. From

Loki's point of view, stealth is the only way that he can get revenge on the blood brother that has betrayed him. He continues to act as if they are all still his friends, but under his smiles he is seething.

First he attempts to undo their immortality by getting Iduna (see Neptune in Virgo) captured; this fails when Thor threatens to kill him and forces him to rescue and return her. Then he decides to rob them of their favorite son. The beautiful god Baldur (Neptune in Libra) has been made immune to all the plants and animals of the world in a deal made by his mother, Frigga. She has missed the tiny mistletoe plant, however, and Loki makes a small but lethal dart from its wood. He convinces Baldur's blind brother Hoder to throw it at Baldur in fun and even offers to aim his hand. The dart finds its mark, and Baldur is slain. The angry and mourning Aesir confront Loki in the hall of Asgard, and in a dramatic final scene he admits to the murder and then treats every one of them to a tongue-lashing. He points out their flaws, their hypocrisies, and every wrong that they have done. He culminates the speech with naming all the Aesir women who have secretly shared his bed while deceiving their husbands about it and criticizes their morals. The other edge of Loki's Geminian tongue is a potent weapon.

The Aesir are humiliated and furious. They seize Loki and bind him in a deep cave. Skadi, the goddess whose heart he has broken (see Pluto in Sagittarius), bitterly places a poisonous snake over him with corrosive venom dripping on his face. His wife Sigyn chooses to stay by his side and hold a bowl beneath the serpent's mouth, catching the venom as it falls. When she has to empty the bowl, he is unprotected, and his pain is so great that the ground shakes from his thrashing.

Loki loses the game that he takes such risks to play, and this is part of the experience of Saturn in Gemini. Mercury is a risk-taker. Conservative Saturn doesn't like risks and punishes risk-taking. Both Loki and Odin are tricksters in their own way, but Odin's trickery is performed subtly, from a place of power within the system, and he is in a position to make it look like necessary politicking. Loki is the trickster who is outcast from the system, fighting it with the only tool he has—the careful and sometimes cruel manipulation of others. Even if his grievances are authentic, he will be seen as a dangerous loose cannon. At their worst, Odin is like the politician who steals the election and Loki is like the terrorist putting bombs in mailboxes. (It is no accident that their representative planets in this book are squared to each other.)

People with Saturn in Gemini will often find themselves outside the mainstream, and not by choice, like Aquarian planets. In any other placement, the Gemini talent for language helps the individual make friends and impress people. With Saturn here, the process is constantly sabotaged and people begin to regard the fast-talking individual as suspicious. All too often they find themselves—as Loki did—using their talent as a way to get some sort of reparation for the wrongs they have suffered. In doing so, they find themselves more outcast than ever.

As a supremely Saturnian fate, Loki is not even allowed to die a relieving death, noble or otherwise. He is bound eternally in torment, a worst-case scenario for active, mobile Gemini. This is the crux of the problem for Saturn in Gemini people. They may be articulate, intelligent people, but somehow those free-flowing Gemini energies get bound up and blocked. They may be able to talk for ages about shallow, informative matters; they may even be able to convince someone else of the validity of their viewpoint, but ask them to speak openly and honestly from the heart and their verbal skill suddenly takes leave of them. They may clam up in bewilderment, or be reduced to third-grade language, or develop an instant stammer or speech disorder.

The best thing that the Saturn in Gemini individual can do—and also the hardest for this placement—is to develop a Saturnian discipline about where to put their words. They need to work less on presentation and more on plainspoken sincerity. They also need to develop better judgment about when and where to use their considerable skill at manipulating situations. Loki's tragedy is that he feels that the ends justify the means, an attitude also held by those who oppose him. Some people may be able to get off with this trick; Saturn, the Lord of Karma, will not tolerate it, because it's sloppy thinking. The most positive keywords for Saturn in Gemini are disciplined mind. If you have that placement, and this doesn't describe you, well, you know what direction to start questing in. It's surely a better fate than being chained in a cave with a serpent dripping poison and knowing that your own bad reactions to other people's bad actions brought you there.

In the Norse pantheon, Loki is the "adversary figure." His spiritual job is to point out the hypocrisies of the ruling classes, which he does brilliantly. In his final speech, nearly everything that he accuses the Aesir of are things that he himself has done—but, he seems to say, at least I admit to it. One can tell how repressed a culture is by how they treat their adversary figure. In Judeo-Christian myth, he has become the Devil, the Lord of All Evil. Loki is still respected in Norse mythos, yet even he is eventually bound, showing their ambivalence about letting this loose cannon of criticism free.

Yet all adversaries are in some way the unwitting tools of fate; although Loki orchestrates Baldur's murder out of anger and vengeance, his act creates the necessary method by which Baldur, safe with Loki's daughter in Helheim, survives Ragnarok to become the king of the next era. Sometimes you can see that happen with Saturn in Gemini people as well; decades after their terrible mistakes, amazing things grow up from the ashes that never would have occurred had they been less willing to thrash about and err. As an example, both of my parents had Saturn in Gemini, and the mistakes they perpetrated on my unwilling child's body eventually deepened into the tools necessary to create this book. Fate sometimes works in mysterious and painful ways. She's a trickster too, you know.

cronos

Saturn in Cancer

Long ago, before the age of the Olympians, there was Cronos the Titan, son of Uranus and Gaea. His mother was the incarnate Earth herself; his father was the Sky and the Air, who spread himself over her every day like a suffocating mass. He was capricious and violent, and he never left his earthy mate alone. By the time she had borne him many children, she was weary of his never-ending advances and wanted nothing more than to be rid of him. She communicated this to her son Cronos, who had grown up watching his father assault his mother in this way.

For his part, Uranus despised his children, who included not only the twelve Titans but three one-eyed Cyclopes and a few hundred-handed monsters. Horrified at what they had created, he shut all the children up in caves in the earth, their mother's body, until Gaea approached them with a plan. She brought out a sharpened sickle and asked for volunteers to slay Uranus.

Cronos took it into his head to save his mother from the abuse of his father, and he attacked Uranus, castrating and killing him. He threw his father's dead body upwards into space, where it became the overarching sky far away, and his severed genitals he threw into the ocean, where they floated for many years on the foam, finally transforming into the goddess Aphrodite. His grateful mother gave him his father's place as king over the created world that she and Uranus had made.

Yet after such a heroic beginning, things began to go terribly wrong with Cronos's reign. He lusted after his sister Rhea and forced her to become his queen, thereby repeating the pattern of his father and mother. Cronos was cannier than his father; he knew that Rhea did not desire him and resented his abuse, and he was not about to let her make a patricidal ally of any of their children. She bore six of them—Hestia, Hades, Demeter, Poseidon, Hera, and Zeus. Cronos was present for the births of the first five deities, and at each birth he seized the baby and swallowed it up, knowing that although he could not kill them, only the prison of his body would hold them securely enough. However, when the youngest child, Zeus, was born, Rhea managed to give birth out of Cronos's sight and presented him with a baby carved out of stone, which he ate.

The child Zeus was raised secretly, out of sight of his father, by two nymphs. When the divine child cried, it was so loud that Rhea sent the Curetes, a sacred band of human warriors, to war-dance around his cradle, striking their shields with their swords in order to drown him out. When he grew old enough, he married Metis, the goddess of wisdom, and she made a magic potion for him that his mother fed to his father, Cronos. The potion caused him to vomit forth all the children trapped in his body, along with one large stone. At this point, Zeus defeats Cronos; in some versions by killing him, in others merely by setting him permanently in chains.

The placement of Saturn in Cancer has one major theme: how families repeat patterns. The abuse of one generation can carry down through several more, if no one takes the time to step away from the familial cauldron and make a conscious effort to change. Cronos grows up watching a violent, abusive father and a weak, spiteful mother; as often happens, Gaea makes her precious son her ally against the bad father and induces him to attack Dad and rescue Mom when he is old enough. Unable to resist this casting of himself as the savior of his beloved mother in the family play, he does her bidding—how could he do otherwise?—and kills his father. However, he is then faced with the emotional dilemma of all sons of bad fathers and smothering mothers . . . is he to be bad, and a man (like his father) or the nice boy that his mother would have him be, but not really a man? He has no positive male role models; "man bad" and "woman good" is all he knows. So of course he chooses to be a man, and to be bad, like his father. Given this bad choice, unfortunately, most boys do. He treats his wife Rhea like his father treated his mother, and she reacts similarly.

Cronos hates and fears his children, as Uranus hated and feared him, because they are independent beings that he cannot control. His attempts to swallow them mirror the attempts of many a controlling father to totally engulf his offspring and allow them no life independent of him. However, his sixth child seems to him a baby carved out of stone—hard and cold, perhaps from watching generations of abuse. The "real" Zeus is raised in secret by his mother, suggesting another emotionally incestuous mother-son bond, and eventually strikes out against him, repeating the pattern. Zeus, however, although he does mistreat his wife, has learned at least one lesson: he honors and cherishes his children, and none of them ever unseats him.

Family patterns of abuse, coldness, and dysfunction, and whether or not to accept or struggle against them, are an underlying theme for a Saturn in Cancer. They may not be the exact pattern of hate that goes on in Cronos's family, but they will be difficult to extract oneself from, especially for family-worshipping Cancer. Dysfunctional families and lack of proper nurturing happen for lots of people, but for the individual with Saturn in Cancer, they are an overriding karmic issue, soaking his entire emotional existence until everything in his life is permeated with them. It is vital—as in, it can mean his very life itself—to commit to two things. First, he must make the struggle to be aware of and rid himself of dysfunctional family patterns. It is just too easy for a Saturn in Cancer to go on miserably repeating what happened to him, taking the role of abuser or abused, or both in turn, because he thinks that it's just the way things are. He has to make an effort to find new role models for human relationships, perhaps forming bonds with people who will treat him as he should have been treated. Whatever he does, he must not idealize anything or anyone from his childhood until he has examined it thoroughly for emotional poisons.

Second, he must find within himself the well of Cancerian nurturing that he did not receive. This sort of quest is so individual that there's no point in giving examples or advice; a Saturn in Cancer must find the path to untainted love himself, step by step. Cronos is defeated and chained by the son he inadvertently created, and his chains symbolize his inability to move from the path his own parents placed him on, even at the end when everything finally fell down. A Saturn in Cancer can follow this path, and it will end in pain and loneliness, because it always does, or he can throw off those chains and creep out onto a new road. Sometimes the way you're used to is not the best, and sometimes the enemy you don't know can turn out to be a friend.

Ahura Mazda
Saturn in Leo

Throughout European mythology, we see the myth of the paired gods who are mirrors of each other. One is usually the Bright God, associated with daylight, the summer months, and the part of the year with long days. The other is the Dark God, associated with winter, the underworld, and the time of the waning daylight. One is the Sun, the other the Black Sun of the underworld. Both take turns being consort to the Goddess that births them. In the lore of the Celts, they are the Oak King and the Holly King. They often ritually fight and slay each other in turn. Yet in spite of this apparent animosity, they are not ranked one above the other. To most of the ancients, each was equally valuable, equally important, and equally good in his own way. Summer followed winter and day followed night, and that was the way it should be. It was a natural phenomenon, and not something to be too deeply anthromorphized.

When the Persian prophet Zoroaster popularized the worship of Ahura Mazda the Sun God, he posited a god of darkness to be his equal opponent, Ahriman. However, after his death, generations of

Sassanian priests slowly crystallized the two into a polarized pair of good and evil influences. Everything that was good or right was attributed to Ahura Mazda; everything that was wrong or harmful was attributed to Ahriman. They became defined by each other rather than by their attributes; the god who was solely anti-devil and the devil who was solely anti-god. This was the first of the bright-god/dark-god pairs to openly proclaim "light good" and "dark evil." As such, they moved away from a description of nature's cycles and became a human abstraction that bore no resemblance to earthly reality.

The teachings of Zoroastrianism formed the basic cosmology for many later religions, including—through the offshoot Manichaeanism—early Christianity. It still survives healthily to this day, to the point where most of us have to fight not being sucked in to its judgmental duality. The older god-pairs were acknowledged to have both positive and negative sides between them. The underworld god was mysterious and brought unseen death from disease and old age, but he was also a comforting guide through sorrow and a teacher of deep, enigmatic wisdom. The sun god stood for light and clarity and bravery, and his light made all things grow, but he was also the bright, hot death that sucked the life out of all plants and animals at the height of his powers, the high summer of those hot semidesert countries. Indeed, his ritual slaying by his darker brother was seen as a relief, for otherwise he would simply become stronger and stronger, until he would burn the whole world. In a sense, as Ahura Mazda's legacy lived chillingly on in the sacred-versus-profane medieval Christian cosmology of the Burning Times, that is exactly what he did.

It's a hard lesson for us to learn, we who live with the unwitting legacy of Zoroastrian dualism. It's so easy for us to forget the hard lesson: this much light must, by definition, create this large a shadow. The more you concentrate on living in the light, while neglecting your own internal shadows, the greater they will become until they leap up and pull down your brilliant daytime façade. As the light becomes stronger, the dark will rise to equal it. As long as you cling to the fallacy of being able to put all good in one place and all evil in another—and make yourself the former container and someone else the latter—you will simply raise the stakes in your own internal war.

This is Saturn's hard lesson for the solar Leo energy. Leo is in its detriment when Saturn resides there, as Saturn is probably the planet who looks—on a surface level, anyway—like Ahriman the Enemy. The Leo Saturn wants many of the things that any other Leo placement wants—admiration, respect, authority, applause— but all too often he has a streak of self-righteousness or feeling of moral superiority that spurs him on to being less of a benevolent monarch and more of a tyrannical dictator. Much of his tyranny may be manifested in attempting to force others to follow a similar moral path. Even simple things like the work efficiency of employees may become a huge moral issue to a Saturn in Leo. Black-and-white dualistic moral codes are a terrible temptation to them, and one that they have to fight hard to extract themselves from.

Traditionally, the dark god's planet in the sun god's sign (or any combination of solar and Saturnian energies) suggests an early life where the child's specialness and identity were ignored in favor of a rigid code of behavior. If he wanted any positive attention at all, he had to pay careful attention to being "good," as opposed to being "bad," by a standard that was probably fairly irrational. As an adult, he works so hard at being "good" by that abstract standard that he resents anyone who acts as though this isn't the most important thing to do. Striving for the light, he casts a bigger and bigger shadow—and since it is behind him, he is rarely aware of it. Paradoxically, the more he seeks acclaim, the less likely he is to get it, until he gives up the crusade against himself.

The solution, of course, is to reintegrate the bright and dark gods within himself. This does not mean that he should dispose of all moral codes, but that he needs to pay attention to the dark places within him. "Monster work," or the practice of appeasing one's inner selfishness in nonharmful ways, is very helpful to this individual. In order to be loved—which is a strong issue of Leo, ruler of the heart—he must first learn to love every part of himself.

The legends of Zoroastrianism are full of the ongoing thousand exploits of Ahura Mazda and Ahriman. Each time the Sun God triumphed, the Black Sun counterattacked, and the battle never ended. The only way to stop the war is to help the brothers remember who they used to be before the age of dualism, when each had value and danger equal to the other. It's not only the Saturn in Leo lesson, but something we all have to look at before the whole world burns.

wayland the smith

Saturn in Virgo

The element of earth is inextricably bound up with the reality of labor. To say that the natural world is carefree and lives an existence of peaceful laziness is a blatant falsehood. Every creature toils, day in and day out, seeking and procuring and processing food, finding water and shelter, attempting to propagate its species, and trying desperately to avoid being eaten by others. In the natural world, nothing serves only one purpose. The romping play of wolf cubs also serves the purpose of teaching them how to hunt and stalk. The songs of birds attract proper mates. Nothing is wasted on mere pleasure. In reality, labor is the modus operandi of the world.

Saturn understands this truth to the core, and so does Virgo. The planet of discipline is at home in the sign of the Monk or Nun, but just because Saturn makes himself at home doesn't mean that it is a comfortable residence. In Virgo, the pessimistic side of Saturn's nature can so thoroughly permeate the individual's life that they submit without negotiation to his ponderous demands. Like its opposite sign, Saturn in Pisces—who expects life to be a string of random, out-of-the-blue sufferings—Saturn in Virgo expects life to be a long, unhappy work week chosen out of duty and guilt. He works not only because he likes to work, but because he believes that it will save him. For Saturn in Virgo people, work is not just their god but their messiah.

The tale of Wayland the Smith comes out of ancient Anglo-Saxon legend, about which we know little. It is mentioned in various Norse sagas, where it remains a tragically ambivalent tale. In the beginning, three swan maidens fly south over the areas of Murkwood and Wolf-dale, where they alight on the shore of a lake and change into their human forms. Three mortal princes, sons of the king of Finland, happen to be watching. They approach the maidens and begin to court them. The swan girls' names are Allwhite, Swanwhite, and Olrun, and they eventually give in to the blandishments of the princes and agree to marry them. They live happily for many years, but in the ninth year the swan maidens decide to return to their own land; they change back into swan-form and fly away. The brothers are devastated; the younger two, Egil and Slagfid, decide immediately to hunt for their lost brides and vanish into the northern forest, although they have no idea where they could have gone.

The eldest brother, Wayland, is a greatly skilled smith, and he has no wish to wander. He misses his wife Allwhite with a passion, but decides instead to wait for her return beside the lake where they met. He sets up his forge by the lake and works daily, making beautiful gifts for her, including a stunningly wrought gold ring.

Mercury-ruled Virgo is all too often taken with airy ideals of perfection, which he will then struggle to achieve. Sometimes he actually succeeds, but usually he falls short. When Saturn passes into this Mercury-ruled earth sign, the individual becomes keenly aware of just how much of a gaping difference there is between his ideals and his reality. Although he strives to fly, he is inextricably bound to the grubby earth. This can result in a number of desperate compensation behaviors, ranging from the person who gives up in despair all too easily to the one who works forever at hopeless tasks that are impossible to achieve. A Saturn in Virgo really does believe that work is the answer to everything, including bringing back lost lovers or dreams or joys, and like Wayland he will keep banging out more gold rings in the hope that this next one will be the Great Work that solves all his problems.

However, those who work too hard often attract those who wish to take advantage of them. A local lord, Niduth, hears of the smith's skill and sends his men-at-arms to capture him. When they approach the smithy, Wayland is out hunting bear, so they steal the golden ring and hide in an ambush. The smith returns, notices the loss of the ring, and for a moment thinks that Allwhite has returned to him. He is struck from behind by the ambushers and falls unconscious. Upon awakening, he finds himself bound and captive and is brought before the greedy lord. When he refuses to work, Niduth has him hamstrung, so that he can only limp on crutches, and imprisons him on the island of Saevarstod. Here he works his forge in fear of death, visited only by the king, and plots his revenge. The ring that was to be Allwhite's is given to Niduth's daughter Bodvild.

Something about the very skill and perfectionism of a Saturn in Virgo seems to lead to the individual's imprisonment in a world of stark duty that he does not enjoy. Sometimes he is imprisoned by his own guilt, as he secretly feels that he is a terrible sinner, and he may use unceasing work to punish himself or to pay off his sins. Virgo is dedicated to service, but Saturn's influence can knock him over the line between sacrifice and martyrdom. He is also susceptible to guilt trips and the manipulation of others, who tell him that he is the only one who is good enough to do what needs to be done, thereby locking him into dutiful overwork. He can also be hamstrung by his own crippling shyness or lack of social skills into exiling himself to the only place where he feels competent.

If he feels alienated enough from people or if they are cruel to him, he may cease to care about the rights of anyone he does not respect or feel is worthy. Years of emotional isolation may also build up a huge font of resentment in him, which may suddenly explode forth. In the legend, Niduth's sons—as greedy as their father—come to Wayland to bribe or threaten him to give them their father's treasure. The resentful smith kills them with his hammer and cuts off their heads, and then makes goblets out of their skulls. These he sends to their father, who is unaware at first of their origin. He also sends along a gift for Bodvild—a necklace made of her brothers' teeth set in gold.

The rigid discipline of a Saturn in Virgo is created in reaction to a huge undercurrent of fear. Every individual with this placement secretly fears that there is a monster within them, waiting to leap out and commit terrible sins. The imagined sins may vary according to the individual, but they are all held back by a stoic front of continual labor. Saturn in this placement can create an amazingly productive life, but it can also be cold and sterile. The heat and emotional action may be locked in a small closet, which is usually already inhabited by the internal monster, and thus all strong feeling becomes associated with violence or loss of self-control.

Eventually the monster must be faced. If its closet is filled with decades of repressed anger and resentment, however, the consequences can be explosive, like Wayland who suddenly erupts in a torrent of violence and vengeance. All too often, in this sign of the Virgin, the most feared activities of the monster have to do with sex and sexual violence. A Saturn in Virgo can be terrified of sexual passion, seeing it as an uncontrollable, destructive force. This repression can explode periodically in impulsive bouts of wild sexual activities that seem to "come out of nowhere," according to their frightened conscious self. In the myth, the maiden Bodvild comes to Wayland out of fascination for the mysterious, talented, tragic smith, and he forces himself on her sexually. The innocent Bodvild and the smoldering Wayland are like the conscious and unconscious levels of Saturn in Virgo: his passion and genius inspire the many works that adorn her daylight life, yet he is hidden, crippled, and despised. Sooner or later Bodvild and Wayland meet, and whether their encounter results in inner violence or a compassionate treaty depends much on how abused that inner monster has been.

At this point in the story, however, Wayland escapes. With the rape of his enemy's last precious possession, his need for vengeance is exhausted. Like the Greek craftsman Daedalus, he builds a pair of great wings that allow him to fly away from the island and make his own way in the world. In a sense, he has gone from being a wounded, ground-crawling creature and has become like his own lost and idealized swan-wife Allwhite. Even if the release of a Saturn in Virgo's inner monster comes with a temporarily destructive upheaval of anger and turmoil, it allows the individual to live a freer life—and gains him the ability to fly through his own achievements.

Wayland the Smith's legend is still alive and well in the county of Berkshire in England, where a stone burial chamber is known as Wayland's Smithy. The legend says that Wayland's ghost still works there, and that a traveler who leaves his unshod horse overnight in the place—leaving, of course, a coin on the anvil stone—will find the next morning that his horse would be magically shod, the stone would be warm, and the coin removed. When a Saturn in Virgo has integrated the urge to work and the passion for life, his talents can seem almost magical, like the wizard who creates displays of delight to entertain the masses. Modest Virgo may still prefer to be invisible and arrange things from behind the scenes, however. To him, adulation is never the point. He knows instinctively that the mind that counts most will always see everything that he has done, for good or ill.

Themis

Saturn in Libra

In the Olympian pantheon of ancient Greece, there is one sedate and unassuming goddess who is often overshadowed by the more flamboyant types. She was honored quietly by civil servants and other citizens, and even the great Zeus listened to her advice, but she tends to be seen as boring and tedious rather than exciting. It's a recurring problem with Saturnian placements. They aren't exciting, what with all the stuff about limits and discipline and duty. Themis was a Titan, one of the demigods borne by Gaea. She was of the generation of the parents of the present Olympians and so was already something of a blue-haired elder, at least in age. In fact, she was the only Titan who was honored rather than hated by Zeus and his followers.

Themis was the Miss Manners of Olympus, the guardian of propriety and civic duty. Her job is to remind us all of our social responsibilities, and it was in this advisory capacity that she sat next to the throne of Zeus and aided him in making decisions of rulership. It's hard to sum up her area of expertise in one word, as our language and culture falls flat when we try to condense her into a single phrase. Some refer to her as the goddess of law, some as that of justice, although that more properly belongs to her daughter Dike. She was concerned with maintaining order and making sure that all ceremonies proceeded properly and with correctness. She was a goddess of wisdom and was given the epithet Eubolos, or "good counselor," but unlike Athena, who dispensed wisdom one on one, Themis as Good Counselor was specifically in charge of giving wisdom to groups of people, and she presided over public assemblies.

Her daughters give us a clue to her personality and values. She gave birth to the three Horae, Eunomia the goddess of rules, Dike the goddess of justice (see Sun in Libra), and Irene the goddess of peace. Themis protected the just and helped to decide sentencing for the unjust, thus acting as a force of karma to the world. Above all, she explained through oracles the proper responsibility one should have toward other people and the gods. A Saturn in Libra is comfortable with social responsibility. She learns the rules about how one should behave so as to grease the wheels of human interaction and make things easier and more diplomatic. She follows these rules precisely and insists that others do the same. Others may accuse her of being dreary and narrow, with her worship of propriety and her insistence on proper social duty, but she has narrowed herself deliberately in order to focus properly on her discipline. The discipline of a Saturn in Libra is, in a word, graciousness.

You will notice that although Themis is a Titan, she does not suffer the fate of her brothers and sisters. The other Titans rebelled against Zeus, who defeated them and locked them up under the earth. Themis prudently did not take part in the battle. In fact, she defected to the Olympian team and thus was on the winning side when the dust had settled. This could be construed as giving her a certain coldness, a calculating lack of moral passion, and indeed this is the sort of accusation that has been leveled against those with Saturn in Libra. The Libran nature is to avoid disharmony, and Saturn in this sign is cynical enough that she may well feel that doomed struggle and tilting against windmills are more trouble than they are worth, something to be indulged in by the somewhat younger in spirit. She also refrains from intervening when Zeus is busy torturing humanity, except to aid them quietly and in oblique ways that could not possibly be construed as disobedience or rebellion. What, a Saturn in Libra rebel against the social order? A Saturn in Libra is the embodiment of the social order. And that means that she can decide that it is whatever she says it is.

In one legend, Zeus decides to flood one area of the earth out of pique toward Themis's fellow Titan, Prometheus. He manages to drown all the people except for one couple, Deucalion the son of Prometheus and Pyrrha the daughter of Epimetheus and Pandora (see Uranus in Pisces). The two escape in an ark, but are distraught when they land and find no survivors. They pray to Themis, and she answers in a riddle: they must veil their heads, unbind their robes, and walk casting behind them the bones of their first ancestor. This stymies them for a while, until they realize that their first ancestor is Gaea, the earth beneath their feet. They walk as Themis has told them, throwing stones—the bones of the earth—over their shoulders. As the stones land, they are transformed into men and women, and the land is repopulated.

Themis is the second wife of Zeus, a brief marriage after his disastrous mating with Metis, but he soon tires of her and puts her aside for other pastures. Unlike Hera (see Jupiter in Libra), for whom divorce and abandonment would be unthinkable, Themis accepts the demotion from wife to cabinet member without more than a shrug. It's not that she doesn't value being in a marriage—all Libra planets want to be in relationship—it's that if the marriage isn't right, she is able to cut her losses and move on with Saturnian aloofness. It is also said that it was the Moerae, or Fates, who brought her to Zeus's attention in the first place and arranged the marriage. Saturn is the planet of karma, and sometimes our karmic relationships don't end up as happily-ever-after lovers. Sometimes one has to learn that being on friendly terms with someone, with no hatred between the two of you, and having learned something about yourself from the affair, is a good definition of success in relationship.

In our world, where we are force-fed the happily-ever-after myth from the cradle on, it's hard for us to accept a friendly breakup unless we can believe that there was never very much passion there to begin with. We find it hard to imagine deliberately disciplining our anger and pain, putting all our effort into trying to salvage some friendship at least, being a good counselor and friend to the one who used to share your life completely. It seems like too much of a demotion, but this is a Saturn in Libra lesson: don't waste a perfectly good friendship just because of a romantic disillusionment. Saturn hates waste, and a Saturn in Libra hates to waste a human connection.

For people with this placement, relationships are the situations where you work out your karmic debts and lessons. They believe in this so strongly, if only on an unconscious level, that they will sometimes avoid relationships entirely because they don't have the strength for yet another learning experience. When they do form bonds, they tend to be drawn to those people who openly flaunt faults that the Saturn in Libra person has herself, but represses and denies. Other people are her harsh mirror, and she is driven to keep looking into it until she finally sees herself in them, whole and happy.

Themis is the embodiment of grace under pressure. In order to cultivate true grace, one has to have some moral spine, some conviction about how things ought to be. One also has to have the strength to actually walk one's talk while not alienating those lesser beings who can't seem to make that struggle work. Saturn in Libra has plenty of grace and graciousness, even though that means a certain amount of distance. Sometimes you have to get a distance on someone to really see them clearly, as who they truly are.

cerridwen
Saturn in Scorpio

Pigs, like Scorpio, have a terrible and undeserved reputation. They are Scorpionic creatures—tough, hardy, omnivorous recyclers of garbage, rooting up the muck in search of interesting things. Originally evolved from semi-aquatic swamp dwellers, pigs are astoundingly intelligent for animals that have been bred to eat a lot and get fat. They can be friendly and affectionate, but they are also the only traditional livestock animal that has been known to eat its owners.

In ancient mythology, the sow goddess was much more revered than her descendants today. Among the Greeks, the word for pig was also the word for female genitalia; this was not an insult but a reference to the sow goddess in her various forms. Since pigs come in the three colors of the Goddess—white, red, and black—they were one of her sacrificial animals. The Celts associate her with Cerridwen, and pigs were eaten at funeral feasts in her honor. There were tales of the oracular white sows who told the future, mortal incarnations of the Lady Sow.

Cerridwen is one of the elder goddesses who have contributed to the "old witch" stereotype. She is a Saturnian old woman, but she is no nice grandmother. Her cauldron bubbles with wonderful and terrible things, gifts and curses and regeneration. Like that of her sister goddess Branwen, slain corpses can be plunged into it and revived again. She is a shapeshifter who can take on animal forms as quick as a blink, and she is ruthless in her own way.

She is a mother, but she is not cuddly. Cerridwen has a son whom she loves very much and a foster son named Gwion Bach whom she treats as a servant. Scorpio is a water sign, and she has to work hard not to naturally play favorites with her loved ones. Cerridwen's son, however, is not an appealing child. He is slow, dull, and halt of tongue, but she loves him anyway. The comparison with the bright hireling boy who does the chores around her cottage must be painful for her, and her treatment of Gwion Bach (later known as Taliesin) probably reflects this resentment.

Cerridwen's response to her son's dullness is to create a magic potion in her cauldron that will give him the gift of speech, language, and intelligence. This potion must be boiled for a year and a day, to which she faithfully devotes herself. One of the clear traits of people with this position is their stubborn, obsessive persistence. The possessive Plutonian nature crossed with the unbending Saturnian energy creates a soul that will doggedly pursue a goal to the bitter end, even beyond necessity or wisdom. Failure becomes a personal affront. The goal must be met, even if it is outdated or destructive. Once they set on a path, they find it almost painful to swerve from it.

I knew one child with Saturn in Scorpio who would work herself into temper tantrums that might last hours, long after the initial slight had been forgotten. It was as if the mood swept over her like a tidal wave, and she found herself unable to stop herself. Adults with this placement have been known to obsess on one small thing until it grows out of proportion in their minds and seems overwhelming, sending them into a downward spiral of anger or despair. On the positive side, however, that emotional surge can fuel long-term goals that a Scorpio in Saturn succeeds with long after others have dropped out or fallen by the wayside.

Death, rebirth, and transformation are the province of Pluto, Scorpio's ruler, and any Plutonian-influenced planet will work with and through and around those energies. The real reason behind a Saturn in Scorpio's obsessiveness is that she is both driven to transform herself (and her energies, projects, and world) and prevented from doing so. Her response is to try again and again until she finally breaks through and turns the situation around completely. The archetypal figure of Cerridwen is both a mistress of transformation—she rebirths people out of her cauldron—and completely, irrationally consumed by her own passions. These are the powerful and powerless sides of this power-fixated sign.

On the last day before the potion is ready, Cerridwen goes out to collect the last few ingredients, leaving Gwion Bach to stir the cauldron. He has strict instructions not to touch its contents. Of course, curious young boys being who they are, he ends up ingesting three drops of the potion, thus taking its magic into himself and ruining Cerridwen's year of work. He flees, using his newly gained magical powers to turn himself into a hare. When the old goddess discovers his theft and the destruction of her son's hopes, she flies into a rage and follows him in the guise of a greyhound. He changes to a fish; she follows as an otter. He changes to a sparrow; she follows as a hawk. No matter how he tries to avoid her, the mistress of transformation manages to adapt, change, and try a new way to approach the situation by transmuting herself into something new.

Finally, he turns into a grain of wheat on a threshing floor and she turns into a hen and eats him. The tenacity of Saturn in Scorpio reflects in Cerridwen's pursuit of Taliesin; the more he eludes her, the angrier she gets. She will not give up until she has consumed him utterly, even though it means that she is forced to give birth to him. Saturn in Scorpio is driven to eradicate their prey as completely as possible, probably with a good deal of overkill.

At this point, it would seem that she has won—completely consuming the problem—but then she finds herself unexpectedly pregnant. She gives birth to a baby boy, and knows immediately that it is the child she ate. Here the tables have been turned: the foster child she rejected is now her own flesh and blood, her true son. Having devoured him, she is forced to rebirth him. This is the way it usually goes with a Saturn in Scorpio. If the problem is solved in a way that does not transform her own self as well as the situation, it will keep presenting itself again in new and unexpected ways. The key is not to change the outside world, but to change the inner one—her reaction to the problem—and then the problem will dissolve.

Cerridwen is faced with a choice. She can kill the child with whom she is so angry or she can raise him as her own, knowing that he will always outshine her dull elder son. She chooses neither path; instead she wraps him in furs and places him in a boat, sending him out into the sea to find a new home. This is the choice that is the hardest of all for individuals with this obsessive combination—just letting go of the whole dilemma and trusting that fate will take care of it. In sending him away, she lets go of her anger and resentment and starts anew.

The child, of course, becomes known as Taliesin (see Mercury in Sagittarius), the greatest bard of Celtic myth. Out of Cerridwen's rage and fear and obsessiveness and constant changing is born the light of inspiration . . . but only because she learned when to rebirth and when to let go.

chiron
Saturn in Sagittarius

Chiron is the name of one of the most important of the asteroids. However, his myth also resonates strongly with Saturn in Sagittarius, so—as I'm not doing all the asteroids in all the signs, which would take another book!—I have chosen to borrow those myths for these purposes. Chiron is a centaur, half man and half horse; in fact, he is *the* Centaur, the one placed in the sky to form the constellation of Sagittarius itself. The half-man, half-horse situation suggests a clash between the physical and the mental, the deep, earth-centered animal urges and the high, airy, mental theorizing, the scholar and the shaman; and this is indeed one of the Sagittarian dilemmas. Which is more of a spiritual experience—reading a holy book or making love to the beloved? This is the sign of religion, as opposed to mysticism, as religion is the place where people turn to answer these questions when they do not have the stomach for the personal quest to find them on their own.

Chiron, however, is not an archetypal Centaur. First of all, he is educated. This alone sets him far apart from his people, as the other centaurs are without exception shown as a rude, barbarous people, delighting in wine and mayhem. The only other noted centaurs in myth are brigands or tribal herdsmen. Sagittarius is the sign of higher education, but in Chiron's case it seems to estrange him from his race. He never dwells among them, but instead lives in Saturnian solitude in a mountain cave, alone except for his royal pupils. His formidable education has been learned from Artemis and Apollo, gods of moon and sun, and it does seem remarkably well-rounded. He knows the arts of warfare and of healing, of lore and music, both the physical and intellectual Apollonian pursuits and the lunar mysteries. His reputation grew so great that he was granted immortality, and every lord wanted his son tutored by Chiron the Wise.

Among his students are Hercules, Achilles, Jason, and the great doctor Aesculapius. On one level, he embodies the Sagittarian archetype of the Philosopher, personifying the sort of scholar that Greek and Roman emperors would hire to teach their sons. Nearly all of his students achieve fame and glory, but one of them—Hercules—causes Chiron's undoing. Hercules seems to be the least refined of the lot of them, the hero whose extreme physicality is his central heroic quality—the one who bashes heads rather than reasons things out. Perhaps, in a sense, he is both Chiron's greatest failure and symbolic of his own repressed animal side.

Saturn has a lot to do with repression, and a Saturn in Sagittarius often seems to split the man/horse conundrum entirely in favor of the man, forcing the wild side deeply into the subconscious. The problem with this is that when something's forced into the subconscious, you may have no access to it, but it has plenty of access to you. It can saw through the floor, so to speak, when you're not looking, and suddenly you fall down into a basement of rage and fear and despair and have no idea how you got there. What is repressed is most dangerous; always-calm and always-reasonable Chiron must have a terrifying dark side.

The only time we see Chiron among his people is the one fateful scene where he is wounded. Apparently he had come home and was staying with other centaurs, and his former pupil Hercules came by to see him. Hercules, always rambunctious, promptly gets into a fight with the other centaurs over a jug of wine and the weapons start flying. Chiron takes no part in the struggle, but a stray poisoned arrow shot by Hercules hits him in the leg. Because he cannot die, the poison does not kill him, and he merely exists in agony. The poison is too virulent for healing by his talents, or even those of his pupil Aesculapius. He suffers for some time, living the irony of the wounded healer who cannot cure himself. At the same time, because he has been granted immortality for his deeds, an endless life of eternal pain seems to be his fate.

The fact that he is wounded in the leg, causing him to limp and have difficulty getting around, is deeply personal to Sagittarius, the sign that rules the moving thighs. Another of the typical Sagittarian archetypes is the Wanderer, signifying the Archer's method of gaining experience, and thus wisdom, by wandering from place to place without a real goal. This is, after all, the sign of travel, yet Chiron becomes too crippled to travel further. In talking to individuals with Saturn in Sagittarius, one can clearly see the ways in which the Wanderer archetype has failed them: some are terrified of the outdoors and hate the uncertainty of travel, others have had long journeys hitchhiking across country that yielded only discomfort and trouble. Often their deliberate attempts to be the free-and-easy wanderer are thwarted by circumstances every time they try—flat tires, lost wallets, and so forth. It is as if Saturn is deliberately crippling them, forcing them to make an inward journey rather than an outward one.

The Wise Teacher archetype, on the other hand, can go one of two ways. If one were to use the Tarot as an example, one path would be represented by the Hierophant and the other by the Hermit. The first path teaches a tradition, inside a specific structure that the teacher in question knows inside and out, backwards and forwards. This can be embodied in someone such as an ordained priest or a martial-arts sensei. The other path is that of the Seeker, who eschews tradition and attempts to find his own way, perhaps wandering through various traditions and taking that which is of use to him, but not staying in any one. He teaches not from a particular structure, but from his own experience; mythologist Joseph Campbell was a good example of this kind of sage. Both are choices of Saturn in Sagittarius, but the first choice seems to have a warning attached to it: that no matter how much you bind yourself to a traditional group, sooner or later you will become unsatisfied with them and be forced by your own conscience to leave.

And so this is the sign of the religious rebel, the inward journey to one's own truth. Although this Saturn placement rarely creates a physical wanderer, it does seem rife with spiritual ones. Sooner or later, it seems, the repressed physical side will leap out, screaming that its own personal experience is not being represented in this faith. Natives of this Saturn placement often end up practically creating their own religions or churches-of-one, as the "top of their mountain" has to resemble that personal, physical, deeply subjective experience. The Hermit, a very Saturnian figure, gets them in the end . . . and often lights the way for others behind them.

At the end of his myth, Chiron decides that he can suffer no longer. He offers to give his immortality to the Titan Prometheus in honor of Prometheus's sacrifice and torment. This offer may not be all that pleasing to the Olympian king Zeus, who chained Prometheus to the rock in the first place. Athena, however, places him among the constellations after his quick death. This symbolizes the breaking-away point of a Saturn in Sagittarius: in order to end that potential unending spiritual pain, he must defy authority and place his energies in a place he finds most deserving. True wisdom does not just hold to the status quo, sharing itself only with the children of the privileged. Prometheus, in this myth, represents the force for the underdog, stealing fire and giving it to the lowest of the low. When a Saturn in Sagittarius finds the right cause and shucks his traditions to follow it, he, like Chiron, can find his way into the stars.

ch'eng-Huang
Saturn in Capricorn

Every large town in China has an incarnation of the god Ch'eng-Huang, the god of walls and ditches. He is the town protector and holy administrator, and his title comes from the walls and ditches that surround a Chinese city or town, creating its boundaries and

protecting it from outsiders. He is a functionary in the holy bureaucracy of the Emperor Lao-Tien-Yeh (see Neptune in Capricorn),
who willingly carries out his duty, visiting a different town or city
each day on a yearly schedule.

The difference between Ch'eng-Huang and most other gods is
that he has many incarnations, all of whom were once mortal
bureaucrats who were especially respected in life. After they have
passed on, the gods arrange for stringent examinations, and if they
pass, they are awarded the prize of becoming one of the many forms
of Ch'eng-Huang. In a way, becoming this god is the ultimate prize
for the dedicated paper-pusher—he gets a highly respected position
of great responsibility in an eternal hierarchy of bureaucrats, which
he keeps for centuries. It is the sort of heavenly reward that Saturn
would dream up and the sort that a Capricorn would end up receiving.

If the dead candidate actually wins the position of God of Walls
and Ditches, he is prevented from reincarnating again until his
replacement comes along. Barred from the Wheel of Life and Death,
he must serve as a divine bureaucrat in what must be a painfully
boring job, possibly for centuries, until someone worthy is found to
be the next incarnation of Ch'eng-Huang. Yet it is assumed that he
considers this an honor, because Saturn would expect nothing less.

Saturn is in its own sign in Capricorn, and here its Saturnian
energies can flow unrestricted by all the nonsense and fluff of the
other signs. Capricorn is paradoxically both quite humble and
incredibly arrogant at the same time. He has a realistic view of his
own shortcomings, but he is quite sure that with enough hard work,
he can and will make it to the top, where he will be in a position of
authority over others. He feels, secretly, that he is morally superior
to most others and that they will be better off under his guidance. If
Leo believes that he is a king, Capricorn is well aware that he is a
peasant—but he firmly believes that he will become prime minister.
As such, he tends to grasp at the trappings of wealth and status, not

so much glorying in them like Leo (who considers them a natural birthright) but deliberately showing them off as proof of his class and worthiness.

The fact that Ch'eng-Huang, as a deity, is less a personality than a position, is telling. Saturn in Capricorn can place more value on success than personal improvement. This placement gives ambitions, whether or not the individual in question admits to them. Ch'eng-Huang always rides into town in splendor, dressed like a high-class Chinese statesman. The governor has always been informed of his visit by the gods in a dream, so the city turns out to welcome him. In spite of his dutiful, pedantic nature, he is a greatly respected god, because he keeps the lesser bureaucrats honest. He is the one that is prayed to when some minor paper-pusher becomes corrupt and abuses his power. Ch'eng-Huang is not a flashy superhero from outside the system who intervenes and saves the day; he is the self-correcting power of the system itself. He is the Internal Affairs whistle-blower; although he will not handle an offense not specifically against the rules, he deals with rule breakers quickly and coldly.

We tend to forget that in order to keep a system fair, it is vitally important to have some element within it who is willing to level penalties and dole out retribution. A Saturn in Capricorn believes in consequences, not luck. If you want to get somewhere, you have to work for it, and he does, often with a vengeance. Workaholism is not unusual with this sign, and neither is success, although it may not come with happiness. Still, a Saturn in Capricorn isn't necessarily trying for success in order to achieve happiness, so it may not affect him the way it does others.

The duties of the God of Walls and Ditches concern themselves with civic propriety. He does not bother with what goes on inside houses—that's more of a domestic Cancerian sphere—but with what occurs outside them. Buildings must be solid; the marketplace must be honest; the politicians must be reliable; the streets must be peaceful, orderly, and well paved; and of course all the walls and ditches must be in order. (Saturn specializes in boundaries and obstacles.) This is Capricorn's realm, that of the world outside the door, and the set of rules that makes a diverse mob of warring individuals get along in some kind of social peace. A Saturn in Capricorn is less concerned with what his family thinks of him than what the outside world thinks of him, and his reputation is as important as if he thought that Ch'eng-Huang was always watching him. That's because his reputation is a tool that he uses to get things done and to get people to trust (or in certain negative cases, fear) him. He doesn't try to charm people into doing what he wants; he shows credentials that prove he knows what he's talking about. Reputation is a large part of that.

Ch'eng-Huang is accompanied by four assistants. Two are his own personal assistants, named—tellingly—Mr. Black and Mr. White. Their names signify that one is the Day Watchman and one the Night Watchman, but they also mirror a deep Saturnian truth— that Saturn, and likewise Capricorn, likes to have things down in black and white, sorted neatly into boxes marked "Satisfactory" and "Unsatisfactory." It's one of their greatest challenges: the struggle to accept things that are vague, ethereal, malleable, erratic, inconsistent, or unpredictable, and still vitally important—things like feelings and aesthetic considerations and the Mysteries. Saturn is the planet of coldness, and there can be a definite chilly atmosphere around someone with Saturn in its own sign. At the very least, he likes his facts cold and dry.

His other two assistants are two demons from hell, which in Chinese mythology is an extremely bureaucratic place as well. They are Horse-Head Demon and Ox-Head Demon, and their job is to carry off to hell any individuals whom Ch'eng-Huang deems to have been so improper as to deserve such punishment. They are allowed to go into the homes of the miscreants to fetch them out, but apparently Chinese mythology has a problem with common garden-variety demons trying to drag away innocent bystanders, so they must carry papers from Ch'eng-Huang that must be shown to every door god and household god on the way in.

Indeed, this is a deity so Saturnian that he can make demons carry paperwork, and one of the Saturn in Capricorn's finer qualities is that he is rarely intimidated by huge, complicated, ugly tasks. He can break them down mentally, organize them, and make the dog and pony sit up and do their tricks. Things don't scare him, and projects are just big things. Anything can be organized down into itemized lists, which may sound cold but is extremely useful in the face of those demons of the psyche that paralyze most people. When panic is extending itself into every crevice of one's being, it can be quite helpful to hear the sharp, stern, and completely unintimidated retort of a Saturn in Capricorn, bringing one back to earth. The earthy energies of this combination are like the ultimate anchors to reality, and like the boundaries set by a strict parent, we are never sure whether to struggle against them or be comforted by them. It's only when we look back, decades later, that we find some appreciation for our own walls and ditches, and how we learned to protect our inner selves.

prometheus
Saturn in Aquarius

Before the Olympians arrived on Earth, it was ruled by a giant race of beings called the Titans. They clashed with the younger Olympians in a great war and lost. Zeus, chief of the Olympian gods, let them live as long as they did not interfere with his plans. For the most part, after their defeat, none of them gave him any trouble again. The sole exception to that rule was Prometheus, whose troublemaking in the name of justice never ceased.

Aquarius is the sign of looking forward, of thinking into the future, and the very name *Prometheus* means "forethought." He was the wisest of all the Titans, and yet he was driven to rebel against Zeus, again and again, in the name of righteousness. Prometheus is one of the creator gods; with his brother Epimetheus, he supposedly re-created the human race after it was carelessly destroyed in a deluge. He re-creates the first new humans out of earth and water; early Greek authors swore that in Phocis there was a hill of broken pieces of clay that had the odor of human skin, supposedly the remains of Prometheus's work.

It is interesting to note that he *re-creates* rather than *creates* the human race. Aquarius is a creative sign ruled by innovative Uranus, but Saturn is more interested in the past than the future. Part of the work of a Saturn in Aquarius is the work of reclaiming; not necessarily creating entire new structures but cleansing and reworking existing ones to better the lot of humanity. To him is given the task of sorting the traditional wheat from the chaff, figuring out what parts of what we do are still useful and what should be discarded. He is the reorganizer, the reformer, willing to re-create human experience in a better light.

Prometheus starts out with an automatic dislike of Zeus and his Olympian authority, which reflects the Aquarian Saturn's dislike of whoever is currently in authority, or sets the fashions, or is popular or "in" at the moment. Not all Aquarian Saturns are progressive; some may rebel against progressive thought and hold to more traditional values. It's all a question of who they are reacting to—main culture or subculture? They can also be clever and canny about how they rebel. The initial act of the rebel Titan is the question of sacrifice: Zeus wants the best part of every animal burned for his benefit; Prometheus knows that this will starve humanity. He divides a carcass in two, enclosing the edible flesh in the ugly stomach and covering the bare bones with a succulent layer of fat, and asks Zeus to officially choose which he wants. The greedy Olympian chooses the fat and bones, and only after the agreement is made does he realize that he has been tricked. There is still a streak of the Uranian trickster in the quietest of Aquarian Saturns.

Prometheus's first issue is a question: to whom does his loyalty go? To the ruling Olympians, whose favor it is important to curry? To his own brother Titans, the losers in the war, who advise patience and forbearance? To weak humanity, cowering in caves? Like any Aquarian, Prometheus goes for the oppressed underdog, because he knows instinctively that they are the ones who need the most help. Aquarius is about group consciousness; every planet in Aquarius will face the challenge of deciding what cliques of society he is or is not part of. Yet constricting Saturn, when placed here, has a different feel to it than, say, the Sun or Venus. The more karmically relaxed Aquarian planets can develop a wide range of friends from many different walks of life. With the Aquarian Saturn, the problem drives the individual to the point of great pain and will be difficult to resolve.

A Saturn in Aquarius is far more strict about his loyalties. His alliances must reflect his morals; his commitments must be not only to a bunch of people but to a cause as well. If, under closer inspection, the experience of belonging to that group disappoints him morally—either because it does not reflect his ethics as well as he thought, or because it does not give him enough reason for a cause, or because the people in it are ethically imperfect—he leaves. A Saturn in Aquarius has a long history of joining and leaving groups, of being an outsider, of pushing his way in unwanted and being thrown out, of championing lost causes, of being alone and lonely for long periods of time. And when he does find a group to whom he can ally in good conscience, the universe does not make it easy for him. Like Prometheus, it often seems as though he is punished.

Prometheus stole fire, against Zeus's explicit orders, and gave it to humanity. They now had a way to cook their food and heat themselves . . . and a potent weapon. Zeus was furious; he had the hapless Titan chained to a rock, and a giant vulture (some say an eagle) came down every night and ate out his liver. As he was a Titan, it grew back again the next day, and the cycle repeated itself in endless torment. The vulture is a creature of recycling and reclamation, and the eagle the symbol of far-ranging thought. Many an Aquarian Saturn will understand the hopeless nights spent being gnawed at by one's own fear of entropy—is anything I do here, with this group or by myself, going to last? Is it worth it? Should I perhaps go into a hole and not bother any longer? Will this group accept me and my ideals or will they be yet another disappointment? Can I make an impact on the world at all?

Prometheus never gives in, stubbornly resisting any hint of capitulation, and Zeus is afraid to kill him outright because Prometheus knows a secret that will affect the outcome of the Olympian king's rulership—that if Zeus has a child by the nymph Thetis, the babe will overthrow him. He keeps this secret to himself as long as he is chained and tortured, martyring himself against Zeus's authority. Rulers don't like martyrs. Often, they are more powerful dead than alive, and both Zeus and Prometheus understand this fact. Unlike Milton's Lucifer, who rebels out of personal reasons, Prometheus is clearly the more principled of the two. A Saturn in Aquarius is not above martyring himself in the name of his principles, even if that martyrdom is social rather than political, a matter of drawing apart and hiding from the very social contact that he craves.

The rebel Titan was finally rescued by Hercules, and Chiron the centaur offered his immortality to Prometheus in exchange for a quick and painless death. Zeus's punishment is thwarted not by any Olympian, but by mortals who recognized the worth of Prometheus's sacrifice. This, too, is the karmic gift of the Aquarian Saturn who does not swerve in his principles: few but loyal friends will be there in the crunch, out of respect for personal worth rather than mere superficial bonds. (After his rescue, Prometheus reveals his secret to Zeus, who arranges to have Thetis married to a mortal; her son was Achilles.) A Saturn in Aquarius must rebel, must suffer for it . . . and must, eventually, be rescued. It is up to him to notice that the friends holding out their hands, regardless of their political motives (Hercules and Chiron were very different people) are, actually, the group he has dreamed of. It is up to him to realize that friendship is an inner, not an outer, bond, based not just on similar lifestyle characteristics but on mutual caring. It is up to him to realize that he is as human as they are and that in the hearts of other imperfect humans lies his own immortality.

odin

Saturn in Pisces

In the Norse/Germanic mythos, Odin is both the chief god and the strangest, a deity of many different faces and actions, some contradictory and some confusing. He is slippery; just when you think you have him nailed down to a single archetype, he does something to give the lie to it. He is hard to catalog, a complex creature, hardheaded and mystical, making great sacrifices one moment and using vicious means for amoral goals the next, a wise ruler and a vengeful warrior, a man of the world and a man of the otherworlds. Like Odin, if there is one sign that is most difficult to put into a box, it is slippery, complex, contradictory Pisces, which appears here in its Saturnian archetype of the Old Man.

The Old Man. That's how Odin's modern followers refer to him, often in confusion, as in, "The Old Man wants me to do this, although I don't understand it at all." Odin has a long and tortuous history that starts not long after the creation of the world in Norse mythic chronicles; in his youth he is a hothead, starting the war with the Vanir that is only resolved by the exchange of hostages between sky gods and earth gods. Of all the Vanir, Odin most strongly encourages Freyja to come stay at Asgard, as she is a sorceress of great worth, skilled in *seidhr*, the woman's prophetic magic.

At some point, Odin decides that what he needs to do is find the wisdom of the universe, no matter what it takes. He does not go armed with shield and spear, but walks unarmed into the wilderness to confront that which is unspoken and unspeakable, and this is where his path diverges from that of the fiery heroes with their swords, the airy fools with their casual adventuring, and the earthy kings who sit on their mountains and rule. He throws those over and embraces the Neptunian oneness, the complete loss of control, and is willing to sacrifice anything for understanding. This is the crux point, the moment where Saturn surrenders to Pisces, the moment when the truth can begin.

Odin's quest is monumental and shamanic. He studies seidhr under Freyja, which includes a year spent living as a woman in woman's clothes, called by the derisive name *Jalkr*, meaning "eunuch." For this year, he sacrifices his manhood and learns about feminine power. He spends years wandering in the wilderness, seeking out wise beings to learn from. He gives up one eye at the Well of Wisdom, exchanging it for the ability to speak all languages, and gains his two allies, the magical ravens Hugin and Munin, Thought and Memory. In a great finale of sacrifice, he gives himself to the Norns, the three Fates in Norse mythology, and they crucify him upon the World Tree for nine days and nine nights, weaving the thread of life out of his running blood. On the ninth night, he has a pain-induced vision of the Runes and suddenly gains true understanding of their meanings. When he returns to Asgard, he is acclaimed King and All-Father for his wisdom and shamanic power.

Over the years, when I read descriptions of the nature of Saturn in Pisces, I found most of them extremely unhelpful. Most astrologers seemed puzzled as to how to put rigid Saturn, who craves boundaries, in the realm of Neptune-ruled Pisces, who wants exactly the opposite. The two of them seem inescapably opposed. One thing that they all said, though: people with this placement have to learn to surrender entirely to their higher (or deeper) power or their lives will never be right. This is the placement of no choice. Only when one gives up all hope of control over fate can one truly find a way to gain it.

One possible keyword for unraveling the mystery of Saturn in Pisces might be disciplined mysticism. Although Saturn in Pisces people will be drawn to altered states and shamanic workings, they inevitably find that they have to do it the hard way. Merely taking the drug or dancing around the fire for a while does not work for them. More likely, they will find themselves throwing up from the drug or becoming addicted to it, and spraining an ankle during the power dance. It's enough to make a paranoid out of you, making you think that the universe is out to get you. Instead, it would be better for them to meditate on the reality of the pain and let that take them somewhere. Saturn in Pisces people do better with the kind of psychic ordeals that most people think you'd have to be crazy to endure. As an object lesson, do not forget Odin, who had to be cross-dressed, humiliated, exiled, maimed, scarred, and crucified to get to his height of wisdom. Isn't there some way he could have done it more easily? No. The pain and difficulty was part of the gift. The discipline of Saturn must be applied to the self-dissipation of Neptune, and that is just never an easy thing.

For this Saturn placement, the ordeal won't wait too long for you to get around to it; if you fight fate for too long, it will come and get you. It might be in the form of a chronic illness, or a debilitating injury, or a medical near-death experience. Most of the people that I've met with a heavily aspected Saturn in Pisces had some form of congenital birth defect. Many would eventually bear scars from corrective surgery or learn to deal with chronic pain. Many spoke of having to both fight and surrender at the same time, which may sound strange to anyone who hasn't been there.

All warriors are honored by Odin and half go to his hall of Valhalla after death, but Odin's special warriors are the berserkers. Named for the *bersark*, or the bearskin they wrapped themselves in as a sympathetic magical armor, these men whipped themselves into a froth of delirium, often with the help of drugs. Under the influence of this delirium, they did not feel pain or injury or fatigue, and plowed through the line of an enemy army, killing and screaming, until they were slain or passed out. One might not think of Pisces as a warrior sign, but it is a very Neptunian thing to require an altered state in order to go into battle.

Of course, Odin is no compassionate Buddha, even after all that shamanic sacrifice. He does both wonderful things and terrible, dishonorable things, all as a means to an end. He is canny and crafty and ruthless; his relationship with Loki is fraught with tension and pain. At first they are blood brothers, but then Loki starts siring children that are too powerful for Odin's tastes. He fears that they will be strong enough to challenge the Aesir, so out of fear he has Loki's wife Angrboda murdered; enspells his child Jormungand, the Midgard Serpent, into a tail-biting circle around the world forever; and locks up his destructive son Fenris. Loki's daughter Hel is too strong to get rid of, so he banishes her to Niflheim and pays her off with the care of dead souls in a kind of standoff. Loki swears revenge on Odin and all the Aesir, and gets it. One can hardly blame him, but Odin feels that the ends—preserving the power of the Aesir—were worth the means.

This shows that even after all the communing with the universe, Saturn is still Saturn. With any other planet in Pisces, the individual will feel compassion and empathy for others whether or not he wants to; he only shuts it off when he becomes embittered and hurt. With the planet of limitations in the sign of compassion, this is something that the individual is lacking and finds difficult to understand. Odin makes bad mistakes and, in alienating Loki, ends up sacrificing his own son, Baldur, among other problems. Like every individual with Saturn in Pisces, his life only works when he surrenders to the Fates and their direction for him. With this placement, one literally has to let go of each thing entirely in order for the universe to allow it to come to them.

Uranus

susanoo

Uranus in Aries

In Japanese mythology, the younger brother of Amaterasu the sun goddess is Susanoo, god of the storm. He is a wild, impetuous god who wreaks a lot of havoc, even while he is also a creative force. When he first climbed the mountain to see his sister, he created such an earthquake that the whole mountain range shook, and Amaterasu took a bow and quiver of arrows with her to meet him, just in case. However, he swore that he had no evil intent, only that he had come to her because the islands were unpopulated and he proposed that they create people. Amaterasu agreed and promptly snatched his sword, which she broke into three pieces and turned into three female beings. He snatched her necklace, chewed the jewels to powder in his teeth, and then spat out five male beings. These became the eight ancestors of the great Japanese noble families.

Of course, they then got into an argument about whose children the beings actually are, and this turns into a full-scale violent war on Susanoo's part. The storm god lost all self-control and thought for others; he ruined rice paddies, filled in irrigation ditches, and threw dung into the temples. As a final outrage, he attacked Amaterasu's house, ripping a hole in the roof and throwing in the skinned corpse of a horse he had killed. One of her weaving-women ended up impaled on the distaff and died; Amaterasu herself fled to a deep cave. Her story (Jupiter in Leo) tells of how she was lured back out by her desperate subjects. Afterward, they decided to punish Susanoo, but were only able to fine him heavily for much gold, shave off his beard and moustache, pull out his fingernails, and banish him for a time. Thus Susanoo became the scapegoat of the Japanese gods.

A Uranus in Aries is the Unconventional Warrior. He has boundless enthusiasm; what he lacks is a good control mechanism. When he is angered, he is ready to slaughter his perceived enemies, but you won't see him running out with a sword. Instead, he'll create a high-tech doomsday device that will laser-zap his enemy from a thirty-story building. Well, not really, but it's what he'll fantasize about. More likely he'll come up with a creative way to sue him. Mars and Uranus energy together can come up with some pretty eye-popping public street theater when he decides to protest something. I read about youths protesting the policies of the Catholic Church by leaving dung on cathedral doorsteps, and I am reminded of Susanoo flinging it into the temples.

Coming back from his banishment, Susanoo happens upon a province where a giant eight-headed serpent is terrorizing and devouring the people. He springs into action, but the snake is too large for him to conquer with a weapon, so he comes up with an innovative plan. Setting out eight bowls filled with rice wine, he tricks the serpent into getting drunk and falling asleep, and then he cuts all the heads off. Inside the snake's body, he finds a magical sword, which he presents to Amaterasu as a reconciliation gift. The story is a good illustration of a Uranus in Aries at his best—brave, inventive, and generous, thinking little of danger to himself. However, he may go back and forth between good and bad behavior until he is older and has learned control. It was said of Susanoo that he had two souls, a good one and an evil one. When the good soul (Nigi-mi-tama) was in control, he was creative and helpful, bringing the rain to grow the crops. When the evil soul (Ara-mi-tama) ruled him, he lost control and wreaked havoc over the countryside, not caring who he injured.

Susanoo at his best can be a testing figure, someone who plants ordeals in people's way in order to measure their worth. When the healer god O-Kuni-Nushi fell in love with Susanoo's daughter, the storm god first made him sleep in rooms full of scorpions and snakes, then trapped him in a fiery field and watched him escape. Finally, O-Kuni-Nushi tied Susanoo's hair to the rafters while he slept and eloped with the girl. The storm god, awakening with a start and accidentally pulling down his house, decided that he had been outtricked, and that this young man was indeed worthy to be his son-in-law. He gave O-Kuni-Nushi advice on handling his rival brothers and was quite good-natured about the whole thing. As he gets older and more relaxed, the Uranus in Aries individual can handle irritations and rivalry better and falls more into the role of elder trickster, devising trials to help the younger ones mature. Fertility means creativity, and Susanoo is a fertile, creative god; he just has to learn not to waste his efforts in reckless anger lest he become a pariah among those he would protect.

The Dagda
Uranus in Taurus

He was called *Eochaid Ollathair*, the Father of All, and *Ruad Rofhessa*, the Lord of Perfect Knowledge. These epithets implied that he was an all-powerful, omnicompetent, paternal deity, yet the Dagda of Celtic myth is nothing like the other "Father-Lord" gods in other pantheons or even among the Celtic pantheon itself. Unlike richly clad Zeus or even polished Lugh, the Dagda at first glance does not seem anything like a Lord-King. He is pictured as fat, ugly, and potbellied, with coarse manners. He wears only the short, rough tunic of a peasant and rawhide sandals. Instead of spear or sword, he carries an immense club, the weapon of the poorer classes.

All Taurus placements are emotionally bound up with money, resources, and property—the Taurus keyword is "I have"—but when Uranus visits this normally stolid sign, it creates a wealth of ambivalences toward it. The individual with Uranus in Taurus both wants money and fears it. He wants the luxuries that it brings, yet is repelled by the attitudes of the upper (monied) classes, whatever they may be in his culture. He may swing back and forth from pursuing wealth to throwing it away; he may be a "trust fund baby" who is guilty about his unearned income; he may pretend to be poor while hiding his wealth or pretend to be rich while actually being penniless. Somehow there's no contempt quite as strong as the repulsion one has for someone you secretly envy just a little.

Like the Dagda, he may be a king who prides himself on just being "one of the people" by rejecting the elaborate trappings of conspicuous consumption, or he may be an "infiltrator" who gets himself fed for free at affluent circles and laughs at the rich fools he is cheating. Uranus turns everything on its head, forcing people to reconsider what they think they know about how class and money should look. The Dagda's peasant manners contrast as well with his "Lord of Perfect Knowledge" title, making us more conscious of the fact that education—and thus knowledge—is all too often a privilege of the monied classes. The idea that someone who lives a peasant lifestyle might know just as much as a college graduate—and possibly even about the same things—makes us uncomfortable. That's what Uranus in Taurus wants us to think about. The individual with this placement may have his own prejudices about people who show off their education, who he perceives as assuming that they are a higher class of human just because they own a sheepskin.

If he is especially inventive, he may find ways to use other people's money. The Dagda owned a great cauldron that continually gave forth food and was never empty; it symbolized his place as nourisher of his people and general fertility god, all good Taurus aspects. Many individuals with Uranus/Taurus combined energy are especially good at getting their humanitarian (or at least innovative) projects paid for with the money of those richer people that they both envy and dislike. It's a combination of practicality and for-ward-thinking inspiration that is more interested in concrete accom-plishments than vague theorizing. Let others worry about feeding the world; a Uranus in Taurus will get a grant and set up a soup kitchen and feed one neighborhood.

Of course, the Dagda's ever-full cauldron—redolent of Taurean love of food and drink—has a Uranian twist to it. At a yearly ritual ordeal on the first of November—the day of the Celtic new year—the Dagda was required to eat an enormous meal of porridge that bubbled up from a hole in the ground, after which he had to make love to a woman. If he was not able to stuff himself with the entire amount and still perform brilliantly afterward, the future harvest would be thin. Fortunately, he was usually up to the challenge. This reflects a Uranus in Taurus's other ambivalence—that of luxury. He may swing back and forth between gorging himself on physical excess and retreating to ascetic self-denial. This is especially an issue with food and sex; he may be prone to the binge-purge behavior, which is worse for the health than merely being fat or thin.

This is also the Taurus placement most likely to have a volatile temper. The Dagda's club was so huge that it took eight men to carry it, and when it dragged along the ground it left a furrow as large as a frontier dyke. When he swung it, he could kill nine men with one blow. A Uranus in Taurus can be noted for incredibly destructive rages, between which he may repress his anger. He may need to learn moderation before he damages himself, his reputation, or someone else. The Dagda was known for his skill in building great fortresses—another link to Taurus the Builder—and a Uranus in Taurus is most often triggered into rage when someone breaches the walls of his carefully protected home, insulting his family or ideals, both of which he considers worthy of extreme defense. He may even be a "radical conservative" instead of a "practical radical," using extreme and unusual methods to promote a philosophy that is actually backward-looking.

The Dagda had one artistic and accomplished side, however; he was a harpist, which is appropriate as Taurus is a musical sign. One of his powers was that he could call the seasons with his harp, a great boon to the farmer who faced a late spring frost or an early autumn sleet. In this way he was called upon by the common folk who made their living from the land; the oxen that pulled the plow were blessed in his name. With the other end of his club—the handle rather than the killing part—he could restore men to life as easily as he had destroyed them, and this is the secret of a Uranus in Taurus. His destructive urges grow out of his need to aid and succor people and eliminate whatever is in the way of his doing that. It will take much careful thinking on his part to be able to do the former without resorting to the latter.

Ellegua
Uranus in Gemini

Among the orishas or deities that were brought over with the African Yoruba people to make a new home in the Americas, many are identified with saints. Yemaya is the Virgin of the Sea, Shango is St. Barbara, Oya is St. Theresa, and so forth. It was a good way to conceal them from the priests who might stick their noses into a house and inquire about suspicious-looking altars. Ellegua the trickster god, called Legba in Haiti and Eshu in Nigeria, is never associated with a saint. In fact, he is sometimes referred to as the devil, even though he is the chief god among all of them.

Ellegua is a first-class mischief-maker. His symbols are chickens, his colors are red and black, and when he possesses one of his dancing worshippers, he has a tendency to spit rum on people. He has his fingers in the pies of all the humans and orishas, interfering, spying, and generally making trouble, and sometimes after the dust settles things are more right than they were before. The other orishas love him or resent him, but he is too powerful to attack, as he is the force who opens the door.

What this means is that Ellegua has the power to open the door between the worlds and allow prayers, magic, and aid to cross between the human realm and that of the gods. Because of this, no matter who a worshipper is invoking, he makes an offering to Ellegua first, in order that his words will get through. Ellegua's special place is the crossroads, where you can stand at the potential for many journeys. He is like Uranus in this way, the lover of all that is new and different and can lead to fresh places and views.

Gemini loves facts and distrusts truth. This may seem like a contradiction to anyone else, but not to Gemini. Facts are his toys, and he knows very well that they can be used to build all sorts of things that pass as truths, many of them mutually exclusive. How do you tell which one is the real truth? It's better to assume that there is none, he says, and thus he is skeptical of people who swear undying anything. After all, everything could change tomorrow, and then where would you be if you had to stick to outdated promises and commitments?

It's said that one of the things Ellegua loves is to make people break their vows and, as such, he operates as a kind of *ha-satanas*, or the adversary who tests people's convictions. One of his most famous legends is about two neighboring men who swore they would always be friends, but their friendship was actually fairly superficial, and both strove not to annoy the other. One day Ellegua walked between them wearing a suit that was red on one side and black on the other. He walked backwards down the road with his clothing and hat on backwards and his pipe sticking out of the neck of his jacket in back. After he had passed, the two neighbors met at their boundary and fell into a fierce argument as to whether that odd stranger had been wearing a red suit or a black one, and whether he had been walking forward or backward. Before the day was over, they were enemies. This may not seem like a particularly good ending, but to Uranus in Gemini it is better to have honest warfare than hypocritical peace.

In spite of his demeanor, Ellegua does have some compassion or at least the wit to know when something is appropriate or not. An example of this is how he handled the situation with Yemaya and Ogoun. Upon coming to their door and hearing Yemaya's cries, he quickly deduced both that Ogoun was attacking her and that to interrupt might gain him a savage assault from a startled leopard god. Instead of barging in, he backed up several steps to the head of the path and then came down it again, singing loudly and tapping the fence with a stick as he went. Ogoun heard the intrusion and slunk off into the shadows. Yemaya straightened herself and greeted Ellegua with a false smile instead of a cry for help, from which he deduced that this was not the first attack, and Yemaya was allowing things to go on in order not to condemn her son.

He returned her greetings politely, said nothing about what he had heard, and then afterward went to Yemaya's other son Shango with the tale. Since Shango was her son as well, he had a better right to bring an injury to trial on behalf of his mother than did Ellegua, who could have been called a liar. His quick thinking and ability to consider several possible consequences ahead saved the situation; this ability to extrapolate on the spot is a typical Uranus in Gemini trait.

Also like Uranus, which is an often androgynous planet, Ellegua has a wife named Pomba Gira, who is often seen as his second self. Pomba Gira appears as a woman dressed in black and red lace; she is the patron of drag queens and is often played by one in parades. Ellegua himself is sometimes played by a girl with a large artificial phallus, another one of his symbols. In fact the very plethora of his disembodied phalluses scattered hither and yon on the altars of his worshippers echo Uranus, the castrated god. Gemini, too, is a dual sign, and appreciates the idea of having a "spouse" who is actually a secret alter ego.

Ellegua the trickster shows us that Uranus can change not only outward situations but inward thoughts, using the manipulation of the concept of truth in order to make people question their own supposed truths. Better to bring it all up into the open, he says, even if you have to trick them into it.

Bes

Uranus in Cancer

The artists of ancient Egypt had specific ways in which they were supposed to portray people, especially gods. Everyone was tall, slim, brown, and perfectly formed. Their eyes were like those of deer or cows, and the men were all clean-shaven except for the pharaoh, who wore a narrow ceremonial beard. This was the way things were supposed to be, and this conservatism of the media image continued for centuries. Although Egyptian art is very beautiful, it is sometimes hard to tell people and gods apart; they all have a serene sameness. Indeed, deities are generally set apart either by glyphs in their heads or by wearing the animal head of their totem beast.

Except Bes. Unlike the tall, slim figures that surround him, Bes is a classic achondroplasiac, a dwarf with a large head and body and short, bent legs. He has huge eyes, a full, fluffy beard, and round cheeks. He wears only a leopard-skin loincloth, and he is always shown full-face instead of in profile like the other figures. Most impertinent of all, his most common expression is with his tongue sticking out in derision. Like trickster figures everywhere, he turns all the rules on their heads and will not be bound by them. After his worship grew to popularity, Bes was made the court jester of the gods and is shown playing a harp, dancing, or tumbling to amuse them. He used his position as fool, as fools did throughout the ages, to say things to the other gods that they would not hear from others.

However, the impunity of Bes comes from more than just his late-comer role of court jester. He was first and foremost a household god, whose sphere was the safety of the home and children, marriage, childbirth, and women's toilets. He had no temples or priests, instead he was honored in the home with a small pillar-altar topped with his statue. He started out as a god of the poorest folk, invoked to help them protect their homes; later his popularity ascended to the middle classes and finally to the royal palace. As a god of the (unimportant) home as opposed to the (more important) work of politics, business, death, or enlightenment, Bes was dismissed as insignificant. It didn't matter how he was portrayed, since his visage would not adorn anything of (supposed) consequence.

Even when his figure was placed over the bed of the pharaoh's wife while she gave birth, however, his main concern was still the protection of the smallest and lowest in society. All children were defended by Bes, especially the children who did not have wealthy parents to defend them—against the bites of scorpions and snakes (much more important in desert Egypt), against attack by crocodiles while fishing or lions while following their parents on a hunt or wild dogs while scavenging. He protected the mother while in child-birth and protected the marital relationship because divorce could break up a family and be hard on the children. He protected the whole family from nightmares, and his visage was often carved on bedsteads for this purpose.

No other trickster god is so domestic in his sphere. To most peo-ple, the job of a trickster is to be wandering about looking for things to complicate, and thus they are inimicable to the idea of a happy hearth and home. This kind of double-take can also be seen when people confront the paradox of Uranus in Cancer. The planet of trickster and innovator, uprooter and disrupter, in the sign of the Parent, the Child, and the Home? It sounds like an uncomfortable situation, and it is. Uranus swerves, in this placement, between being extremely protective of itself to wanting to break away from the bonds of home and tradition. In a sense, the ongoing dialogue of Uranus in Cancer is that of an overprotective parent arguing with a rebellious child . . . only Uranus plays both parts, forcing the individual into a back-and-forth of whether to cling to the ways you learned as a child or find entirely new and innovative ways to do things.

Bes is also associated with the beauty toilets of women, and at first this, too, is jarring. Why pray to an ugly dwarf for beauty while applying your makeup? His grinning face was carved on the handles of mirrors and jars of unguents, so that no woman could fail to notice him while making herself beautiful. It seems strange that one with no apparent sense of aesthetics could grant attraction, but it must be remembered that the primary value of Bes is guarding and taking care of the household and family. To him—as to any planet in Cancer—the only real point, at bottom, of making oneself attractive is to create the spark for a committed relationship that will form the basis for a family. Bes is more interested in the emotional than in the physical, and his outwardly ugly, inwardly kind presentation drives this home. He warns the beautifying woman not to get so caught up in Venusian values of beauty that she mistakes the packaging for the internal reality. Looks aren't everything, he says; in fact, they have very little to do with emotional security.

Like Uranus's lightning-bolt nature, Bes sometimes goes overboard when being protective. He is shown wielding a knife, an evil grin on his face, as often as he is shown capering, suggesting that he is willing to go the extra mile to protect those he loves. Even after the old gods of Egypt had fallen by the wayside and Christianity had taken over, rumors held of the terrible dwarf-monster that would leap out of alleys and strangle you if you were cruel and laughed at the deformities of others. Bes the trickster probably delighted in being the bogeyman who struck in defense of the weak and helpless. So does Uranus in Cancer; it is no accident that during its last transit, TV sets began to proliferate in every home, showing children tales of good guys who appeared out of nowhere, aided the underdog, and vanished again into the night. Is there a bit of Bes in Superman and Batman, or at least in Clark Kent?

coyote
Uranus in Leo

We all think of Leo as being the archetype of the King or Performer, but few of us remember that it is also the archetype of the Divine Child, associated with the fifth house, which rules children. When the golden Leo veil is draped over Uranus, we are forcibly reminded of the presence of the Divine Child in the guise of the Trickster. A Uranus in Leo has a wacky, self-centered sense of humor—the love of practical jokery, the desire to goose those that cramp his style, and he never forgets to be young. There is an eternally childlike aspect to his nature . . . as long as the child is Bart Simpson or Calvin. He may be a kid at heart, but nobody said that he was one of the well-behaved *good* children.

Coyote is the infamous trickster god of the Southwest Native Americans, and he is both the innocent fool and the sneakiest bastard in the valley. His overriding quality is his ego, which drives him to ever more grandiose antics. He sniffs out every nuance of hypocrisy and yet is blindly susceptible to flattery. Like all tricksters, his trickery is on some level meant to teach others about questioning their preconceived notions, but for Coyote it's something that he does inadvertently rather than consciously.

In one of Coyote's myths, he is taking a walk during a dark, moonless night, and he comes across a field of what he thinks are people dancing, waving and swaying back and forth. He leaps in, crying that he is the best dancer of all, and dances for hours. The other dancers seem tireless; no matter how long or hard he leaps and cavorts, they ignore him and keep going to their own simultaneous rhythm. By dawn, he is utterly exhausted and can barely lift his feet, but the dancers have not stopped for a second. As the sun breaks across the horizon, he realizes that he is standing in a field of bulrushes, waving and bending with the wind, and that he has danced himself into exhaustion competing with a bunch of plants.

This is the Fool side of a Uranus in Leo. When he is in command of the chart, the individual leaps into things without thinking, obsessed with his own brilliant idea, which is the most amazing thing he or anyone has ever thought of before, and will save the day, and cover him with glory. He sweeps aside all argument and leaps straight into the fray . . . and sometimes he is brilliant and sometimes he falls flat on his face. But it's as if he needs that unthinking charge in order to get up the gumption to do the deed. If he thinks too much about it, goes his unconscious reasoning, he just might find a reason *not* to do it, and then what would he do? In his hurry, he often doesn't take the time to see other people as real humans with needs and wants, not just spear-carriers in his production. The Child is the center of his own universe, and he has not yet learned that he is only one of many. This can result in years of dancing with bulrushes, mistaking ordinary circumstance for personal insult.

In another of his myths, Coyote sees the women of a tribe go off together in the woods, forbidding men to follow them. He decides that he will get into their group and seduce them, one way or another. Like all trickster gods, he is a shapeshifter, so he takes off his penis and becomes a woman. He lends the phallus to an under-endowed friend for the night, with the promise that the friend would give it back when Coyote was ready for it. He sneaks into the group of women, gains their trust and then, when one agreed to go off into the trees with him, he went in search of the holder of his phallus. The friend was nowhere to be seen, having found a willing partner and gone back to her hut. Coyote went in search of him, and by the time he was found hours later, the women had moved on and the effort was ruined.

Coyote demonstrates another quality of a Uranus in Leo: he feels entitled to go anywhere he wants. On some level, his Uranian urge to upset the status quo is because they will not let him in. This can lead to brave protests against unfair discrimination—Uranus transiting through Leo saw the rise of the civil rights movement—or it can lead to him bullying his way into places where he isn't wanted and probably shouldn't be invading merely on principle. This Leonine sense of entitlement cuts both ways. In the myth, Coyote's efforts are foiled by circumstance; in real life, he can annoy people by messing in their business. A Uranus in Leo doesn't even try to excuse it as being for their own good. It's for his own good—to make the world a better place for him to be in, and incidentally help others as well. This was the attitude that spawned, with Pluto's help, the Me Generation.

To be fair, Coyote is brave. He has little fear, and he is not afraid to fail. Of all the Leo planets, Uranus is the least affected by Leo's need to keep his dignity. He loves to be seen and applauded, but if rotten tomatoes are thrown, he doesn't waste time on being humiliated. He simply packs up and moves on to the next audience with trusting faith that they will be more appreciative. If Leo is the Performer, Uranus in Leo is the Comedian, pouring out his heart into his wisecracks. His motives are transparent, because he trusts the universe enough that he doesn't need to hide them.

His resilience is amazing. Knocked down, he bounces back up. Coyote is constantly dying through stupid accidents and misadventures, but he doesn't die like a sacred king or a dying and reborn god. He dies like a cartoon character, like Wile E. Coyote who gets up from a charred mess, shakes off the ashes, and is fine again. He dies not as if death is a great transformation, but as if it is a momentary inconvenience. Likewise, a Uranus in Leo keeps coming back for more, without becoming cynical and giving up. Somewhere in that trickster's heart is the Divine Child who never really dies, not really. If there is one phrase that sums up this placement, it is faith in change. To look at all change as a good thing is to look through the eyes of the Divine Child who lives in all of us.

Lilith

Uranus in Virgo

There are two stories of Lilith from two different civilizations. According to the Sumerians, Lilith was a goddess of the desert, personified by the sandstorm. She took up residence in a great huluppu tree, between a dragon at the base and an eagle at the top—reminiscent of the Norse Yggdrasil—symbolizing her essence, which was poised between earth and air. She lived there until Inanna, the queen of heaven, decided that she wanted the tree for furniture and asked Gilgamesh to evict the squatters. The hero threw out the dragon and the eagle. Lilith realized that she was not strong enough to best him and fled, destroying her home in the process. From that time on, she lived banished to the desert wilderness, a goddess of barrenness.

The Hebrews have her cast in a somewhat different role: Adam's first wife, who refused to be subservient to him and fled in anger when both he and Jehovah insisted. She supposedly became a hairy, shapechanging, lustful goddess who birthed incubi and succubi, the demons who bring wet dreams. She was also a bringer of barrenness who would slip into the marriage bed between the husband and wife, lying with them both and making them both barren. During the medieval era, she was demonized as the "baby-killer," murdering children in their cradles.

Virgo, the sign of the Virgin, is considered by many to be the least sexual of all the signs and quite incompatible with capital-L Lust. In some signs, this may appear on the surface to be true. Since Virgo is about discrimination, someone with an inner planet in

Venus may turn down the unsatisfactory partner rather than bother with a second-rate experience. Uranus, however, turns everything on its head. A Uranus in Virgo is driven to try many sexual situations that she normally wouldn't, because she's seeking sexual perfection. She is also seeking perfection of thought and analysis—this sign is ruled by Mercury—and that's why Lilith is not only the goddess of lust but the asker of hard questions. She is related mythologically to the Sphinx of Greek mythology, who asked deadly riddles, and the Queen of Sheba, who visited Solomon to grill him about his beliefs.

Virgo is an earth sign, but it is ruled by airy Mercury, and when cast over equally airy Uranus, it creates the fusion of earth and air that Lilith symbolizes. She lives between dragon and eagle, between body and mind, between mental theory and physical experience, and she knows the hard truths. Virgo's weapon is not the sword but the needle, as anyone who has experienced Virgo's nagging can sheepishly affirm. Needles can be dangerous. They can stitch up wounds or holes and fix things like nobody's business, but they can also jab, prick, and pop overblown egos. And they can inject things. In Uranus's case, those things can be new ideas that poke holes in old concepts, deflating them. Uranus in Virgo is the sign of the mental injection, new ideas introduced so quietly that no one notices—until they run rampant and unobstructed through the social bloodstream. Often these ideas have to do with health—of the body or the planet—and choices.

Lilith's barrenness is also a Virgo issue, and not just because real virgins don't breed (if they do, they obviously aren't virgins) or that plants seeded in a Virgo Moon come late to fruition, if they fruit at all. Birth control, as a social practice, is part of Virgo's discriminatory practices. Birth control, when practiced properly, requires a good deal of analytical thinking. Can I afford to breed? Who should I do it with? What should their genetic and social markers be, for the best offspring? How many can I afford to have? How many can the earth support? If it's not wise to breed right now, what method

should I use to stop it? Virginal abstinence? Alternative sexual practices? A partner who can't physically reproduce with me? Technological birth control—and if so, what sort? And, of course, if there
is an unwanted pregnancy, should it be terminated? Lilith is the
"baby-killer" in medieval culture because of her association with
abortion, which was reviled by the church. Her ultimate question,
which has not yet been answered with complete success, is this: Do
you own your body, or not?

In the 1960s, the sexual revolution was fueled partly by Uranus
in Virgo and partly by the onset of widespread birth control. It
equalized relationships between the sexes, took away the threat of
pregnancy, and encouraged independence and nonmonogamy. It
also gave people a view of sexuality that was not ruled by procre-
ation and was therefore pleasure-centered. Masturbation was reex-
amined and proclaimed no longer sinful (a good solitary Virgoan
sexual practice, reminiscent of Lilith's incubi and succubi), and people were given more positive choices in sexual activities and partners. Although some parts of society have since tried to backtrack,
the sexual revolution has never quite been countered. Its mark is
indelible. Lilith lies down with us and will not be banished.

Another Uranus in Virgo issue of the 1960s is the health of the
planet that we walk on. Ecology came into its own during that
period, and particularly the first appearance of a fierce, unswerving
ecology that chained itself to trees and sabotaged industrial
processes. Uranus trumpeted that it was not enough to work to
merely fix holes in the rapidly growing disaster. Immediate and
drastic action must be taken. This battle cry can be taken overboard, usually in the direction of Virgoan self-sacrifice, such as the
bumper stickers proclaiming "Friends don't let friends eat meat."
When Virgo errs, it is in taking her own sacred self-discipline and
attempting to force it bodily onto others. Lilith is also the virago,
who will sweep down like the sandstorm and kill anyone in her
path. She is a force of nature, and she is for nature—and its beauty,

and its life, and its cruelty. Earth as mother who eats her children is present in Lilith's character, and that is a force we cannot rationalize away or judge as good or bad. It is simply life, as swift and random as a Uranus transit.

The original meaning of "virgin" did not just imply someone who was physically untouched. It meant someone who remained unmarried and unattached regardless of who she was sexual with. This is Lilith's venue: she lies with many, but partners with no one. No child holds her down; no mate tells her what to do. She is not a kind or compassionate goddess—as one of the Death Maidens, she is more coldhearted than giving—but she is strong and independent and fierce, and not afraid of the truth. She asks you, and everyone, the hard questions about who you are and what you believe. Earth and air, sand and wind, body and mind. Can you face her?

Eris

Uranus in Libra

Eris loves me, this I know,
For my headache tells me so!
—*Modern pagan chant by Heather MacArthur*

There are two manifestations of Eris, the Greek goddess of chaos and strife. In her ancient form, she is one of the daughters of Nox, goddess of the night. She was at first purely a personification, but gradually she began to take on something of a true character. She is said to accompany Mars, the god of battle, on his excursions, and she was mentioned more in fear and warding-off than in reverence. Eris is attributed as having a huge litter of children, including Sorrow, Forgetfulness, Hunger, Disease, Combat, Murder, Massacre, Quarrel, Lies, and Injustice. Her youngest daughter, named Ate, was a trickster figure who followed people about, trying to get them to do foolish things.

She must have learned that from her mother, because Eris is a trickster deity of the highest sort. She has today been reborn in the pseudo-faith of Discordianism, named after her Roman title Discordia. In this version, she is a mocking creature who plays tricks on humanity largely to show them their own stupidity. It's not an uncommon pattern with tricksters; the Sacred Trickster is at heart a teacher, if sometimes a cruel one. If Eris manages to show people their own stupidity, they must have some to be revealed.

Uranus, the Sacred Trickster, loves to upset apple carts, and when it moves into Libra, the cart to be pushed is that of love and justice. If you're not sure what love has to do with justice, then you probably don't have a heavy Libra influence in your chart. Libra knows it all too well: love makes the world go round, and justice makes sure it doesn't collide with too many other worlds in the process. In other words, how emotionally intimate individuals actually treat each other is a good indicator of how their society in general treats its denizens. In a very real sense, love is the litmus test of equality, and Libra is obsessed with equality.

Although the Goddess of Chaos and Strife is mentioned briefly in many writings, her only real cameo does manage to clearly show her connection with relationship and consequences. She is often blamed for starting the Trojan War, and although one could make a case that she was the catalyst, every deity and human in the story was theoretically an independent adult who was responsible for making their own bad choices. *The Iliad*, the tale of the Trojan War, starts with a wedding, an appropriate place for something sparked by the sign of marriage and partnership. The demigoddess Thetis is marrying the mortal prince Peleus, much to the relief of everyone who has heard that she is destined to bear a son greater than his father. Eris, jealous at not being invited and playing the part of the archetypal evil faery, tosses a perfect apple of solid gold through the roof. It is marked "For the fairest," and three goddesses claim it at once. There is a general fight, and the wedding is ruined.

One can immediately see Eris's status as outsider grating on her. The Uranus perspective is often one of being the outcast, the one who can see all that is wrong with the system from her place outside it. As she can't even get invited to a wedding, Eris obviously has no chance at being seen as "the fairest," something that beauty-oriented Libra desires. Like the ugly schoolgirl who throws dung on the prom queen's dress, she protests this unfairness with a stunt clearly designed to appeal to the worst in everyone there and show the strife hiding just below the Olympian veneer. To exclude Eris from your wedding is to ban the unflattering outsider perspective from your relationship, and that is courting trouble.

The three goddesses who claim it—Hera (Jupiter in Libra), Athena (Sun in Aquarius), and Aphrodite (Venus in Libra)—symbolize three different ways of being female in the male-dominated world. Hera is the archetypal wife, Athena the tomboyish but non-sexual companion in intellect and adventure, and Aphrodite is the sensual lover. All three act with equal immaturity, dropping their dignified exteriors to squabble over a trinket. Of course, the title— "For the fairest"—is not inconsequential; its winner will hold the public admiration of the important people in the world—men. Eris's nasty stunt immediately proves that all three of them are not nearly as independent or powerful as they claim to be; all are so dependent on male public approval that her stunt sets them to childish bickering. In one fell swoop, she exposes the single weakness that they all share. Smiling cynically, she sits back and watches the fun.

The three goddesses ask Paris, the prince of Troy, to judge their contest, as the male Olympians wisely exempt themselves. All three further demean themselves by trying to bribe him—Hera with power and fame, Athena with wisdom and skill, and Aphrodite by promising him the most beautiful mortal woman in the world for his wife. It's all quite consensual. They don't have to do it, but they do. Paris doesn't have to choose with his gonads, but he does. Aphrodite doesn't have to give him Helen, who happens to be married to another man, but she does. Helen herself doesn't have to run off with Paris, goddess or no goddess, but she does. The war begins, and it does not really end until long after *The Iliad* and *The Odyssey* are over, in the final volume, the *Oresteiad*. The gods are called to judge whether an abused wife and mother is more important than the abusive spouse that she murders. Athena casts the final vote in favor of the man and so seals in the fate of patriarchy for the next several hundred years. Again, the story is all about love and justice. Anything started by Eris eventually gets around to that.

A Uranus in Libra turns the concept of marriage on its head, often seeking new and unusual forms. She doesn't do it merely because of a love of innovation or boredom or thrill-seeking; she does it because she is in search of real equality in relationship. The ordinary social masks are not good enough for her; as an outsider she can see behind them, and she tends to rip them off and expose the ugly unfairness underneath. By the end of Eris's war, women are no better off, but their oppression has been publicly stated. All hypocrisy is ended; the tyranny is out on the table. Perhaps this means that someday, someone will be able to do something about it.

Sometimes this urge for equality can be taken to extremes, like the Uranus in Libra couple who calculated out every ounce of ice cream and divided the price up by that amount, so that neither should have to pay for one drop more than they consumed. One Libra Uranus said dolefully to me, "I need a lover who's just as emotionally screwed up as I am, or we can't be equals." Uranus isn't averse to being weird or downright bizarre in the ways that she explores new alternatives, which can lead to a variety of broken liaisons as she makes her way through the minefield of sex and social assumptions.

To be a real innovator in love is, all too often, to spend a lot of time alone. People tend to be more conservative in love than in anything else, because they don't want to get their hearts broken. A person with Uranus in Libra is willing to risk heartbreak for real equality and true justice, and that's something worth admiring. They're even willing to risk balance and harmony, and that's unique among Libra placements. Eris isn't a comfortable goddess, and she often drives them to extremes of pain and loneliness while they seek their ideal. Still, if there's one karmic rule that proves true about love, it's that the universe gives you what you're willing to settle for. To have the planet of chaos in the sign of harmony means that you're just not going to settle at all, ever, and the universe had better not ask you to, or who knows how many apple carts are going to go spilling out across the street?

Anubis
Uranus in Scorpio

Society, by its nature, can only be a collection of agreed-upon rules that serve to lubricate the masses of people so that they don't all die or kill each other. Sometimes, society has to repress things—relegate them to the collective underworld—in order to make society run smoothly. Some of these things are sexual issues, aggression, psychological dysfunction, spiritual mystery, and the transformation of morality—all items that make Scorpio sit up and take notice. Uranus, on the other hand, Cosmic Trickster and planet of change, doesn't like to see anything repressed. Censorship is his anathema. Put the two together and you have a keen-nosed astrological detective, alert to the scent of secrets, ready to ferret them out, dig them up, and expose them naked, the more shocking the better.

In Egyptian mythology, Anubis is one of the gods of the underworld. However, his job is not to rule over the dead, but to guide them down. He is a mischievous psychopomp, seeking out each flustered soul and then coaxing it down into the dark depths, where it is left to its fate. Likewise, a Uranus in Scorpio is happiest when dragging innocent bystanders down into the depths of some amazing and horrific and controversial discovery; he doesn't so much care what reaction he gets so long as he gets one. The stripping away of blissful ignorance and the forced witnessing of the forbidden are his bread and butter; they are how he proposes to change the world.

Anubis is shown as a jackal, one of the wild dogs of the Egyptian desert, and sometimes as a jackal-headed man. Uranus in Scorpio shows an uncanny ability to sniff out rot and dig up dirt, whatever its form, and like a jackal he tends to gather on the fringes of death and disaster, curious and waiting for a piece of rotting carrion to chew on. He is not easily shocked and is often fascinated with unpleasant things that others might choose to sweep under the rug. Like Anubis, he chooses to live in the barren desert rather than the comfortable town, because that's where people aren't looking, and something normally unseen might be going on.

Dead things especially fascinate him, whether they are dead religions, dead civilizations, dead languages, dead people, or the mystery of death itself. He doesn't just want to contemplate them, either; he wants to take them apart and see what makes them tick. Anubis was the god of embalming, the first really serious mortuary business, and he aided Isis in reassembling his dead uncle Horus, with the aid of Thoth the doctor, in order to give him a semblance of life just long enough to conceive a child from this Frankenstein god. Whatever the suffering of Isis was, no doubt Anubis found it terribly interesting.

We must recall that past eras of Uranus in Scorpio have given us such cultural icons as the X-ray, the steam engine (water and air), the first American book on psychiatry, the fall of Napoleon, Goethe's *Faust*, the first writings of Freud, spiritualism, and the discovery of radioactivity. Uranus is always a harbinger of discovery, but one of the hallmarks of the discoveries of a Uranus in Scorpio is that they always lead to some sort of loud moral controversy. Scorpio is more interested in getting abominations out of their holes than thinking ahead to what will be done with them when they're out; no doubt he figures it will be good for everyone to rush around dealing with their monsters, and often he's quite right. Anubis has a trickster streak, and it tickles a Uranus in Scorpio to watch people's hypocrisy exposed.

Anubis was the son of Set, the "divine enemy of the gods," and Nephthys, the goddess of the winnowing basket, Isis's darker sister, one of the four Deaths. While Isis collects the souls of pharaohs and people of high rank, Nephthys is in charge of the common man's dead. When Set murdered Osiris and claimed his throne, wife and son both defected in moral outrage and followed Isis's family into exile. Child of two dark powers, Anubis must choose between the murderous authority and the deathlike exile; not content to watch injustice, he prefers the high ground of moral conviction and ostracism. He still serves the darkness, but in such as way as to bring justice and not subvert it.

A Uranus in Scorpio lives in both the schlocky pulp reporter, putting hidden cameras in people's windows, and the serious researcher on the fringe of science, psychology, or mysticism. The difference between the two is his commitment to a long-term goal of betterment for the world, rather than a short-term psychic peepshow. Anubis, after all, had an important job: as psychopomp and guide to the underworld, he saved newly dead souls from wandering forever in the upper world as voiceless ghosts. It is this sense of purpose, linked to a larger goal for all humanity, that makes the difference between profane sensationalism and sacred discovery.

♅♐

Uranus in Sagittarius

Lightning and thunder and rain and wind. Stolen fire in a pot. Smashed crockery. The whirl of purple cloth and copper beads. A swarm of locusts, a charging water buffalo. A glass knife slashing, a spinning top. A tornado sweeping the sand clean and white. The darkness and peace of a cemetery, headstones gleaming in the moonlight. If those images flashed by, unconnected and chaotic and yet somehow falling into place, then you've experienced a little bit of the planet of sudden change and chaos in the sign of truth.

Oya is the weather goddess of the Afro-Caribbean Yoruba religion. Capricious as the lightning strike, one calls on her at one's own risk. It is said that if you ask for a new job, she'll get you fired first; if you ask for a new home, she'll burn down your old one. Her nine sacred items delineate her nine powers and titles. As Lady of the Winds, she holds a glass knife with a sharp edge. As Lady of the Rain, she brandishes a rainstick. As Oya the Queen, she holds the copper crown. One of her totems is the locust, whose swarms devour everything; the other is the female water buffalo, who charges through anything in her path. The buffalo's horn is her fourth sacred object.

In many cultures, the deity who rules the winds is also the deity who rules the dead, as dead souls are said to ride the air. Oya is la Dueña de la Cemetaria, the keeper of the dead souls. Her son Egungun is the faceless embodiment of the legions of the dead. Her sacred items in this regard are a small pot of graveyard earth and a purple cloth, used to pull over the head for meditative purposes. This side of Oya is the one whose priests seek out and destroy evil magicians, who is not only capricious but ruthless. We think of Sagittarius as being jovial and easygoing, but there is a callous side to this sign, the part that shoots out the arrow of truth even when they know that it might slay the target. When Uranus is behind that energy, there may even be a bit of grim satisfaction in the slaughter. This placement would rather kill something cleanly—a project, an idea, a cherished illusion—than let it live on corrupted, even if others are hurt in the process of spiritual excavation.

One of Oya's titles translates to "swept clean" and another to "nearly white," symbolizing the idea that her tornadoes are a purifying force that clean away debris and uncleanliness and leave the sand spotless. Her sixth item, corresponding to this title, is the black horsehair fly whisk used for purification. One of her tales recounts how she sent tornadoes to the houses of two rich but greedy and dishonest men, swept away all their belongings, and dumped them in the yard of a poor but honest worker. There is a similar streak of the Robin Hood syndrome in a Uranus in Sagittarius; it is a rare individual who has these two energies combined and doesn't secretly wish that they could rob from the unworthy and give to the deserving.

Oya is an independent-minded goddess; one might in fact call her the most bloody-minded female deity in the Yoruba pantheon. She is also sexually independent; she has had several husbands and lovers and sometimes appears as a prostitute. She is the patron of bargains, Lady of the Marketplace, and she holds as that symbol the prostitute's mat rolled up around a pile of smashed crockery. This symbolizes that her favors are for sale, but woe betide him who tries to cheat her. This is an attitude that the Sagittarius Uranus will be familiar with. This placement often gives an interest in maverick types of commerce, and is more likely to see sex as something that should be free to dispose of as one wants, even if that is for money—but your partners had best play fair or else.

Her first marriage was to intense and taciturn Ogoun (see Mars in Capricorn). While he treated her as an equal, he was so immersed in his work that she became bored with him. The moment the fiery Shango (see Mars in Sagittarius) came by Ogoun's forge looking for spearpoints, she made eyes at him and they ran off together. Ogoun pursued her in a rage; instead of hiding behind Shango she faced him down and they fought, striking each other with their various weapons. She broke Ogoun into four pieces and he broke her into nine. They managed to pick themselves back up and called it a truce, and she went home to be Shango's wife.

However, Shango had taken on more than he bargained for. First she stole some of his fire, hiding it in a pot and keeping it secretly in her room; her eighth item is the container of fire, a small pot filled with ash and candles. Then, jealous and mischievous, she goaded his gentle wife Oba (see Venus in Pisces) into cutting off her ear and serving it to their mutual husband in a soup in order to enspell his love. This is the dark side of Uranus in Sagittarius; the line between malice and mischief can be pretty fine, and usually erupts when they are bored. This placement tends to lack compassion for others, and they can convince themselves that they are just playing an innocent trick or even that they are teaching someone a useful lesson, when they are actually being hurtful.

The horrified Shango threw Oya out, and she was judged before the council of orishas. For her crime against Oba, she was sentenced to share her duties as Lady of the Cemetery. Oya gets the headstones and the bodies of those who are buried above ground; Oba takes whoever is buried in the earth. This reflects the dilemma of the fiery person whose impatience with earthiness and humbler people may lose them their own connection with the earth. Oya flies through the air and rarely touches ground; a Uranus in Sagittarius may also have a harder time coming down to earth and may alienate others as a result.

Oya's final item is the mirror, in which she shows people the truth of their souls. For the person with this energy, it is imperative never to forget that what is good for others is also good for them. It does no good to inflict on anyone else the painful truth that you are unwilling to see in yourself, even if it does knock you down to the level of all the earthbound crawlers for a while. Truth is as sharp as the clear glass knife, and it has two edges—one for the speaker and one for the listener. To be truth's avatar is to hold that blade very close to your own heart and risk the symbolic death as much—or even more—than those whose lives you seek to change.

Arawn

Uranus in Capricorn

In the Celtic myth of Pwyll, the hero is putatively a young mortal lord who meets a stranger, but it is actually the stranger who rules the story. His name is Arawn, and he is lord of a magical kingdom underground, another form of the Celtic underworld. While Pwyll is out riding and hunting, he comes across a pack of strange hounds pursuing a deer. The hounds are snow white with red eyes and ears, and they set up an unearthly baying. Pwyll shoots and claims the deer, but then the hounds' master approaches and chides him. He identifies himself as Arawn, king under the earth of the realm of Annwn, and he is a dark Saturnian figure whose regal bearing impresses Pwyll. The young lord offers to make up for the lost kill in any way he can.

Arawn then makes him an offer. He suggests that the two of them trade places for a period of one year. With his magic, he will make Pwyll look like him and vice versa. Pwyll will rule the magical realm under the earth, and Arawn will rule Pwyll's mortal kingdom. At the end of one year, they will return, and Arawn will be in Pwyll's debt.

Pwyll is newly come to lordship in his realm. There is some suggestion that it is not a happy or prosperous place, and also some suggestion that this is due in part to his inexperience and ineptness at ruling. Arawn implies that he will set everything to rights, and Pwyll jumps at the chance. He is duly transformed, and the two switch horses and ride off to be welcomed into each others' kingdoms.

Saturn is all about rules, and Uranus is all about change. When the two of them collide (in both Uranus in Capricorn and Saturn in Aquarius), it could be considered to be about merely breaking the rules when they have grown too stagnant. This would far underestimate the complexity of this unlikely partnership. Saturn is capable of making new rules as fast as Uranus is capable of breaking old ones. After all, the Trickster's goal is not mere chaos. That's Neptune's realm. Uranus is a teacher who teaches through mental sleight of hand, with the ultimate goal of improving things through innovation. When Uranus is shoved into Saturnian shoes, he can still play his tricks and turn things upside down, but he must do it in the service of structure. His tests must be bound with honor, and his lessons must be about the rules and how to work them.

This is what Arawn does. His offer turns Pwyll's world upside down, literally—Annwn is underneath the earth, and it is always twilight there. The earth's crust is their sky. Yet Pwyll is still bound by the rules of the game and by his honor. Arawn has told him not to reveal the switch, and he does not, but the dark lord has not advised him on how to deal with Arawn's beautiful wife. She weeps when Pwyll rejects her sexually, thinking that her lord no longer loves her, but he holds firm; to take her would be to dishonor his host's marriage, and to reveal himself to her would be to break his word. It is one of those terrible contradictory situations that one can only hope to wait out, and so he does.

There is also some implication that relations with Arawn's wife may be more than just dishonorable. The wife of the Lord of the Underworld, in many European mythic traditions, is the Queen of the Underworld, the Lady of Death, the Black Darling. Although she is sometimes shown as beautiful, she has another side that is terrible and devouring and that no callow youth can survive. She symbolizes the terrible parts of the darkness that can completely drag down the visitor to any underworld. Pwyll's honor, and the sudden urge to Capricornian asceticism, may be what saves him from destruction.

He is also seized with a sudden urge to rule Arawn's kingdom as well as Arawn had. Far from being a vacation from responsibility, his sojourn in the underworld becomes a drive to excellence. He throws himself into Arawn's work with diligence and, to his surprise, becomes competent at it. However, Arawn has a hidden agenda that he has not told to Pwyll. Another immortal king, Havgan, whose realm borders on Annwn, has threatened to kill Arawn sometime that year. It has been prophesied that if the two meet, Arawn will not survive. On the last day before Pwyll goes home, Havgan attacks and Pwyll slays him in a close battle. Arawn's Capricornian practicality and reserve has left the encounter as a Uranian surprise for his replacement.

When the day comes for his return, Arawn shows up as promised. Pwyll returns home to find that his kingdom is peaceful and prosperous, and that he himself has gained a reputation as a wise and just lord—a reputation created by Arawn that he must now live up to. Arawn, in his turn, is touched by the fact that his wife has not been violated. He reveals the events of the past year to her, and she is relieved of her fears and grateful for Pwyll's honor.

Uranus in Capricorn creates a situation where an individual is driven by choice or circumstance to question and change rules that are not working—and replace them with rules and codes of honor that do work. Often he finds himself being unexpectedly tested, over and over, forced to revise his ethics and competence into excellence. He will be forced to tear down structures and forced to rebuild them again. Any attempt to escape structure altogether will simply rebound back onto him and trick him into a situation where he must strive for personal excellence or face heartbreak. In the process, Uranus in Capricorn tricks him into climbing the high mountain of achievement in such a way that he is surprised to reach the top and find it like coming home.

Anansi

Uranus in Aquarius

When Uranus, sign of the forward-thinking Trickster, goes into its own sign, it channels a clear stream of inspiration that is at once confusing and marvelous. This is the placement of the Inventor, the one who thinks up the gadgets that make things work. The creativity of this placement is different from the creativity of its opposite sign, Leo; instead of a way to express himself, the aim is discovery and reaching actual goals, in that order. This is the period that gave us such varied ideas as vitamins, the Geiger counter, the assembly line, and Einstein's theory of relativity. A Uranus in Aquarius tackles the problem with amazing ingenuity, figuring out a solution that no one else would have thought of. This is the ultimate think-outside-the-box placement.

The African spider god Anansi is an ingenious trickster of the highest sort, who is never thwarted for long in his adventures. He is the hero of dozens of tales that were brought to the West in the voices of African slaves. He was a favorite of the transplanted Africans, who had need of an archetype of irrepressible cleverness and imagination. In his most famous stories, Anansi wants to buy some magical stories from the sky god, who is the repository of all lore. (It's not inappropriate for this double-air placement to get inspiration from the spirits of the sky.) The sky god charges high prices, however; in fact, they would be almost impossible for most people. He wants a python, a leopard, a hive of hornets, and a wood spirit—all alive and unharmed.

Anansi immediately tackles the problem, and quickly figures out a way to manage the impossible. First he finds a python wrapped around a branch; he waits until it is sleeping and then wraps a vine around both snake and branch so many times that the python is completely wrapped except for its head. The clever spider then breaks off the branch and delivers it to the sky god. The leopard is caught by digging a pit, lining it with a net, and baiting it with a deer; the cat jumps in and is quickly wrapped and hoisted.

The hornets are a little harder; Anansi fills a gourd with water and convinces them that it is full of nectar. When they fly into it, he corks the gourd. The wood spirits, who are basically African fairies, are tougher still. For this, he creates the figure of a wood spirit out of sticks and tar, and poses her standing with her open hands offering cooked mashed yams, an apparent favorite food of the wood spirits. When some wood spirits come along, they pounce on the mashed yams and eat them. Then, realizing their own rudeness, they politely thank the tar fairy, but become angered when she refuses to speak to them. One wood spirit is annoyed enough that she punches the interloper, and her hand sticks. Other blows simply manage to get her more thoroughly stuck, at which point her sisters flee in terror and Anansi can take charge of the immobilized creature. After this, the sky god willingly sells him as many stories as he likes, and Anansi becomes a renowned storyteller.

One can gain some further insight into the pure Uranian character from these stories, besides the fact that Anansi is brilliant and competent. First, every method that he uses to obtain these creatures allows him to capture them at a distance, with no chance of confrontation. He prefers to do his dirty work at arms' length. This is one major flaw in the unadulterated Aquarian energy of Uranus: his dealings have a certain amount of coldness to them, and he prefers to keep a distance between himself and others. One notices that Anansi did not consider even for a moment the feelings and desires of the creatures that he kidnapped and sold. Sometimes when a Uranus in Aquarius is on the track of an important goal, the individual wants and needs of the people involved become secondary or even beneath consideration. At his worst, he may be of the opinion that they ought to see how important the work is and be willing to sacrifice themselves for it.

Another point that we notice is his handling of the wood spirits. Unlike more empathic planets or signs, a Uranus in Aquarius is not afraid of confrontation. Although he doesn't like to get emotionally involved in it, he is adept at using it as a tool to get his way. Actually, the fact that he isn't likely to be emotionally involved plays in his favor; he can keep his cool and keep baiting the other person into overreacting and doing something foolish. Uranian types love civil disobedience and public street theater, and not only because it is an effective tool for getting your message heard. It delights him because it touches his instinctive understanding that a trickster's sacred job is to stir things up. Ironically, although he is an excellent planner, he is also impulsive enough to forget to plan beyond the end of the project or for anyone else's reaction. This means that he may not see retaliation coming until it is right on top of him.

Uranus takes his name from the god of the heavens, and Aquarius is an air sign. This clever sign needs to learn to come down to earth once in a while, or he will become disjointed from the rest of the human race, and possibly his own humanity as well. He cannot just hang from a thread above the world like Anansi, observing and interfering but not braving the muddy ground. Besides, some of those grubby earthbound types could use his ingenuity, and they might even be willing to put up with his tricks in exchange.

pandora

Uranus in Pisces

When the Greek Titan Prometheus (see Saturn in Aquarius) stole fire to give to humanity, he was punished for his temerity by being chained to a rock while a vulture ripped out his liver. His brother, Epimetheus (whose name means "afterthought," as opposed to Prometheus's "forethought"), had aided him in this task. However, Epimetheus's part was less blatant, and the gods could not prove that he had actually done anything, although they suspected it. Instead of a terrible punishment like that of the activist Prometheus, the subtle Epimetheus deserved a subtler punishment to fit the crime, or so the gods decided. For this, they created Pandora and sent her to Epimetheus to be his wife.

Her name means "all-gifted," and her body was created out of clay and fire by Hephaestus, the smith god, at Zeus's command. All the gods gathered around to give her gifts—beauty from Aphrodite, clever speech from Hermes, and music from Apollo. Hephaestus placed a golden crown on her head that he had engraved with magical symbols, and the Horae wreathed her in fair flowers. She was the loveliest mortal woman that had yet been placed upon the Earth, humanity being young and Helen yet to be born. However, the last gift given to her was from Hera, goddess of marriage, and it deserves attention.

It may be that Hera disliked the idea of creating a passive, malleable virgin to pawn off as a helpless bride on some unsuspecting man. She herself (see Jupiter in Libra) was no passive wife; although her "harridan" reputation is usually denigrated in classical and modern myth, she is the image of the woman who fights to be heard and not dismissed in marriage. To her, the conjugal relationship is something to be actively engaged in, even if it brings fireworks. She was constantly rebelling against the stereotype of the humble, obedient wife, and the creation of this live sex doll may have gotten on her nerves. At any rate, she gave Pandora the gift of insatiable curiosity.

Of all the signs, Pisces is the most likely to get trapped in passivity. This is especially true for female Pisceans, although the males are by no means immune. When you hate conflict as much as this Neptune-ruled sign, it's sometimes just easier to smile, let people fuss, and appear to do what they want, while quietly working behind the scenes to your own ends. A Piscean can be willing to sacrifice honesty for peace, and they justify it by telling themselves that it will be better this way, that people would rather have unwitting smooth sailing than uncomfortable, conflict-ridden truth. A Piscean often gets so caught up in seeming nice to people that she loses her own nature in their needs and convinces herself that it didn't matter anyway. Pandora is the constructed woman who is perfect in every way; she smiles and obligingly submits to the enthusiastic Epimetheus—who, of course, falls in love with her at first sight. Many a Piscean has hidden behind this kind of façade and fooled everyone . . . even the people they were married to.

There's something about constructed women in myths that is a warning to us. (As a comparative example, see the story of Blodeuwedd, the wife of Llew, in Pluto in Gemini.) It's as if the myths warn us to be wary of someone who is too perfect, whose shell is a false face, because it will eventually crumble and show its inhumanity. Perfection, the myths say, seems too good to be true—because it is. To make a "dream girl" is to indulge in a selfish fantasy that is doomed to catastrophic failure. Perhaps it is Hera's curse on those who might prefer an empty, vapidly smiling spouse to a real, although flawed, human being.

Of course, the forces of Uranus are not going to stand for this sort of thing. Uranus doesn't like subtlety, and he wants to strike fast and openly and attract as much attention as possible. Uranus prefers to rip the covers off of the Mysteries and have them all revealed naked, to be probed and measured. Unlike when Neptune is in Aquarius and he triumphs over the veiled planet, when he transits Pisces he is forced to use Piscean methods, and it is maddening—both to him, to people with this placement, and to people who are enduring the transit. This combination is known for its long, slow repressions, behind which builds up a great seething cauldron ready to burst out. The individual with Uranus in Pisces may not even be consciously aware of this until the doors open and everything explodes. "But she was so quiet and nice," everyone thinks as they pick up the pieces of shrapnel. Often the reaction will come from a direction hitherto ignored, as creative, unconventional Uranus seeks desperately for a hidden outlet.

When Uranus was last in Pisces, alcohol (a Neptunian substance) was restricted due to Prohibition. Instead of booze, technological Uranus gave us a new addiction—the movies, a more total sensory immersion in fantasy. Television was invented during this time as well, although its addictive qualities were subtler yet and would not show their colors for decades. In other words, because of Neptunian sacrificial repression, Uranus dragged us via Piscean illusions into a new culture of social change (Uranus), which ultimately culminated in a sound-bite generation, digesting their fantasies in lightning-fast sound-bite forms. Who won the battle . . . Uranus or Neptune?

Certainly the myth of Pandora illustrates the long fuse and final explosion. When she is sent to Earth to be with Epimetheus, she is given a dowry of a strange lidded jar full of supposed gifts (the original jar was transformed into a box in later versions of the myth). The gods have filled it with all the horrible things that plague a mortal's existence—disease, injuries, birth defects, accidents, and ill luck. They tell her not to open the jar or in some cases Epimetheus, suspecting foul play, orders her never to touch it. For a time, she agrees and plays the part of the perfect submissively obedient wife. Eventually, however, she can no longer contain her curiosity and opens the jar . . . and as everyone knows, all the ills of humankind flew out and have troubled us ever since.

One thing remained in the bottom of the jar, and that was Hope, who we have with us always. When we are troubled by disease and death, it is hope that keeps us afloat. Hope is a wonderfully Piscean thing, the best quality of the sign whose keyword is "I believe." It is brought to fruition by Uranus, dweller in the future, who learns, through this slow and frustrating partnership, what hope really means. It's simple; without hope for a better future, no one would ever move forward. Sign of dreams, planet of change . . . in order to dream the change, you must first change the dream.

Neptune

Hercules
Neptune in Aries

The God of War and the God of Dreams and Madness do not work together well. Mars often feels powerless and impotent in Neptune's sign, Pisces, and Neptune does not like Mars' sign, Aries, any better. He is uncomfortable there, and the myth of Hercules is an uncomfortable one too. Wherever Neptune sits, he tends to idealize things. It's as if his misty veils of illusion rub off on anything close at hand, and so the Neptune-Venus combination idealizes love until mere humans won't qualify, and the Neptune-Mercury combination spends three-quarters of their time in a haze of fantasy. When Neptune goes into Aries and joins Mars's influence, he idealizes warfare and strife in all its forms.

The hero Hercules, greatest and most revered of all the Greek heroes, was deliberately spawned by Zeus in order to create a special protector for humankind. In practice, Hercules killed as many innocents as he protected. It was as if Zeus's grand experiment to create the Ultimate Hero went entirely wrong, creating a super-strong, drunken, half-mad idiot who saves and massacres people by turns. Of course, much is blamed on Zeus's jealous wife Hera, who hated Hercules and constantly tried to get him killed, but this line of excuses has the ring of a late-addition, devil-made-me-do-it pretext. The hero's very *name—Heracles* in the original Greek—means "glory of Hera," and it is patently obvious that he is actually her special hero, the one who acts out her repressed aggressions in a quite satisfactory way.

Hercules is basically a loose cannon. His adventures are peppered by brutal killings, often accidental or done in a fit of temper. He starts by killing one of his childhood tutors and eventually permanently injures another one accidentally—the wise centaur Chiron, who bears a poisoned wound for life. The twelve labors are placed on him by his kingly cousin Eurystheus because he kills his wife and children. This is supposedly due to a madness placed upon him by Hera, but this madness seems to recur throughout his life. It's a terrible irony—the one man who is stronger than all the other mortals has a case of periodic mental illness that makes him dangerously violent.

Neptune in Aries is the dream of the Hero. It's about the glory that one is supposed to accrue through warfare and physical courage. We're no stranger to this dream; we've all been fed the idea, at one point or another, that the only good death is one in battle, and that even dying in battle is a good thing as long as your deeds were heroic enough that you will be remembered. It's an ambivalent dream. We feel its pull even as we shy away from it. We are seduced by it even as we speak out against it. It makes us jittery, even when we adore it. Like Hercules, it is mixed blessing and curse. Individuals with Neptune in Aries may find themselves inadvertently slipping into the mindset of the Holy Hero over insignificant annoyances; if they're not careful, anything can trigger a Hercules episode. On the other hand, they are happily willing and even enthusiastic about rushing into battle for a holy cause, as long as they can be convinced—and to be fair, often they don't take much convincing—that the cause is indeed sacred.

Hercules is, of course, finally done in by a woman. While traveling with his wife Deianeira, she is accosted by the centaur Nessus, who carries her off to rape her. Hercules shoots him as he runs away, and Deianeira is saved—but the dying centaur whispers to her to soak up some of his magical blood with her skirt, and if ever Hercules should seem to be straying, she should weave it into a shirt for him to wear. She takes him at his word and saves some of his blood. Not long afterward, Hercules decides to steal a princess named Iole, whom he has loved for many years, and replace Deianeira. She becomes frightened and makes the shirt, but the centaur has played a cruel trick on her. When Hercules dons the shirt, it burns him so fiercely that he bursts into flame and dies.

After his death, however, things change. He is brought up to Olympus, where he is made an immortal and marries Zeus's daughter Hebe. His character completely changes at this point; he ceases all violence and becomes instead a magical protector that people call on in times of need. The cult of Hercules was incredibly popular throughout the Hellenistic era, and not necessarily because people wished to imitate him. As a divine protector, he was invoked frequently by frightened travelers and the oppressed; his checkered past simply made him a god who knew what it was to be human and imperfect, and therefore would be more likely to aid other imperfect humans.

When Neptune went through Aries, the line between spirituality and militarism became blurred. The Salvation Army was founded, and the Ku Klux Klan. "Onward Christian Soldiers" was written, as was "The Battle Hymn of the Republic." Tent revivals, often preaching fire and brimstone and handling poisonous snakes, were rampant. Neptune blurs the boundaries, and the Aries Neptune who desperately wants a cause may take up with the first one that comes by, forgetting to turn on his skepticism. Yet we do need heroes in this world—meaning those who are willing to put themselves in harm's way to make the world a better place.

It is no accident that Hercules had to die before he learned self-control. Sometimes the would-be hero has to undergo a terrible experience that strips his soul and his assumptions to the bone, forcing him to start over as someone entirely different, before he can see the truth through the propaganda. To be the divine hero, one has to have been the imperfect, messy, half-mad mortal hero, and then one has to die—often painfully—to that existence, in order that one might both know it well and be done with it. Only then can the hero fulfill the dream of Glory that was promised out of the nebulous cloud that held out the sword. Hercules must learn the hard way, because that is Mars's way and Neptune's as well. In the end, it is the one thing they have in common.

Jack o' the Green
Neptune in Taurus

Throughout history, the Green Man winds his way quietly through the archetypes and symbols, showing himself in a myriad of designs yet always fundamentally unchanging. He is Nature personified. His hair and beard are leaves, his body is a tree, his speech is vines, his eyes twinkle merrily—human and yet not human—out of a body of verdure. He is the forces of Earth that surround us given arms and legs and a face. No child has lived around trees and not seen his face peering from the rough bark, his form bending its limbs over a fence or tapping against a window. He is every tree who ever danced in the wind, every vine that moved up a window with a will of its own. He is the constant spirit of the plant kingdom we share this Earth with, who gives us our very breath as we give it ours. He is the May King, erecting the phallic Maypole in the fertile Earth on Beltane, when the Sun is in Taurus.

Appropriate for a Neptunian figure, he has few concrete myths and stories, and his character is elusive if one only looks at literature to find it. If one looks at the natural world, especially that of plants, it is easy. Everyone instinctively knows all about the Green Man's character. It's so obvious. We assume that it's obvious, and then we forget about it and have to go looking all over again. The best place to look for him is not in the world of words, but in the Neptunian world of imagery and experience.

Like all the green world, it starts with roots. The Green Man has roots, even when he is up and walking. He can instantly reroot himself, making himself into tree or plant or vine, and then no one can move him, except to chop him down and kill him. The place that he chooses to grow is his home, and you can evict him only over his dead body. This ability to put down roots anywhere and make the place your own, to refuse to be moved, is one of the gifts of Taurus. When Neptune moves into this earthy, sensual, slow-moving sign, it creates the dream of Earth, the green world where everything is natural and abundant, where human strife does not intrude. The Green Man, Jack o' the Green, is the king of this green world of woods and wild.

Even when Christianity became ascendant in Europe and images of all the other gods were banned, the Green Man was still an acceptable figure to carve on and in a church wall. In fact, some of the most beautiful Green Men remaining today are in churches. This ability to quietly infiltrate established institutions and get accepted there is a Taurean art, even when it's Neptune. The Green Man is a profoundly mystical and pagan symbol, and it is also profoundly physical and reflective of the mundane world. In spite of this, he sneaked into the status-quo art of a repressed, anti-Earth, and anti-physical religion for centuries, because Neptune will enter any crack, like smoke, if you let him. Taurus can often give him just enough respectability to do it, too.

The one story that shows the ambivalent nature of the Green Man most clearly is the Arthurian tale of Sir Gawain and the Green Knight. In this story, the Green Knight shows up at King Arthur's court as a giant green-skinned knight who challenges the king and his knights. He roars that any man may strike his head from his shoulders, as long as he agrees to meet and fight with him in a year's time. Sir Gawain takes up the challenge and beheads the strange knight, who promptly picks up his head, tells Gawain to meet him at a particular castle on a particular date the next year, and stalks out. The Green Man, being the spirit of verdure that constantly dies and is reborn, cannot be killed by such ordinary means.

Gawain goes sadly to his appointed time and place, finding a great castle with a merry host who does not resemble the Green Knight at all. The host has a new bride who is young and beautiful and promptly starts flirting with Gawain. They feast and entertain him for three days, during which time the young wife tries hard to get him into her bed. He refuses out of propriety, but does exchange a kiss with her. On the third day, he goes down to the river and the Green Knight meets him. They fight, and Gawain loses; the Green Man spares his life, but gives him a small nick in the side of the neck—for kissing his wife, he says, revealing that he was the merry host. If Gawain had actually climbed into her bed, he would have been killed. The entire situation was merely a test of his honor.

The Green Man, in his form as the Arthurian Green Knight, symbolizes absolute trust in Nature and its mysteries. He is willing to have his head struck off—remember that Neptune has much to do with sacrifice—because he knows that he will be able to put it back on his neck and be reborn. He understands about facing death with immutable hope and trust, of a kind so bedrock-strong that only Taurus could hold it. He inspires Gawain to the same trust and tests him accordingly. Gawain's breach of honesty and trust resulted in a wound, but because it was not serious, he did not have to face real death—from which, it is implied in the story, the Green Knight could have raised him back alive anyway.

The Green Man often issues vegetation from his mouth in carvings; his words are leaves and vines. The idea of speech as something other than speech is very Neptunian. To understand the ultra-mystical planet Neptune in the ultra-concrete sign Taurus is to understand that what is most concrete, most real, is not actually the manmade world of rent and taxes and electric bills and money. These things are associated with Earth, but they are actually an abstraction of what Earth really is. The element of earth, when it is real and not abstract, is the ground we walk on, the planet that we are dependent on for food, the bodies we inhabit whose archaic and exuberant needs we cannot—and should not—repress or eliminate. Neptune in Taurus gifts the ability to touch this truth, to clearly feel one's place in the natural—real—world, and to make one's words and deeds grow abundantly from this rooted, peaceful, dangerous, cyclical place . . . the green world that is Jack o' the Green's true home.

мimir and нoenir

Neptune in Gemini

The well is dark and deep, with the scent of clear water and earth floating up from its open pit. Torchlight glints off of the water's surface. As you lean over it, you see a face rising up through the water. It is the head of an old man with long white hair, skull-like, disembodied. He asks you, in a cracked voice, what it is that you seek, and you ask your question in a trembling voice. He laughs at you, creakily. Perhaps he answers. Perhaps he doesn't, merely sinking out of sight in a trail of chuckling bubbles. Knowledge is not always easy to come by.

Not all sacred water is seawater; sacred wells have long been a source of devotion and inspiration. When watery Neptune enters airy Gemini, the focus becomes the dream of the Well of Knowledge. The Well of Knowledge is deep, dank, and dangerous, like Neptune; however, it always seems to have a voice of some sort, a guardian being whose words echo up from the deep. Gemini gives words to misty Neptune in this placement, although the words may be somewhat incomprehensible to those without the correct experience.

Mimir is in some myths an Aesir—one of the gods of the sky, who well suits an air sign. In other myths, he was a giant who stood with the Kjolen Mountains on his shoulders, somewhat like the Greek Atlas. His name means "memory," and he is indeed a memory of the tradition of oracular severed heads. These heads have been found in bogs and temples; Mimir is akin to Orpheus (see Mercury in Pisces), whose severed head was installed as an oracle at a temple in ancient Greece, where it sang continually. Throughout Indo-European history, the magical, disembodied, severed head appears as a giver of knowledge.

Like all the air signs, Gemini is more than a little uncomfortable about living in a limiting and annoying physical body; perhaps only Aquarius dislikes it more. Any Gemini planet will strengthen the tendency to live entirely in the head, dispensing interesting information yet not connecting to the practical and grinding world. When Neptune comes into this sign, its job is not to bring Mercury's sign any closer to earth; watery Neptune's aim is to bring the mind and intellect into the obscure places of mystery. In the process, the disembodying effect can be exacerbated, so natives with Neptune in Gemini—or people undergoing transits with similar energies—need to work doubly hard not to become "talking heads," all searching and words and no belly and heart.

Hoenir, on the other hand, is referred to as "the most timid of the gods." When Odin blew life into the first humans, Hoenir thought to give them a soul. He is a quiet god and little is known about him, like all matters of soul. When the Aesir (the warrior sky gods of Asgard) and the Vanir (the agricultural fertility gods) had a great war, a truce was called only by the exchange of hostages. Odin, the king of the Aesir, demanded the accomplished love goddess Freyja, in order to learn the mystical art of seidhr from her. The Vanir demanded someone equally wise in return, and Odin sent them Mimir and Hoenir, as a pair. Their new hosts, however, soon found them less than useful: Hoenir insisted on keeping silent about any wisdom he might have had, and the few words that he would say aloud were merely phrases parroted from the more loquacious

Mimir. Like all matters of soul, he was not easily accessible, and his wisdom was not something to be conveniently learned from others.

Disgruntled, the Vanir killed Mimir and sent his severed head back to Asgard, where Odin (see Saturn in Pisces) reanimated it by throwing it into the Well of Wisdom. There Mimir stays, a disembodied head, but he learns all the secrets of the well and gains the ability to prophesy the future. When Odin goes wandering in search of wisdom, one of his stops is Mimir's well. Here the mysterious Mimir demands that Odin give up one of his eyes in exchange for some of Mimir's wisdom; Odin capitulates and is given the two ravens Hugin and Munin in exchange.

The two figures, Mimir the knowledgeable and Hoenir the silent, form the dichotomy of mind and soul—that which lights the way into the dark cave and that which is part of the dark cave and flees the pursuing light. Of course, Gemini has a recurring theme of opposites changing places or melding with each other, so it is almost appropriate that the airy Mimir ends up down the well in the mysterious depths. Here he connects with all the low, dark, terrifying things that make Gemini uncomfortable, yet are Neptune's stock in trade—and here he becomes the sacred voice for those who seek those dark places and require a guardian and guide. Mimir travels to the land of soul and gives it a voice; Hoenir stays in the upper world, but remains silent. It's a Gemini paradox.

People with Neptune in Gemini often find themselves being mouthpieces for the mystical, explaining murky ideas and clarifying mysterious paradoxes. Sometimes they can be brilliant; sometimes they can degenerate into indecipherable mental scribbling. Either way, this is the placement of the Sacred Voice, the God-Mouth as the ancient Norse called it. To listen to them is to hear an echo down the long, long shaft of Mimir's well, an echo of memory that brings wisdom and prophecy—for all that has happened before is still part of the pattern of what will be.

poseidon

Neptune in Cancer

The symbol for Cancer is the Crab, which lives on the seashore, between ocean and land. Although Poseidon was the ancient Greek god of the sea, ruling all its denizens, he also has links to the land and shore. He is watery and yet earthy; his animal totems included the horse, which was said to be visible in the white tidal waves—considered "Poseidon's horses"—and the great bull, which caused earthquakes. He took both forms on occasion, plus that of the more normally aquatic dolphins and fishes. He was called Enosichthon, "earth-shaker," and earthquakes were all attributed to him. He rules not only the seas, but in a sense the earth itself, for the earth was sustained by water. He could split mountains with his trident and roll them into the sea to form islands.

Yet in many ways, his watery, emotional nature makes him still very much an oceanic deity. Poseidon was famous for his volatile rages and excessive vengeance. When Odysseus kills one of his sons, Poseidon deliberately delays his journey home for fourteen years and nearly gets him killed in the process. Those who insulted him courted terrible wrath. One wonders about his early childhood, spent inside the belly of his father, Cronos. Each of Cronos's children seem crippled in some way that follows from early neglect and abandonment—Hades and Hestia withdraw from the world; Hera is codependent; Demeter clings to her child. Only Zeus, who escapes, is fully able to act with conscious knowledge, and he is doomed to identify with the father he kills and become the tyrant. Poseidon's character, however, is one of uncontrolled feeling. He does not act so much as react, often entirely out of proportion to the offense. He feels everything with the keenness of the water element, on a scale as large as the entire ocean.

After the death of their father Cronos, the three brothers Zeus, Poseidon, and Hades all split the rulership of the world between

them. Zeus the leader chose the sky and lived on the highest mountain. Hades, in what could be considered either Saturn-born unluck-
iness or Capricornian practicality, chose the underworld with all its
riches. Poseidon chose the water and the earth, the middle plane
most home to all of us. Although a Cancer can go far in his chosen
field, climbing to the top of the mountain or conquering death is
not his first choice. He wants a place he can call home, land under
his feet, a safe hearth with a river of love running through it.

Yet Poseidon lives in the most inaccessible place in this most
accessible plane—the bottom of the sea. Neptune puts the Cancerian dream of the perfect home-castle out of reach, in a dreamy, idealized, obscure realm that you can drown in. The planet Neptune is
itself named for the Roman counterpart of Poseidon. Although it
actually has a closer affinity with Pisces, the sea god's planet likes
being in a water sign. Water flows and water distorts. Water has
incredible passive strength, and water destroys by enveloping and
drowning. Water also gives life to dry lifelessness. Neptune does all
these things, too, including the drowning part. To come to terms
with Poseidon, one has to come to terms with the passionate tidal
wave as well as the generous Giver of Fishes.

One of Poseidon's less attractive traits was his greedy possessiveness; he kept trying to claim more coastal cities for himself. When
he lost to another deity, he would often flood the city in a fit of
pique. He reacted the same way to the women and goddesses with
whom he tried to have his way. Cancer's possessiveness and grabby
behavior isn't about gaining more wealth or land so that you can
move up in the world or gain social status or even self-worth; it's
about emotional security. Money or land or resources or love
becomes a hedge for them against all the bad things that could happen to them and, as such, there can never be enough of it, because
they can always think of more bad things that might happen. When
they are thwarted, they perceive it as you making them less safe in
the world, and the Crab hides in his shell and starts nipping with all

his might, hanging tightly on to what he has and snapping at the apparent enemy. Sometimes his defenses may end up attacking the wrong person or creating overkill.

Neptune placed in this sign can make things especially fuzzy when it comes to discerning friend from enemy, because Cancer is closely associated with the unconscious mind. This is the part of ourselves that was programmed in childhood and is so hard to see clearly enough to control or change. (During the last run of Neptune in Cancer, the art of psychoanalysis was invented and popularized.) Like Poseidon, a Neptune in Cancer reacts instinctively, with primal emotions. The word "primal" is key here. Cancer, ruled by the Moon, has close links to childbirth and infancy, the most primal time of life. The ocean is the birthplace of all carbon-based existence on Earth, the most primal time of life. To touch Neptune in Cancer is to go back a long, long way—because this sign also rules the past. Neptune in Cancer holds an idealized view of the past, because Neptune idealizes and distorts everything it touches.

This placement also holds an idealized view of home and relationships, too. Poseidon's wife was a nymph named Amphitrite, about whom we know little except that she was long-suffering, ignored her husband's infidelities, and seemed content to remain in the background of his undersea palace. On some level, a Neptune in Cancer may secretly wish for this kind of perfect relationship, where hot soup and forgiveness are dished out on a daily basis, regardless of bad behavior. A more enlightened Neptune in Cancer, however, can use the ideal of a perfect relationship not as an excuse for poor behavior or a club to beat a lover over the head with but as a goal to strive for, preferably as a team. It can also teach deep and enduring lessons about the history of the psyche, both personal and collective.

A Neptune in Cancer has a strong drive to understand the beginnings of things, how they started and how they got to where they are today. Poseidon's manifestations echo both the chaotic fluctuation of the primal beginnings of life and its reflection, the chaotic fluctuation of the psyche. He is instinct and emotion, upheaval and gentle flow, and he can change at any moment. He has no reasons for this; like Neptune, he never asks why. He simply is. It's one of those mysteries that the Neptunian mystics keep talking about. Sometimes one has to go a long way through the planetary influences—all the way out to Neptune's great, slow, oceanic orbit—to find the oldest mystery of all.

Lugh
Neptune in Leo

Leo is the sign of the sun, the golden light that burns eternally overhead, the biggest thing in the sky. In Neptune, that sun energy is idealized into the dream of a perfect performance, a perfect form of self-expression, perfect grace mixed with perfect self-worth. This sort of thing is seen as something that is gifted to people as a kind of sacred birthright, and the world gets divided into the haves—a very small number of people who manage to convince the rest of the world that they are avatars of this solar energy—and the have-nots, who watch half in fascination and half in resentment at the sparkle and glamour of the living embodiments of Light. Indeed, the word *gifted*, with all its connotations, can pretty much sum up the dream of a Neptune in Leo.

Or so it seems. In reality, no one is all-gifted. People may have talents, but if they don't polish them or strive to better them, they will never be seen. People may have personality, but if it doesn't stand up to the wear and tear of the world, they will dissolve into mere petty tyranny, the bane of Leo placements everywhere. "Look at me" can become a desperate way to say, "Love me, because if you don't love me I can't love myself." Neptune in Leo can be a way to mystically connect with the solar hero, or it can be a prison of self-doubt that you futilely attempt to escape from by convincing yourself and others that you actually are the untouchable solar hero. And while we all walk in myth and archetype, we are also all human, and identifying too closely with any one myth can take you out of the realm of humanity. In other words, it can kill you.

Lugh Sun-Face is the golden Celtic hero-king whose story weaves around the edges of this archetype and its issues. His mother is the beautiful daughter of the terrible Balor, a god-monster with one enormous eye. His eye is so heavy that the eyelid can only be lifted with the aid of others, and its baleful rays slay everyone it touches. The great eye is clearly the negative aspect of the Sun, burning and drying up all that it touches. This can be seen in the Leo ability to completely intimidate shyer and more sensitive individuals. Hearing that he would be killed by his grandson, he locked his daughter up on an island with her maidens, but a young mortal youth named Kian sailed out in a boat and seduced her. Balor threw the child into the sea, but he floated to land and was adopted by a mortal couple. Already we see the Leo myth of specialness at work—the idea that one has an exclusive destiny that protects one from the ordinary annoyances of life, like being drowned in the ocean.

Lugh grows faster than most children, another sign of his specialness, and soon has so many talents that they cannot be counted. He goes to King Nuada's court at Tara and asks to be let in, listing all the things he can do—carpenter, weaver, warrior, poet, scholar, etc.—only to be told that they have some of each of those. Lugh points out that they may have specialized labor, but they do not have anyone who can do all of those things at once. Realizing his virtuosity, he is allowed into Tara. Nuada takes one look at him, knows prophetically that this is the man who will be king after him, and immediately abdicates in his favor. This is the way that a Neptune in Leo would like to be treated, and in his unconscious he believes that this is how it should be. Often, when people cannot automatically see his worth, he becomes sullen and angry, feeling as if he is surrounded by fools who will never appreciate him. Even the most retiring Neptune in Leo person has a secret belief that the world owes him automatic appreciation, which his common sense may or may not check.

Soon after he is made king, Lugh plunges into battles with the Fomorians, chief of which is his own grandfather. This too is a Leo problem, as Leo rules children and often refuses to identify with the adult authority figure, even when they are being the adult authority figure. A Neptune in Leo can believe that they are battling the evil tyrant long after they have become the evil tyrant, and it is hard for any Neptune placement to face up to Saturnian truths about elders and authority. Lugh, however, is besieged on both sides. Not only does he have to continually battle for his borders, but his men snipe at each other and start feuds. Behind the court of the golden Sun Face all is not sunny. His own father, Kian, gets into a feud with three brothers, who kill him and bury the body secretly. The deed would have gone unpunished except that the stones covering Kian's body cry out for vengeance, and Lugh hears them while on a scouting mission and discovers the murder.

Whatever a Neptune in Leo's faults may be, one of his best qualities is the ability to think creatively. Lugh swears vengeance on the killers, but as they live in his own hall, he cannot slay them without violating rules of hospitality, so he comes up with an ingenious punishment for them. He orders them to bring him a fine of three apples, one pigskin, one spear, two horses and a chariot, seven pigs, one hound, a cooking spit, and three shouts to be given from a hilltop. They are elated at the light sentence until he explains that each of these is a specific magical item with some great power, owned by someone who will not give it up easily. Any one of these quests could get the three brothers killed.

This shows a great deal of canniness on Lugh's behalf. If he tried to steal the items himself, he would be risking his life and his reputation, but by forcing the three brothers to do it, he puts the blame on them and gets his revenge. If they fail, he is rid of them; if they succeed, he has new weapons with which to fight the Fomorians. A Neptune in Leo would prefer not to soil his hands with the nastier tasks in life, especially those that might besmirch his reputation. As it turns out, the brothers get all the magical items but the last, at a cost of great bloodshed. The final quest is to make three shouts from the top of a hill, which is actually a sacred place, defiling it. This is a sacrilegious order, and the brothers are killed by the site's guardians. Lugh uses the new weapons to defeat the Fomorians and kill his grandfather, fulfilling the prophecy.

This story has a happy ending for the ethically ambiguous Lugh because it is part of the Leo dream, where Leo the Sun always wins, no matter how. But if we go back in time to the older myth cycles, the ones that are less allegory than metaphor, we find that the summer festival of Lughnasad, named for Lugh, is the celebration of the sacred Corn King. In other words, all Lugh's omnicompetent talents and brightnesses are only leading up to him becoming, eventually, the perfect sacrifice. If this seems jarring, remember that Neptune is the planet who rules Pisces, the sign of sacrifice itself. This is the key to harnessing Neptune in Leo positively. This placement needs to remember that the more perfect you are, the more appropriate a sacrifice you are as well. The sacrifice you offer need not be your death, but your life—using all those talents selflessly for the common good of humanity. This is the only sort of use that you will eventually be allowed by gentle, fragile, merciless, inexorable Neptune. Self-aggrandizement will eventually be swallowed up, either by self-delusion or by a new search for self-effacing service. In order to be a truly talented servant, you must be both fully aware of your own talents and also of how little they matter if they are not used for a sacred purpose.

ıduna

Neptune in Virgo

The Aesir deities of Norse myth never age and die; they stay hale and youthful forever. This is not due to their divinity; it is due to the patient and laborious efforts of Iduna, the goddess of the apple orchard. She grows and tends the magical apple trees whose fruits keep the gods of Asgard young forever. She is a divine maiden goddess, akin to the maiden goddesses of spring and flower and fruit who bring the first blossoms of fertility onto the land. However, Iduna does not merely walk across the field and watch fertility spring up in her footsteps. What sets her apart from the other archetypal maidens is that she works. Iduna has a full-time task—keeping the other gods young and healthy—and it is her labor that ensures their immortality.

When Neptune, the planet of dreams, goes into Virgo, it takes on the dream of Sacred Labor. This dream can mean that all honest work is sacred, or it can speak of specific kinds of work—perhaps done with special mindfulness—that transport one to a sacred space. This is echoed in the monastic ideal of labor as a productive meditation, whether it be European monks digging in their medicinal gardens or Shinto monks raking spirals around rocks in a meditation garden. Work, and especially repetitive work, can become a method through which one achieves a state of inner peace and serenity, backed up by the assurance that one is also making a positive practical impact on the world.

Virgo, being an earth sign, likes things practical and concrete. Neptune is just the opposite, which is why it is in its detriment in this discriminating, detail-oriented sign. Virgo attempts to bring down the ethereal Neptune energy into something useful; Neptune just hears the words "bring down" and reacts somewhat negatively. The meditative nature of sacred work seems to be the compromise between these two energies, and like all compromises, it does not come easily or naturally. One has to pursue it, work at it, try and fail and try again.

Sacred work can be anything from washing dishes to digging trenches, but when we think of it in archetypal terms, the first image that classically springs to mind is a garden, with someone lovingly tending the plants. Iduna is the divine gardener whose humble work sustains the louder, showier members of Asgard. Although she is not a nun in the Christian sense—she is married, and anyway celibacy was not particularly important to the ancient Norse—there is something vaguely monastic about her. She is content to stay home, doing her sacred work. She stays modestly in the background, allowing her gift to be taken for granted—until, suddenly, it is withdrawn and everyone faces ill health and dramatic aging. She is usually portrayed as maidenly, but there is something ageless and old about her meticulous diligence.

Virgo is ruled by Mercury, the planet of speech, and Iduna's husband is Bragi, the divine *skald* or bard of Asgard. One version of her myth claims that she engraved runes on his tongue in order to give him the gift of fine speech and song. Some folk who have worked with her energies relate that she is linked with herbal medicines and the growing of plants to maintain health, which is a very Virgo issue. In fact, one thing that a Neptune in Virgo cannot resist is new (and especially mystical) methods of healing people. This may be psychic healing or physical but alternative healing methods. Neptune provides the dream/goal of curing the body (Virgo) and mind (Mercury) by nonphysical means; this can create amazing breakthroughs or complete fraudulence. This placement has to be careful not to see Iduna's golden apples in mere hedgefruit.

Iduna was once stolen and held captive by the giant Thiazi, who coveted her gift of eternal youth. The gods began to age, and panicked. Although they presumably still had Iduna's orchard, they were unable to get the immortality effects without her, which suggests that it was her powers, not the mere existence of the trees, that created the magic. Loki flew to rescue her in the form of a bird, borrowing Freya's magic falcon coat. He found her imprisoned in Thiazi's home, changed her into a nut, and flew away with her.

The nut is a typical Virgo symbol—small, compact, modest, earthy, nutritious, and springing with new life. It is the little thing that grows big things. From small moves come big changes, whispers this planetary placement. Little things, done one at a time over a long period, can change the world. Virgo is the master of little, day-to-day things. Iduna is a goddess of the natural cycles, which every gardener understands. She can show how to fall blissfully in love with each tiny element of the natural world. Her work is evident not just in the gardener, but in the scientist who lovingly catalogues fifteen specimens of mosquito, all in the distant hope of someday improving the world with his knowledge. Another pitfall of the Virgo Neptune, of course, is getting so lost in the details that you forget the world. The lab or research library or computer can become a kind of monastic hermitage in its own right. The dream of Sacred Work, when it is practiced faithfully, can extend itself to a sense of everyday small things being sacred—the new leaves slowly unfolding, a bit more each morning; the way a seed pushes up from the earth; the smell of rain; the way the sun moves in a slightly different arc as the seasons move on. Why hunt for supernatural miracles, Iduna asks us, when the true miracles are all around?

Baldur
Neptune in Libra

Of all the gods in the Norse pantheon, Baldur was the most perfect. He was so stunningly beautiful that he shed light all around him. Talented, loving, charming, fair, and always good-natured, he was the darling of Asgard, and especially of his powerful mother Frigga. His archetype embodies the Venus-ruled ideal of Libran goodness. Baldur is a good picture of what a Libra wants to be like when he or she grows up, complete with the adoring mob of fans. When Libra colors Neptune, she creates the dream of Beauty. However, from Neptune's point of view, the perfect being has only one purpose: to be the perfect sacrifice.

> It is the nature of sacrifice
> To be difficult.
> If it was easy to throw away,
> It was no sacrifice.
> If you did not miss it,
> It was no sacrifice.
> If it was not the best you could give,
> It was no sacrifice.
> If it was not agonizing to choose,
> It was no sacrifice.
> If it did not make you waver
>   at least once in your choice,
> It was no sacrifice.
> If it did not make you weep,
> It was no sacrifice.
> —*Lammas invocation, Pagan Kingdom*
>   *of Asphodel, 2002*

One finds this theme again and again in mythology: The ideal sacrifice is someone who has mastered the art of being perfect, who shines with light wherever he goes. He is also, strangely enough, valued not for what he *does* so much as what he *is*. Although Baldur is beloved of all, he is not actually recorded as doing anything specific. He simply smiles and bestows his charm on others, and they bloom in response. It is also important that he is the son of a mother goddess, another qualification for sacrificial kingship. Somehow, Baldur is overidealized in his perfection; he is simply too good to be true, or at least real.

Of course, Libra's answer to this is that it isn't *fair*. Sacrifice never is. "Why should our dear Baldur have to die?" cry the gods, and so when their golden boy starts having dreams of death and destruction, they immediately rush to his aid, making every living being swear not to harm him. To show off his newfound invulnerability, Baldur turns it into a game: he lets people throw objects at him and laughs as they bounce off harmlessly. Of course, Frigga in her hurry has missed one plant; she felt that one tiny mistletoe was too young to be forced to swear an oath. Loki finds the plant, makes a dart out of it, and tricks the blind god Hoder into throwing it at Baldur, who is killed.

The gods are horrified and seize Loki. They send Hermod, another son of Odin, down to Helheim to plead for Baldur's return. He travels for nine days and nights and finally comes to Hel's realm, where she receives him graciously but is adamant that Baldur must stay. When Hermod begs for his brother's life, she gives one condition: all things on the earth must weep for him. The Aesir receive the news with their usual hopeful flurry of activity, and the effort that once swore all things to harmlessness now encourages them to beg for the return of the God of Light. One old hag, however, holds out and claims that she will not weep for Baldur, and the effort fails. He is condemned to stay in the Land of the Dead until the coming of the New Era.

Neptune in Libra is not only the dream of Beauty; it is also the dream of Justice. Here, where justice and fairness are idealized, they are shown to be two different things, often mutually exclusive. It's a question that has dogged many philosophers: when the fox eats the mouse, is it fair or good? In reality, of course, both the fox and the mouse are part of an ecosystem cycle that is often harsh and cruel. Sometimes the fox kills the mouse; sometimes the mouse gets away and the fox kits starve. Both endings can seem awfully unfair if you are the fox or the mouse being asked to sacrifice, and neither work well under anthropomorphic human ideals of "fairness."

We humans like to imagine that we do not live in the same system as the fox and the mouse; we pretend that they are denizens of some other world that we can peer into on wildlife TV shows, ensconced in our concrete and plastic and good/bad thoughtforms. But we do live in that system, as long as we inhabit flesh bodies on this earthly planet, and the moment we take off our blinders we are assailed with the truth: Nature is already perfect. She's had billenia to work the kinks out of her system of natural selection, and it is self-reassessing and self-adjusting. It is also no fairer to us than to any other organism, which means from the human point of view that it's terribly unfair. That's the truth that Libra has a love-hate relationship with—that perfection is inherently unjust. Want perfection? asks Neptune. Fine. How much are you willing to sacrifice for it?

Neptune also asks Libra to take a longer look at justice than merely that of a human lifetime. What was not immediately apparent in the gods' angered grieving is the knowledge that Ragnarok was soon to come, and the Aesir are nearly all slaughtered by their nemeses. Had Baldur been among them at that time, he would not have lived to see the next world—the world where he is destined to be king. In order to keep him safe for his destiny, he had to be removed from imminent doom. The safest place for him in all the nine worlds is Helheim, Land of the Dead. It is the point at which justice meets dire necessity, and it is telling that all the figures who arrange for his future are keepers of storm and trouble and death— Loki, Hel, and the adamant old woman who says, "Hel must keep her own." Neptune asks justice-obsessed Libra to take the long view and look far into the misty, vague, turbulent future to see the pattern that will, in time, turn out to be just.

Of course, we humans have a terrible time doing this. We are required to have faith, another Neptunian quality, and to believe that all things will turn out for the best. Individuals with Neptune in Libra will find this to be their biggest seesaw of indecision. When faced with apparent injustice, is it better to assume the worst and jump in, or to wait and hope that things will get better on their own? There is, of course, no correct answer that will work in every situation. At worst, this dilemma so frightens them that they hide in an artificial dream of sweetness and light, the sort of thing that created the aesthetic of the 1950s. At best, they accept that nothing can ever be truly fair, but it is in everyone's best interest to at least strive to alleviate obvious injustice in the here and now—the sort of thinking that created the United Nations. Both came out of Neptune in Libra, and only the future will show their place in the long view of time.

Dionysus
Neptune in Scorpio

In ancient Greece, the cult of Dionysus was both revered and feared, sometimes more of one or the other, sometimes both at once. Its adherents engaged in sexual orgies with no thought to marriage and indulged in mind-altering substances, wine first and foremost, but also psychedelic mushrooms and plants. They overthrew traditional sex roles—women were definitely in control at their rituals, and men ran the risk of being torn to pieces if they argued. Some gatherings were women-only, or women and castrated men only, and were fiercely guarded. Others allowed "satyrs"; wild men who were in touch with their earthy, animal-like side. Heterosexuality was not necessarily the rule in their orgies, either. Their leaders and priests were often androgynous, to honor the castrated cross-dressing god Dionysus, known as "the womanly one." They frequently used music and dance to achieve altered states, trance-dancing wildly to drumming and music for hours on end; they did not hold down ordinary jobs, preferring to move from town to town in their dancing bands and beg for food. Ordinary citizens looked upon them with distaste and fear and often banned their public rituals.

The last time this sort of thing happened in Western society, it was the late 1960s, when Neptune went into Scorpio. Sex, drugs, and rock-and-roll exploded in a great wave across America and Europe, and dancing, long-haired hippies in festive clothing and pockets full of pot and shrooms and acid festooned impromptu music festivals in city parks. Mythologist Joseph Campbell went to a Grateful Dead concert and claimed that it was the rebirth of the Dionysian ritual all over again. Feminism gained serious speed during this time, and the spirituality of altered states was fodder for experimentation for the first time in centuries, not to mention the spirituality of sex. The "free love" concept of Neptune in Libra became the tantric promiscuity of Scorpio, for whom sex is far more than just a way to get an orgasm or bond with a lover. Sex, for this intense sign, is about connecting with something deeper than oneself or even one's partner, or it's somehow unsatisfying.

Scorpio is paradoxical in that it is also the sign of elimination, ruling the colon and anus. Part of the strangeness around Neptune in Scorpio is the constant veering between excess and asceticism. Both hippies and ancient Dionysians practiced excess of sex and drugs and altered states, yet ascetically gave up a hold on money, jobs, and material objects (all ruled by Taurus, Scorpio's opposite sign). This experimenting with what should be done to death and what should be thrown away is Scorpio's way of finding its balance. It is an entirely different method of balance from Libra's Golden Mean, more a way of seeing if different intensities can cancel each other out. Add Neptune's inherent ethereality and compulsion to move further from the material world rather than closer to it, and the spirit of this placement drives itself toward the gates of the underworld, where the material world has no place or importance.

Dionysus was the youngest child of Zeus. His mother was accidentally burned to death while carrying him, so Zeus rescued the fetus from the dead mother's womb and enclosed him in his own body until he could be born. Dionysus is referred to as "twice-born" because of this, and he gives Zeus the feminine experience of carrying and bearing a child. Torn apart by beasts, he is reassembled by the gods. He is hidden from Hera's wrath by being raised as a girl, and as a youth is bribed to mutilate the androgyne Agdistis. Spilling the hermaphrodite's sacred blood drives him mad, and he runs through the countryside spreading madness wherever he goes. This is part of the deeper experience of Neptune in Scorpio. The followers of Dionysus used to refer to the "greater madness" and the "lesser madness"; the first was the delusion that the mundane world with its ordinary chores and materialism was all that existed, and the second was the temporary madness inflicted by an altered state that could lead to awareness of deeper realities.

The path of Dionysus is, in part, the shaman's path. The shaman is twice-born, dismembered and re-membered, and faces a hard choice: either he must live a life of Spirit or go mad. Dionysus also faces this choice. In mutilating the sacred hermaphrodite he has attempted to kill a more fully manifested version of his own androgynous self, and he has committed a sin that he can only expiate with eternal sacrifice. He goes to the temple of Cybele, where he is castrated and dressed in women's clothes, and regains his sanity. He then goes about spreading vine-culture with his dancing band of sex-crazed Maenads and satyrs. His castration, on the one hand, and his reputation as an orgiastic deity, on the other, are not mutually exclusive—at least not to Neptune in Scorpio, who understands the tantric truths about sexual energy. Sometimes blocking the ordinary procreative urges, or holding back or disciplining the instinctive compulsions, can bring physical ecstasy into the realm of spiritual revelation.

This does not mean that everyone born in the Neptune in Scorpio generation is going to be a sexual mystic or drug guru or anything close to a shaman. Sometimes Neptune's aura can distort things until the individual simply drowns in a watery Scorpionic swamp of alcoholism or drugs or self-delusion. Addiction is probably the biggest trap in the illusive veils of Neptune in this placement. Scorpio's intensity does mean that if the native starts down the Path, they are either going to have to embrace it strongly, or sink into that swamp, or turn back . . . if they can. Dionysus is an incredibly powerful god, and he demands sacrifice, as he has been sacrificed himself. He shows how altered states are a door into the cosmic web, but one that must be approached with respect. This path can never be made completely clear and safe, and that is part of Neptune's challenge. The Path of the Vine God will always be hung with shadows and dangers, and at its end is the gate of rebirth.

Herne
Neptune in Sagittarius

Our most distant ancestors gather around a campfire, where a mammoth roasts in hot, bloody chunks over a bonfire. Talk is hushed. A man steps out of the shadows wearing the skin of the mammoth, tusks balanced on his shoulders. He trumpets his defiance to the sky and begins a slow mammoth-dance around the fire. Another man leaps out of the shadows, spear in hand, and mimes striking the mammoth-man, who trumpets and falls to the ground. The tribe converges on the meat, thanking the God of the Hunt with their cries of pleasure.

Move forward to a medieval era. "Herne was the Lord's best huntsman," the old crone recounts to her grandchildren. "He was treacherously murdered because he saw an evil deed done and would have up and told the Lord of it. Now his spirit rides with the Wild Hunt, a great forbidding man with great antlers that pierce the moon, astride a black horse, surrounded by hounds with red eyes. Their baying can reduce a man to shivers, my ducks. He rides in search of evildoers, those who try to stop the truth from being told." The children look at each other guiltily. "No matter how big the lord or king, when he hears Herne come sweeping across his country at night, he knows his days are numbered! Herne the Huntsman will hunt him down, chase him like a deer through the woods, until his hounds bring him down at last."

He may well be the oldest god of all, perhaps second only to the Great Mother. The Horned Lord of the Hunt moves down through history and prehistory, dancing across cave walls and early pottery, with his rack of antlers and his spear. The paradox of his mystery is that he is both hunter and hunted, both killer and prey. He understands the tearing cruelty of the predator and the running fear of the deer, and how any of us can, at any time, be either or both. He is lord of the animals, protector of the wild things, the dream of the Wild. He is the animal nature within us, all the "brothers of the tribe" who died that we humans might live, and all the humans who declared themselves brothers to the animal world. He is the totemic tribal god of the hunter, and he has fed our species for millennia.

He has had many names and shapes, some of them subtle or hidden. He is related to the Greek hunter Actaeon, who saw the hunting goddess Artemis (see Moon in Sagittarius) bathing naked in a pool; she turned him into a stag and his own hounds tore him to pieces. The Celts called him Herne, or Kern, or Kernunnos. He lived in the tale of Herne the Huntsman and the myth of St. Hubert, who saw a cross glowing between the antlers of a stag and became the name that Herne was secretly venerated under. He is stern and forbidding, yet kindly to the wild creatures that he both protects and culls.

When Neptune moves through Sagittarius, the dream of Neptune becomes the dream of the Wild, a vague shape of utopia where things are always true and real, and uncluttered with the detritus of human opinion. Sagittarius broadens the horizons, and Neptune inspires mystical seeking. At its best, the combination can create a philosophical search for new meaning, tracking it down with the intensity of any hunter's god. In some cases, the search never ends; the individual keeps seeing and finding and discarding and moving on for the rest of his life. Herne has no home; he never stops moving; all the world's wild places are his home.

Sagittarius has an implacable side that can be just as inflexible as Taurus and as uncompromising as Scorpio, in spite of the fact that it is a mutable sign. It's the side that comes in when a Sagittarian gets that fanatical religious gleam in his eye and starts talking about Truth with a capital T. He doesn't want to hear about there being many truths, some contradictory; this is always a hard existential pill for the Archer to swallow. He wants there to be One Truth, one basic reality that he can hunt down, catch, and keep forever, uncontradicted. In a sense, the only place where there is such a Truth is the realm of nature, which is also cruel and uncompromising. It's human truths that are myriad and confusing. Since Neptune is the very planet that specializes in myriad and confusing, the native with Neptune in Sagittarius can get sidetracked into a philosophical quicksand of What Is Right And True, trying desperately to find that one gem that is more real than all the others. Herne's Wild Hunt runs down evildoers, including those who disagree with him, without mercy.

There is more than a little streak of fanaticism in this combination. During the reign of Neptune in Sagittarius, the animal rights movement picked up steam and became a social force, for good or ill. Herne might have been happy, or he might have shaken his head. In the dream of the Wild, there is only one Truth, and it is the Truth of predator and prey in a delicate balance, a chain that should not be broken. There is an inherent order to all things, even if it is crueler than we as humans would like. Neptune in Sagittarius both longs for Herne's world, where things are simple if brutal, and fears it, because it does not allow for all of human variation. His nature forces him to keep widening and expanding his world-view, and the more he does this, the more he loses Herne's focused track.

In the end, the choice for Neptune in Sagittarius may be the hunter's mind. By being both predator and prey, Herne is able to understand both the hunter's need to eat and the need of the hunted to escape, and appreciate them both. This can lead to a greater Neptunian compassion, which can soften the hard Sagittarian search for unbending Truth. Herne is elusive as a wild animal and yet universal; all our ancestors knew him in one form or another. When we understand this, we understand a fundamental Neptunian mystery about the line between human and animal, the dream of Truth and the dream of the Wild.

Lao-tien-yeh
Neptune in Capricorn

In ancient China, the emperor was a living god who presided over an immense edifice of bureaucracy, with literally thousands of officers who reported about anything and everything. Being a part of the royal bureaucracy was far more than just a job, it was a sacred duty. Men were supposed to dedicate themselves to it with all the fanaticism of religion. For some jobs, the government went so far as to require castration as part of the job requirements, so that no distraction of family ties should interfere with their job performance. Individuals chosen for these often high-paying, high-esteem jobs were ordered to show up for the first day of work with their testicles in a jar.

One of the interesting things about the Chinese heavenly pantheon is that it exactly resembles the earthly bureaucracy, only in a more perfect and idealized way. At its head was Lao-Tien-Yeh, Father-Heaven, also known as Yu-Ti, the August Personage of Jade. He was the divine figure that the actual emperor on earth was supposed to embody. Almost no one prayed to him, though, since he was far too busy to actually listen to the average Chinese peasant. He was said to have created the first humans out of clay, but since that time a variety of lesser gods were supposed to look after them.

Lao-Tien-Yeh's legions of bureaucrats are almost uncountable. There is the Ministry of Thunder, headed by the thunder god Lei-Kung and staffed by rain gods, wind gods, and the four dragon-kings whose job it is to allot specific amounts of rain to each of the Chinese provinces. There is the God of Literature and the God of Examinations, followed by several lesser deities who help pupils with their studies. The Ministry of Happiness consists of three gods: Shou-Hsing, the god of long life; Fu-Hsing, the god of generalized happiness; and Lu-Hsing, the god of salaries. They are not to be confused with Ts'ai-Shen, the god of wealth, who works out of a different ministry.

The chancellor and second-in-command of the great Lao-Tien-Yeh is the Emperor of the Eastern Peak, T'ai-Yueh-Ta-Ti, who heads up over eighty divine offices, mostly dealing with class issues—determining the births, deaths, marriages, number of children, and class and social position of each poor mortal, and also registering the good and bad deeds and their appropriate retributions during and after life. He needs so many subordinate workers that he has to recruit them from the souls of the dead; some are working there at menial tasks to pay off their bad deeds, and others were given honored positions due to their good works during life.

There is even a specific demigod who is in charge of local towns, called the Lord of Walls and Ditches (see Saturn in Capricorn). The difference between him and the common protective town or city deities of other cultures is that he gives solemn written reports to the deity who is his provincial executive officer, and thus on to the top of the bureaucracy. On an even smaller scale, each household has a kitchen god whose visage hangs on the wall next to the hearth; he is periodically burned and sent to heaven where he, too, will make his written report on the deeds committed in the house, and household-ers will often smear his lips with honey before burning him as a bribe to make him say only sweet things.

In this cosmology, it is very hard for a god or goddess to refuse to be involved with the heavenly bureaucracy; indeed, if they stray independently at all it is only in the unwatched rites of peasants. The levels and levels of divine surveillance seem to create an atmosphere both of security—knowing that nothing will ever change, and wrongdoings will be seen and somehow punished—and constant worry, as the hapless peasant cringes from the all-seeing eyes of each god. At its best, Lao-Tien-Yeh's heavenly staff are like an idealized system that is always perfect and makes all the trains run on time; at its worst it is a faceless, unforgiving Big Brother of religious systems.

This ambivalence perfectly sums up the contradictions of Neptune in Capricorn. Practical, orderly, status-conscious Capricorn does not like to live on dreamy, elusive, mystical Neptune. Not one bit. Not for a minute. Unfortunately, he has to spend one piece of his time there, and so his compromise is to create a kind of idealized bureaucracy, the way that things could be if everyone in society was just willing to stop fussing and settle down and work for the greater good, as mandated by the people who have the authority to know best. Capricorn likes being the Authority, whether it's the Authority over people or the Authority on some sort of information. Lao-Tien-Yeh is not an emperor who conquers or even one who brings in new innovations. He is a chief bureaucratic executive officer of an immense corporation that runs like clockwork. All-wise, all-capable, and firmly ensconced in the top niche of the hierarchy, he is a Capricorn dream, and that's part of Neptune's magic too.

Neptune in Capricorn doesn't have to be all about idealized bureaucratic dystopias, although that's its danger, its dark side. It can also be about the dream of a hierarchy that works, that is responsive to its members, that finds a safe place for everyone in every class. One of the good things about the heavenly Chinese system is that it is possible to climb through merit and hard work, which is always recognized. If one has to work within a hierarchical system, one had better get busy making sure that people can actually move around within it and that they reach their places based on being able to do the job rather than nepotism or flattery. Neptune in Capricorn's idealized hierarchy does this, and although it is a perfection that we perhaps can never achieve—and perhaps may never want to—we can at least be inspired by Lao-Tien-Yeh's insistence on merit and hard work and apply that to our own experiences on the ladder of system and tradition.

Tiresias

Neptune in Aquarius

Neptune, the dreamy planet of illusions and cosmic consciousness, loves to dissolve boundaries, especially ones that prevent us from empathizing with each other. Uranus, the lightning-strike planet of violent innovation, loves to demolish boundaries, especially the ones that prevent us from changing. Their methods may be different, but they agree on one thing: walls were made to be destroyed.

One of the biggest walls in our human experience is the line between male and female. We defend it rigidly, fanatically, almost hysterically. To pass things back and forth over the line is to court social opprobrium, as those who try to loosen up stereotypical gender roles discover. To try to move the line is to create a general uproar, as those who try to deconstruct the nature of gender discover. To cross the line yourself is to put your very life in danger, as transgendered people have discovered. To erase the line completely is to bring on a frenzied attempt to erase and obliterate you, as intersexed people know to their despair. It's a truth that shapes so many people's worlds that to show it to be other than an impenetrable barrier is like removing the earth from beneath their feet.

Yet in many ancient and indigenous cultures, to cross the gender barrier was to move into a kind of permanent altered state. By ceremonially moving between genders, one could magically become a

374

Walker Between Worlds. In some cultures, those who transgressed gender boundaries were shamans by default and developed special powers. Once the rigid boundary of gender was removed, other boundaries might soon follow—for instance, those between human and animal, the living and the dead, the world of material objects and the world of spirit. Shapeshifting—a Uranian talent—was the key to learning how to inhabit bodies and worlds other than one's own, and all too often it started with crossing genders, as if this "sacrosanct" line was the key to turning one's world-view completely upside down.

The story of Tiresias starts with a wager made by Zeus (see Jupiter in Aries) and Hera (see Jupiter in Libra), warring spouses who embody the distrust, alienation, and deep-seated anger between men and women both then and now. Both insist that the other sex has more pleasure during lovemaking and a long-standing argument ensues. In order to end the debate once and for all, Zeus hits on an idea: they will pick some hapless mortal, magically change their sex, and order them to reveal the truth. Tiresias, a mortal man, is the unlucky recruit. He is given his orders, changed into a woman, and sent on her way. In seven years, she is told, she must return to Olympus and her former shape will be restored. At first she is resentful of the gods' game, but eventually she grows to prefer being female.

Seven years later, Tiresias returns to chronicle her adventures to the Olympian throne. She reports that, indeed, women did have the greater enjoyment in sexual relations. She also asks to be allowed to remain a woman, rather than have her original gender reinstated. Zeus and Hera are both furious—she because the well-kept secret of female pleasure is supposedly out and he because Tiresias traitorously rejects the male sex. Zeus denies the mortal's request and turns her back into a man—or, in some cases, a somewhat hermaphroditic figure—and his enraged wife strikes Tiresias blind and flings him off of Olympus.

He is rescued by Athena (see Sun in Aquarius), who is a gender-crossing figure herself. The goddess is unable to undo either curse, but she grants Tiresias the gift of second sight, and s/he becomes a famous seer and soothsayer. One can imagine that much of hir wisdom comes not only from Athena's gift but from hir own double past. The cosmic energy of Neptune, immersed in the far-seeing Aquarius nature, can indeed bring second sight, a precognitive glance into the future. Once the boundaries of male and female have been challenged, not much still stands unassailable, including the future as we know it.

As I write this, Neptune rides through Aquarius. These last few years have seen a drastic increase in sex reassignments, especially for younger people; the rise of the transgender revolution; the creation of a movement for the rights of intersex people; tumultuous arguments in academic circles about gender, sex, culture, and biology that rival the debates of Zeus and Hera; and scientific studies that link the rising tide of physical and mental hermaphroditism in both animals and humans to environmental pollution by "endocrine disruptor" chemicals. If, as some say, the degradation of the environment is part and parcel of the same mindset that demeans both women and the earth that they are made to represent, then the gods are using our own weapons against us in a singularly appropriate way.

There is another version of the story of Tiresias. In this older story, Tiresias sees a pair of snakes coupling, and the sight magically transforms him into a woman. This is curiously reminiscent of the sort of wild dreams that presage a shamanic rebirth, which a consciously spiritual sex change can actually be. Serpents are themselves associated with an intersex state—it is very hard to sex a snake, and they have been symbolic of both the straight phallus and the "writhing" female genitals. They are found associated with such gender-transgressing deities as Athena, Shiva, and Lilith. They are symbols of death and rebirth, as they shed their skin and renew themselves; the power of "snake medicine" is to take poison into yourself and transform it.

This is the true use of Neptune in Aquarius's ability to glimpse the future. To navigate the waters that we have mined with physical and social poisons will take people who are strong in snake medicine. This placement is the dream of the Future and, like Tiresias, people with this placement will not put up with arbitrary walls. Not only will they challenge them, they will refuse to accept their very existence. Of course, also like Tiresias, they may be so wrapped up in visions of the future that they are blind to the very real fears and limitations of people around them. This may mean that the future they envision might not come about in their lifetime, which is always a disappointment to a visionary.

Tiresias is an ambiguous figure. Starting as a Neptunian victim, s/he becomes a Uranian seer. Like any shaman, altered states are thrust upon hir by a higher power, yet s/he triumphs by accepting and using them. It doesn't have to be this way, s/he says. Look at me. I'm not like that, and I survived. You can too. Those walls were put up by humans; they can be dismantled by humans. We don't really need them any more. I can promise you that. I can see the future, and so can you . . . in my eyes.

Tiamat

Neptune in Pisces

In the beginning, there was chaos. That's how most of the founding creation myths of Western culture start out. They describe roiling, turbulent chaos that sprayed random life about without any integral order. You'll notice that creation doesn't superimpose itself on a state of empty nothingness; there's always something there. It's just undesirable because it's chaotic. Usually, it's described as endless heaving waters, as if humanity somehow carried prehuman history in its race memories. Did our ancestors somehow remember how we stumbled into the ocean as small tree-climbing monkeys and emerged an era later as upright tool-users? Or perhaps they might have remembered even further back to the primal waters from which crawled the first primitive life. Somehow, they understood— as do we, on a deep level—that water was the original source of life.

Tiamat is the Babylonian goddess who personifies this primordial chaotic ocean. Little is known of her physical attributes, but she is referred to as "dragon" and "she-serpent." She births several gods and a pair of giant serpents, and begins the dynasty of the Babylonian pantheon. Tiamat is said to represent two kinds of primordial waters; one is the water that covers the world and the other is the "celestial" water that fills where the air should be. In this cosmological story, everything is swirling, chaotic water. The upper and lower waters suggest that Tiamat brings forth rampant creativity in both earthly and spiritual matters. Her waters are, in many ways, a personified womb from which everything springs forth.

When the planet Neptune goes into its own sign, Pisces, it is expressed truest to its nature. I do not use the term most clearly, because there is nothing clear about either Neptune or Pisces. The three water signs—Cancer, Scorpio, and Pisces—are all concerned most with emotion, but in Pisces the flow of feeling transcends personal boundaries and becomes instead a sense of the numinous, a need to open to the ethereal. This can result in profound mysticism or profound delusion, and Neptune does not seem to care which. "In the end, what does it matter? All things are one," Neptune says. This is a hard answer for more clear-cut types to tolerate.

We tend to imagine that since Pisces is generally a passive sign, a Piscean figure would be less than effective as a warrior. One look at the level of bloodshed in the last two millennia—the Piscean Age— will show this to be a falsehood. Unlike Aries, when Pisces decides to fight, she does not intend to be a hero. She expects to win or to become a martyr, and one outcome may be as satisfactory as the other. Martyrs, of course, have little to lose and thus are more dangerous than heroes who tend to prefer survival. Neptune is always more interested in the nebulous hereafter than in practical survival. It's why her martyrs so often win; it's hard to stand against that kind of spiritual fatalism.

During the last pass of Neptune through its own sign, movements such as the Transcendentalists and the Spiritualists sprang up. Table-tipping mediums were all the rage, and Lourdes had its famous vision of the Virgin. Under all the charlatanry was a human populace desperate to believe in something. The mundane world was no longer enough; people were drawn into the swirling mists of mysticism and were often not prepared for what they found. The Neptunian urge to be at one with the universe is a two-edged sword; in order to get there, you have to let go, but letting go can blind you to a false messiah or movement. Any dealing with the energies of Neptune in its own sign can signal a "faithquake," a spiritual experience so sudden and powerful that it feels forced, driven, engulfing. We have no choice but to endure it; we can only attempt to choose our reaction.

At any rate, things do not go well with Tiamat's descendants. She and her consort complain of their noise, crying out that they cannot sleep with the riotous antics of their children and grandchildren. At first, of the two of them, Tiamat counsels patience and does not wish to destroy her offspring. Apsu keeps complaining (rather peevishly, in fact) until the offspring in question hear the rumor and start discussing the possibility of removing the elders instead. They start by capturing and imprisoning Apsu.

Tiamat is enraged when she hears this and begins to give birth to an army of dragons, serpents, and scorpion-men. She chooses her faithful son Kingu to lead it, creating for him the Tablets of Fate as a magical weapon, and they march on their upstart progeny. Ea and Anu both fail against Tiamat's onslaught, and everyone else is terrified of her. She is the force that is not only irrational but transcendent, that connects the most primitive parts of our brains with the

All That Is, leaving rational mind out of the loop altogether. Whenever this kind of spiritual assault descends on us—and more often than not, it descends because we have been studiously ignoring it—we are completely overwhelmed. Our everyday mode of thinking deserts us, ill equipped to handle the tidal wave from the Otherworld, the Elder World of primordial awe.

Marduk (Mars in Gemini), the warrior of the winds, finally steps forward and agrees to take on Tiamat, although he blackmails all the gods into giving him complete authority and unquestioned rule if he succeeds in slaying her. Desperate, they agree. This, too, plays out archetypally in our lives; when the overly intense karmic experience comes to get us, we fall back on fire and air, will and thought, the warrior of the winds, to save us. We will promise him anything to get us out of the bottomless sea that we have fallen into, including things that will constrict us later. Sometimes he loses, in spite of everything, and we are swept away.

Sometimes he wins, at least temporarily. Marduk slays Tiamat, but her body is so huge that it cannot be made to go away. Instead he carves it into two pieces, turning one into the earth below and one into the sky above. Different parts of her body become dwelling places for gods, men, and other beings. From the castrated corpse of her son Kingu he forms the bodies of humankind. The act of destruction becomes, in the end, an act of creation.

The myth of Tiamat is usually read as a sorrowful slaying of the Mother Dragon by the nasty warrior. Neptune, in its inscrutable transcendence, sees it differently. To Neptune and to Pisces belong all sacrificed beings, hero and heroine, parent and child, willing and unwilling. To be a sacrifice is in Neptune's eyes the greatest honor one can have. Tiamat's fate is in this sense glorious rather than ignominious. Like all shamanic stories, she is dismembered, and her parts are used in the creation of all new things. Marduk's reign might pass, but Tiamat became the entire world that we live in. No matter what happened after that, everyone would be surrounded inescapably by Tiamat. In the Neptunian way of things, no matter what happened, Tiamat could not lose. To understand this truth is to touch for a moment the crystal heart that lies deep within the blurring cloud of Neptunian energy. It is more than merely victory through surrender. It is why Pisces will always be the last sign standing.

♇ pluto

pan
Pluto in Aries

The mountains of Arcadia loom large and awesome in the legends of ancient Greece. Later eras record the word "arcadian" as implying peaceful, bucolic pleasures; images of romping shepherds and shepherdesses in an unspoiled pastoral setting come to mind. However, the ancient Arcadia was a place of harsh mountains and dark, trackless forests. This was the country of the Wild Things, including wolves and bears that prowled on the hunt for food. There were no roads and few hamlets; Arcadia as untamed wilderness was anything but safe. Into the fringes of this frightening and mountainous country would come small bands of herders with their precious sheep and goats, searching ever farther up the steep slopes and into the dreaded forests for fresh fodder. It was a dangerous lifestyle, and the men who followed it were often the poorest and most outcast of their lowland villages, willing to brave the wilderness in order to eke out a living.

Their patron god, Pan, was as ambivalent and challenging a figure as the mountains they traveled. Goat-footed and goat-horned, he protected and terrified the beleaguered herders by turns. The sound of his pipes could lull them to sleep or send them into a panic, the word created from his name. To understand Pan is to understand the world of the universal ancient herder, dependent on his flocks yet forced to keep moving constantly in order to feed them. Shepherds and goatherds did not have an easy life, despite any stereotypes to the contrary. Isolated and solitary for most of the year, some went mad from the lack of human contact, startling at every noise as if it was a wolf come to devour them. Others merely grew unused to polite human customs and found themselves still outcasts for their eccentric behavior when they returned to civilization. Their world was an ever-vigilant circle around their helpless and wayward charges; a circle surrounded by known and unknown dangers that could spring on them at any moment. For them, Nature was very close. She fed and succored them and also slew them without warning. Pan, Lord of the Wild Things, was her avatar and servant. His very name—"all"—suggests that he is the symbol of all that is male and wild in nature.

As a phallic deity, he made their animals fertile. We forget how important sexual fertility was to our ancestors; if the livestock didn't go into rut, there would be no young. Milking females would dry up, and future meat would never appear. Creatures who went into heat regularly and enthusiastically would ensure enough food for survival. Thus, Pan's greatest blessing was his rampant virility, with which he ensured the continuity of the flocks and herds. We tend to wince, today, at the figure of Pan with his erect penis and huge grin, ready to leap out and get on with it. This sexual urge is too much, we think; too aggressive . . . too animal. It terrifies us, not least because we all recognize it.

When we describe Mars, the ruler of Aries, we modern astrologers tend to stress the traits of "action" and "assertiveness," and forget that part of that Mars energy is sexual in nature. Mars is not the sexuality of Venus, which tempts and attracts; Mars is the part of oneself that is willing to run after the prey and capture it. Part of Pan's contradictory nature is that although his form is half that of a vegetarian herd animal, he has a strong streak of the predator in him. He does not chase in order to kill, however, but for purposes of sex . . . even if that sex turns out to be rape. Indeed, he doesn't seem to make a distinction between the two, and that terrifies us as well.

Pluto, the ruler of Scorpio and the eighth house, has a lot to do with sex as well. To Pluto, sex is a way to tap into a powerful force, for good or ill. The negative side of Pluto uses it for power over others; the positive side seeks to harness the energies in order to magically improve the world. Add Martial aggression to the mix in the form of impulsive Aries, and it can tip the balance toward violation for the sake of selfish experience. Pan's myths are fraught with tales about him assaulting nymphs, often in the form of a dazzling white ram or great-horned goat, and we tend to think of him in context with sexual violation. However, these days it is often the pristine wilderness that is being violated. The last time that Pluto was in the pioneering sign of Aries, the American wilderness was "opened up" and settled by the people who would eventually tame and transform it. Pan's fierce protectiveness of his lands and animal subjects is a little more understandable in this light; he is the guardian who violates intruders so that they will not violate his territory.

Pan is fully aware of his own vulnerability, which is the manifestation of the vulnerability of the wilderness. He is, after all, made in the image of a creature who is prey, not predator, even if he is fierce. To Pan—and to Pluto in Aries—the best defense is a good offense. Pan is the spirit of the wilderness fighting back with every weapon it has, and that includes the war he wages within us, using our sexuality as his weapon. Pan demands respect while in his territory, and the wilderness of sex is part of that realm. When we lose our respect for its sacredness and mystery, when we "open up" and sell and barter and generally commoditize our sexuality, he strikes back with a host of sexual dysfunctions, from rape to frigidity. If you try to violate me, I will violate you in turn, he says—and that includes the part of you that is me.

In practical terms, this means that people with Pluto in Aries must fight a constant border war with Pan. The Arian urge to explore something "just because it is there," regardless of the consent of the virgin territory, is fueled by a Plutonian need for power and can create a personality that violates both land and people for their own gain. On the other hand, the internal Plutonian urge to transform and purify dark urges—even painfully—is fueled by the Arian drive. This placement can live out the story of the fall from hubris, where the individual selfishly wrongs others and then is smitten by the great realization of what he has done. Sometimes those realizations can change a life and sometimes they merely trigger a wave of guilt that passes quickly, and the offender forgets and goes back to his old ways. With the Pluto-Mars influence of this placement, however, the battle gets replayed over and over until some kind of death occurs—that of the individual or that of the behavior pattern.

Pan will always be an ambivalent and uncomfortable figure. We admire him, envy him, and fear him. There is something primordial about any planet in Aries, and the intense Plutonian Pan is no exception. He stampedes us into a panic whenever we confront the biological wilderness of our hormones and instincts. Pan's dark forests grew when our primate ancestors first began to learn the concept of action instead of mere reaction. It was an era when danger was everywhere, territory was made to be defended violently, and sex was simply relief from tormenting urges installed in us by a ruthless goddess of evolution. Her only dictum was to propagate the strongest of the species, no matter what the cost. Pan symbolizes the part of us that still carries out her dictum, no matter how we try to delude ourselves that our decisions stem from measured thought and not programmed neural wiring. In Pan's world, we are shocked to find out how animal we still are. Be grateful for it. A world without the goat-footed god would be a sterile horror indeed.

osiris

Pluto in Taurus

Most underworld gods are dark or pale. Osiris is green. The Egyptian god of the dead is shown as a mummy wrapped in his bandages, but his face and hands are exposed, and they are green—not the green of rot, but the green of verdure, of the land. It's the hardest part of the Pluto in Taurus mystery to grasp: that the Green Man of the world above feeds on corpses.

Neptune passing through the earth sign Taurus moves like the Green Man of the woods, the dream of the Green World. Osiris takes the Green Man lower down, beneath the earth itself. His face is green because it is the ground, the part of the earth that we see. His body is enclosed in the depths that we are blind to, unless we dig deep . . . and then we find riches, resources, Taurean wealth. It is no accident that the last time Pluto was in Taurus, the first oil well was drilled into the earth's crust.

His face may be green, but his body is dead. Osiris was slain by his brother Set. The first time he was shut into a coffin, which floated downstream and grew into the trunk of a tree; his dedicated wife Isis (see Moon in Libra) searched for and found the tree, and brought the coffin back to Egypt to resurrect. Set attacked his escort en route and cut the body into fourteen pieces, which he scattered far and wide. Isis attempted to resurrect him, but a Nile crab had eaten his phallus, the giver of life, and he could not be brought back. Distraught, Isis sought the help of Thoth, and the two of them invented the magical rites of embalming, designed to keep the flesh preserved forever. This gave him just enough life to father a posthumous child on her, whom she named Horus and raised to avenge his father, and then Osiris passed into the underworld to rule it forever.

Osiris carries as his symbols the shepherd's crook and the flail used in separating grain from the stalks. This is an echo of Taurus's archetype of the Farmer; of all the underworld deities, Osiris is the only one who openly carries agricultural implements. When Osiris was among the living and ruling Egypt, his first act was to teach his savage hunter-gatherer subjects the arts of agriculture. He invented the making of bread, wine, and especially beer. People make a great fuss about these items being the symbols of Egyptian kingship, but they often seem to miss why they were so important: they are the items by which the growing of food is accomplished. The shepherd's crook indicates the king's magic as he who makes the animals fat and fertile, and the grain flail is used in the processing of the body of the Corn King, he who dies and is reborn again.

Taurus is the Builder as well as the Farmer, and Osiris also taught his people how to build large and impressive monuments, many of which became houses for the dead, his eventual subjects. More Taurean clues can be glimpsed in the Egyptian death cult that focused itself around Osiris. His cult seemed intensely bound up with material objects, or "phys-obs," to put it in MIT slang. Egyptians were buried with as many of their worldly goods as possible. When you went to live with Osiris, you took all your stuff with you, even your physical body, which was carefully preserved. This Taurean preoccupation with stuff is another Pluto in Taurus clue; remember that Taurus is associated with the second house of material resources . . . and stuff.

Stuff weighs you down. It makes you slow. It forces you to move deliberately, step by step. If you have more than you can carry, you have to make tedious arrangements to get it from one place to another. Before you can get anywhere quickly you have to drop it, sacrifice it. Pluto moves through Taurus more slowly than through any other sign, especially when compared to its comparative whiz through Scorpio, the sign of elimination. It plods ponderously through Taurus for thirty-one years, weighted down with the chains of stuff. (In the Victorian period, when Pluto last visited this sign, fashionable houses were crammed with so many material objects that they resembled the average wealthy Egyptian tomb.) Another difference between Osiris and the other dead gods is that they, at least, can move. Hel is a rotting corpse and walks slowly, but she moves. Osiris is a wrapped mummy, totally immobile. He is never shown in any other position than bound and motionless like the rooted tree that his coffin grew into, like the green plant he resembles. In death he becomes not a mobile human but a sessile plant, and this too is a nature mystery of Taurus: when you die, your body goes into the ground and feeds the plants, which your descendants eat. Your body will one day be their food, your rotting flesh their bread, and you will live again in them. This much life can only have grown out of this much death.

When Osiris becomes the judge of the dead, he is a good and kind god, much like his attitude when he was a living pharaoh. Taurus is, after all, ruled by Venus, and Venus does not generally love battle. In fact, Osiris is said to have conquered other countries during his reign as pharaoh without any violence or battle; he peacefully won over the subjects of each new country with songs and the playing of musical instruments, many of which he had invented. It is the tale of a Venusian war campaign, aided by the Taurean archetype of the Musician. However, Venus is not generally comfortable with Pluto, as her goal of peace and harmony is antithetical to Plutonian upheaval and violent transformation. Osiris is a dying and reborn god, and as such goes through a Plutonian transformative experience, but it is followed by a long, slow immobility.

Indeed, it is as if slowness is Osiris's power, something which a Pluto in Taurus individual can relate to. When a soul comes before him, freshly dead, the intake process is long and tedious. The dead soul must face forty-two animal-headed judges in turn and tell his story to each one. He then tells it to Osiris, and much deliberating is done about his truthfulness and moral righteousness. Then his soul must be weighed in the balance by Ma'at, the goddess of justice, and finally a decision is made. Transformation, when Taurus is in charge, seems to take forever. Social opinions freeze during its era, and change is only brought about with great deliberation . . . but it is thorough. Sometimes slowness can be for the best, especially when one is debating the moral rightness of something or someone. Hurrying, says Taurus, is only more likely to create mistakes.

The gift of a Pluto in Taurus is the ability to take change slowly, at a more peaceful pace. It's the ability to say that if you have a lifetime commitment to something or someone, then one can afford to take it at a leisurely walk right now. It's not the transformation of being consumed in flames and turned from matter to energy, or being drowned and dissolved, or struck by lightning. It's the transformation of buried matter, flesh or flower, slowly and inexorably rotting into the earth to fertilize the next generation. It's the knowledge that human time is just a fleeting thing and that we could all do well to listen to the earth's calendar. It will live on when we are gone, and it will forgive us almost anything, if we wait long enough.

Gwydion
Pluto in Gemini

Pluto is a planet of transformation, they say. What that's a euphemism for is rebirth, and what's behind rebirth is death—not the abrupt loss and long, slow stasis of Saturn; Pluto's transits are like a series of labors, in the sense of birthings. Ask anyone who's given birth without anaesthetic: it hurts. It goes on and on, and you despair of being done with it, you want to beg for it to stop, but you know there's no way to make it stop. You fear for your ability to hang on until the end, yet there is no way to walk away short of your own death. Every minute feels like an hour; every hour feels like a lifetime. Then it's over, and suddenly you have this beautiful baby in your arms and you are transformed into a new being: Mother. That's why mothers get together and swap war stories; it really feels like you've been through a war and come out the other side, irrevocably changed.

A Pluto transit cannot be bargained with, or fast-talked, or tricked, or weaseled around, and this is especially difficult for Gemini, as these are his main coping mechanisms. The story of the ambivalent Celtic hero Gwydion shows the transformation of a Mercurial trickster: Gwydion is a great poet, speaker, and illusionist. He specializes in the Mercurial magic of glamour, making things look other than they are. At first, he uses this gift for havoc; when his brother Gilvaethry wants a particular maiden who is the beloved ward of the great sorcerer Math, Gwydion offers to help get the girl and decides to start a war for distraction. He bargains for the magic pigs of the great king Pryderi, paying for them with mushrooms enchanted to look like magical shields and squirrels made into great horses. No sooner does he leave Pryderi's country when the enchanted objects change back, and Pryderi, infuriated, marches an army against Math's country.

While the armies are clashing—eventually causing the death of the great Pryderi—Gwydion and Gilvaethry sneak into the castle and the maiden's bedroom. There Gilvaethry rapes her while Gwydion guards the door. When Math comes home, the girl cries out against them, and the infuriated Math sentences them to three years of a terrible punishment. For the first year, Gwydion is turned into a stag and Gilvaethry into a doe; they learn fear and vulnerability fleeing from hunters, having neither powers nor strength to protect themselves. It is a hard lesson, especially when Gilvaethry goes into heat during the rutting season, and Gwydion finds himself unable to resist taking his doe-brother. Thus Gilvaethry learns what it is to be sexually assaulted, and both brothers learn that such an act is only worthy of an animal. In a year's time, they return with a fawn, which Math turns back into a child and raises at his court.

The second year, they are turned into wild boar and sow; this time they are still hunted, but they also have tusks with which to rend their hunters. Again, during the season of rut, Gwydion is unable to resist taking his brother and they return after a year with a piglet, which Math turns back into a human and adopts. The third year they are wolf and she-wolf, and they learn what it is to be a predator. They return with a wolf-cub, which Math humanizes and adopts, and he declares their penance to be enough. This series of painful transformations is typical of a Pluto transit, which often forces one's feet into strange shoes. Whatever one's ordinary coping tricks are will be found utterly useless, and one will be made, often against one's will, to learn hard lessons.

Gemini is the sign most concerned with duality; it is said that each Gemini has a light twin and a dark twin, who fight for control. In this myth, the two sides of Gemini are enacted in collusion by the two brothers. There is the twin who wants bad things and the twin who does the fast-talking to get them; the twin who does bad deeds and the twin who stands by and witnesses; the twin who repents and the twin who makes excuses for him. Both brothers come out of the ordeal changed and humbled; Gilvaethry retires in shame, but there is still some craftiness left in Gwydion.

In order to please and placate Math, whose alliance he wants, Gwydion offers to bring him another virgin to replace the one his brother has despoiled. The purpose of the virgin at court was to hold Math's feet in her lap, magically preventing his power from draining away into the earth. Gwydion goes to his sister Arianrhod, who lives locked up in a tower with her maidens, and talks her into being Math's foot holder. She is not thrilled with the idea, but agrees to do it for him. However, although she has not actually lain with a man, she has had relations with an ocean spirit and an eagle spirit; since they left her maidenhood intact, she does not know that she is with child by both of them.

Math quizzes her on her virginal status, and she swears that she has not lain with a man. When he tests her by tapping her crotch with his magic wand, however, she suddenly drops two babies onto the floor. One Math seizes and releases back into the sea, realizing it for a selkie creature; the other one Gwydion snatches up, hides, and gives to a wet nurse. Arianrhod is humiliated publicly and refuses to speak to Gwydion ever again. He, however, has a new thing in his life: love. For the first time, selfish Gwydion, the fast-talker, has someone whom he cherishes more than himself. He loves his adopted son with a fierce passion and wants only the best for him. Through this child, he feels, all his mistakes will be redeemed.

The problem is that Gwydion still has not let go of the idea that the ends justify the means. His ordeals in the forest have taught him enough that he can now love someone unselfishly, but he is not yet ready to learn how to treat those he loves less. When the child is six years old, Gwydion takes him to Arianrhod and presents him as her son. Still angry with him and refusing to admit her affairs, she denies the child. Gwydion asks her to give him a name, the prerogative of mothers, and she refuses, saying that he shall have no name until she gives him one, which will be never. Undaunted, Gwydion disguises them both and manages to inadvertently trick a name out of her—Llew Llaw Gyffes, or Llew of the Skillful Hand. Furious, she says that the boy shall have no weapons until she arms him herself, but using other disguises, Gwydion tricks her into unknowingly doing this as well.

At this point, her wrath at her deceitful brother knows no bounds. He, in turn, honestly believes that he is only doing what is best for his adopted son, but it does not occur to him that using dishonest means is not the best role-modeling or form of care. In a sense, Llew Llaw Gyffes symbolizes the open, naive, vulnerable part of Gemini, which he desperately tries to hide and protect with illusions and mirrors, not accepting that this is the part that needs to be laid open to the universe. Arianrhod's final curse is that he shall have no living woman as a wife for the rest of his days. At this point, Gwydion realizes that he can use and trick her no further; she has won—this round at least.

He has a plan, but he needs help from Math. The old sorcerer agrees, although he chides Gwydion for driving Arianrhod to such rage instead of patiently offering the hand of friendship over and over again, heedless of insult. The two of them decide to create a woman out of flowers to be Llew Llaw Gyffes' wife—oak for her bones, broom for her hair, meadowsweet for her flesh, and many flowers of the field for her eyes and lips. They bring her to life, name her Blodeuwedd, and Llew takes her to wife, madly in love with her beauty. However, although she seems quiet and sweet and every man envies him, she is inhuman and amoral, with no heart. As soon as she sees another man she desires, she arranges for him to kill Llew. Struck by a spear, Llew turns into an eagle and flies away, to be found almost dead by Gwydion, who nurses him back to life.

As soon as Llew is healthy, Gwydion raises an army and marches on Blodeuwedd and her lover, who by now is tired of her endless and inhumanly persistent entreaties for attention. He is killed by Llew, and Gwydion turns the heartless Blodeuwedd into an owl, to fly the night and swoop on small creatures. In her capacity as the symbol of cruel nature, Blodeuwedd embodies the merciless Pluto energy. Gwydion pays for trying to cheat fate; rather than beg forgiveness of his humiliated sister, he will play god and make life himself. In the process, he not only loses Llew's Frankenstein bride, but almost loses Llew himself and ends up no better than he had been before, except for his gratitude at his son's continued existence.

Pluto is a harsh mistress, and Pluto in Gemini connotes a transformation in the arrogance around one's intelligence. The idea that one can outsmart everything, even one's own karmic consequences, is a falsehood that must be painfully broken. Pluto implacably points out the flaw that one can have control over everything, and yet Pluto is about control of one's own soul. Had Llew gone alone to Arianrhod, without Gwydion's interference, the story might have been very different. Sometimes the part of oneself that must face karmic wrath is not the most intellectually sophisticated, but the most innocent of all.

sedna

Pluto in Cancer

In the myths of the Inuit people of Alaska, there was once a beautiful young girl named Sedna. Her family was very poor, and when a terrible famine came, they decided that they had to get rid of their children. The youngest they exposed to the elements, but as Sedna was just old enough to be married off, they proposed to give her to an older male hunter. Sedna wept and refused to marry him. "Do not make me leave home," she begged her parents. "I am too young to marry." She flung herself on the ground and refused to go. The next day her father took her out on the boat with him, ostensibly to help him with the fishing. However, his true intention was to rid himself and his wife of this intractable girl.

As soon as they were out of sight of land, Sedna's father threw her overboard into the ocean. She clutched desperately at the side of the boat, and he chopped at her fingers with his axe, severing them. Three times he chopped, and three times bits of her fingers flew into the water. The first time, the bits of flesh became seals; the second time, fish; the third time, deep-sea creatures. Finally Sedna fell with a cry of anguish into the ocean and drowned. There, she transformed into a sea goddess; she grew very large, and her hair grew so long that it flowed through all the depths of the sea bottom, entangled in the seaweed. The Inuit pray to her for good fishing and calm waters.

In many cultures, the underworld is ocean or water rather than underground, especially in those that have a strong economic survival tie to marine food. For the Inuit, who never dig because the ground is almost always frozen, the deepest place that one can go is to the bottom of the ocean. For them, as for the Cretans and the Aleuts, the *bottom* is the sea bottom. The watery concept of the underworld suggests a place where things are distorted and indistinct, crowded and floating, a source of life as much as the fertile earth. Although Cancer is a water sign, the Crab rules the shoreline, where water meets earth. For her to descend all the way to the uncertain depths is a rare thing, usually prompted by a major transformative trauma. Pluto, of course, deals in major transformative traumas.

When Sedna's father betrays her and cuts off her fingers, one of the things he cuts is the lifeline to family and clan, to hearthside and the love of others. She is left drifting, and since she cannot swim alone, she drowns. Being rejected by the family of origin is the hardest thing that can happen to any Cancerian person, and few walk away without going through a period of drowning in their own emotional responses. The Pluto experience in Cancer brutally cuts that umbilical cord, be it to the parents themselves or to the world views they espoused or to the illusion of them as good, loving people. A Plutonian transit in aspect to a Cancerian planet can result in the death of a parent or just the death of parental bonds of love.

So Sedna lives at the bottom of the ocean, and when she is lonely or sad, which is often, she weeps and kicks her feet and causes great waves that sink ships. Sometimes the ocean is full of fish and seals for the Inuit to eat, but sometimes it runs dry and no creatures are to be found. When that happens, it is because the creatures have gotten tangled in Sedna's long hair like lice and fleas, and she cannot comb it out with her mutilated hands. A shaman must then journey astrally to the depths of the sea and offer to comb her hair for her. She will be grateful for his help, and he can comb out the long, long strands of her hair, freeing the marine creatures that will feed his people.

Pluto in Cancer focuses society on the issue of how children are treated. Part of its milieu is the transformation in attitudes about childrearing and child abuse; the field of child psychology became a mainstream idea during the last transit of Pluto through Cancer. For the individual with Pluto in Cancer, childhood is a particularly intense time, an especially imprinting era that affects her attitudes for the rest of her life. We are all molded to an extent by our youthful experiences, but the Pluto in Cancer native finds it even more difficult to let go. An example of this is the famous Depression-era children who grew up having issues with wealth and poverty and frugality. Like Sedna, they may need many years of weeping to get around their early pain. They may also seek to transform that pain in a Plutonian manner—the scrimping and saving of the Depression-era generation was the main reason why the Pluto in Leo generation was able to make the kind of splash that they did.

On a personal level, Sedna is the wounded child who passes through the ordeal and becomes the important supernatural being on whom everyone else depends. She is still fairly helpless, though. The removal of her fingers indicates that her ability to act is limited, especially her ability to care for herself. Even though she is powerful, she is still a victim. The way in which she strikes back at others in revenge for lack of care is very Cancerian: she threatens their food supply. "Take care of me," she seems to say, "or you will all starve." This reflects the damage done to a wounded Pluto in Cancer: nurturing must be exchanged for nurturing, or it will be held hostage. Pluto is, after all, about power, and there is very little power as great as food and care and its withholding.

It is also no accident that Sedna's demands must be met by a shaman: one who has died and been reborn, who has passed into the underworld and out again, who knows about Plutonian depths and has gained the ability to heal from Plutonian ordeals. The shaman is the symbol of evolved Pluto, and s/he knows how to care for the wounded victim who cannot seem to recover from her hardship. The shaman also knows that the universe does care and that someone will always be sent to help when help is asked for—s/he is living proof of that truth. This is the final lesson of Pluto in Cancer—learning to recover from the wounds enough to trust again, to ask openhanded for help and aid, and to grant it in turn without threats or manipulative withholding. As a sea goddess, Sedna was put in touch with the source of life; she must eventually learn that it is truly inexhaustible, even if that lesson takes ten thousand years to learn.

Durga
Pluto in Leo

She rides out of the sky on the back of an enormous and bitterly fierce tiger. Every one of her ten arms holds a weapon, and she wages war on the forces of evil. Yet although she comes across in every other way as the implacable warrior, Durga is always shown with a serene smile on her face. Nothing, not even the struggles of cosmic existence, mars her supreme self-confidence. She is both the lady and the tiger, and one of her titles is "The Inaccessible." Strong Leo energy can make a person warm and approachable, or they can swing to the other direction and look down on all the "commoners" from a place of high detachment and pride. Durga is a virgin goddess, not in the sense that she has no sexual relations, but that she belongs to no one fully. Unlike a modest Virgo-type virgin, however, she is a formidable warrior, and there is nothing retiring about her.

This implacable lady is one of the consorts of Shiva the Destroyer, and she shares a job with him: slayer of demons. Unlike Shiva and Parvati, their relationship is remarkably nonsexual; instead, they are comrades in arms. They ride out together to destroy the legions of evil that constantly threaten the earth. In Hindu thought, however, demons are not otherworldly creatures that come to plague innocent humankind; instead, they come in two varieties: fears and illusions. The two are brother and sister or perhaps parent and child, as one springs from the other. Scratch an illusion and you'll find its progenitor, the fear that it was created to hide.

Proud, brave, egotistic Leo is constantly beset by fears. You wouldn't think it to look at them, but behind the bright show is a legion of small demons, each nibbling away at Leo's self-esteem. Am I good enough, am I competent enough, am I talented enough? Most of all, do they like me? Am I loved? Am I worth anything in their eyes? In a way, the show is the equivalent of a spirit fetish, hung up to frighten off the demons. Sometimes it works. Sometimes it just hides the problem still deeper.

In the Leo Sun section, we discussed how the light is both the gift and the curse of Leo—that this much light must cast an equally huge shadow. When Leo moves into the realm of Pluto, the home of the gods of darkness, the façade is turned around to clearly reveal that dark side. It is teeming with small demons of fear and illusion. They swarm like cockroaches, and from this side it is easy to see how beleaguered the light actually is, how fragile is its life. The Superhero—one of the ultimate Leo archetypes—is constantly in danger of being eaten alive from within. In order to be a real Superhero, the first enemies you must take on are those internal demons, or they will eventually sabotage you. Durga does not pretend that everything is fine, that those demons are held at bay in a far land. She goes after them with a fierce immediacy that proves she knows their real power. They are her first priority, her first opponent.

It's a purifying act, slaying fears and illusions. In reality, the second bunch generally have to be slain first, and their dead bodies are the evidence pointing to the fears that they mask. It's hard for any Leo planet or person to admit that they are so imperfect as to need a constant discipline of demon destruction. Yet this is the difference between real self-confidence and the feigned version: to leap just as bravely upon the internal demons as the external ones. Part of the problem is that you get no applause for dealing with internal demons. Nobody sees the terrible battle, no one is awed at your bravery, and most people don't even seem to think that you've accomplished anything particularly impressive. That lack of applause can keep an insecure Leo-type person hiding from their demons for years. After all, one gets so much more public acclaim from burying your demons and looking good on the surface. The inner work can wait until later, they decide.

When you put Pluto in a sign, you intensify whatever quality that sign craves. It becomes an issue of overwhelming, life-and-death importance, and thus Pluto in Leo spawned the Me generation. This particular litter of humans craved visible importance and applause, including all its socially assigned trappings—money, power, expensive gadgets, a luxurious lifestyle. Yet now, as they move into their later decades, many have grown out of that early materialistic hysteria and are seeking something deeper, something else on which to base their self-esteem. Like Durga, they are finding the serenity that comes in battling your demons. Through all of it, they are adept at keeping their pride and dignity.

In the myth, Durga comes forth to slay a great demon that has literally dethroned all the gods, and they are cowering from its fury. It's certainly a Superhero calling, being the one to ride out to save the day, yet this is no easily disposed of monster. It changes shape from one destructive visage to another. First it is a great trampling buffalo, then an enormous elephant, then a giant with a hundred hands. She must change her attack each time, not letting it fool her, until finally she manages to spear and kill it. This shapechanging demon is a good facsimile of the social demon that a Pluto in Leo faces; it comes in many forms, and they are all frightening. One might be the sneering face of disapproval, another the averted yawn of boredom, still another the impatient face of annoyance. Social expectations, whatever they may be, are a many-faced trap that it is all too easy for someone to fall into. They can also hamstring whole parts of a society's psyche and that of the individual psyches within it.

This is the kind of Superhero we need. It is someone who is strong enough to brave the demons of social approval and disapproval and destroy the monster who embodies those irrational and harmful rules. In an ironic twist, the hero whose karmic job this is happens to be terribly vulnerable to just that demon. She must steel herself and swing true, even as he changes shape and comes at her again with a new insult, a new cutting comment, a new attempt to kill her self-confidence. It's the kind of power that can dethrone gods, since those who lose simply become its minions. Everyone with Pluto in Leo is destined to fight this battle, for both themselves and for the larger society. We all hope and pray that in the end, they can find a way to win.

Hel
Pluto in Virgo

Virgo is the only sign where the central glyph-figure is undeniably female and unutterably alone. When looking through the many underworlds from different cultures, one and one alone stands out as the place where a female figure has ruled in unbroken power from the very beginning, and that is Hel, the Lady Death of the old Norse pantheon. Her name is one of the most frequently invoked deity names today, as the Christians stole it to refer to their own underworld. Still, one wonders what kind of power it must be to be invoked so many times every day, even if unwittingly and probably in negative situations? After all, Pluto is about power, and Hel's very name makes people sit up, or flinch, or at least take notice. Perhaps it's for different reasons than it used to, but does that matter? Hel will make do with what power is given her. She always has. This, too, is a Virgo trait, making do.

Hel lives on the plane of Niflheim, which is as cold and dark as a Scandinavian winter, and her kingdom is Helheim, or "Hel's home." Unlike status-conscious Valhalla and Sessrumnir, where worthy fallen warriors are taken, Helheim takes in all the great mass of human dead together. It doesn't matter if the likes of Odin and Thor scorn those who died the "straw death" in their beds. Let the other gods worry about who gets to sit above whom at the table; Hel isn't interested in these foolish games. Everyone in Helheim is equal, which is also a change from the Greek underworld of Hades, where the inmates are ranked according to their deeds and separated out into various levels of torment or peace. Hel does her best to accommodate everyone; her table is meager, but everything is shared equally, and she is said to be as kind as possible to the vast horde of unwilling subjects that she has been saddled with.

Hel had no temples; she shares with Virgo an indifference to the adulation of humanity and prefers to do her work quietly, behind the scenes. With Pluto, the planet of transformation, in the sign of work, Hel's lesson is that transformation does not just come on the backs of camels while you loll about. It is work, hard work, and although she is willing to help with that work, she is not impressed by laziness. Hel has a job to do, and she does it to the best of her ability, and she expects the same from others. She has been called cold, an epithet also used against Virgo.

The Norse Lady Death ruled alone, not in a pair. A consort named Valraven has been theorized by some researchers, but he would at best be a secondary figure; Hel does not share her throne or her power. Unlike Ereshkigal, no king is ever forced on her by patriarchal invaders; Odin seemed content to keep his small tithe of souls elsewhere and not interfere with Hel and her realm.

She does have a variety of servants; one of them, Mordgud, is a dark maiden who stands as guardian at the bridge to Helheim; her presence is another echo of Virgo. Then there is Hermod, a mortal traveler who braved Hel's realm to convince her to free Baldur, and ended up staying for a while, possibly as her lover; his is the classic shamanic journey-to-the-underworld-and-back tale. He is a psychopomp figure of the Hermes mold, and his presence in her myth reminds us that Virgo is ruled by Mercury. Another reminder is that Hel is the daughter of a trickster god.

The other interesting thing about Hel, and the thing that sets her apart from other gods, is that she is generally blatantly ugly. Her most common form is a beautiful woman on one side and a rotting corpse on the other. Another is a deathly pale girl of great beauty who smells of rot, and still another is a half-blue, half-skeletal woman. She is Lady Death, and she does not hide that fact; nor does she glamorize it. She simply Is, both ugly and beautiful, both kind and terrifying.

Virgo is associated with the health of the body, and Pluto in Virgo is especially concerned with how we treat that body, both our own and the one of the earth beneath us. Visions of Pluto are often the Powers That Be simultaneously showing us the best and worst that could possibly happen, and Hel is an obvious example of this with her half-beautiful, half-rotted body. Which will it be? she says. What will you do with your body? What have you already done? Virgo is concerned with cleanliness, so it seems strange that her appearance would be less than sterile, but Hel's purpose is an object lesson. This is death, she says. It may look horrific to us, but it is part of life. We tend to forget that it is worms and bugs that "clean up" the carrion in the environment and that Virgo rules them.

Virgo is the sign of discrimination, in the sense of cutting things apart into their component bits. Virgo is also an earth sign, and for all we go on about how Earth is beautiful, we like to forget that when you bury something in the earth, it rots. Rotting can be compared to the ultimate breaking down into one's component pieces, which can then be used to build new life. Look at the trees around you, says Hel. Look at all that green and all that beauty. This much life can only have grown on that much death. It is a lesson we have to remember: that compost is essentially a rotting process, and someday our physical bodies will go through this as well. Hel points out that we must pay attention to and respect that part of the cycle, including in our own psyches—the long, slow rotting down of our memories and experiences into fodder for new ideas. These things take time, says Hel, who moves slowly and carefully and does not see a need for hurry.

In Virgo, the Plutonian energy transforms our ability to think about breaking things down in preparation for building them up differently. It is no accident that this placement brought on the chaotic sixties. It is also said that Hel saves all the fingernail parings of her deceased guests, as they are being used to build a great ship in which she and her hordes will sail in order to be reborn at the end of the world. Only a Virgo could save and catalog the nail clippings of that many dead people and still have something useful to do with them afterward, something that will even help them to start a new life. Lady Death, after all, wastes nothing.

Ereshkigal
Pluto in Libra

Libra is the sign of relationships—between partners, between friends, and between members of society—and Pluto is the sign of total transformation, so when the two come together it is to somehow transform the relationships in life, sometimes painfully or destructively but always for the best in the end. Pluto is not comfortable in Libra, as Libra prefers harmony and agreement, which Pluto is utterly indifferent to; the touch of Pluto in this sign is anything but harmonious. Pluto despises superficiality and would rather destroy a relationship than see it wander along blindly with only the most shallow of connections. Pluto would gladly drag people down to the underworld and make them truly look at each other, even if it means the end . . . because the end is always a beginning.

The Babylonian underworld is ruled by Ereshkigal, the queen of the depths. She is the twin sister of Inanna (see Venus in Scorpio), and as told in Inanna's story, she receives her sister when Inanna comes down to meet her. She seems to know that Inanna is coming and has already made up her mind not to show her any mercy; the guardians of her gates strip Inanna of her jewelry and trappings (a very Plutonian thing to do) and bring her before Ereshkigal. The Queen of the Dead nails the hapless Inanna with the dark magic of her gaze, killing her, and she is hung on a great meathook above the throne of the dark queen.

Of all the death goddesses, Ereshkigal seems most peculiarly involved with the issue of companionship. Inanna's journey is prompted by the funeral of Ereshkigal's husband, Gugulanna, the Great Bull. There is also a hint of jealousy (another Plutonian trait) in that Inanna still has her lover, Dumuzi. However, Ereshkigal does not set out only to destroy the sacred marriage of Inanna and Dumuzi, only to transform it by any means necessary. On some level she knows that Inanna's "perfect" marriage isn't, and she means to show it to her. In this way, she functions like Psyche's sisters, pointing out the glaring errors in a dreamy, unquestioned relationship.

Ereshkigal is not a happy goddess. Besides being the Queen of the Dead, which is portrayed as a thankless, tedious job, she has recently lost her husband, a matter of terrible gravity for Libra. For a sign as together-oriented as the Scales, the death of a lover is like the end of the world. Into her deep mourning walks Inanna, with her complacent illusions, and Ereshkigal sets out to ruin them. However, when the two androgynes created by Enki to rescue Inanna appear, she is startlingly moved. The nature of the two androgynes is important: they represent what both Inanna and Ereshkigal want, the two-in-one status of a sacred Libran marriage, only they contain it within themselves. On top of this, they are paired, doubly married, in a partnership yet not dependent on each other for completion. They balance each other, in Libran completion. They are reminiscent of the transgendered Babylonian priest/ esses, the *galatur* and *kurgarra*, who wore a costume that was masculine on one side and feminine on the other, the sides being reversed for masculine women and feminine men. They also recall the custom of the transgendered *hijras* of India who bring good luck at weddings, symbolizing in themselves what the bride and bride-groom are striving for. From their perspective of two-in-oneness, they are able to tell exactly what Ereshkigal wants, and they weep tears of sympathy for her loss and her loneliness.

She is so moved that she gives Inanna back to them, but on one condition: the first person she meets who is not glad to see her must take her place. Ereshkigal knows that Dumuzi is making merry in Inanna's place in the palace and is still determined to teach the love-blinded Queen of Heaven a lesson about denial and hypocrisy. As told in Inanna's story, Dumuzi is surprised to see his dead lover again and not altogether pleased at having to explain himself; the demons of Ereshkigal who have accompanied her leap upon him and drag him down to the Queen of the Dead.

Now Ereshkigal is no longer alone and indeed she has taken Inanna's lover for her own. Dumuzi is fated to spend the rest of his life with her—and one would assume with her Plutonian personality she is less likely to put up with foolishness—and Inanna weeps in spite of her anger at him, until his sister Ninshubur offers to spend half of Dumuzi's time in the underworld for him. Thus Ereshkigal has him for half the year and his sister as a companion to the other half, and does not seem dissatisfied. Inanna has undergone a sacrifice, not only of part of her dignity and life while she hung on the hooks, but also of her marriage of blindness, and in doing so learns to share her lover with her sister.

However, Ereshkigal's story does not end there. In later times, it was decided that the female gods in the pantheon needed strong male consorts to rule with them, but apparently Ereshkigal did not take well to this idea. For all her longing for a mate, she preferred them to be lesser and weaker than her, like Dumuzi and his sister. Pluto's weakness is power, the more absolute the better, and Ereshkigal was used to being the unquestioned mistress of her entire domain, teaching hard lessons to others but not learning from them herself. Then, according to the later myths, the warrior god Nergal invaded her realm with the aid of fourteen demons and demanded her hand in marriage and an equal rule in her kingdom. She refused, and he threw her down from her throne; in terror she agreed to his terms, and he became King of the Underworld at her side.

This story may make people wince, and certainly on one level it is an example of the negative rule of patriarchy. On another level, however, it is reminiscent of Shiva giving himself up to be trampled and eaten by Kali. If you are the bringer of destruction, you must at some time offer yourself up for destruction by another. People who look at Pluto as one of the markers of reincarnation point out that those who are victimizers in one life are victims in another and vice versa. You must be familiar with both sides of the power dynamic, says Pluto. No one gets to be all one or the other, even the mighty Ereshkigal, Queen of the Dead. More than anything, she wanted another consort, and she was given one who was weaker than her and one who was stronger. The Scales always balance with Libra, even in the powerful and terrible language of the Plutonian underworld.

Kali

Pluto in Scorpio

She is black-skinned as the night sky and the fertile earth and the deepest chasm. Her body is emaciated, her ribs jutting, her hair long and wild. Around her neck she wears a string of skulls, her skirt is made of thigh bones, and her belt is formed of severed human hands. Her four arms hold a sword and a severed head on one side, a flower and a mudra on the other. Her eyes are fierce, her dance frenzied, and her tongue lolls from her mouth. She was labeled a "destroying demon" by Victorian westerners who were appalled at her terrifying aspect, unable to comprehend how such a deity could command reverence.

She dances on the prone body of her lover Shiva (see Sun in Scorpio) or sometimes mounts his erect penis while disemboweling him and eating his intestines—sex and death combined. As the Kalika, dressed in red, she is the bringer of disease. She is worshipped in cremation grounds; her altars are bedecked with skulls. She created the ocean of blood that birthed the world and she will dance the world into its ending and rebirth when her era ends. Blood is Kali's favorite substance; she demands blood sacrifices, and to invoke her you must shed some of your own.

She is both Creatrix and Destroyer; she is called the Mother Who Eats Her Own Children, the earth who brings everything forth and sucks everything back in. She is the rawest part of Nature, the part that does not care about humanity any more than it cares about a parasite or bacteria or virus; to think that we are somehow more valuable in her eyes than the creature that kills us is to be guilty of naive hubris. There are many visual conceptions of Mother Death from many places in the world, but none—with the possible exception of Hel—surpass Kali's grotesqueness, and none outstrip her fierceness.

When Pluto goes into its own sign, Scorpio, its intense transformative energy cycle comes through straight and direct, like pure ethyl alcohol with no additives for flavoring. And, like straight booze, it has no flavor to identify it, except how much it burns going down and how easily just a little of it knocks you into a wall. Pluto is merciless and uncompromising; pain is just another part of the deal, as far as Pluto is concerned. We are born out of pain—labor hurts—and we die out of pain. That same simple equation works regardless of whether the birth and death that we speak of is physical or experiential. Pluto is the natural ruler of the eighth house, which encompasses sex, death, karma, and all the Mysteries. It is a dark and frightening place to most of us, but it is Kali's palace.

Life and birth are always bound up with death and destruction. We say it casually, but we flinch from the reality of it. What if we were always aware of it? What if, whenever we began something, we were already thinking ahead to its end? What if, before we got married, we wondered, "How will I cope when this person dies?" or "How will they cope when I die?" or even "What sort of an ex will they make?" What if, when we give birth to a child, we were to look at its helpless body and see the helpless elder that it might become, equally unable to control their bodily functions, deteriorating in a strange reverse of their infant years? What if we were to think like this? Would it make life all the more sweet and urgent or would we simply give up and go mad?

With Pluto in Scorpio, it's like having that inner dialog going on in an undertone all the time. It might be unconscious or it might be something that the individual lives with and is used to. To those of us who are not used to the straight undiluted Plutonian energy, this may seem horrid, but tantric sages claimed that one could not truly appreciate Kali's loving, caring side until one had willingly embraced her terrifying aspect. Kali is also known as the Mother of Karuna, which is the Hindu concept of all-embracing maternal love. Karuna is the love that all other love is based on, as we initially learn how to love from the being that first holds us to her breast.

What does love have to do with sex and death? Well, we can probably link it without too much difficulty to the first one, but what about the second? Fear of death is like a plague in our culture. We go to incredible lengths to hide it—and people who remind us of it—yet we are simultaneously fascinated by it and worship it in our media. In order to break out of this love-hate denial relationship with Kali Ma (Mother Kali), we need to begin to see Death as the loving mother welcoming us in, even when we are also seeing the terrifying side. Pluto in Scorpio individuals have a streak of this dual vision in them; they tend to live life on the raw edge, repelled by superficiality and always seeking to embrace the fertile darkness. It can be an even stronger urge than those with Sun in Scorpio; to the former group Kali is a friend, to the latter she's more like a wife.

They may go through crisis periods when strong emotions lie on them and eat their guts out, and the only way to get through these periods is to let go of something, to let some part of yourself die—never an easy task for Scorpio.

Pluto in Scorpio people simultaneously long to hold on to things and are compelled to throw them out; they are drawn to confrontation and crisis. They prefer the burning ground to the comfortable couch because it's more real. The closer they are to the edge, the "realer" life feels to them. This can bring them to self-destruction or, if they survive, it can bring them the kind of tempered power that is impossible to bring down. Kali Ma's gifts require the soul to walk through many fires, through volcanic eruptions, through storms of ice, through punishing drought, all unflinching, and at the end she waits there herself, for better or worse, our greatest collective fear and the wellspring of that without which we cannot survive.

skadi
Pluto in Sagittarius

One of the recognizable aspects of Pluto in any sign or ruling any planet is that the temperature changes rapidly from blazing hot to bitterly cold and back again. Pluto is neither fire nor ice, but both—often without the benefit of the more comfortable points in between. Pluto drives people to extremes, giving them courage and audacity in the face of desperate situations. This planet is not a force for objectivity; Pluto feels everything intensely and reacts accordingly.

In fiery Sagittarius, sign of the Archer and the Philosopher and the Explorer, Pluto becomes the Destroyer of Lies, the Defender of the Truth . . . as they happen to see it. And therein lies the rub. Truth can be a cold thing, and defending one's own personal truth against all comers is a pretty cold place to be. That's why the Norse goddess Skadi is the deity of the mountain snows.

First and foremost, she is a hunter. One tends to forget this basic truth about Sagittarius, what with all those pretty pictures of archers aiming their arrows at some remote part of the sky. In reality, no one fires random arrows at the sky, and if you are firing at the faraway horizon, it is because you have a target in range. We also tend to forget what arrows are meant to do, which is to kill things. Like the Scorpion's sting, like the horns of the Ram and Bull and Goat, like the teeth and claws of the Lion, Sagittarius is one of the signs that goes openly armed. Skadi is a hunter, and so is the essence of Sagittarius. We tend to think of Scorpio as being a detective; it is true that the Scorpion may sneak around peering into dark corners, but the thrill of the long-range hunt for truth belongs to the Archer.

The problem is that while you're focused on the hunt, you may miss things. The Archer's keyword is "I see," and many of their issues are built up around vision. To focus on that far point, you have to close one eye and narrow your gaze down to that point and nothing else. This shuts out the broad spectrum of vision that is normally attributed to Jupiter's sign; the usual criticism about the Sagittarian field of vision is that they tend to go for breadth rather than depth. Having Pluto in this sign means that the broad focus is narrowed down to a laser point, and woe betide anything it lights upon.

Skadi was a giantess, the daughter of a Jotun chieftain. When her father Thjiassi was killed in a skirmish with the Aesir, she marched up to their palace in her snowshoes, armed to the teeth, and demanded *weregild*, or payment for the death of her beloved father. Apparently she seemed so powerful and formidable a warrior that the Aesir quailed and decided to pacify her. When Odin asked her what she wanted, she retorted that they must make her laugh, and they must give her a husband. Odin lined up all the unmarried gods behind a curtain and made her choose one by his feet. She chose the one with the handsomest feet, hoping that it would be beautiful

Baldur, but it turned out to be Njord, the sea god. This is a good example of what happens when choices are made based on a narrowed field of vision. Skadi attempts to live with Njord by the seaside, but cannot stand it there; he tries to live with her in the mountains, but is equally uncomfortable.

They finally agree to part, as neither could bring themselves to make that much of a sacrifice. Sagittarius is not the most self-sacrificing of signs, and when Pluto is in the vicinity, they much prefer to sacrifice the whole deal than any part of themselves or their preferences or world-views. Skadi goes back and forth between fire and ice, courage and coldness. Above all, she is as uncompromising as a winter storm, as is a Pluto in Sagittarius.

As I sit here, Pluto is going through this sign and opposing Saturn in Gemini. Buildings are exploding, people are waving fists at each other, and everyone seems to be blinded by their own convictions, however good they may be. The world seems to be changing yet again as the planet of transformation in the sign of the implacable Hunter faces off with the planet of limitation in the sign of the Trickster. If we look to Norse mythology to see Skadi's relationship with the Trickster Loki—who wanted to be associated with Saturn in Gemini—we find a stormy and ambivalent relationship.

When Skadi demanded a good laugh for part of her weregild, it was Loki the Trickster who stepped in to do the dirty deed. Tying his testicles to a goat, he staggered around howling in pain until the rope broke and he fell into Skadi's lap. Apparently this painful slapstick mollified her, and they actually seem to have had an affair—at least, Loki claims to have done so in one archaic text. Somehow, however, the affair went terribly wrong—we have no idea how or why—because by the time of Loki's next appearance in her life, he is making reference to their affair, and she hates him bitterly, with the kind of hatred often found in a woman scorned.

Her hatred of him goes so deep that when he is captured by the Aesir and chained up beneath the earth for his murder of Baldur,

Skadi places a serpent over him to drip poison on his body for the rest of his existence. This is the kind of tunnel-vision intensity that a Pluto in Sagittarius brings, accompanied by anger, explosions, fire, and ice. In Pluto's defense, it can also inspire amazing discoveries in the obsessive hunt for truth. Its manifestations range from the fanatic with the bomb to the scientist who declares war on a disease—and wins. It can obscure the very truth it seeks by its own blindness, and it can tear away the veil on the mysteries of other people's truths.

In the sign of nuclear power, the missiles of the Hunter/Archer can be lethal, as we've all found to our dismay. We must always remember, however, the way in which Loki managed to defuse her anger—he gave her a good laugh. Humor is the cure for tunnel vision, even if it means that we have to sacrifice some dignity to do it. Skadi's intense feelings are evident in the miasma of hurt and resentment and betrayal that swirls about us today; if we are lucky, we'll find a goat and do the dirty deed before everything turns poisonous and bitter.

Hades
Pluto in Capricorn

There was no Valhalla in the ancient Greek scheme of things. With the very rare exception of those mortals who were chosen for their great feats to be made into demigods, everyone who died ended up in the realm of Hades, called by the Romans Pluto. His Greek name means "unseen," his Roman one "wealthy," and these two epithets summed up the two most important cornerstones of his nature. First, he was not showy. He did not walk in the upper world often, and when he did, it was with a helm of invisibility. Second, he was master of all the underground riches—gold, silver, iron, jewels. Everything found beneath the earth was his and was given up only by his leave.

The horoscope of the United States has Pluto in Capricorn, and this has always been a country where everyone is equal . . . except the wealthy. Our class system is based almost entirely on money. To an extent, it is affected by the jobs that are high status versus low status, but almost inevitably one finds that "high status" either makes a lot of money or used to make a lot of money, and low-status jobs are either low-paying or used to be low-paying in days gone by when physical labor was cheap. Inevitably, as time goes on, if a career becomes higher status, it is because it has made a lot of money for long enough that no one living can remember when it didn't.

At this time, as we draw near to our country's Pluto return, we find that this reverence for wealth has created a system where the greatest influences in our lives are the immense amoebic corporations, which spend their time eating each other and the smaller fish. This plutocracy, for such it can be called, is also mostly unseen, or at least its workings are unseen enough that it is able to sneak things by us all the time . . . pollution in our food and water and ground, devious business practices, paid-for laws and politicians that do not serve the majority of the people. We scratch our heads and ask ourselves, when did this happen? I didn't see it coming. And with Pluto, you rarely do.

In both the Greek and the Roman versions, Hades/Pluto was identified with his country; he and it carried the same name. It was said that his true name was unspeakable; to say it was to strike something dead. As Hades he was terrifying and merciless; as Pluto he was considered generous and bountiful. These two sides of his nature correspond to the worst and the best of Pluto in Capricorn. At best, the Capricorn Pluto is a gatherer of riches and wealth, which is then spread quietly through society; at its worst, it is ruthless, miserly, and willing to dispose of anyone in order to get to the top of the heap.

Status is also important to Capricorn, and the realm of Hades had definite class distinctions. The best wandered the Elysian Fields;

the worst were tormented in Tartarus, and there were many grades in between. Hades did take care of his dead as best he could, but life in his realm was said to be rather sad and mournful, and living visitors had to take care not to be swept in by dead souls begging for help. Capricorn as a sign leans more toward asceticism than comfort, and in spite of his wealth Hades was not said to live a particularly lavish lifestyle.

The "best and worst" scenario is also apparent in the many versions of the myth of Persephone's abduction. In the later Hellenic myths, the daughter of Demeter was snatched from the fields where she played with her childhood companions, carried off into the underworld by Hades in his chariot, and there held until he could get permission for her to marry (which her father Zeus gave) and get her to relent and agree (which he finally did; she ate from his hand six seeds of the pomegranate, the fruit of the womb, thus agreeing to enter a mature phase of sexuality with him). Although there is no evidence in any version that he sexually raped her—indeed, he seems to have gone to great lengths to make her happy and get her to agree to his attentions—it is usually referred to as a rape.

In the earlier myths, we get such variants as Persephone hearing the voices of the ghosts wailing underground; following them out of pity, she finds a door to the underworld and makes her way to Hades. He tells her that she cannot leave, and she says that she will stay, but only as queen, to which he agrees. In the Orphic mysteries, Orpheus says, when he comes before Hades and Persephone enthroned, "If the legends are true, you two were brought together by love." Even if the worst version of the tale is the "most true," as if any such thing could be said for any myth, I disagree with modern attempts to make the story of Hades and Persephone into a tale of the molested female child, if only because the story ends with Persephone going willingly back to Hades after being reunited with her mother, and spending half the year there with him, forever. He is not something she escapes, but something she embraces.

At any rate, no one ever tells the story from Hades' perspective. Whether Persephone comes to him willing or unwilling at first, she represents something that he needs and desires, a complement to his nature. As Queen of the Underworld, she is the Divine Counselor, and sympathetically listens to the sorrows of the dead souls, comforting them and helping them to achieve rebirth. It is clear that what Persephone has that Hades needs is the power of compassion, something that makes the difference between being the pitiless death-dealer and being the distributor of wealth. With her as an example, he makes the transformation for Hades to Pluto.

Pluto, whatever its sign, is always about transformation, and in Capricorn the ongoing transformation is the change from obsessive acquisition of wealth and power to the use of that wealth and power to do good in the world and learning to place the second quality above the first. It is not a matter of getting away from wealth and power; this is Pluto we are talking about and not Neptune, and Pluto ruled by a constricting Saturn. Saturn does not like people who respond to their power struggles with avoidance. It is better and cleaner to keep up the struggle and find a way to redeem it, to bring the grasping urges that we all have into the service of benevolence and bounty.

Baphomet
Pluto in Aquarius

No one is really sure about the mysterious origins of the modern god Baphomet. Some say his name comes from the Arabic *abu-fihamet*, meaning "father of knowledge," and that he was a pre-Islamic Arabic god. Some say that his name comes from the Greek *Baphe Metis*, meaning "baptized in wisdom," and that he came out of the Greek Orphic mysteries. Still others claim that he was invented out of whole cloth by crusaders in the Middle East, as a conglomerate Horned God deity that would symbolize everything opposite to their worldly Christian faith. The earliest of his cult relics date back no further than the thirteenth century, and aside from giving him the form he wears today, they tell us little about his worship.

He seems to have been reinvented by ceremonial magicians in the nineteenth century, and it may well be that everything we know about him today dates back only a century or so, and certainly not past the Middle Ages. This makes him the youngest and most modern god in this whole book, a phallic fertility deity for the modern industrial era rather than the ancient world. Rather than being a handicap, his relative modernity makes him more accessible to contemporary magicians and pagans, who need a deity that addresses the important concerns of today.

Baphomet is shown as a hermaphroditic Pan; he has horns, hooves, and fur, along with breasts and double genitals. He is the figure most closely related to the androgynous devil of the medieval Tarot deck. Sometimes his head is that of a goat or ass, sometimes of a goat-horned human. He is a Plutonian figure of sex and death and power, yet his androgyny and comfort with the urban world of steel and concrete—as well as abrupt change—show his affinity with Uranian energies as well. His modern resurgence of popularity came about in the 1960s, when Pluto was conjunct Uranus.

The blatant hermaphroditism of Baphomet is troubling to many people, but radically important for today's Plutonian lessons. Some attempt to explain it away as merely "symbolic merging of male and female to embody the entirety of humanity," but Baphomet's androgyny is far more than that. First of all, he is very different from other Aquarian androgynes and the social image of the androgyne in general. Our culture tends to be most comfortable with androgyny when it is youthful and undeveloped—e.g., boy-girls or girl-boys—and especially if it is sexless. We grow nervous around hermaphroditic figures that combine the characteristics of mature men and women—large breasts and beard or body hair, muscles and long hair, wide shoulders and wide hips, erect phallus and devouring vagina. Baphomet is usually (but not always) referred to as "he," because he looks masculine to us with his muscular form and hairy body. Seeing him as equally male and female gives us discomfort, because these are gender cues that we have been taught should not be present in one body.

Why the discomfort? It's about power, of course; a Plutonian specialty. Because we as a culture prefer our people to be safely separated into little boxes marked "male" and "female," we require any diversion from those roles to be neotenous (or at least passive and feminine) and thus powerless. Baphomet combines the mature sexual cues because he is anything but powerless. One of his titles is *Rex Mundi*, King of the World, symbolizing his rulership over the realm of the physical. He stands arrogantly and demands that we respect him. His androgyny is blatantly sexual. *I can take you any way there is,* s/he says to us, showing that s/he combines the traits not only of mature male and female, but dominant male and female as well. S/he is the patriarchal divisionary committee's worst nightmare and, as such, s/he is vitally important to our understanding of the basic divisions in our culture—gender, sexuality, and power.

Baphomet is known as the Lord of Perversions, a title borne to connote his ability to teach through what one fears most. He is especially adept at defeating repressed people through their own fears and personal shadows. His philosophy is that taboos are there to be broken and that in doing so one learns more about oneself and others. It's a harsh ideal, because Pluto in Aquarius is not a comfortable place. Its mutual-reception energy partner, Uranus in Scorpio, likes to force people to witness uncomfortable things; Pluto in Aquarius takes it one step further and forces people to experience them. Where your fears are, there is where you can learn the most, says Baphomet. In studying perversion you learn what is true.

It's a philosophy reflected in the left-hand tantric path of ancient India. In order to get people ready to confront their repressed sexuality and thus be ready for magical sexual-energy use, the tantric masters first forced them to eat a feast of meat, fish, wine, and parched grains. The meat and fish were a taboo for many vegetarian Hindus and the wine for Muslims. Afterward, assuming they had passed that test, it was then explained that the meat symbolized male organs and the fish female ones, the wine stood for sexual fluids, and the parched grains for the friction of bodies rubbing together—all of which they must also consume without fear. The food taboo broke down the resistance to the sex taboo and opened the doorway to tantric mastery.

Baphomet is fine with being a bogeyman. Sometimes he is shown carrying a whip or scourge, reminiscent of the ordeals in the Dionysian Temple of the Mysteries. He is scary because he is always urging you to confront yet another idea that you thought was set in stone. Saying "Oh, I could never do that!" is a challenge to him, yet all his challenges have to do, ultimately, with changing social mores—by changing people's minds, one person at a time.

When the planet of transformation rules the sign of social change, it makes for a person or a situation with no patience to wait for the long, slow conversion. A Pluto in Aquarius wants it to change now, by force if necessary. This placement does lack compassion and tends to react to the horror of others with arrogant amusement, which practically guarantees that their transformative ideas will be shunned by the timid and conservative. However, it is also a placement of great charisma and fascination—the allure of the dangerous. People who are changed by this energy look back and say, "It's not nearly as dangerous as I thought it would be . . . except that it totally changed my life." Baphomet merely smiles and beckons, the flash of white human teeth in an animal's face, the ambivalent body that lures and terrifies. S/he has us by a hold on our dark places and in order to resist we must go down and confront them, which is the whole point of that iron grip anyway. Sooner or later, Baphomet will win, because Pluto always does.

peɾsephone
Pluto in Pisces

Demeter the goddess of the grain has only one daughter from her former marriage to the much-married Zeus. This is Persephone, sometimes called merely Kore or Maiden, and Demeter loves her more than anything else on Earth. Indeed, Demeter's love is a near-smothering intimacy that seeks to create the perfectly idyllic childhood for her daughter. Persephone in her Kore form starts out as the goddess of spring, born on the spring equinox that marks the final day of Pisces. Flowers rise from her footsteps and new green sprouts from where she walks. She is in a sense the Maiden personified, and little more. Laughing and joyful, she lives her dreamy one-day-much-like-the-next life with other maidens, weaving garlands of blossom in her paradisiacal home. She is undifferentiated, passive, and eternal. Her mother's love has sheltered her so fiercely that she has never had a single challenge to face.

The transformative energy of Pluto loves to upset an apple cart as perfectly balanced as this one, and Persephone is no exception. One day she finds a beautiful white flower and plucks it; the ground opens up and out shoots a great dark chariot pulled by black horses. The driver seizes her and carries her off, screaming, and the earth closes up after them. It is Hades, lord of the underworld, and Persephone's perfect life is shattered once and for all.

Demeter's actions and mourning, and how she brings about her daughter's release, can be read about in the section containing her myth (see Sun in Cancer), but here we focus on Persephone's side of things. Although originally dismissed as a mere seasonal myth and later exaggerated into a symbol of rape and incest, Persephone's story is at bottom the tale of a young girl's coming of age. Unlike fierce virgins such as Artemis or Athena, Persephone has been the innocent Kore for so long that she does not know how to be anything more at first. She sits paralyzed in a corner of Hades' realm, neither responding to his attempts to woo her nor trying to make an escape. She is waiting, in fact, for someone to rescue her so that she will not have to actually make an active decision.

Pisces is often accused of being the most passive of the signs, and Persephone does indeed start out as a passive victim who bad things happen to. However, somewhere down in the underworld, something happens to her, and it is catalyzed not by her abductor/suitor but by the ghosts of the dead. There is an implication in the myth that Persephone takes pity on the weeping spirits, that she listens to them, soothes them, and they love her in turn. Her later titles clearly show her as the counselor for the dead, the compassionate one who is not afraid to comfort the endless weeping of the ghosts. She moves from being a helpless captive to having an actual purpose in that dark place, and her view of the world changes as well. For the first time, she has something to do that is important, that is unique to her, and that is not dependent on her mother. In other words, she is growing up and becoming independent.

A Pluto in Pisces, when trapped in the underworld, can either revert to a kind of sentimental victimhood (complete with depressed poetry and music) or she can take her experience of grief and loss and use it to develop compassion for others. That Persephone takes up a position of service to the wounded and psychically injured is no coincidence. Like Virgo, Pisces has a strong undercurrent of service, even to the point of self-sacrifice. For Pisces, however, the service is usually not so much practical or physical as it is spiritual. Although not every member of the Pluto in Pisces generation will want to become a therapist or counselor, the way out of the underworld for each of them does lie in some sort of compassionate help for their fellow prisoners, even if it is only support for a close circle of friends or family.

At some point, Persephone's opinion of the underworld changes. Instead of being a terrible place where she is trapped against her will, it becomes a place where she can do some good—the source of a career, if you will. Up until this moment, she has eaten nothing, knowing that eating will trap her in Hades' realm forever. But when he offers her a pomegranate, the fruit of the underworld that is red like the womb of rebirth, she accepts it and eats six seeds. The later versions of the myth, seeking to turn Persephone into nothing but the helpless victim all the way through the tale, maintain that she was tricked or seduced or otherwise ate those seeds under false pretenses. This attitude makes no sense when compared to the fact that Hades and Persephone do seem to have a happy—and eternal—marriage. Although she rejoins her mother for the spring planting, she returns to her husband in the fall and does not seem unhappy to leave the upper world. In his song to them, Orpheus says, "If the tales are true, you two were brought together by love."

When Hermes does appear to rescue her, sent by Zeus in response to Demeter's agricultural sit-down strike, she greets him gladly and is borne to her mother in triumph. Their reunion is happy, with many tears and embraces. Then Demeter—assuming that her child is returned and all will be as it had been before—asks about food and drink, and Persephone reveals that she has accepted the pomegranate seeds. The red pomegranate has strong sexual connotations, implying that she has also given Hades her virginity and therefore her self-enclosed innocence. Besides, no one can remain innocent after being the counselor to the dead. Demeter weeps and rages again. Her world is ruined; her child must leave her and go on to an uncertain future, as must all children. A mothering urge this strong cannot easily let the offspring go. It may be that Persephone's protestations that she was seduced come out of her compassion for her mother, allowing her a white lie to make her feel better. This is a classic Piscean technique of getting what you want; a Pisces believes that it is better to tell a comforting lie than to face a stormy confrontation. Although Persephone has overcome some of her passivity, she cannot bring herself to say, "Mother, I am no longer a child. I am a woman now, and I have decided to take the position of

Queen of the Underworld that has been offered to me. I have a purpose now, and a destiny, and I realize that Hades in all his ambivalent dark glory is part of that destiny." Instead, she lies and prevaricates, and stays the innocent victim in her mother's eyes.

This kind of gentle deception does not sit well with Pluto, the avatar of radical honesty. Pluto finds it difficult to work through the Neptune-ruled Pisces, as it must go much slower in its transformative machinations. It can be likened to a volcano erupting at the bottom of the sea; its lava is immediately cooled, its explosion is muffled and undramatic, and it is noted only as a bit of turbulence on the upper waves, if that. While in Pisces, Pluto often has a much subtler effect than when in other signs. Its transformative violence is subdued, taking place largely in the personal and collective unconsciousness. Still, although Persephone may tell one last passive lie to her mother, her attitude when she is revered as Queen of the Underworld is very different. None who descend find her absent or uncompassionate; she stares clear-eyed to the bottom of the soul and concurs with the hard truths of her husband's pronouncements. In the underworld, the place of darkness, she finds herself.

This is true for Pluto in Pisces people as well. It is in the dark, silent, overlooked places of the human experience that they will find the keys to their own souls. The turbulence must be tracked to the bottom of the psychic ocean, where the leaking volcano is being smothered. Its message is about the group rescue of the human soul—how we rescue each other and, by doing so, find our own way out.

appendix
Basic Archetypes of the Planets and Signs

If you know nothing about astrology, I strongly recommend *The Inner Sky* by Steven and Jodie Forrest as the best possible primer in basic astrology. If you're looking for more simple information on just the planets and signs, *Meet Your Planets* by Roy Alexander is another good one to look at. There is no way that I can teach you basic astrology in one tiny chapter at the end of this book, so I'm not going to try. Instead, I'm going to give you the planets and signs from an archetypal point of view, and let you use your imagination.

You'll find below a list of archetypes associated with each of the signs, and another list associated with the planets. Some of these are drawn from the above books; others are drawn from my own experience or that of fellow astrologers. As Roy Alexander suggests in his book, you can start by thinking of the planet as a cartoon character, and the sign as the job to which it is assigned. Start by looking down the list of a particular planet; it's likely that one particular archetype will leap out at you. That's probably the one that best fits how that planet manifests itself in your chart (but keep in mind that other people might lean more toward other aspects of it, if you're trying to interpret someone else's chart). Any planet, of course, can manifest in any of the archetypes at any given time in anyone's life, as well as some I haven't thought of yet. Then look down the list for the sign that it's placed in, and imagine that character stuck in one of the assigned jobs for that sign. Some of them will fit well together; others will take some imagining to visualize the unique way in which this particular character does the job that they've been forced into by time and universal synchronization.

You'll notice that some of the signs and planets have archetypes in common, or ones that are very similar. This is because certain signs are "ruled by" certain planets, meaning that they are in affinity with them. For example, the Lover, is an archetype common to both Venus and Libra. The difference in how you'll treat them in this chart is that for Venus, being the Lover is part of her nature. Listed under Libra, it's about doing, not being; it's a job that any of the planets can take on in their own unique ways. For example, how Saturn does the Libra Lover job will be a lot different than how Mars does it. It will also look different, to a lesser degree, depending on whether someone's Saturn is manifesting as the Old-Fashioned One, or the Depressed and Despairing, or the Ascetic. The first manifestation of Saturn in Libra might just want a faithful and solid commitment, with a traditional wedding and living quietly ever after. The second one might have a continuing series of terrible affairs, each of them ruined by the other person's inability to be inhumanly perfect, and become awfully bitter about love in general. The Ascetic might boycott the Lover job entirely as being too indulgent and instead put all its focus into other jobs of that sign, such as the Injustice Fighter.

On the other hand, different sign jobs will bring out different aspects of a planet. Let's take an example of the planet Venus in the sign of Scorpio, which is a difficult place for her to be in general. Looking down the "job list," one might see how Venus as Lover might get caught up in the job of the Extremist and have a love life heavy with emotional or sexual psychodrama. On the other hand, the job of Mystery Seeker might bring out the Sacred Whore, seeking to experience sexuality and sexual service as a sacred rather than a profane experience. The job of the Hypnotist might attract the Beautifier or the Artist, who might use it to create "spooky," mesmerizing art forms of some kind.

Archetypes of the signs

Aries

The Leader
The Warrior
The Pioneer
The Daredevil
The Survivor
The Innocent

Taurus

The Farmer
The Builder
The Rock
The Musician
The Solid Citizen
The Sensualist

Gemini

The Clever One
The Witness
The Teacher
The Storyteller
The Networker
The Journalist

Cancer

The Baby
The Nurturer
The Homemaker
The Sensitive
The Invisible One
The Protector

Leo

The Boss
The King/Queen
The Aristocrat
The Performer
The Adolescent
The Clown

Virgo

The Servant
The Monk/Nun
The Martyr
The Analyst
The Critic/Perfectionist
The Worker

Libra

The Injustice Fighter
The Devil's Advocate
The Lover
The Artist
The Lawyer
The Diplomat

Scorpio

The Extremist

Sagittarius

The Gypsy
The Priest
The Philosopher
The Explorer
The Anthropologist
The Judge

Capricorn

The Authority
The Hermit
The Disciplinarian
The Prime Minister
The Strategist
The Executive

Aquarius

The Rebel
The Scientist
The Revolutionary
The Truth Sayer
The Exile
The Genius

Pisces

The Sacrifice
The Mystic
The Dreamer
The Poet
The Healer
The Romantic

Archetypes of the planets

Sun

The Self
The Observer
The Head of the Show
The Center
The Natural One
The Ego

Moon

The Emotional One
The Inner Parent
The Inner Child
The Heart
The Nurturer
The Keeper of Memories
The Wounded One

Mercury

The Communicator
The Traveler
The Curious Little Brother/Sister
The Geek/The Expert
The Gossiper
The Writer
The Keeper of the Thinking Process

Venus

The Lover
The Partner
The Aesthetic One
The Artist/The Dancer

The Sacred Whore
The Beautifier/The Layer of Glamour
The One Who Looks to Others

Mars

The Action Guy/Girl
The Fighter/Aggressive One
The Decision Maker
The Athlete
The Adventurer
The Sexual One
The Keeper of Anger

Jupiter

The Generous Gift-Giver
The One Who Thinks Big
The Impulsive One
"Have I Got a Deal for You"
The Keeper of Luck
The Christmas Present (à la Scrooge)

Saturn

The Naysayer
The Old-Fashioned One
The Strict Teacher
The Ascetic
The Depressed and Despairing
The Stumbling Block
The Keeper of Discipline

Uranus

The Futurist
The Freethinker
The Crazy One

The Nonconformist
The Maker of Radical Change
The Catalyst
The Keeper of Ideals

Neptune

The Visionary
The Anchorite on the Mountain
The Mystical God-Toucher
The Addict
The Delusional One
The Clouded Obscurer
The Keeper of Dreams

Pluto

The Destroyer
The Rebirther
The Pain Giver
The Power Seeker
The Purifier
The Death God/dess
The Guardian of the Gate of Mystery
The Keeper of the Depths

This, plus a copy of your birth chart, will give you an idea of how the planets and signs function within yourself. In the following chapters, the myths themselves will fill out the meanings of the planets and signs with stories that you can remember. If you need to refer back to these charts as a way to better anchor the information, go right ahead. You'll see how Mars in Capricorn's main character, Ogoun the Afro-Caribbean hunter and smith, puts the archetype of the Keeper of Anger into the role of the Hermit and the Disciplinarian; whereas the main character of Mars in Pisces, the Greek maiden Psyche, puts Mars's face as the Adventurer first into the role of the Sacrifice and then as the Dreamer. The important thing to remember is to let the stories and the characters unfold in your mind.

Bibliography

Alexander, Roy. *Meet Your Planets*. Llewellyn, 1997.

Anderson, William. *The Green Man: Archetype of Our Oneness with the Earth*. HarperCollins, 1990.

Bulfinch, Thomas. *Mythology*. Dell Publishing, 1959.

Campbell, Joseph. *Myths to Live By*. Bantam Books, 1972.

———. *The Hero with a Thousand Faces*. Princeton University Press, 1949.

Carlyon, Richard. *Guide to the Gods*. Quill Press, 1982.

Downing, Christine. *The Goddess: Mythological Images of the Feminine*. Crossroad Publishing, 1981.

Dundes, Alan. *Sacred Narrative: Readings in the Theory of Myth*. UCLA Press, 1984.

Evelyn-White, Hugh G. *The Homeric Hymns and Homerica*. Harvard University Press, 1914.

Forrest, Steven, and Jodie Forrest. *The Inner Sky*. ACS Publications, 1989.

Gleason, Judith. *Oya: In Praise of the Goddess*. Shambhala Press, 1987.

Graves, Robert. *The Greek Myths*. Penguin Books, 1955.

Greene, Liz. *Saturn: A New Look at an Old Devil*. Weiser Press, 1976.

Hamlyn, Paul. *Larousse Encyclopedia of Mythology.* Hamlyn Publishing Group, 1970.

Ions, Veronica. *The World's Mythology in Color.* Chartwell Books, Inc., 1987.

Kaldera, Raven. *Hermaphrodeities.* Xlibris Press, 2001.

Knight, Richard Payne. *A Discourse on the Worhsip of Priapus* (1786). Republished in *A History of Phallic Worship.* Dorset Press, 1992.

Moore, Marcia, and Mark Douglas. *Astrology: The Divine Science.* Arcane Publications, 1978.

Paris, Ginette. *Pagan Meditations.* Spring Publications, 1987.

Stone, Merlin. *Ancient Mirrors of Womanhood.* Beacon Press, 1979.

Teish, Luisah. *Jambalaya.* Harper & Row, 1988.

Vermaseren, Martin. *Cybele and Attis.* Thames and Hudson, Ltd., 1977.

Von Franz, Marie-Louise. *Creation Myths.* Spring Publications, 1972.

Wright, Thomas. *The Worship of the Generative Powers in the Middle Ages in Western Europe* (1866). Republished in *A History of Phallic Worship.* Dorset Press, 1992.

) LLEWELLYN ORDERING INFORMATION

Order Online:
Visit our website at www.llewellyn.com, select your books, and order them on our secure server.

Order by Phone:
- Call toll-free within the U.S. at 1-877-NEW-WRLD (1-877-639-9753). Call toll-free within Canada at 1-866-NEW-WRLD (1-866-639-9753).
- We accept VISA, MasterCard, and American Express.

Order by Mail:
Send the full price of your order (MN residents add 7% sales tax) in U.S. funds, plus postage & handling to:
Llewellyn Worldwide
P.O. Box 64383, Dept. 0-7387-0516-0
St. Paul, MN 55164-0383, U.S.A.

Postage & Handling:
Standard (U.S., Mexico, & Canada). If your order is:
Up to $25.00, add $3.50
$25.01 - $48.99, add $4.00
$49.00 and over, FREE STANDARD SHIPPING
(Continental U.S. orders ship UPS. AK, HI, PR, & P.O. Boxes ship USPS 1st class. Mex. & Can. ship PMB.)

International Orders:
Surface Mail: For orders of $20.00 or less, add $5 plus $1 per item ordered. For orders of $20.01 and over, add $6 plus $1 per item ordered.

Air Mail:
Books: Postage & Handling is equal to the total retail price of all books in the order.
Non-book items: Add $5 for each item.

Orders are processed within 2 business days.
Please allow for normal shipping time. Postage and handling rates subject to change.

MAPPING YOUR FUTURE
Understand and Maximize
Your Potential

KRIS BRANDT RISKE

Includes CD-ROM to calculate your birth chart
and forecast your future!

Predictive astrology is a tool for mapping the shortest route to your goals. From marriage to moving cross-country, it can show you when to act, when not to upset the status quo, and when you may encounter road blocks from the universe.

The step-by-step method in *Mapping Your Future* explores your birth chart as the foundation that supports your ever-evolving life. From there, you will learn basic predictive techniques—progressions, eclipses, and outer-planet transits—and then learn to recognize how specific events are triggered by New and Full Moons and the inner transiting planets. Subsequent chapters examine relationships, money, career, relocation, and health in detail.

0-7387-0501-2
240 pp., 7½ x 9⅛, illus., includes CD-ROM $19.95

To order, call 1-877-NEW-WRLD
Prices subject to change without notice

TO write to the Author

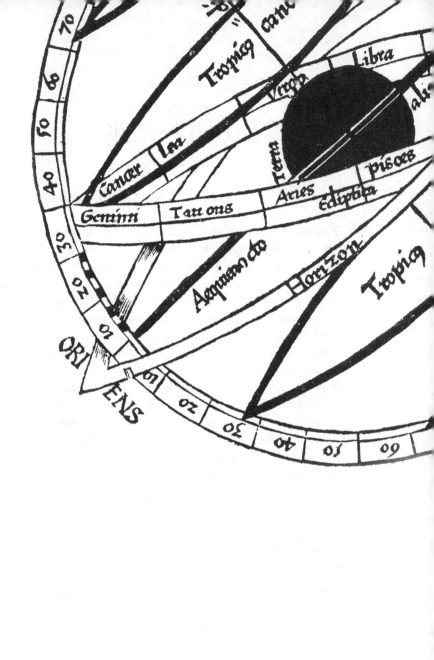

For readers of

Mythastrology
only

FREE Birth Chart Offer

Thank you for purchasing *MythAstrology*. There are a number of ways to construct a chart wheel. The easiest way, of course, is by computer, and that's why we are giving you this one-time offer of a free birth chart. This extremely accurate chart will provide you with a great deal of information about yourself. Once you receive a chart from us, *MythAstrology* will provide everything you need to know to interpret your chart from a mythological perspective.

Also, by ordering your free chart, you will be enrolled in Llewellyn's Birthday Club! From now on, you can get any of Llewellyn's astrology reports for 25% off when you order within one month of your birthday! Just write "Birthday Club" on your order form or mention it when ordering by phone. As if that wasn't enough, we will mail you a FREE copy of our fresh new book *What Astrology Can Do For You!*

Complete this form with your accurate birth data and mail it to us today. Enjoy your adventure in self-discovery through astrology!

Do not photocopy this form. Only this original will be accepted.

PLEASE PRINT

Full Name:_____

Mailing Address:_____

City, State, Zip:_____

Birth time:_____ A.M. P.M. (please circle)

Month:_____ Day:_____ Year:_____

Birthplace (city, county, state, country):

_____

_____

Check your birth certificate for the most accurate information.

Complete and mail this form to:
Llewellyn Publications, Special Chart Offer,
P.O. Box 64383, 0-7387-0516-0, St. Paul, MN 55164

Allow 4–6 weeks for delivery.